Managing DIVERSITY and INCLUSION

SAGE was founded in 1965 by Sara Miller McCune to support the dissemination of usable knowledge by publishing innovative and high-quality research and teaching content. Today, we publish more than 750 journals, including those of more than 300 learned societies, more than 800 new books per year, and a growing range of library products including archives, data, case studies, reports, conference highlights, and video. SAGE remains majority-owned by our founder, and after Sara's lifetime will become owned by a charitable trust that secures our continued independence.

Los Angeles | London | Washington DC | New Delhi | Singapore

Managing
DIVERSITY
and INCLUSION
an INTERNATIONAL PERSPECTIVE

edited by

JAWAD SYED and MUSTAFA ÖZBILGIN

Los Angeles | London | New Delhi
Singapore | Washington DC | Boston

Los Angeles | London | New Delhi
Singapore | Washington DC

SAGE Publications Ltd
1 Oliver's Yard
55 City Road
London EC1Y 1SP

SAGE Publications Inc.
2455 Teller Road
Thousand Oaks, California 91320

SAGE Publications India Pvt Ltd
B 1/I 1 Mohan Cooperative Industrial Area
Mathura Road
New Delhi 110 044

SAGE Publications Asia-Pacific Pte Ltd
3 Church Street
#10-04 Samsung Hub
Singapore 049483

Editor: Kirsty Smy
Editorial assistant: Molly Farrell
Production editor: Tom Bedford
Copyeditor: Andy Baxter
Proofreader: Salia Nessa
Indexer: Silvia Benvenuto
Marketing manager: Alison Borg
Cover design: Francis Kenney
Typeset by: C&M Digitals (P) Ltd, Chennai, India
Printed and bound by CPI Group (UK) Ltd,
Croydon, CR0 4YY

Library of Congress Control Number: 2014956398

British Library Cataloguing in Publication data

A catalogue record for this book is available from
the British Library

ISBN 978-1-4462-9463-5
ISBN 978-1-4462-9464-2 (pbk)

At SAGE we take sustainability seriously. Most of our products are printed in the UK using FSC papers and boards.
When we print overseas we ensure sustainable papers are used as measured by the Egmont grading system.
We undertake an annual audit to monitor our sustainability.

Contents

About the editors and contributors

Jawad Syed is Professor of Organisational Behaviour and Diversity Management at the University of Huddersfield. Previously he held the positions of Reader and Senior Lecturer in Human Resource Management (HRM) at the University of Kent, UK where he worked for seven years. Jawad received his PhD in HRM from Macquarie University, Australia, and completed a Postgraduate Certificate in Higher Education at the University of Kent. In addition, he received a Masters of International Business from the University of Western Sydney, Australia. With a professional and academic career that spans over 20 years in academic institutions and business organisations in the UK, Australia and Pakistan, Jawad examines HRM and diversity from relational, contextual and interdisciplinary perspectives, and focuses on critical integration of theory with practice.

Mustafa Özbilgin is Professor of Organisational Behaviour at Brunel Business School, London. He also holds two international positions: Co-Chaire Management et Diversité at Université Paris Dauphine and Professor of Management at Koç University in Istanbul. His research focuses on equality, diversity and inclusion at work from comparative and relational perspectives. His work has a focus on changing policy and practice of equality and diversity management at work. He serves as the editor-in-chief of the *European Management Review* (EMR), the official journal of the European Academy of Management (EURAM).

Faiza Ali is Senior Lecturer in Business Management at Liverpool John Moores University, UK. She completed her PhD in management from Macquarie University, Australia. Faiza has written widely on business and HRM in a wide range of publications. Her main academic interests include gender and diversity in organisations, international HRM and cross-cultural management issues. In particular, she is interested in exploring gender equality related issues in the workplace in Muslim majority countries such as Pakistan, Saudi Arabia and Turkey.

Kurt April is a tenured Professor of Leadership, Diversity and Inclusion at the University of Cape Town (SA), an Associate Fellow of the University of Oxford (UK), Research Fellow of Ashridge (UK), Faculty of Duke CE (USA), and Visiting Professor at London Metropolitan University (UK). Kurt is also an Owner-Director of LICM Consulting and Helderview BMW, Non-Executive Director of the Power Group and Achievement Awards Group, as well as DIAC Chairman for Novartis International. He is an editorial board member of numerous, global academic journals, and holds a PhD, Cert (Japanese Production), MBA, MSc (ElecEng), HDE, BSc (ElecEng), NDip (EE) and NDip (LS). He has published over 130 academic works and written eight books.

Erhan Aydin is a PhD student in Brunel University and Research Assistant in Usak University, Turkey. He has received his MBA degree from Dokuz Eylul University, Turkey and he has three bachelor degrees from the field of Business Administration (Eng), International Relations (Eng) in Dokuz Eylul University, Turkey and Public Administration in Anadolu University, Turkey. His research interests include diversity, equality and inclusion in organisations, religion in business and entrepreneurship. Erhan is acting as a member of the Work and Organisation Research Centre (WORC) at Brunel Business School. He is also a member of the Academy of Management (AOM) and British Academy of Management (BAM) since 2013.

Darren T. Baker is studying for a PhD in management at King's College London. His research focuses on the enablers and inhibitors to the career progression of men and women in the finance and accounting sectors. He is collaboratively funded by the ACCA and the ESRC. His academic supervisor is Professor Kelan, who is an expert on women in business. He is also a teaching assistant and guest lecturer at King's College London. Prior to this, Darren was a Management Consultant, designing and delivering strategies for FTSE companies, including diversity and culture change programmes. Darren read geography at the University of Oxford where he received his MA.

Mustafa Bilgehan Ozturk is Senior Lecturer at Middlesex University Business School. His research is focused on equality, diversity and inclusion issues in contemporary workplaces, with particular reference to the challenges and barriers faced by sexual orientation and gender identity minorities. His previous work appeared in leading journals in the field, such as *British Journal of Management*, *Human Relations* and *International Journal of Human Resource Management*.

Charmine E.J. Härtel Charmine E.J. Härtel is Professor of Human Resource Management and Organisational Development at UQ Business School, Australia. Professor Hartel is an internationally renowned organisational psychologist and management scholar with almost 30 years of experience working in the public and private sector, including consultancies in Australia, Europe, Asia and the US. She is recognised internationally as one of the originators of the study of emotion in organisations and as a leading expert in the development and application of theories about the strategies, systems and practices underpinning positive organisational change, leadership development, engagement, workplace wellbeing, and diversity and inclusion. She has published numerous books, several government and industry reports, over 60 book chapters, and nearly 100 refereed journal articles in leading international management and psychology journals, including *Academy of Management Review, Journal of Management, British Journal of Industrial Relations, Journal of Applied Psychology, and The Leadership Quarterly*.

Elisabeth K. Kelan is a Chaired Professor of Leadership at Cranfield School of Management. Her research focuses on women and leadership, generations in organisations, leadership and diversity and inclusion. She has published two books and numerous peer-reviewed articles in academic journals. She is an associate editor of *Gender, Work and Organization* and on the editorial board of the *British Journal of Management*. She has worked at King's College London, London Business School, the London School of Economics and Political Science, and Zurich University. She holds a PhD from the London School of Economics and Political Science.

Olivia Kyriakidou is Assistant Professor of Management and Organizational Behaviour in the Department of Business Administration at the Athens University of Economics and Business. Her current research interests are focused on the field of equality, diversity and inclusion at work from interdisciplinary, international and comparative perspectives. She is also interested in the remaking of the contemporary workspace with a special emphasis on social enterprises, organisational change, knowledge, innovation and creativity, and culture. More specifically, she studies the functioning of gender at work and the possibilities and impossibilities of organisational change.

Clifford Lewis is a licensed psychologist and human resource practitioner. He is currently pursuing doctoral studies at the School of Business and Management at Queen Mary University of London. His research interests are in equality and diversity within the leadership structures of organisations. His PhD research focuses on the ways under-represented groups in South Africa construct the concept of organisational leadership. Clifford holds several academic awards, including a Stellenbosch University Leadership Bursary, a Studentship from the Centre for Research in Equality and Diversity at Queen Mary University and an award for Best Paper that he received at the Conference on Equality, Diversity and Inclusion in Munich in 2014.

Hélène Mountford undertook her PhD in the department of marketing and management, Macquarie University, Sydney, where she now works in the Learning and Teaching Centre, and teaches human resource management and industrial relations at the University of Western Sydney. As an older worker, she was curious about the lack of literature at the time on why older workers retired early or could not gain employment when they wanted to. This has changed since the global financial crisis, but she still researches the need for changing human resource practices to employ and retain older workers. Before becoming an academic, Hélène was a journalist and a lawyer.

Peter A. Murray is an Associate Professor in Management at the University of Southern Queensland with previous affiliations at Macquarie University and University of Western Sydney. Peter is an applied researcher in strategic change and diversity management and lectures more broadly in strategic management, change management and human resource management. His most recent book is entitled *Contemporary Strategic Management: An Australasian Perspective* which was published in 2014. He is currently conducting applied research in local government and is a member of the Australian Centre for Sustainable Business Development and the Australian Human Resources Institute.

Jennifer M. O'Connor completed her Postgraduate Certificate in Research Methodology, School of Social Sciences, and her Bachelor of Arts Degree majoring in Psychology, Sociology and Human Movements both from the University of Queensland. She received commendation from the School of Social Science for outstanding performance and is currently employed as a Research Assistant at the University of Queensland Business School. Her work involves research projects in the area of organisational behaviour and employee well-being, with research interests including physical, psychological, social and emotional well-being.

Nick Rumens is Professor of Organization Behaviour at Middlesex University London, UK. His research uses queer theory to examine lesbian, gay, bisexual and transgender (LGBT) sexualities, workplace friendships, intimacies and identities in organisation. He has published on these topics in journals, including *Human Relations*, *British Journal of Management*, *Organization*, and *Human Resource Management Journal*. He has also published a number of books, including *Queer Company: Friendship in the Work Lives of Gay Men* (Ashgate, 2011), *An Introduction to Critical Management Research* (Sage, 2008, co-authored with Mihaela Kelemen) and *Sexual Orientation at Work: International Issues and Perspectives* (Routledge, 2014, co-edited with Fiona Colgan).

Ahu Tatli is Reader in International Human Resource Management at Queen Mary University of London, UK. Her research explores intersectionality of disadvantage and privilege at work; inequality and discrimination in recruitment and employment; diversity management, agency and change in organisations. She has widely published in edited collections, practitioner and policy outlets and international peer-reviewed journals such as *Academy of Management Review*, *British Journal of Management*, *Canadian Journal of Administrative Sciences*, *European Journal of Industrial Relations*, *Entrepreneurship and Regional Development*, *International Business Review*, *Human Relations* and *International Journal of Management Reviews*.

Selcuk Uygur is a Lecturer in Business Ethics in Brunel Business School. He has received his PhD degree from Brunel Business School on management researches. Selcuk holds an MBA degree from Baskent University and a BA degree from Inonu University, Turkey. His research interests include work ethic, business ethics and social responsibility, influence of religion in business, enterprise culture and entrepreneurship. He is a reviewer for the *Journal of Business Ethics*. Selcuk is acting as a member of the Work and Organisation Research Centre (WORC) at Brunel Business School. He is also a member of the European Business Ethic Network (EBEN) since 2007, and of the Institute for Small Business and Entrepreneurship (ISBE).

Harry J. Van Buren III is Professor of Business and Society, holds the Jack and Donna Rust Professorship in Business Ethics and serves as a Daniels Ethics Fellow at the Anderson School of Management, University of New Mexico, USA. Harry holds a PhD in Business Environment, Ethics, and Public Policy from the University of Pittsburgh's Katz Graduate School of Management, an MSc in education for sustainability from London South Bank University, an MDiv from Princeton Theological Seminary, an MS in Finance from the University of Illinois at Urbana-Champaign, and a BS in managerial law and public policy from Syracuse University. His research interests include the ethics of contemporary employment practices, preventing human trafficking in global supply chains, the intersection of religious and business ethics, and the relationship between accounting and stakeholder theory.

Foreword

Professor Stella Nkomo

The field of diversity management had its origins in the United States. Over the years the field developed with a focus on diversity issues within that country and the business interests of its organisations. The large body of knowledge developed during the past several decades evolved from an earlier focus on US employment discrimination and the need for theories and practices to overcome workplace exclusions based on race, gender, national origin, sexual orientation and physical ability. This was also the case for textbooks. A number of articles can be found critiquing the US-centric nature of diversity theory and practice. Despite the growing critique, it is only recently that scholars have begun to develop theoretical frameworks to guide thinking about how context, particularly national contexts, shape and influence questions of diversity and difference. It is so easy to be unaware of how one's own context, values, assumptions, and interests affect how we perceive and understand diversity. *Managing Diversity and Inclusion: An International Perspective* could not have come at a better time. In tandem with an increasing emphasis on the globalisation of organisations, products and services, there is a critical need for a book that will expand how students and managers alike understand diversity and inclusion beyond the context of the US. Multinational organisations have become a dominant feature across the globe and today they are not only US based. Thus, it is important to understand both intra-country and inter-country diversity issues.

It is clear from the chapters in this book that national context shapes not only the salience of particular categories of diversity but also policy and organisational practices. While issues of diversity in Europe are central to this book, it also provides valuable insight into other important national contexts ranging from the BRICS countries (Brazil, Russia, India, China and South Africa) to Poland, Greece and Australia. The contrasts between regions illuminates how historical, social, culture, economic and demographic factors influence diversity. For example, increasing immigration in European countries, particularly immigrant populations from former colonies, underscores the lingering effects of colonialism on current diversity issues and tensions. New immigrants are not finding a warm welcome despite labour force shortages due to ageing populations in many European countries. Debates also exist about the national status of ethnic minorities who are native born citizens. The book's inclusion of BRICS countries provides additional insight into the contextual effects on diversity. As transitional economies, issues of diversity, difference and inclusion are closely linked to aspirations for economic transformation. There is a strong desire by emerging market countries like India, Brazil and South Africa to ensure economic transformation which also contributes to a reduction in poverty and inequality. The magnitude of demographic diversity in BRICS countries presents complex ethnic, race, gender and class dilemmas with significant implications for doing business in these countries. For example, South Africa's focus on transforming the country from legislated racial segregation and deeply embedded patriarchy has resulted in robust legislation for preventing discrimination and ensuring economic empowerment for the black majority population and women. All companies wishing to do business in the country are subject to these laws and have to learn quickly how to navigate the lingering effects of historical racial and ethnic faultlines.

In writing an international text that seeks to overcome universalism, it is sometimes easy to over-particularise the unique aspects of diversity in different countries. The authors deftly avoid this by illuminating the macro-economic and historical forces that determine salient diversity dimensions in different countries. This approach provides a valuable lens for understanding why diversity and organisational practices differ across the globe. Further, students will recognise diversity issues are not fixed in time but evolve as the context changes. The cases in each chapter contain complex contemporary diversity issues ranging from religion in the workplace to intersectionality challenges. They provide an opportunity for students to consider how managers and leaders should approach difficult diversity issues. The chapters are written by prominent scholars in the field ensuring that students and other readers will have access to the most current knowledge and debates.

I believe *Managing Diversity and Inclusion: An International Perspective* will be a valuable resource for acquiring a different perspective on diversity and inclusion. Moreover, its critical and analytical treatment of the dominant theories of diversity provides an opportunity to seriously ponder their applicability in different contexts. The book is a welcome volume for those of us who teach diversity in regions of the world featured in the text. It is also an important resource for those in the US who teach international human resource management courses. *Managing Diversity and Inclusion: An International Perspective* will help students gain a much needed comparative understanding of diversity and its management.

Professor Stella Nkomo
University of Pretoria, South Africa

Acknowledgements

I would like to thank all the authors for their valuable contributions to the book and also for their engagement with the spirit of diversity and inclusion, my colleagues at the University of Kent and the University of Huddersfield for their dedication and support of my research endeavours, and my ever cooperative children, Haider and Pernian, wife Faiza, mother Khalida, and sisters Sajida and Zahida, who continue to inspire and enthuse me. Special thanks are also due to Kirsty Smy, Senior Editor at SAGE Publications, for her faith in this book project right from our first meeting a few years ago. Thanks are also due to Tom Bedford (Book Production Editor) and Molly Farrell (Editorial Assistant) fot their hard work, professionalism and persistence in making this project possible.

Jawad Syed

Guided tour of the book

Intended learning outcomes

After reading this chapter, you will be able to:

- Understand the guiding concepts in a psychological and sociological study of diversity
- Discuss the major debates in social science concerning the study of diversity
- Explore some theoretical building blocks, such as prejudice and discrimination
- Define targets of prejudice and discrimination and understand the effects of prejudice
- Explain the dominant theoretical paradigms utilised by scholars to understand diversity in organisations
- Describe the cultural diversity discourse and practices in Greece
- Identify good practices directed at organisations and policy makers

Introduction

The study of diversity has a long history encompassing a variety of perspectives, philosophical assumptions and prescriptions. As with most areas of theoretical endeavour it is not without controversy. There has been much debate over the years about the possibilities and practices of 'effective' diversity management, the import of diversity to organisational functioning, the links with power in organisational settings,

interaction, and we are given meanings and values for these categories by our social institutions, peers and families. What we learn depends on the culture in which we live as well as on our place within that culture. Further, how we are defined by our culture often determines how we experience our social world. As W.I. Thomas noted, if we 'define situations as real, they are real in their consequences' (1966: 301). For example, when we define one group as inferior to another, this does not make that group inferior, yet it may result in them being experienced as inferior. To illustrate this, consider the vicious cycle that results from the assignment of substandard resources to people who are poor. For example, low-income housing is generally located in geographic areas that lack quality resources such as good state schools and access to adequate health care. Lacking such quality resources results in further social disadvantage, which can perpetuate the poverty of this group. Thus, although reality is initially soft as it is constructed, it can become hard in its effects.

Discussion activity 1.1

Can you provide examples of how privilege and disadvantage concerning race, or gender, or any other system of advantage and disadvantage, have been socially constructed in your culture?

Intended learning outcomes

Each chapter starts by setting out clearly what key information you should soon understand, so you can easily track your progress.

Discussion activities

These activities are designed to get you to think about key issues and interesting scenarios, and will hopefully provoke constructive debates between you and your classmates.

increasingly take on masculine roles there will be substantial change in gender stereo-types. However, the converse may also occur: as a traditionally male role becomes increasingly occupied by women, that role may become less valued. Finally, we should not lose sight of the fact that in general men still have more socio-political power than women to define the relative status of different roles in society. Not surprisingly, women can find it difficult to gain access to higher-status masculine roles – a phenomenon called the 'glass ceiling'. One explanation is that male prejudice, or backlash against women with power, constructs the glass ceiling (Rudman and Glick, 2001). Again, either sex can hit a glass ceiling if gender stereotypes are inconsistent with the organ-isation's norms. For example, Young and James (2001) found that male flight attendants hit a glass ceiling because, to put it simply, stereotypes about men prevent people from expecting men to make 'good' flight attendants – male stereotypes block promotion.

Organisational insight 1.1

Addressing prejudice at Weyerhaeuser

For Weyerhaeuser, one of the world's largest forest products companies, ensur-ing an environment that is truly diverse and inclusive is a top priority. So when the company made the important decision to look into combating prejudice

(Continued)

Organisational insights

These boxes provide examples of how companies and organisations confront diversity issues in a huge variety of ways, sometimes successfully and sometimes generating problems.

Summary and recommendations

This chapter has sought to highlight some of the key tensions and paradoxes in the management of diversity in organisations overtime and across different geographies. We have identified three prevalent organisational models or paradigms to diversity management for organisations. The discrimination-and-fairness paradigm, linked to the Civil Rights Movement in the US, ensures equitable recruitment, retention and support structures for minority groups. The access-and-legitimacy paradigm focused on how organisations can increase business profitability through effectively leveraging and aligning minority demographics with clients, products and markets. The contemporary learning-and-effectiveness paradigm focuses on integrating diversity into all aspects of business performance, and measuring progress against multiple organisational metrics.

In this chapter, we have also identified two approaches to diversity management and linked these to legislative demands at the national and supra-national level. The liberal approach to diversity is recognised for increasing the representation of certain minority groups in the workforce, particularly further down within the organisational hierarchy. EU non-discrimination law, for example, upholds liberal approaches to diversity management as it supports a meritocratic culture and, therefore, demands that employers act fairly in all employment issues. However, we have argued that, despite best practice policies and procedures, the liberal approach fails to contend with the underlying processes of discrimination and bias within organisational cul-tures. On the other hand, we argue that a radical approach, which focuses on targets and quotas, provides better equality outcomes, specifically in the representation of minority groups in senior positions, which can have a positive spillover effect further down within organisations. The US has more radical legislation in place than in the EU to deal with discrimination. Affirmative action has arguably been one of the most effective ways to redress employment injustices suffered by minority groups. An inde-pendent federal agency promotes equal opportunities in employment through administrative and judicial enforcement of federal civil rights laws, education and

Summary and recommendations

These sections at the end of each chapter summarise the content and outline the key lessons to which readers and organisations should pay attention.

Discussion questions

1. Compare and contrast the four major debates outlined in the chapter, i.e. essentialism versus social constructionism, universalism versus cultural relativism, reductionism versus complexity, and identity versus coalition politics. How does each debate contribute to our understanding of diversity issues in organisations? How can these debates be used by management in order to develop policies for diversity management?
2. As a manager, how would you address the challenges faced by minority employees?
3. What is the glass ceiling and why do you think it has proved to be such a barrier to women and minorities?
4. Have you been associated with an organisation that made assumptions associated with a monolithic orientation? Describe the culture.
5. How would you apply social identity theory, embedded intergroup theory and demography approaches in preparing an organisation to accept diversity?
6. How might critical and postmodern approaches contribute to the advance-ment of women and minorities to higher-level positions in an organisation?
7. As a manager, how would you accommodate the special needs of different groups – such as single parents, older workers, or employees with poor English language skills – without appearing to show favouritism?
8. Have you ever tried to team up with people from a racial/ethnic, class, religious, etc., background very different from your own? What happened? If you have not had such an experience, why do you think that was? How can the theo-retical approaches in this chapter help you reflect further on that experience?
9. What knowledge or skills would you need to be able to take action against an instance of racism? How could the theories presented in this chapter enable you to take action against racism?

(Continued)

Discussion questions

Pull your learning from the chapter together to determine how you think the scenarios and conundrums presented in these questions should be dealt with.

CASE STUDY

Multi-level experiences of Pakistani women in the workplace

Considering the limitations of the equal opportunity approach, it can be argued that the approach ignores the significant societal- and individual-level factors that exist beyond the organisational level but at the same time impose imperative effects on organisational practices and the effectiveness of diversity management (Syed and Murray, 2009). As mentioned earlier in this chapter, the mainstream single level of diversity management with an emphasis on law and legislation fails to develop a comprehensive understanding of an array of factors influencing gender equality at the workplace. A multi-level framework as suggested by Syed and Ozbilgin (2009) would be of paramount importance in filling this gap. This chapter will therefore use Ali's (2013) paper as a case study for the discussion of a multi-level perspective on equal employment opportunity for women in organisations, and its presentation of the framework in Pakistan. Ali carried out

(Continued)

Case studies

Each chapter covers a major diversity issue in depth in its case studies, so you can get a full picture of the various nuances of the situation.

Further reading

This section highlights books and articles that will help to broaden your understanding of that chapter.

References

A wealth of further reading material is available here, as all the sources that have collectively informed the writing of the chapter are gathered in one place.

Companion website

In addition to the wealth of information and activities contained in this book, further useful resources for both lecturers and students are available from the companion website. Simply head to http://study.sagepub.com/syed to discover the following resources:

- Instructor's Manual containing key points and indicative answers to questions in each chapter
- Videos of the contributors discussing their research and chapters
- Links to useful websites relevant to each chapter
- Access to SAGE journal articles cited in the book
- PowerPoint slides for instructors.

List of figures and tables

Figures

Tables

List of case studies

Introduction

Theorising and managing diversity and inclusion in the global workplace

Jawad Syed and Mustafa Özbilgin

Welcome to *Managing Diversity and Inclusion: An International Perspective*. The idea of this book surfaced a few years ago at an informal meeting of diversity instructors from across the globe at the 2011 Annual Meeting of the Academy of Management (San Antonio, Texas). One common observation made by several instructors was that there was a need for a textbook which would capture world-wide organisational and national examples of gender, race, sexuality, age and other dimensions of diversity, taking into account important elements of societal and relational context, and integrating the theory of diversity with its organisational practice. It was at that point that the editors of this book decided to start working on this project and were encouraged by the warm reception of the idea by SAGE Publications.

After approximately two years of hard work, which involved refinement of the book and its various chapters in the light of thorough reviews and comments by noted diversity scholars and instructors, identification of important dimensions of diversity and the topics to be covered within each dimension, recruitment of expert authors for each dimension, integration of theory with organisational and country examples from across the globe, particularly from BRICS countries (Brazil, Russia, India, China, South Africa), the end product is in your hands. The volume is packed with fresh insights, new theorisation and empirical evidence on diversity management (DM), which experienced rapid pace of change in practice over the past three decades.

More formally, the book offers an authoritative text on current theories, issues, practices and developments in managing diversity, equality and inclusion in organisations in a broad European and international context, with a special focus on BRICS countries, Australia and the UK, along with other countries. The book will provide the reader with an in-depth and contextual understanding of workforce diversity and its relevance to managing people and organisations.

The demographics of the population and the workplace in Europe, Australia, BRICS countries and other continents are changing drastically because of a number of factors, such as an increasing number of ethnic and religious minorities, women, older persons and single people with caring responsibilities in the workforce (Bisin et al., 2011). Accordingly, there is a need to understand and effectively manage workforce diversity not only to enhance business outcomes but also to create an inclusive workplace in a socially responsible manner (Syed & Kramar, 2009). There is also a need to create institutional and organisational structures and cultures to enable employee inclusion in the work group as involving the satisfaction of the needs of both belongingness and uniqueness (Brewer & Silver, 2000; Syed & Boje, 2011).

Bringing together eminent international scholars, this book places a premium on critical thinking and analytical abilities that can be successfully applied to DM. Our take on the theory and practice of DM is far from US-centric; our choice of topics as well as geographies covered in the text is an attempt to situate and understand DM in the European context and beyond.

What we know of diversity at work predominantly emanates from the industrial democracies of the world (Syed & Özbilgin, 2009). While some industrialised countries have adopted a voluntary approach to issues of diversity at work, others have developed sophisticated regulatory measures (Özbilgin & Tatli, 2011). One significant example is the European Union (EU) countries. Diversity in the workplace is an issue which is coming to the fore in all EU member states and the EU is undertaking legislative initiatives in the area of diversity. The EU legislation banning discrimination on grounds of racial or ethnic origin, gender, religion, disability, age and sexual orientation is bound to have a major impact on businesses across the EU. Article 13 of the European Community Treaty states:

> Without prejudice to the other provisions of this Treaty and within the limits of the powers conferred by it upon the Community, the Council, acting unanimously on a proposal from the Commission and after consulting the European Parliament, may take appropriate action to combat discrimination based on sex, racial or ethnic origin, religion or belief, disability, age or sexual orientation. (EUR-Lex, 2002)

The above provision is quite empowering as it enables the EU to take action against diverse forms of discrimination and inequalities. The EU has, pursuant to Article 13, adopted several Directives to combat discrimination. For example: Council Directive 2000/43/EC prohibits racial discrimination in the fields of employment, education, social security, health care and access to goods and services; Council Directive 2000/78/EC establishes a framework for equal treatment in employment and occupation on the grounds of religion or belief, disability, age and sexual orientation (EC, 2014).

While each member country has developed its own national anti-discrimination law, issues, challenges and trajectories of DM in each country remain different.

However, legal measures are not popular internationally. In parts of Europe, not unlike the US, currently there seems to be movement away from equal opportunity (or in German '*Chancengleichheit*') and affirmative action towards a more voluntary, organisational approach geared towards business outcomes of diversity. This approach, however, is not easy to put into practice. In the absence of legal enforcement, diversity officers would find it difficult to convince organisational leaders to support diversity interventions. There is heterogeneity of political positions and discourses such as multiculturalism, integration, assimilation, tolerance, national values and citizenship which currently shape DM policies and practices across Europe. These debates and related economic and social issues obviously cannot be overlooked as they are embedded in complex macro-national, global and industrial contexts. This complexity entails understanding and assessing each unique diversity constellation of any particular organisation, community or country. For example, the different historical and social roots of diversity in organisations in Turkey and France cannot be dissociated from the actual management of equality and diversity in the workplace. At the same time, examples of best practices (positive action for gender equality in Scandinavian countries, attention to older workers and pensions in Germany, etc.) are equally relevant and important.

Consistent with the business case paradigm, the European Commission (EC) has encouraged employers to put DM more firmly on their strategic business agendas and has supported their activities across the EU through numerous actions over the past few years. Such actions include: (a) launching and maintaining a platform for EU-level exchange between Diversity Charters in Europe; (b) developing and implementing a European diversity award at the workplace; and (c) developing a diversity benchmarking system for and in association with businesses. Previously, the EU's EQUAL Community Initiative (2000–6) focused on supporting innovative, transnational projects aimed at tackling discrimination and disadvantage in the labour market (EC, 2011). Despite these initiatives and policies, it is a fact that organisations in the EU, as elsewhere, remain deeply gendered and racialised. Concepts such multiculturalism and diversity are currently subject to much criticism and debate. Social stereotypes, prejudices and tensions, which are not unusual in the political and media landscape, are also visible in the workplace, thus posing a major challenge to leaders and managers of a diverse workforce.

Similar attention to DM as a governmental policy is evident in other countries, e.g. Australia. The Australian Government's Multicultural Australia Policy (DSS, 2014) clearly states the government's emphasis on the country's multicultural character and the competitive edge it offers in an increasingly globalised world.

There are cross-cultural and cross-country variances in terms of approaches to and outcomes of DM. For example, women's advancement into senior management roles globally is much less in the G7 group of developed economies, according to

2013 research from the Grant Thornton (2013) International Business Report (IBR), a survey of 6,600 business leaders in 44 countries. IBR data reveals that globally, 24 per cent of senior management roles are now filled by women. However, in the G7 economies just 21 per cent of senior roles are occupied by women, compared to 28 per cent in the BRICS economies and 32 per cent in South East Asia. The US ranks in the bottom eight performing countries for women in senior management at 20 per cent, along with Japan at 7 per cent and the United Kingdom at 19 per cent. It is, therefore, important to develop a contextual understanding of policies and outcomes of DM.

Similar attention to DM is evident in India, China and other emerging economic giants, e.g., Ye et al.'s (2010) study of Chinese listed firms on the impact of gender on earnings, and Cooke and Saini's (2010) and Syed and Pio's (2013) studies of diversity management in South Asia.

Each chapter in this book addresses a core topic and reflects the current state of scholarly activity in the field, highlighting some enduring theories and approaches, and then pushes the boundaries of DM to critically situate such theories and approaches in the global context. The book identifies and challenges assumptions, develops an awareness of the context, seeks alternative ways of seeing a situation and relates these to real-world examples of DM in contexts as diverse as the UK, Germany, Turkey, Poland, Australia and the BRICS countries.

While the book has been designed and written primarily for students, we believe it will be equally useful to academics, research scholars and practitioners who want to understand and meet the increased challenges facing DM in the current global crisis and beyond.

Overview of chapters

Chapter 1 titled 'Sociological and psychological perspectives on diversity' deals with the development of diversity from a psychological and sociological perspective as an arena of discourse and managerial practice. It highlights the key ideas and debates that have characterised the field, aiming to develop a common conceptual vocabulary through which relationships between different diversity categories can be explored in greater depth. It also examines the ways in which prejudices and negative stereotypes arise in and influence diversity. It places and discusses diversity in an organisational and workgroup context in order to examine how diversity interfaces with topics of current interest within business and management. The workplace is a strong situation that enables subtle prejudice and stereotypes to manifest as unfair discrimination and systematised bias. The chapter presents several major theories such as social identity theory, embedded intergroup relations theory, demography and critical and postmodern approaches, with particular attention to understanding what happens when groups with different identities come together in an organisation. As a contextual example, the chapter presents the current debates on cultural diversity in Greece and offers cross-cultural comparisons with other national contexts. Greece is an excellent example to highlight important issues of cultural diversity, as during the past two decades it has become host to more than a million immigrants who pose major diversity challenges to the country.

Chapter 2 titled 'Leadership and diversity management in a global context' explores the interplay between diversity and leadership in its contextual specificity. Theoretically, it provides a critical review of the academic literature on leadership, explores competing definitions of leadership, introduces key approaches to leadership and discusses these approaches in relation to workforce diversity. In order to highlight the link between theoretical debates and real-life situations, it presents country-specific examples derived from the UK and South Africa. The UK has a long-standing equality and diversity tradition both in terms of the public debate around the issue as well as anti-discrimination legislation. South Africa, on the other hand, has a unique history of Apartheid, which was followed by a significant legal, political and economic push towards promoting equality, diversity and inclusion. Yet, both countries experience leadership challenges in terms of diversity of leadership, i.e. lack of diversity in corporate leadership as well as in relation to leadership for diversity, i.e. commitment to diversity from the organisations' leaders. These two country examples will help the reader to understand the convergence and divergence of diversity and leadership issues internationally.

Chapter 3 titled 'Policy and practice of diversity management in the workplace' examines the policy approach to DM in the workplace and its persistent tension with forces and factors of discrimination. The chapter defines diversity management by situating it in a fluid, highly contested and often contradictory discourse. It discusses how different approaches to DM have influenced non-discrimination legislation in the EU and the US, and organisational policies and practice, and how these have changed over space and time. It outlines temporal changes in the meaning of diversity, and in particular critically explains the business case for DM.

Chapter 4 titled 'Gender equality in the workplace' discusses and critically evaluates theories of gender segregation at work and the related ideologies of gender equality, and contrasts them with organisational practice. It examines how these theories approach employed and unemployed workers, men and women, in a society. The chapter presents the case of gender at work in a South Asian country, Pakistan, to explain the role of prevailing employment norms in a society and gender segregation of the labour force arising from those norms. The chapter also offers an overview of the Marxist, radical feminist theories, dual system theories and their critique from a post-structuralist and human capitalist perspective. The chapter also discusses the change ideologies related to the issues of gender equality within employment contexts.

Chapter 5 titled 'Race and ethnicity in the workplace' explains the notions of race and ethnicity and their implications for DM in organisations. In particular, the chapter explains why there is racial or ethnic discrimination, and how issues of racism and stereotypes affect equal opportunities at work. Issues of institutional racism, racialised organisations, intersectionality and migrant workers will also be explained. It also explains how legislative, historical and demographic contexts in a specific country affect organisational approaches to race and ethnicity. The chapter also offers cross-national examples, particularly from South African and Indian contexts.

Chapter 6 titled 'Age diversity in the workplace' presents a number of facts and key reflections relating to the importance of older workers (those aged 45 years or more) in the overall labour market. Here, the focus is largely on Australia with worldwide implications noted. The chapter outlines cross-cultural issues within the context of research on ageing and the importance of policy debates and strategies for ageing. It explains how classical approaches to age diversity have evolved to more contemporary approaches adopted in modern organisations. It takes into account various socio-economic, legal and demographic factors in determining age diversity policies, analyses and applies age diversity principles to practical case problems, and specifies how to develop age diversity practices in contemporary settings.

Chapter 7 titled 'Disabled persons in the workplace' provides the reader with an overview of the research and practice relating to disabled persons in the workplace, with a view to promoting evidence-based understanding and practice as well as stimulating new thinking. It presents classic theories and key concepts underpinning the study of disability in the workplace, and also explains the key obstacles disabled individuals face when gaining and maintaining effective employment. The chapter presents data from several countries, demonstrating the extent of the issue relating to disabled persons at work, and provides real-world case examples of disabled persons at work.

Chapter 8 'Religious diversity in the workplace' deals with religion and spirituality in the workplace through theoretical and empirical studies. In order to understand religious diversity and discrimination with regard to DM, the chapter focuses on Turkey and the UK as specific cases in terms of religious diversity and discrimination in a legislative-based approach. The value of creating such a comparison among those countries is due to the differences between state and legislative structures of both countries. This chapter also indicates the secular conservative thought of Turkey and non-secular liberal thought of the UK in accordance with content analysis of the legislations of both countries, and international research centres' reports on religious minorities in both countries.

Chapter 9 titled 'Sexual minorities in the workplace' deals with sexual minorities, i.e. lesbian, gay, bisexual and transgender (LGBT) persons in the context of workplace relations. It reviews the contributions made by a range of theoretical traditions to our understanding of the type and extent of discrimination faced by LGBT employees. It also explains how the impact of context on the workplace experiences of sexual minorities is useful in understanding that sexual stigma and prejudice do not exist in a vacuum. Rather, they take particular forms and expressions depending on a range of social, legal, political and organisational contextual factors. The chapter argues that an analysis of the employment experiences of sexual minority employees remains incomplete without adequate attention being devoted to underlying relations of sexual and gendered power within the workplace, which may constrain or encourage the development, shape and purpose of organisational practices designed to give sexual minority employees a voice in the workplace, and which may allow them to participate openly as LGBT in organisational life. The chapter ends with recommendations for good practice in addressing the inequalities experienced by sexual minority employees at work.

Chapter 10 titled 'Work–life balance' discusses the issue of how to manage work–life balance (WLB) by organisations and employees in an increasingly global competitive environment. It discusses the notion of WLB and examines the factors that have caused an increase in attention to WLB and how the issue is addressed within DM. It identifies important changes within society and organisations which have contributed to an increased focus on WLB within organisational policies. The chapter explores organisational examples in order to assess how DM policies address WLB and how this affects employees and organisations. The chapter offers a critical review of the literature and identifies some gaps in diversity policies surrounding the issue of WLB.

Chapter 11 titled 'Intersectionality in the workplace' discusses the development of intersectionality as a concept (including the three types of complexity that inform work in the area) and discusses some of the current critiques of intersectionality research. It then considers the EU and US context vis-à-vis intersectional analysis, focusing on the forms anti-discrimination legislation takes and how an intersectional approach would be a useful addition to existing legislation and regulation. Illustrated by a case study focusing on veiled Muslim women in the EU, the chapter discusses approaches to using intersectional analyses in organisations and concludes with a set of recommendations.

Chapter 12 titled 'Conclusion: Future of diversity management' provides a critical overview of the key themes presented in the book. It also presents a number of elementary questions to contextualise and manage diversity in different international spaces and situations. The chapter outlines a number of key challenges and possibilities for the future expansion and enhancement of DM.

Unique features of the book

1. International text, written for British, European, Australian and audiences from BRICS countries, with the ability to be adapted in other countries.
2. Suitable for undergraduate and graduate teaching programmes on general human resource management (HRM) as well as for specialist modules on gender, diversity, work psychology and cross-cultural management.
3. Provides a contextual approach to DM. Each chapter offers a substantive section on contextual insights, evaluation and recommendations.
4. Detailed case studies and organisational examples in each chapter.
5. The book takes into account diverse issues and challenges facing DM in public, private and voluntary sectors, and also in large and small-to-medium organisations.

6. Critical text integrating theories of DM with organisational practices and examples. Jargon free but cutting edge research; easily accessible to scholars from non-English-speaking backgrounds.
7. Contributions by eminent scholars and academics in the field.
8. Equally valuable for academics, students, researchers and practitioners.
9. A common structure for all chapters.

Structure of the book

Comprising 12 chapters (excluding this Introduction), the book is divided into three parts – Concepts (three chapters); Dimensions of Diversity (six chapters); and Future of DM (three chapters).

Each chapter shares the following common structure:

1. Intended learning outcomes
2. A brief introduction to the chapter and its contents
3. A critical overview of theories and key concepts
4. Contextual (demographic, socio-cultural, legal, institutional, macroeconomic) information about a specific dimension of diversity in a specific country or organisation
5. In addition to the provision of the country-specific contextual information and examples, cross-cultural comparison with other countries, comprising information about regulatory measures, institutions, organisational interventions, etc.
6. Attention to issues of power, voice, hegemony and silence
7. Practical examples of a company or country
8. In-text discussion activities, which raise questions designed to encourage critical thinking
9. Critical analysis and discussion
10. Summary and recommendations, including the identification of any good practices directed at organisations, managers, employees and policy makers
11. Further reading: up-to-date, easily available books, journal articles and online resources
12. End of chapter questions and class activities
13. Case study: a major part of each chapter focuses on one or more organisational or country case example. The aim is to provide detailed case examples of how the issues have been applied or handled in a specific situation
14. References: all cited material is fully sourced and acknowledged

Index

The book has a subject and author index.

Instructor's manual and slides

The book is accompanied by an instructor's manual providing key notes per chapter and PowerPoint slides for instructional and exercise purposes.

Companion website

There is a companion website including access to free full-text SAGE journal articles linking to relevant chapters. Each chapter and case study has web links, author podcasts (highlighting key points for chapters, key debates, etc.) and additional cases studies where applicable. There is also a section on policy and law updates.

References

Bisin, A., Patacchini, E. Verdier, T. & Zenou, Y. (2011) Ethnic identity and labour market outcomes of immigrants in Europe. *Economic Policy, 26*(65), 57–92.

Brewer, M.B. & Silver, M.D. (2000) Group distinctiveness, social identification, and collective mobilization. *Self, identity, and social movements, 13*, 153–171.

Cooke, F.L. & Saini, D.S. (2010) Diversity management in India: a study of organizations in different ownership forms and industrial sectors. *Human Resource Management, 49*(3), 477–500.

Department of Settlement and Social Services (DSS) (2014) *Settlement and Multicultural Affairs. The People of Australia – Australia's Multicultural Policy.* Available at: https://www.dss.gov.au/our-responsibilities/settlement-and-multicultural-affairs/publications/the-people-of-australia-australias-multicultural-policy

EC (2011) *European Commission EQUAL.* Available at: http://ec.europa.eu/employment_social/equal_consolidated/

EC (2014) *Joint Report on the Application of Council Directive 2000/43/EC and Council Directive 2000/78/EC.* Brussels, 17.1.2014, COM(2014) 2 final. European Commission. Available at: http://ec.europa.eu/justice/discrimination/files/com_2014_2_en.pdf

EUR-Lex (2002) *Treaty Establishing the European Community (Consolidated version 2002). Access to European Union Law.* Available at: http://eur-lex.europa.eu/legal-content/EN/TXT/?uri=CELEX:12002E/TXT

Grant Thornton (2013) *Mature Economies Lagging Behind Emerging Markets in Advancement of Women.* Available at: http://news.grantthornton.com/press-release/mature-economies-lagging-behind-emerging-markets-advancement-women

Özbilgin, M. & Tatli, A. (2011) Mapping out the field of equality and diversity: rise of individualism and voluntarism. *Human Relations, 64*(9), 1229–1253.

Syed, J. & Boje, D. (2011) Antenarratives of negotiated diversity management. In Boje, D. (ed.), *Storytelling and the Future of Organizations*, 47–66. New York: Routledge.

Syed, J. & Kramar, R. (2009) Socially responsible diversity management. *Journal of Management and Organization, 15*(5): 639–651.

Syed, J. & Özbilgin, M. (2009) A relational framework for international transfer of diversity management practices. *International Journal of Human Resource Management, 20*(12): 2435–53.

Syed, J. & Pio, E. (2013) Guest editorial: rediscovering 'anekta mein ekta' or 'kasrat mein wahdat': South Asian management through unity in diversity. *Equality, Diversity and Inclusion, 32*(3), 236–244.

Ye, K., Zhang, R. & Rezaee, Z. (2010) Does top executive gender diversity affect earnings quality? A large sample analysis of Chinese listed firms. *Advances in Accounting, 26*(1), 47–54.

PART I

CONCEPTS

Part I Contents

Sociological and psychological perspectives on diversity

1

Olivia Kyriakidou

Intended learning outcomes

After reading this chapter, you will be able to:

- Understand the guiding concepts in a psychological and sociological study of diversity
- Discuss the major debates in social science concerning the study of diversity
- Explore some theoretical building blocks, such as prejudice and discrimination
- Define targets of prejudice and discrimination and understand the effects of prejudice
- Explain the dominant theoretical paradigms utilised by scholars to understand diversity in organisations
- Describe the cultural diversity discourse and practices in Greece
- Identify good practices directed at organisations and policy makers

Introduction

The study of diversity has a long history encompassing a variety of perspectives, philosophical assumptions and prescriptions. As with most areas of theoretical endeavour it is not without controversy. There has been much debate over the years about the possibilities and practices of 'effective' diversity management, the import of diversity to organisational functioning, the links with power in organisational settings, and even whether the concept of 'diversity' has any utility (please see Chapter 3 for a comprehensive review).

This chapter will chart the development of diversity from a psychological and sociological perspective as an arena of discourse and managerial practice. It will begin by highlighting the key ideas and debates that have characterised the field, aiming to develop a common conceptual vocabulary through which relationships between different diversity categories, such as for instance race, gender and class, can be explored in greater depth. Next, ways in which prejudices and negative stereotypes arise in and influence diversity are presented. Third, diversity will be discussed in an organisational and workgroup context in order to examine how diversity interfaces with topics of current interest within business and management. The workplace is a strong situation that enables subtle prejudice and stereotypes to manifest as unfair discrimination and systematised bias. Several major theories will be presented, such as social identity theory, embedded intergroup relations theory, demography and critical and postmodern approaches, with particular attention to understanding what happens when groups with different identities come together in an organisation. Moreover, this chapter will introduce students to the current debates on cultural diversity in a specific national context (the Greek context) and will provide cross-cultural comparisons with other national contexts. Greece is an excellent example to highlight important issues of cultural diversity as during the last two decades it has become host to more than a million immigrants who pose major diversity challenges to the country. We close the chapter with a discussion of how the field of diversity could be developed in order to address multiple forms of oppression.

Overview of classical theories

Useful concepts for studying diversity

Understanding diversity from a psychological and sociological perspective necessitates the development of a conceptual vocabulary and the acquisition of some basic tools through which diversity can be explored in greater depth. The extant research and theory on diversity is built around four major concepts that need preliminary explanation:

1. Essentialism versus social constructionism
2. Universalism versus cultural relativism/historical specificity
3. Reductionism versus complexity
4. Identity versus coalition politics

Essentialism versus social constructionism

This is one of the oldest ongoing debates in social science, one that counterposes beliefs in unchanging ongoing essences of phenomena to an equally passionate conviction that social life, as we know it, results from interactive processes over which human beings exert control (e.g. Acker, 1992; Alvesson and Billing, 1997). In most countries there are systems of stratification that are based on many categories of difference, including race/ethnicity, social class, sex/gender and sexuality. These systems are viewed as fixed because of the assumption that these categories are unchangeable. Such assumptions are often based on a belief in essentialism – the tenet that human behaviour is 'natural', predetermined by genetic, biological or physiological mechanisms and thus not subject to change.

A different perspective however notes that categories such as race/ethnicity, social class, sex/gender and sexuality are socially constructed. Peter Berger and Thomas Luckmann, on whose work this premise is based, state that 'social order is not part of the "nature of things", and it cannot be derived from the "laws of nature". Social order exists only as a product of human activity' (1966: 52). Social construction theory suggests that what we see as 'real' (in this case, cultural categories of difference and systems of inequality) is the result of human interaction. Through such interaction we create aspects of our culture, objectify them, internalise them, and then take these cultural products for granted.

Adopting a framework based on social construction theory means understanding that we are not born with a sense of what it means to be male, female or intersexual; with a disability or not; black, Asian or white; gay, straight, asexual or bisexual; or rich, working-class, poor or middle-class. We learn about these categories through social interaction, and we are given meanings and values for these categories by our social institutions, peers and families. What we learn depends on the culture in which we live as well as on our place within that culture. Further, how we are defined by our culture often determines how we experience our social world. As W.I. Thomas noted, if we 'define situations as real, they are real in their consequences' (1966: 301). For example, when we define one group as inferior to another, this does not make that group inferior, yet it may result in them being experienced as inferior. To illustrate this, consider the vicious cycle that results from the assignment of substandard resources to people who are poor. For example, low-income housing is generally located in geographic areas that lack quality resources such as good state schools and access to adequate health care. Lacking such quality resources results in further social disadvantage, which can perpetuate the poverty of this group. Thus, although reality is initially soft as it is constructed, it can become hard in its effects.

Discussion activity 1.1

Can you provide examples of how privilege and disadvantage concerning race, or gender, or any other system of advantage and disadvantage, have been socially constructed in your culture?

Universalism versus cultural relativism/historical specificity

A universalistic view is one that prioritises how a given social experience or practice recurs across any, and perhaps all, social contexts we can imagine. Thus, the experience of death, for example, seems indeed to be universal: do we know of any society, at any time, which has managed to avoid this for even one of its members indefinitely? Analogously, one could say that human beings universally require to be fed and to drink lest we die; humanists might go further yet to contend that all human beings are born with rights whether or not properly granted and realised. Moreover, in the study of gender, for instance, many feminist theorists have used the notion of patriarchy or male domination as a basic structural characteristic of societies, one that applies universally to all societies (Millett, 1970).

On the other hand, commentators who have stressed cultural relativism and historical specificity emphasise variations in human experiences and practices in different places and at different times. Thus, a cultural relativist may be less interested in death's obvious universality than in how – in relation to a given nation, ethnic, racial or religious group – perceptions and reactions to our mortality decidedly differ. A party whose concern is historical specificity may also, or instead, be interested in whether attitudes on death have stayed the same over decades or centuries. As far as the study of gender is concerned, the relativists argue that claims to patriarchy's universality overlook that practices appearing to manifest male domination may, in some societies, be perceived quite differently – for example, as reflecting a mutually agreed upon gendered division of labour.

Reductionism versus complexity

Reductionism can be defined as attributing the causes of a particular social phenomenon to a single factor rather than to a complex of causes. On the other hand, complexity demands the investigation of a host of possibly relevant influences to explain a phenomenon at hand. Regarding the issue of gender, for example, Marxist feminists severely critique radical feminists about omitting sufficient attention to class (Hennessy and Ingraham, 1997). Some Marxist feminists believe that radical feminists reduced the study of women's subordination to a function of gender – or male domination – alone. In so doing, capitalism's contribution to that subordination, and the relevance in general of class differentials to understanding women's situation, was overlooked. Ironically though, this accusation of reductionism (or attributing the cause of one type of discrimination primarily to one factor) was also exactly the objection radical feminists lodged against previous Marxist perspectives (Firestone, 1979). According to their critique, Marxists traditionally assumed that women's subordination was entirely a product of the capitalist system. In this sense, they argue that many

Marxists reduced gender oppression to a function of class, attributing primary explanatory power for gender biases to class-based inequalities rather than to a more complicated combination of social factors.

Identity versus coalition politics

This last concept brings a more explicitly political dimension into the conceptual vocabulary presented here, since studying diversity points toward social movements that have played an enormous role in bringing many forms of diversity to public notice. Most crucial to the emergence of this field were movements of identity politics. This term refers to social movements that saw as their prime purpose advocacy for individuals and groups directly affected by forms of discrimination (Evans, 1970). Often these forms of discrimination are based on the physical characteristics or sexual practices of such individuals or groups. Thus, the feminist and civil rights movement fought against prejudice towards women and racial minorities respectively; the gay and lesbian rights movement defined itself around advocating for sexual freedom and against homophobic biases. Identity politics, therefore, presumes that the people most likely to push for social recognition are individuals whose 'identities' depend on these movements' successes.

For some people, identity politics have been replaced by a wider coalition politics wherein a wide range of people may march in public arenas to support various causes. This perspective has led to queer theory, which questions any notion of essence of sexual identity that appears to be fixed. Thus, practitioners of coalition politics may well criticise identity politics as being essentialistic. For such critics, the categories 'woman' or 'gay' can appear fixed and unchanging, thereby partaking of the very rigidity which sustained discriminatory systems in the first place. Queer theory insists that all sexual behaviours, all concepts linking sexual behaviours to sexual identities, and all categories of normative and deviant sexualities, are social constructs, sets of signifiers which create certain types of social meaning. Queer theory rejects the idea that sexuality is an essentialist category, something determined by biology or judged by eternal standards of morality and truth. For queer theorists, sexuality is a complex array of social codes and forces, forms of individual activity and institutional power, which interact to shape the ideas of what is normative and what is deviant at any particular moment, and which then operate under the rubric of what is 'natural', 'essential' or 'biological' (for a more comprehensive review on the issue of sexual minorities please refer to Chapter 9). Indeed, this is precisely the perspective Judith Butler proposed in her work on feminism, *Gender Trouble* (1990). For Butler, there is no essence of woman, or gay for that matter. Consequently, in her view, social movements are more potentially liberatory to the extent that they do not reinforce or reify the very social categories which led to their creation.

Prejudice and discrimination

This section examines several constructs that are often used to express psychological processes and actual behaviours involved in intergroup relations. These constructs are defined as 'mechanisms by which advantaged and disadvantaged group members perceive and interpret interactions that appear to be based on their category membership rather than on their individual characteristics' (Taylor and Moghaddam, 1994: 159). As the basis of both intergroup attitudes and behaviours are the diversity categories used to make the distinction between the advantaged and the disadvantaged in each society. These constructs are helpful in clarifying central aspects of diversity that could lead to the dominance or advantage of one group over another.

As the term prejudice literally means 'prejudgement', it is usual to consider prejudice as an attitude where the attitude object is a social group (e.g. women, Chinese, politicians). In this sense, prejudice could be considered as an unfavourable attitude towards a social group and its members. A traditional view (e.g. Allport, 1954) of prejudice is that it has three components:

1. Cognitive – beliefs about the attitude object,
2. Affective – strong feelings (usually negative) about the attitude object and the qualities it is believed to possess,
3. Conative – intentions to behave in certain ways towards the attitude object.

Certain groups are the enduring victims of prejudice because they are formed by social categorisations that are vivid, omnipresent and socially functional, and the target groups themselves occupy low power positions in society. These groups are those based on race, ethnicity, sex, age, sexual preference, and physical and mental health. Most research on prejudice has focused on sex, race/ethnicity and age but only touches on handicap and disability, homophobia or discrimination based on sexual preference.

Sexism

Almost all research on sexism focuses on prejudice and discrimination against women (Deaux and LaFrance, 1998) (for a more focused review on gender in the workplace please refer to Chapter 4). This is because women have historically suffered most as victims of sexism, primarily because of their low power position relative to men in business, government and employment. However, it should be noted that gender roles, i.e. behaviours deemed sex-stereotypically appropriate, may have persisted because although they provide men with structural power they have provided women with dyadic or interpersonal power (Jost and Banaji, 1994). Research on gender stereotypes has revealed that both men and women believe that men are competent and independent and women are warm and expressive (Fiske, 1998). These are really consensual stereotypes – widely shared and simplified evaluative images of a social group and its members. Presumably, competence, independence, warmth and expressiveness are all highly desirable and valued human attributes. However, earlier research suggested that female-stereotypical traits are significantly less valued than male-stereotypical traits (Broverman et al., 1970).

Might gender stereotypes accurately reflect gender differences in personality and behaviour? Perhaps men and women really do have different personalities? Traditionally, men and women have occupied a different gender role in society (men pursue full-time out-of-home jobs, while females are 'homemakers'). Gender roles can be described as social norms, or rules and standards that dictate different interests, responsibilities, opportunities, limitations and behaviours for men and women. Informally, by virtue of living in a social world, individuals learn the appropriate or expected behaviour for their gender. For this reason, individuals inevitably internalise conventional and stereotypic gender roles and develop their sense of gender in the face of strong messaging about the correct gender role for their perceived body. Gender differences, if they do exist, may simply reflect roles not sex, and role assignment may be determined and perpetuated by the social group that has more power (in most cases, men).

In this sense, one reason why stereotypes persist is that role assignment according to gender persists. Certain occupations become labelled as 'women's work' and are accordingly valued less. At the same time, there is the possibility that as women increasingly take on masculine roles there will be substantial change in gender stereotypes. However, the converse may also occur: as a traditionally male role becomes increasingly occupied by women, that role may become less valued. Finally, we should not lose sight of the fact that in general men still have more socio-political power than women to define the relative status of different roles in society. Not surprisingly, women can find it difficult to gain access to higher-status masculine roles – a phenomenon called the 'glass ceiling'. One explanation is that male prejudice, or backlash against women with power, constructs the glass ceiling (Rudman and Glick, 2001). Again, either sex can hit a glass ceiling if gender stereotypes are inconsistent with the organisation's norms. For example, Young and James (2001) found that male flight attendants hit a glass ceiling because, to put it simply, stereotypes about men prevent people from expecting men to make 'good' flight attendants – male stereotypes block promotion.

Organisational insight 1.1

Addressing prejudice at Weyerhaeuser

For Weyerhaeuser, one of the world's largest forest products companies, ensuring an environment that is truly diverse and inclusive is a top priority. So when the company made the important decision to look into combating prejudice

(Continued)

(Continued)

within its corporate walls, the move made perfect sense. The company's Chief Diversity Officer (CDO) believes that prejudice can and will show up in many areas of the workplace. Prejudice can show up in hiring, promotions or even in daily interactions around the office. A critical point in addressing prejudice is in first recognising and acknowledging that it exists. 'You have to be able to recognise the kinds of issues or situations where people feel disrespected and devalued and look for these subtleties that other people might not always look for', explains the company's CDO. Weyerhaeuser's managers are expected to encourage women, minorities, veterans and individuals with disabilities to apply for positions for which they are qualified. Further, the company's leaders are expected to maintain a work environment that supports the success of all employees. Each member of the company's senior management team, for example, develops an action plan based on his or her individual diversity leadership assessment and is held accountable for follow through.

In addition to some of the blatant ways that prejudice manifests itself, there are many subtle ways in which prejudice appears. Prejudice, the CDO points out, can show up in generational differences within the workplace. Younger workers may make assumptions about older workers, and vice versa, leading to unconscious, yet impactful, attitudes and actions. The same goes for assumptions across – and within – racial and ethnic groups, as well as management levels. 'We did a survey amongst our company employees to see what they thought about [prejudice] and how they thought it showed up, and the feedback we got back from them was that employees felt that managers who didn't mention diversity did not have an interest in the topic or a stake in the topic', said the CDO. 'At Weyerhaeuser, we know that there is no easy framework for this, but what we have tried to do is create a culture within our organisation where people feel included and where our management team is held accountable when we fall short of this.'

Adapted by CDO Insights (www.diversitybestpractices.com).

Racism

Discrimination on the basis of race or ethnicity is responsible historically for some of the most appalling acts of prejudice (the issues around race and ethnicity are described more thoroughly in Chapter 5). Because explicit and blatant racism (derogatory stereotypes, name calling or ethnophaulisms, abuse, persecution, assault and discrimination) is illegal and thus socially censured, it is now more difficult to find. However, racism may not only have gone 'underground', it may actually have changed its form. This new form of racism has been called 'aversive' racism (Gaertner and Dovidio, 1986), 'symbolic' racism (Sears, 1988), 'regressive' racism (Rogers and Prentice-Dunn, 1981) and 'ambivalent' racism (Hass et al., 1991). Although there are differences between these theories, they all share the view that people experience a conflict between deep-seated emotional antipathy towards racial outgroups and modern egalitarian values, which exert pressure to behave in a non-prejudiced manner (Brewer and Miller, 1996). According to Sears' (1988) notion of symbolic racism, negative feelings about blacks blend with moral values embodied in the Protestant ethic to justify some anti-black attitudes and therefore legitimise their expression. According to Kinder Sears (1981: 416):

> symbolic racism represents a form of resistance to change in the racial status quo based on moral feelings that blacks violate such traditional American values as individualism and self-reliance, the work ethic, obedience, and discipline. Whites may feel that people should be rewarded on their merits, which in turn should be based on hard work and diligent service. Hence, symbolic racism opposes to political issues that involve 'unfair' government assistance to blacks; welfare; reverse discrimination and racial quotas.

Generally, racism reflects how people resolve an underlying antipathy based on race with their belief in equality between groups. This is achieved by avoidance and denial of racism – avoidance of the topic of race, denial of racial advantage and thus opposition to affirmative action or other measures to address racial disadvantage.

Ageism

Elderly people are generally treated as relatively worthless and powerless members of the community. They are denied many basic human rights and their special needs go untended. Young adults may consider people over 65 to be grouchy, unhealthy, unattractive, unhappy, miserly, less efficient, less socially skilled, overly self-disclosing, overly controlling, feeble, egocentric, incompetent, abrasive, frail and vulnerable (Noels et al., 2003). Furthermore, the young generally have little to do with the elderly, so intergenerational encounters tend to activate intergroup rather than interpersonal perceptions, which reinforce negative stereotypes that lead to avoidance and minimisation of intergenerational contact. The cycle continues and the elderly remain socially isolated and societally marginalised (please refer to Chapter 6 for a focused review on issues around age diversity in the workplace).

Discrimination against homosexuals

Prejudice against homosexuals is widespread (see Chapter 9 for a comprehensive review). In general, since the late 1960s there has been a progressive liberalisation of attitudes towards homosexuals. Against this background, continued liberalisation often reveals deeply entrenched homophobia in certain sectors of the community. For example, Gay Pride, which is the world's largest public celebration of homosexuality, repeatedly provokes fierce public reaction from a number of religious groups – there is good evidence for a correlation between prejudice and traditional or fundamentalist Christian attitudes (Batson et al., 1993).

Discrimination on the basis of physical or mental handicap

Prejudice and discrimination against the physically handicapped has a long history, in which such people have been considered repugnant and subhuman (Jodelet, 1991). Overt discrimination against people on the basis of physical handicap is illegal and unacceptable in most Western societies. People generally no longer disparage the physically handicapped, but often they are uneasy in their presence and uncertain about how to interact with them (Heinemann, 1990). This can unintentionally produce patronising attitudes, speech and behaviour that serve to emphasise and perpetuate handicap (Fox and Giles, 1996). The improvement of attitudes towards physical handicap has not extended to mental/psychological handicap. Western societies prefer to overlook the existence of mental illness and to abdicate responsibility for the mentally ill. This is reflected in remarkably low funding for research into most mental illnesses and poor resourcing for the care and therapy of psychiatric patients.

Another facet of prejudice against the mentally ill is the use of the 'mad' label to dehumanise and justify discrimination against minority-status groups as a whole. 'Different' becomes 'mad'. Research indicates that the stereotypical behaviour of women does not conform to what people consider to be the behaviour of a typical, well-adjusted, adult human being (Broverman et al., 1970) – in this sense, women are 'maladjusted'. A similar process, in which cultural difference is made pathological by the dominant white middle-class group, occurs with respect to blacks and other racial/ethnic minorities (Nahem, 1980). There is a further twist to the story. Prejudice often creates brutal conditions of existence (poverty, poor health, low self-esteem, violence, etc.), which may produce certain types of psychiatric disorder in minority groups. In this way, fear and ignorance about psychiatric illness dovetails with and may amplify ethnic or racial prejudices.

Forms of discrimination

There are three more types of behaviour that do not look so obviously like discrimination but nevertheless may conceal underlying prejudice:

- *Reluctance to help*. Reluctance to help other people to improve their position in society, by passively or actively declining to assist their efforts, is one way to make sure they remain disadvantaged.

- *Tokenism*. Tokenism refers to a relatively small or trivial positive act towards members of a minority group. The action is then invoked as a defence against accusations of prejudice and as a justification for declining to engage in larger and more meaningful positive acts or for subsequently engaging in discrimination. Typical examples include purposely hiring a non-white person in a mainly white occupation or a woman in a traditionally male occupation. In the US, there has been criticism of the token employment of minorities (e.g. African Americans, Latinos) by organisations that then fail to take more fundamental and important steps towards equal opportunities. Such organisations may employ minorities as tokens to help deflect accusations of prejudice. Tokenism at this level can have damaging consequences for the self-esteem of those who are employed as token minorities (Chacko, 1982).
- *Reverse discrimination*. A more extreme form of tokenism is reverse discrimination. People with prejudiced attitudes may sometimes go out of their way to favour members of a group against which they are prejudiced more than members of other groups. Because reverse discrimination favours a minority group member, it can have beneficial effects in the short term. In the long run, it might have some harmful consequences for the recipients and there is as yet no evidence that reverse discrimination reduces or abolishes the deep-seated prejudices of the discriminator. Reverse discrimination may affect self-esteem. Fajardo (1985) had white teachers grade essays that were designed to be poor, average or excellent in quality and were attributed to either a black or a white student. The teachers evaluated identical essays more favourably when they were attributed to black students than to white students. In the short run, this practice may furnish minority students with self-confidence. In the long run, however, some students will develop unrealistic opinions of their abilities and future prospects, resulting in severe damage to self-esteem when such hopes collide with reality. Reverse discrimination may also prevent students seeking the help they sometimes need early in their academic careers, with the consequence perhaps of contributing to educational disadvantage.

Discussion activity 1.2

Peter is convinced that he is not anti-gay – he just doesn't much want to talk to gays or about homosexuality. As proof of his 'good will' he donates five pounds each year to AIDS charity collectors. Do you think that Peter is prejudiced, and how would you go about explaining whether he is or not to someone who disagrees with you?

Effects of prejudice

The effects of prejudice on the victims of prejudice are diverse, ranging from relatively minor inconvenience to enormous suffering.

- *Social stigma.* Crocker et al. (1998: 505) define stigma as follows: 'Stigmatised individuals possess (or are believed to possess) some attribute, or characteristic, that conveys a social identity that is devalued in a particular social context'. The targets of prejudice and discrimination are members of stigmatised groups, and thus they are stigmatised individuals. The subjective experience of stigma hinges on two factors: visibility and controllability. Visible stigmas, such as race, gender and obesity, mean that people cannot easily avoid being the target of stereotypes and discrimination. Controllable stigmas are those that people believe are chosen rather than assigned: for example, obesity, smoking and homosexuality are thought to be controllable – people are responsible for having chosen to be these things. Uncontrollable stigmas are those that people have little choice in possessing: for example, race and sex. Controllable stigmas invite much harsher reactions and more extreme discrimination than uncontrollable stigmas.
- *Self-esteem and psychological well-being.* Members of stigmatised groups tend to internalise the negative images and can form an unfavourable self-image that can be manifested in relevant contexts as low self-esteem. For example, research reveals that women generally share men's negative stereotypes of women, often evaluate themselves in terms of such stereotypes, and under circumstances where sex is the salient basis of self-perception actually report a reduction in self-esteem (Hogg and Turner, 1987).
- *Stereotype threat.* Because stigmatised groups know exactly the negative stereotypes that others have of them, they experience what Steele and Aronson (1995) have called 'stereotype threat'. Stigmatised individuals are aware that others may judge and treat them stereotypically, and thus, on tasks that really matter to them, they worry that through their behaviour they may even confirm the stereotypes. These concerns not only increase anxiety but can also impair task performance. Stereotype threat has been found in many different contexts, for example women and mathematics, low socio-economic status and intelligence, the elderly and memory, women and negotiation skills, and black and white men and athletic performance (Wright and Taylor, 2003). One way of coping with stereotype threat is domain disidentification – that is, reducing the degree to which our identity is tied to the performance that may attract negative feedback (Major and Schmader, 1998).
- *Failure and disadvantage.* The victims of prejudice belong to groups that are denied access to those resources that society makes available for people to thrive and succeed, such as good education, health, housing and employment. Discrimination thus creates clearly visible evidence of real disadvantage and of manifest failure to achieve the high standards set by society. This sense of failure can be internalised by victims of prejudice so that they become chronically apathetic and unmotivated: they simply give up trying because of the obvious impossibility of succeeding.

- *Attributional ambiguity*. Stigmatised individuals are very sensitive to the causes of others' treatment of them (Crocker and Major, 1989). 'Did she fail to serve me at the bar because I am black, or simply because someone else shouted louder?' 'Was I promoted quickly to comply with an affirmative action policy or because of my intrinsic ability?' Attributional ambiguity can quite obviously lead to suspicion and mistrust in relationships.
- *Self-fulfilling prophecies*. Prejudiced attitudes covertly or overtly produce discriminatory behaviour, which cumulatively, across time and individuals, creates disadvantage. In this way, a stereotypical belief can create a material reality that confirms the belief: it is a self-fulfilling prophecy.

Discussion activity 1.3

Stereotype threat is the feeling that we will be judged and treated in terms of negative stereotypes of our group, and that we will inadvertently confirm these stereotypes through our behaviour.

Self-fulfilling prophecy is where the expectations and assumptions about a person influence our interaction with that person and eventually change their behaviour in line with our expectations.

Are minority students more vulnerable to self-fulfilling prophecy? Why would stereotypes drive teachers' estimation of students' efforts in school but not their assessment of the students' grades?

Diversity in organisations and workgroups

Given the review of the major concepts and debates that underpin most of the literature on diversity, we turn now to the extant research and theory on diversity in organisations and workgroups. Social identity theory, embedded intergroup theory and organisational demography have been the dominant theoretical paradigms utilised by scholars to understand diversity in organisations and workgroups.

Social identity theory

Social identity theory (SIT) (Tajfel and Turner, 1979) continues to be one of the theories scholars utilise to examine diversity in organisations and workgroups (Ashforth and Mael, 1989). SIT is a cognitive theory which holds that individuals tend to classify themselves and others into social categories and that these classifications have a significant effect on human interactions.

In her model of communicative interactions in culturally diverse workgroups, Larkey (1996) utilised Cox's (1991) continuum of organisational types, from monolithic organisations (which are homogeneous with few minority employees, and where formal policy alone is utilised to incorporate diversity), to multicultural organisations (where the integration of minority employees and perspectives is ideal). Larkey (1996) predicted categorisation processes as a function of the organisational culture within which workgroups were embedded. For example, monolithic organisational and workgroup types were theorised to make salient identity group boundaries, with negative and divisive norms resulting among workgroup members. Multicultural workgroup orientations were theorised to produce specification, where individual group members are perceived and assessed based on their personal attributes and characteristics, rather than stereotypes generally attributed to their relevant social groups (e.g. race, gender). Specification and its influence on group and organisation culture were to result in more inclusive norms among workgroup members.

Hogg and Terry (2000) provided an integration of SIT and its extension, self-categorisation theory. Self-categorisation theory is used to explicitly describe the process by which depersonalisation of the self occurs through the internalising of group prototypes – one's representation of the features that best describe their group, often in the forms of exemplary members. To the extent that they identify with, value or want to be accepted by the group, individuals internalise and attempt to conform to these prototypes. These prototypes also serve to maximise similarities within and differences between groups, satisfying individuals' identity-based needs for self-enhancement and uncertainty reduction. Mutual influence between majority and minority group members was theorised to be a function of the extent to which individuals fit organisational and workgroup prototypes. Accordingly, minority members can potentially face difficulty because of the lack of fit between their identity group memberships and organisational prototypes for roles such as leadership, which are often white and male.

Organisational insight 1.2

Sodexo

Sodexo, with strong CEO commitment and a refocused diversity initiative, remains a world-class leader in diversity and inclusion. Sodexo is the only company to have been in the top two of the DiversityInc Top 50 for five years in a row. It has become the model for other companies through its use of diversity dashboards and scorecards to accurately measure and improve initiatives. The company's streamlined and valuable metrics enable its top leadership to get

(Continued)

(Continued)

better and are used to show other organisations, including its clients, how to grow and assess diversity initiatives. A hallmark of the efforts of leadership is strong accountability factors, with 25 per cent of top executives' and up to 15 per cent of senior management's bonus compensation directly tied to diversity goals – and paid regardless of the financial performance of the company. In 2014, a realignment has focused both on workplace diversity efforts, including strong emphasis on recruitment and talent development, and on marketplace connections and supplier diversity. External efforts include its Diversity and Inclusion Business Advisory Board, which includes leaders of multicultural nonprofit organisations, the private sector and former government leaders. Sodexo continues to improve its best-in-class Impact mentoring programme and uses its talent development efforts to bolster the diversity of its talent pipeline in all its business units.

Source: www.diversityinc.com

Embedded intergroup relations theory

Alderfer and Smith (1982) proposed embedded intergroup relations theory which posits that two types of groups exist within organisations: identity groups – groups whose members share some common biological characteristics (e.g. sex), equivalent historical experiences, and thus have relatively consonant world views; and organisation groups – groups whose members share common organisational positions and participate in equivalent work experiences, resulting in relatively consonant world views. The significance of the theory is its attention to the effects of diverse identities within a larger organisational context. The identity of individuals in organisations is said to be determined not only by organisational categorisation but also by identity group membership. It recognises that individuals don't leave their racial, gender or ethnic identities at the door when they enter an organisation.

In a qualitative study of three large service-oriented organisations, Ely and Thomas (2001) considered the embedded nature of workgroups in organisations as they sought to determine the conditions under which workgroup diversity yielded positive, negative or neutral outcomes. Their research identified three primary organisation and workgroup orientations toward diversity, each with different implications for sustained effective diversity management. The 'discrimination and fairness' orientation uses primarily human resource policies such as affirmative action, sensitivity training and formal mentoring programmes. Under this paradigm, minority members are expected to assimilate and organisational members are trained and encouraged to take a 'colour-blind' perspective to establish the principle that demographic differences do not matter. Under the 'access and legitimacy' orientation (or the business case for diversity), employees' demographic differences are used to gain access and legitimacy with diverse markets. Organisational structures that typify this orientation include special divisions or business units largely comprised of female or minority employees dedicated to the service of emerging niche/minority markets. Finally, organisations operating under the 'integration and learning' orientation seek to incorporate diversity throughout the organisation, vertically and horizontally, inclusive of the nature of the organisation's approach to processes, strategy and work.

Demography

Demography research refers to the study of 'the causes and consequences of the composition or distribution of specific demographic attributes of employees in an organisation' (Tsui et al., 1995: 4). Research in demography has extended from the initial work on organisational demography, which focused on the macro level of analysis (Tsui et al., 1995), to include the group and relational levels of analysis. Group demography research examines group processes and outcomes as a function of group composition along various dimensions of identity, in terms of 'visible' or 'surface-level' variables, such as race, gender, age and other readily identifiable traits, and 'non-visible' or 'deep-level' variables such as attitudes and personality, which are typically only recognised over time (Harrison et al., 1998). Relational demography research focuses on individuals' demographic similarity to a given group, assessing each member's similarity by taking into account the demographic characteristics of others in the group.

Demography researchers have established that minority and majority status in diverse workgroups is not experienced equivalently across sex, race or age, among other dimensions of diversity. Both Chattopadhyay (1999) and Riordan (2000) observed that there is strong theoretical and empirical support for the need to incorporate asymmetrical predictions for the effects of relative demographic similarity in demography research. Early demography work by Tsui et al. (1992) also supports this convention. They found that white male employees reported adverse reactions to increasing minority representation in workgroups, while women and racial minorities did not. Chattopadhyay (1999) reasoned that organisation-specific power dynamics, and expectations with regard to the make-up of the most favourably perceived workgroups drive these effects. In organisations where males occupy the most powerful or prestigious positions, such as executive management, organisational members likely perceive workgroups predominantly composed of males more favourably. Therefore, women who are placed in these groups may likely perceive these assignments positively from a career and organisation-specific perspective. However, in this same organisation, males placed in groups comprised largely of women, or in groups where female representation is increasing, likely perceive these groups as lacking in power and status. Their placement in these groups is taken as a signal that they are not on track to achieve greater power within the organisation.

Postmodern and critical perspectives on diversity

The work discussed previously fits squarely within a positivist paradigm. According to the positivist paradigm the nature of social reality is seen to be stable, with pre-existing patterns just waiting to be discovered. The result is that theories on gender identity remain decontextualised from the social, economic, political and ideological environment. Postmodern and critical theories question the tendency to essentialise gender, race and other categories of identity (e.g. Acker, 1992; Calas and Smircich, 1996; Alvesson and Billing, 1997; Benschop, 1998). Interest is in the subjective social and organisational meaning of gender. These scholars argue that the reification of gender as 'women' has resulted in a general neglect of understanding gender relations and power in organisations. Mills and Tancred (1992) argue for a theoretical stance that recognises that organisations are not spaces into which people enter but, rather, networks of relationships that are deeply gendered. For example, Fletcher (2001) in a study of female engineers shows that emotional intelligence and relational behaviour, even when they are in line with stated organisational goals, are often viewed as inappropriate because they collide with powerful, gender-linked images of good workers and successful organisations. This means that images of good workers and successful organisations are considered as primarily 'masculine'.

Work by Collinson and Hearn (1996) and Cheng (1996) explicates the nature and practices of masculinity. Cheng (1996) uses the concept of hegemonic masculinity to describe the masculinist ethos that privileges what have traditionally been seen as natural male traits. According to Cheng (1996: xii), 'writing about masculinities need not be about the male sex. Masculinity can be and is performed by women. Women who are successful managers perform hegemonic masculinity'. For example, executive-level women have reported that developing an interpersonal style 'comfortable for men', accepting more risky assignments, and meeting higher than normal performance expectations were critical to their success (Nelson and Burke, 2000), indicating the gendered and masculine nature of their organisations, and the necessity of explicit recognition of this dynamic in order to succeed. The recognition of the hegemonic masculinity of organisations raises the question of just how much 'diversity' can really flourish in organisations.

Discussion activity 1.4

Nora Petrou has been working for Intertrust for nearly 20 years, first as a clerical worker and later as an accountant. As a division of a national communications company, Intertrust offers good salaries and benefits in a part of

(Continued)

(Continued)

northern Greece where unemployment is typically high and wages are low. Nora, a single mother of two, has always felt lucky to have the job.

However, recently a young accountant, Thomas Demetriou, has suddenly been promoted to a job that Nora – and everyone else in the department – thought she was better qualified for. The job had never been advertised inside or outside the company. Instead top managers had suddenly boosted the position's pay scale five grades and given the job to Thomas. After a few days, Nora went to the controller and applied for the position, insisting that she should be given an interview. Weeks went by with no word, until Nora requested a meeting with the controller and general manager (GM). The controller tried to pacify her by saying he had not interviewed her because he knew she wouldn't be happy in the position. 'You'd get bored in a week, Nora', he said. 'The job isn't nearly as interesting or challenging as what you're doing now'. Nora disagreed and pointed out that the pay was much higher. In addition, the higher profile would give her a better chance for future promotions. 'Look honey', the GM soothed, putting his hand on her shoulder, 'the decision has already been made. Thomas is a good man, and he fits in well with the other top guys around here'.

Discuss reasons for this situation.

Cultural diversity in Greece

Until 20 years ago, Greece was considered largely a mono-ethnic, mono-cultural and mono-religious country, a true 'nation state'. The dominant definition of the nation was ethno-cultural and religious, while civic and territorial elements were of secondary importance in defining who was Greek. The Greek state formally recognises only the existence of a religious Muslim minority in western Thrace, while the relatively large Roma population suffers discrimination in all spheres of life and is largely marginalised. During the past two decades Greece has become host to more than a million returning co-ethnics, co-ethnic immigrants and foreigners. Minority groups in Greece can actually be classified into three broad categories in terms of their closeness to the majority group. The term 'national majority' identifies Greek citizens born of Greek parents, in Greece, who are Christian Orthodox.

Co-ethnics

In terms of the national identity and citizenship conception, *omogeneis*, that is co-ethnics, are the minority groups that differ least from the national majority. There are two populations within the larger category of co-ethnics: Pontic Greeks[1] and ethnic Greek Albanians. Pontic Greeks are considered to be similar to native Greeks as regards their national consciousness, culture and religion. They only differ from natives in terms of their language and, at least for the first generation, in terms of the socio-economic system that they had been brought up in. It is clear that the cultural and linguistic difference of the Pontic Greeks is not perceived as challenging the national unity (Kokkali, 2010). Ethnic Greek Albanians differ from native Greeks mainly in their citizenship and to a lesser extent in their language. The ethnic, religious and cultural proximity of ethnic Greek Albanians with native Greeks makes them a minority group that is gradually assimilating into Greek society and poses no strong cultural diversity challenge to the country. At the same time their presence forces clarification of how national and cultural unity and homogeneity is pretty much constructed rather than given, depending often on beliefs in common genealogical descent more than actual cultural proximity.

Native minorities

The second category of minority groups are native minorities, that is people who are ethnically, culturally and religiously different from the national majority but which have formed part of the modern Greek state since its creation. These include the Muslims of western Thrace who are Turkish speaking, followers of Islam and largely self-identify as ethnic Turks. There are also three more native minority groups, the Macedonians of Greece, Greek Jews and Greek Roma who are Christians.

Diversity challenges

The Turks of Thrace pose an important ethnic and religious diversity challenge for Greece as they bring into question its ethnic and religious homogeneity. They share with other Greek citizens neither their genealogical descent nor their religion – they differ in the two fundamental elements that define the dominant vision of Greek national identity and citizenship. Their claims for collective recognition of their ethnic identity have generally been met with intolerance and rejection. At the same time Greece has been pressurised by the policies of the Council of Europe and by the European Court of Human Rights to adapt and update its policy towards its largest native ethnic minority. It has thus abolished the infamous article 18 of the Greek Nationality Code which had been used discretionarily to unilaterally deprive members of the minority of their Greek citizenship.

Overall, Greek policies towards the minority have become more liberal, defending the equality of individuals before the law and the state no matter what their collective

---

[1]Pontic Greeks are an ethnically Greek group who traditionally lived in the region of Pontus, on the shores of Turkey's Black Sea and in the Pontic Alps, in north eastern Anatolia and the former Russian Caucasus province of Kars, and also in Georgia.

affiliation is in terms of religion. These policies however have been defended in the name of the common, compact and unitary national interest that is the Greek Christian Orthodox majority's interest (Anagnostou, 2005), not by reference to human rights norms. There is no re-consideration or re-definition of what it means to be Greek nor a sort of collective level recognition of the existence of minorities that are part of the Greek nation state. There is as yet no room for these minorities to contribute to the definition of what it means to be Greek in the twenty-first century.

Migrant populations

The third category of minority groups in Greece are migrant populations. Five different populations can be identified: Albanians, as the largest group; Georgians and Ukrainians as the second and third largest nationalities among immigrants; Asian immigrants and asylum seekers (Pakistanis, Bangladeshis, Filipinos and Afghanis) who are Muslims from southeast Asia; and last but not least Sub-Saharan Africans who come from many different countries and are Christians in the large majority.

Diversity challenges

All immigrant groups raise important identity challenges to the Greek majority to the extent that they are ethnically different from the Greek nation. However, these challenges have been most acutely felt in relation to Albanian citizens for a number of reasons: because Albanians are by far the most numerous immigrant community in Greece, they are visible in the labour market, in schools, in leisure, among youth, in culture and the arts. Albanians also challenge Greek identity and culture because they are very close to it: the two groups share a common history (of conflict and coexistence), common culture and traditions (of the wider Balkans). Albanian immigration touches the most sensitive points of Greek national identity as it challenges the authenticity of the Greek nation and its symbolic boundaries with its neighbouring nations. Thus, it forces the Greek Christian Orthodox majority to re-consider both its internal and external boundaries: it obliges public opinion and a variety of social institutions such as schools, the welfare state, the labour market, state authorities defending equality in the labour market and in society to re-consider what it means to be Greek today (when 10 per cent of the population are of immigrant origin, a vast majority of whom are Albanian) and what are the rights of immigrants in Greek society and polity. It is interesting to note that the religious diversity of Albanians (when it was the case) has been largely invisible or indeed blurred not least because they have opted for an assimilatory path in this (but also in other) respect(s). By their silenced otherness they did not challenge the values and the practices of the dominant society. They are thus actually considered – and in this respect they are indeed – the most integrated migratory group in Greece (Kokkali, 2010). The debate that arose in December 2009 and January through to March 2010 with regard to the citizenship law reform is an interesting point in question, which highlights the predominantly ethnic diversity challenges that immigration raises for Greece.

Other groups of immigrants from Eastern Europe (Ukrainians, Georgians) have not posed important ethnic or religious challenges to Greek society because they largely share with the Greek majority the Christian Orthodox faith.

The immigrant groups that have most recently raised important diversity challenges in Greece by their visibility in the urban space are Asians. While Pakistani, Bangladeshi and Afghani immigration has been largely male only (and hence has not yet posed issues in school life for instance) and is overall numerically rather small, their largely illegal entry into Greece (crossing the Greek–Turkish borders with the help of migrant smuggling networks), their concentration in downtown Athens, and most importantly their instrumentalisation during the past few years (2007 onwards) by the Greek authorities has converted them (in the media and policy discourses) to the epitome of the 'migration evils' that Greece suffers. Since 2011, the major political parties and the media have been constructing immigration as a security issue, citing the case of 'illegal' immigrants accumulated in the centre of the capital.

Cultural diversity, power relations and inequality in Greece

The minority issues for long have been treated in Greece as taboo; they have thus stayed outside the public sphere and the public debate, permitting the emergence of non-transparent, arbitrary and oppressive regulations. Even if some non-governmental organisations (NGOs) and politicians (mainly of the left) support minority rights, the public discourse is dominated by fearful attitudes about 'national dangers' that correlate any claim of a particular linguistic and/or religious identity with foreign interests and irredentist aspirations (Cholezas and Tsakloglou, 2009).

According to Iliadis (2013) after 1990, the political discourse on the minorities in Greece has been characterised by:

- A formalistic invocation of the principle of fairness and egalitarianism.
- An obsession with national homogeneity and the fear of otherness.
- Suspicion towards minorities, which *a priori* are thought to constitute a threat to the country's territorial sovereignty.
- A legalistic approach: only minorities recognised by international treaties, such as the Muslim religious minority of Thrace, are officially recognised by the state.
- A selective reference to the ethnic dimension. For example, while the Slavic origins of the Pomak language are emphasised with a view to distinguishing the Pomaks (who are Muslims) from the ethnically Turkish majority of the Muslim minority in Thrace, the Slavic language and cultural identity of the Slavic-speaking Macedonians of Greece are not recognised by the Greek state.

Despite the above situation regarding minorities, the linguistic and religious differences come unavoidably into light, imposed by the undeniable socio-demographic changes that migration has brought to Greece. As a result, in recent years, there is an increasing debate about interculturalism, multiculturalism and cultural difference. However, despite the ongoing discourse on multiculturalism, the understanding of Greekness (and, thus, of the Greek national identity) as mono-cultural and mono-ethnic seem to impede the 'opening' of the Greek system to the cultures of its foreign population. Indeed, as Gropas and Triandafyllidou (2011) point out, a frequent understanding of what interculturalism is, implies the foreigners' assimilation to the Greek culture without involving any redefinition of the latter. Therefore, the so-called intercultural policies are plural in the letter of the law but rather assimilatory in their daily practice, thus reflecting the dominant understandings of what is Greek national identity more strongly than the more general principles of respect for and recognition of cultural diversity, in spite of the fact that those principles are currently regarded as integral parts of a liberal democracy such as Greece.

More generally, while multiculturalism in Greece is gradually being accepted as a fact, multiculturalism is seen as a normative approach that predicates the parallel (but not integrated) co-existence of different ethnic and cultural communities. By contrast, Greek policy makers and scholars tend to favour intercultural dialogue: notably the integration of individuals (not communities) into Greek society. In the Greek debate, the intercultural approach is seen as favourable to societal cohesion and as a normative and policy approach that is in line with modernity and liberalism. In practice, however, there is little change in education, anti-discrimination or political participation policies towards this (Triandafyllidou and Gropas, 2009).

The debate on the 2010 law on citizenship and the immigrants' brand new right to vote in the local elections is indicative of this discordance, which is again related to the understanding of Greekness. While an attempt to differentiate national identity from citizenship gradually came to light in the public discourse, reference to national history, the Greek ideals and national heroes is dominant. In this respect, the role of education is put into debate. For those in favour of civic citizenship, education is the means for becoming Greek, whereas, for those in favour of an ethnically based Greek nation, education should reinforce the existing ethno-religious conception of the nation, but cannot convert to Greeks those who were born 'foreigners', that is to say of foreign parents. In this sense, the cultural difference is understood as ethnic, linguistic and religious, all three echoing the ethnic conception of the nation.

The media and parliamentary debates regarding the construction of a mosque in Athens, on the occasion of the 2004 Olympic Games, are indicative of the dominant understandings of difference in Greece and of how religious difference, in particular, should be accommodated. In their analysis of the debates in the press, Triandafyllidou and Gropas (2009) point out that, while it was generally considered that constructing a Mosque was not only a reasonable religious freedom but also a necessary venue for the needs of the Muslims who desired to practise their faith, a significant underlying unease still existed. This latter partly concerned geopolitics and identity, thus linking the religious aspects of Islam (the construction of a mosque) with the question of national security and the relationship between Turkey and Greece. As such, the question of the mosque became intertwined with Greece's most significant Other (Turkey) and the West's most significant threat (violent Islamic fundamentalism) rather than being treated as part of internal arrangements within Greek society. In other words, cultural and religious differences were defined as coming from outside and/or necessarily related to a sense of threat – both military and symbolic – to the nation and its well-being.

In this case, another central issue was the disassociation of religious and national identity, as 'modernity' was at stake, meaning that the establishment of a temple of worship for another faith was considered necessary in a 'European' and democratic country like twenty-first century Greece. The terms 'tolerance' and 'democracy' were thus repeatedly mentioned. However, as Triandafyllidou and Gropas (2009: 969) maintain, diversity (and the tolerance of it) were recognised only as an individual private matter and not as an issue associated with the recognition of collective rights.

In the above debates, the term *tolerance* was either not used at all or very scarcely. In the Greek context, tolerance corresponds to *liberal tolerance*, notably the will to tolerate practices, beliefs or behaviours with which one does not agree although one has the power to suppress them. The use of the Greek term for tolerance is so far not connected to any sense of egalitarian tolerance, notably to acceptance, let alone respect of cultural diversity. Terms such as *pluralism* or *liberalism* are not used in the Greek political debate on migrants and minorities. There are no arguments made in the name of pluralism (let alone religious pluralism), nor in the name of liberalism. Liberalism is understood in the sense of right-wing neoliberal ideology and not as part of a diversity discourse. The terms *national heritage*, *national identity* and *the nation* are often used and hotly debated, and indeed in relation to issues pertaining to migrant diversity accommodation, integration or assimilation.

In truth, it is the term *integration* that is mostly used in Greek political and policy debates on ethnic minority and immigrant diversity. Conveniently, its meaning is often not clarified and hence can range from:

- integration in a multicultural perspective (focusing on the incorporation and participation of immigrants and ethnic minorities into state and society, taking into account their modes of ethnic and religious difference, reconsidering the meaning of national identity, and pluralising national identity – but these views are held by a very small minority of left-wing parties and intellectuals); to
- integration in an intercultural perspective (focusing on the integration of individuals rather than collectivities, integrating individuals as bearers of specific cultures, promoting the dialogue between cultures, acknowledging a multitude of cultures that co-exist within the society, and accepting and respecting 'other' cultures – such a perspective however does not permit the incorporation of collective difference into

Greek society in the sense that it does not allow for the reconsideration of the Greek national culture and identity, nor of the fact that for instance migrant or minority children are of 'hybrid' cultural upbringing); and/or to

- assimilation understood as the peaceful and welcoming but still total cultural, ethnic and linguistic assimilation of immigrants and minorities into the dominant Greek national culture and language.

Discussion questions

1. How can the theories described in this chapter be used to understand cultural diversity in Greece?
2. Compare the cultural diversity context in Greece with that in your own country. Which similarities and differences do you identify?
3. How could such a context affect diversity management policies in Greek organisations?

Discussion

As this chapter demonstrates, scholars have relied on multiple theoretical and research perspectives to understand diversity from a sociological and psychological angle. Despite a proliferation of academic research, there is still much to do about diversity.

First, scholars need to pay attention to the categorisation of diversity into deep-level diversity and surface-level diversity characteristics, as studied mainly by group demography research. Race and gender are placed within the surface-level category whereas personality traits and values fall within deep-level diversity. The hypothesis is that over time deep-level diversity may be more important to workgroup dynamics than surface-level diversity. There is real danger in reducing diversity to benign differences among people. To imply one type of diversity is 'surface' while another is 'deep' overlooks the role of conflict, power, dominance and the history of how race, gender and other socially marked categories have been created and maintained. Positioning race and gender as surface diversity can also end up reducing them to biological constructs without any social meaning. For example, Zanoni and Janssens (2003) argue for the development of a non-essentialist reconceptualisation of diversity that acknowledges power.

More analysis is needed of the complex power relations in which gender and race are embedded. A case in point is the work of Collinson et al. (1990). In their study of 45 companies in five industries in the UK, they show how sex discrimination can be reproduced, rationalised and resisted by those in positions of domination and subordination within the recruitment and selection processes of the organisation. At the same time, scholars need to recognise the intersectionality of race, gender and class in understanding inequality. Despite calls for this type of analysis (e.g. Bell and Nkomo, 2001), there is a tendency to study race or gender, and rarely both together or both with class. The concept of intersectionality offered by black feminist theory underscores that everyone in every context has race, gender and class (Hooks, 1984). Black feminists also suggest that people are oppressed and social hierarchy is maintained by a number of bases, including ethnicity, sexual orientation, age and physical ability. Categories of domination are relational concepts and gain meaning in relation to one another. Hence, differences among groups must be viewed as systematically related.

Finally, one cannot engage with a world of inequality from insular disciplinary languages, positions or frameworks, and for that reason our theorising has to be multidisciplinary. Interdisciplinarity is not only about learning from different disciplines for a more complex engagement with the problem of inequality. It is also a way for keeping in view the needs for change in frames of thinking and understanding, as those problems evolve partially as a result of prior ways of understanding and acting upon them. Complexity rather than simplification is the aim, as much as change rather than stability is. In emphasising, perhaps more than in the past, the very material conditions of inequality continuing to be produced by a number of power relations all around the world, we are also attempting to advance the possibility of a different kind of understanding of diversity. We need a field that allows us to ask: What prevents change? Who keeps the gates closed? Whose knowledge is allowed? What kinds of politics are the politics of knowledge in the sociological and psychological field of diversity?

Discussion activity 1.5

How would you evaluate the following advice – 'Re-phrase the conversation: while diversity has traditionally been thought of in terms of demographic diversity (e.g. gender), the conversation is shifting to diversity of thought as a way to describe the desired end game: where different perspectives become the point of valued difference rather than our visible characteristics.'

Summary and recommendations

We have attempted to map the theoretical terrain around the psychological and sociological approaches used to study diversity. This chapter suggests that understanding diversity requires an approach that recognises its complexity and multiple orientations. We also tried to point to some of the continuing dilemmas. Perhaps it will be frustrating to some that we do not offer a single passageway out of these dilemmas. Instead we feel that we need to pause to reflect upon the slippery slope of how we conceptualise and research diversity.

We also feel it is important that we reflect upon the strategies for change emanating from the perspectives that we use to study diversity. Perspectives rooted in social identity and demography largely suggest strategies of increasing contact between people with different identities (premised upon the contact hypothesis), manipulating demographic composition (e.g. cross-cutting job assignments) and changing cognitions. On the other hand, postmodern and critical theories imply far more radical approaches to changing organisations from structures of exclusion to inclusion. While both perspectives are highly sceptical about change emanating from positivist prescriptions, critical theorists see hope in attending to the social, historical and political contexts of diversity as means of achieving inclusion and equality (Alvesson and Deetz, 2000).

Discussion questions

1. Compare and contrast the four major debates outlined in the chapter, i.e. essentialism versus social constructionism, universalism versus cultural relativism, reductionism versus complexity, and identity versus coalition politics. How does each debate contribute to our understanding of diversity issues in organisations? How can these debates be used by management in order to develop policies for diversity management?
2. As a manager, how would you address the challenges faced by minority employees?
3. What is the glass ceiling and why do you think it has proved to be such a barrier to women and minorities?
4. Have you been associated with an organisation that made assumptions associated with a monolithic orientation? Describe the culture.
5. How would you apply social identity theory, embedded intergroup theory and demography approaches in preparing an organisation to accept diversity?
6. How might critical and postmodern approaches contribute to the advancement of women and minorities to higher-level positions in an organisation?
7. As a manager, how would you accommodate the special needs of different groups – such as single parents, older workers, or employees with poor English language skills – without appearing to show favouritism?
8. Have you ever tried to team up with people from a racial/ethnic, class, religious, etc., background very different from your own? What happened? If you have not had such an experience, why do you think that was? How can the theoretical approaches in this chapter help you reflect further on that experience?
9. What knowledge or skills would you need to be able to take action against an instance of racism? How could the theories presented in this chapter enable you to take action against racism?

(Continued)

(Continued)

10. Brainstorm a list of what constitutes 'women's work' and 'men's work' in your country of origin and then critically discuss the difference in the valuation of each.

11. A neighbourhood group in Athens, Greece, proposes to send the children of new immigrants to a special school, where first they can learn to speak Greek and later continue the rest of their education. The group says that this is for the good of the children. Would you have any concerns about this?

12. When African-American employees at Oilco filed a racial discrimination lawsuit against the company, top executives took quick action to defend the company against the charges and tried to save Oilco's reputation. But as the drama unfolded, it soon became clear that Oilco's lawyers were facing an impossible task. A top official had secretly taped meetings of managers freely using racial epithets and discussing how to make incriminating documents 'disappear'. In addition to exposing blatant acts of racism by Oilco managers and employees, the lawsuit revealed several examples of institutional racism, such as hundreds of minority employees being paid less than the minimum salary for their job category. With mounting evidence staring it in the face, Oilco settled the case and set up an independent task force to monitor its diversity efforts. However, the real challenge would be to root out and destroy the racism that permeated the organisation. Modest diversity efforts and promises weren't going to cut it. Top executives would have to come up with solid plans to make supporting and valuing diverse employees a key element of Oilco's culture. If you were a top manager at Oilco, what steps would you take to make Oilco a company where minority employees feel valued, respected and supported? You should base your plans on the theoretical approaches presented in this chapter.

CASE STUDY

Filipina domestic workers in the Greek family space

On Monday morning at 6:54 a.m., Klara was ready to leave her apartment in the centre of Athens, Greece. Her four-year-old son was sleeping in his bedroom and so was her husband. It was one of the most important days in her

(Continued)

(Continued)

career as she was organising a major event at work with colleagues from abroad. She could not leave though before Anabelle, her Filipina domestic worker, had returned from her Sunday break to take care of her son. At 6:55 a.m., Klara was feeling really stressed because Anabelle had not arrived yet. 'She is late, and I was explicit that she has to be here early in the morning, around 7:00 a.m. Where is she?', Klara thought and sat anxiously at the stairs waiting for Anabelle. She was paralysed for a couple of minutes and could not think or do anything. These couple of minutes seemed like a century to her.

At 7:00 a.m. sharp, Anabelle put the key in the door. When Klara heard the beautiful sound of the keys, she stood up, put on her coat, took her bag and moved towards the door. Every day she used to talk to Anabelle for a few seconds, repeating the same phrase almost mechanically looking at her for a couple of seconds: 'Good morning Anabelle, is everything OK?'. Anabelle never replied with more than a couple of words just trying to satisfy her employer and answer her question. Anabelle was not loud at all, in fact silence was the basis that structured this specific employment relationship, as if talking was an inappropriate expression of professionalism in the domestic environment. Not absolute silence, however, as she used to sing softly beautiful songs or hymns during the performance of her household duties. However, Anabelle was more than simply a person in this apartment who did not talk. Anabelle cared. This was actually what she was doing for a living, her job was to care for other people. And she cared in silence. She was trying on her part to create a good relationship with her employer, her 'ma'am', not as a relationship of equality, but as a communication practice that is shaped through the tacit exchange of interest, creating reciprocal positive feelings of love, affection and sympathy.

Today, however, something was different. Klara could feel it by looking at the expression of Anabelle's face and by listening to the way her body 'sounded' during the performance of the household tasks. 'I think that I can see on her body the signs of sadness ...' Klara thought for a few seconds. 'What a weird thought ... but she is very quiet today, so much that it becomes deafening! I need to ask her what is going on when I come back home from the event.'

Klara was thinking of Anabelle throughout the day even though she was so busy with her guests. She thought of the first days of her employment relationship with Anabelle where she was really surprised when after only three days Anabelle was running the domestic duties just like she did herself. Anabelle was doing exactly what Klara used to do at home without any guidance, without

(Continued)

(Continued)

any information provided by Klara about how she should perform her duties. 'How did this happen? How did she know everything without any practical advice and any guidance?' Klara had never thought about this before and it crossed her mind that it was simply through observation. Anabelle was a very good observer, she was carefully observing the habits of the family, the habits of her 'ma'am', so that she could subsequently anticipate and satisfy them without any specific guidance from her employer. 'So this is what her job is about. She tries to record the ways through which me and my husband, but especially me, structure our day and our lives in the domestic space. What time do we wake up and what exactly do we do when we wake up? Do we cut the bread in thick or thin slices when we have our breakfast? What time does ma'am take her pills? Do I leave them on the refrigerator or in the bathroom? How do I arrange my clothes in the closet? What is our favourite cup for our afternoon coffee? However, I think that it is more than that. Anabelle was not only observing our daily practices and habits. She was also observing with great attention our emotions, our emotional state. That's how she cared! She is discreet, so professional! I was so right when I made the decision to hire a Filipina.'

When Klara came back home that night, she observed Anabelle for a couple of minutes and she could clearly hear this deafening expression of sadness on her face and body. 'What is wrong, Anabelle?' 'My mum died ma'am.' 'What? When? Why you did not say anything? Oh, Anabelle, I am so sorry ... You should have told me in the morning ... What can I do? How can I help? I think that you should go home and take next week off ... Let me know if you need extra money ...' Anabelle was crying quietly and she left immediately. She had to take care of everything back home. She took care of her mother when she was alive as she was indebted to her forever. Her mother sacrificed her life for her daughter and now her daughter sacrificed her life for her mother by reciprocating her mother's care when she was growing up. On the other hand, Klara was very loud, she was shouting, she was very upset and at the same time quite angry with Anabelle because she had not mentioned anything. The whole neighbourhood could hear what was going on in the house. Klara was so loud expressing her feelings and her thoughts as if the intensity of her voice indicated who was the boss in the domestic space, who was the native and who was the foreigner.

'Oh my god', Klara thought, 'it feels as if Anabelle, a foreigner, is a member of my family ... Anabelle is not just discreet. I think that she loves me and I feel that she is like a daughter to me ...' Klara hesitated for a while as the

(Continued)

(Continued)

thought that her domestic worker, her 'kopela', was like a daughter to her really shocked her. 'Could she ever be my daughter? I don't think so, but she could be my daughter-in-law! That's it!' This revelation was even more shocking for Klara as she realised that she treated Anabelle as her daughter-in-law. The daughter-in-law is traditionally considered in the Greek symbolic sphere as a 'foreigner', who has moved into the family of her husband and has to live with him and his mother. The relationship is hierarchical and there are conflicts regarding the performance of the domestic duties and the children's upbringing. The domestic worker, just like the daughter-in-law, has to obey the employer–mother-in-law and most of all she needs to work for her. She is not independent, she is not fully respected and she is always a 'foreigner'.

'Actually, if I want to be honest with myself, I never really cared about her true emotions and her emotional state. Even though I used to observe her intensively, especially at the beginning of our relationship, I was not looking at her emotions, as it is also very difficult to understand the emotional expressions of a Filipina, but the way she was performing her duties. I could not say anything about her mood, but I knew exactly whether there was any dust left on the bookcase, what exactly she ate for lunch, whether she got some rest with her legs on the couch.' Klara ran into Anabelle's room as she felt that it was going to reveal more things about this important employment relationship. There were no signs of her personal identity in the room, it was left unchanged. The decoration was impersonal and dry, just like a hotel room. 'My house has never become home for Anabelle, it is an interim station between her boarding house and her family house back in the Philippines. Besides, I think, that unconsciously I would not have allowed any changes to her room, I am not sure how I would have reacted if Anabelle started to personalise her space. It feels as if I have swallowed and digested Anabelle.' And with this thought Klara went to bed.

After a week, Anabelle came back home. Everything was under control and she seemed to be a little happier. However, Klara was wondering how she could frame differently her employment relationship with Anabelle after the realisation of the nature of that relationship with her domestic worker.

Questions

1. How would you describe this employment relationship? What is the basis of this employment relationship?

(Continued)

(Continued)

2. How is diversity constructed in this employment relationship? How is gender and race enacted in this employment relationship?
3. How could we use each of the debates presented at the beginning of this chapter to understand this employment relationship?
4. What is the role of 'care' in this employment relationship? How is care perceived in the Filipino and Greek culture?
5. How does a foreign woman employed as a domestic worker become a 'member of the family'?
6. How could this employment relationship be framed differently?

Further reading

Feminist Review, www.feminist-review.com

Johnson, A.G. 2005. *Privilege, power, and difference,* 2nd edition. Boston: McGraw-Hill.

Making diversity count, www.adl.org/education/mdc

McMahon, A.M. 2006. *Responses to diversity: Approaches and initiatives.* Retrieved March 13, 2014, from www.shrm.org/hrresources/whitepapers_published/CMS_017028.asp

Mor Borak, M. 2005. *Managing diversity: Toward a globally inclusive workplace.* Thousand Oaks, CA: Sage Publications.

What does it mean to be white? The invisible whiteness of being [VHS & DVD, 60 min.], Microtraining Associates, www.emicrotraining.com

References

Acker, J. 1992. Gendering organizational theory. In A. Mills & P. Tancred (Eds), *Gendering organizational analysis.* Newbury Park, CA: Sage, pp. 248–60.

Alderfer, C.P. & Smith, K.K. 1982. Studying intergroup relations embedded in organizations. *Administrative Science Quarterly,* 27: 35–65.

Allport, G.W. 1954. *The nature of prejudice.* Reading, MA: Addison-Wesley.

Alvesson, M. & Billing, Y.D. 1997. *Understanding gender and organization.* London: Sage.

Alvesson, M. & Deetz, S. 2000. *Doing critical management research.* London: Sage.

Anagnostou, D. 2005. Deepening democracy or defending the nation? The Europeanisation of minority rights and Greek citizenship. *West European Politics,* 28(2): 336–58.

Ashforth, B.E. & Mael, F. 1989. Social identity theory and the organization. *Academy of Management Review,* 14: 20–39.

Batson, C.D., Schoenrade, P. & Ventis, W.L. 1993. *Religion and the individual: A social–psychological perspective.* New York: Oxford University Press.

Bell, E. & Nkomo, S.M. 2001. *Our separate ways: Black and white women and the struggle for professional identity*. Boston: Harvard University Press.

Benschop, Y. 1998. Covered by equality: the gender subtext of organisations. *Organization Studies*, 19(5): 787–805.

Berger, P.L. & Luckmann, T. 1996. *The social construction of reality: A treatise in the sociology of knowledge*. Garden City, NY: Doubleday.

Brewer, M.B. & Miller, N. 1996. *Intergroup relations*. Buckingham, UK: Open University Press.

Broverman, I.K., Broverman, D.M., Clarkson, F., Rosencrantz, P.S. & Vogel, S. 1970. Sex-role stereotypes: A current appraisal. *Journal of Social Issues*, 28: 59–78.

Butler, J. 1990. *Gender trouble: Feminism and the subversion of identity*. New York: Routledge.

Calas, M. & Smircich, L. 1996. From the 'woman's' point of view: Feminist approaches to organization studies. In S. Clegg, C. Hardy & W. Nord (Eds), *Handbook of organization studies*. London: Sage, pp. 218–59.

Chacko, T.I. 1982. Women and equal employment opportunity: Some unintended effects. *Journal of Applied Psychology*, 67: 119–23.

Chattopadhyay, P. 1999. Beyond direct and symmetrical effects: The influence of demographic dissimilarity on organizational citizenship behavior. *Academy of Management Journal*, 42(3): 273–87.

Cheng, C. 1996. *Masculinities in organizations*. Newbury Park, CA: Sage.

Cholezas, I. & Tsakloglou, P. 2009. The economic impact of immigration in Greece: Taking stock of the existing evidence. *Southeast European and Black Sea Studies*, 9: 77–104.

Collinson, D.L. & Hearn, K.J. 1996. *Men as managers, managers as men: Critical perspectives on men, masculinities, and management*. Thousand Oaks, CA: Sage.

Collinson, D.L., Knights, D. & Collinson, M. 1990. *Managing to discriminate*. London: Routledge.

Cox, T. 1991. The multicultural organization. *Academy of Management Executive*, 5(2): 34–47.

Crocker, J. & Major, B. 1989. Social stigma and self-esteem: The self-protective properties of stigma. *Psychological Review*, 96: 608–30.

Crocker, J., Major, B. & Steele, C. 1998. Social stigma. In D.T. Gilbert, S.T. Fiske & G. Lindzey (Eds), *The handbook of social psychology*. New York: McGraw-Hill, pp. 504–53.

Deaux, K. & LaFrance, M. 1998. Gender. In D.T. Gilbert, S.T. Fiske & G. Lindzey (Eds), *The handbook of social psychology*. New York: McGraw-Hill, pp. 788–827.

Ely, R.J. & Thomas, D.A. 2001. Cultural diversity at work: The effects of diversity perspectives of work group processes and outcomes. *Administrative Science Quarterly*, 46: 229–73.

Evans, S.M. 1970. *Personal politics: The roots of women's liberation in the civil rights movement and the new left*. New York: Vintage Books.

Fajardo, D.M. 1985. Author race, essay quality, and reverse discrimination. *Journal of Applied Social Psychology*, 15: 255–68.

Firestone, S. 1979. *The dialectic of sex: The case for feminist revolution*. London: Women's Press.

Fiske, S.T. 1998. Steroetyping, prejudice and discrimination. In D.T. Gilbert, S.T. Fiske & G. Lindzey (Eds), *The handbook of social psychology*. New York: McGraw-Hill, pp. 357–414.

Fletcher, J.K. 2001. *Disappearing acts: Gender, power, and relational practice at work*. Cambridge, MA: MIT Press.

Fox, S.A. & Giles, H. 1996. Interability communication: Evaluating patronizing encounters. *Journal of Language and Social Psychology*, 15: 265–90.

Gaertner, S.L. & Dovidio, J.F. 1986. The aversive form of racism. In J.F. Dovidio & S.L. Gaertner (Eds), *Prejudice, discrimination and racism*. New York: Academic Press, pp. 61–89.

Gropas, R. & Triandafyllidou, A. 2011. Greek education policy and the challenge of migration: An 'intercultural' view of assimilation. *Race, Ethnicity and Education*, 14(3): 399–419.

Harrison, D.A., Price, K.H. & Bell, M.P. 1998. Beyond relational demography: Time and the effects of surface- and deep-level diversity on group functioning. *Academy of Management Journal*, 45(5): 1029–45.

Hass, R.G., Katz, I., Rizzo, N., Bailey, J. & Eisenstadt, D. 1991. Cross-racial appraisal as related to attitude ambivalence and cognitive complexity. *Personality and Social Psychology Bulletin*, 17: 83–92.

Heinemann, W. 1990. Meeting the handicapped: A case of affective–cognitive inconsistency. *Journal of Applied Psychology*, 70: 379–88.

Hennessy, R., and Ingraham, I. 1997. *Materialist feminism: A reader in class, difference, and women's lives*. New York: Routledge.

Hogg, M.A. & Terry, D.J. 2000. Social identity and self-categorisation processes in organisational contexts. *Academy of Management Review*, 25: 121–40.

Hogg, M.A. & Turner, J.C. 1987. Intergroup behaviour, self-stereotyping and the salience of social categories. *British Journal of Social Psychology*, 26: 325–40.

Hooks, B. 1984. *Feminist theory: From margin to center*. Cambridge, MA: South End Press.

Iliadis, C. 2013. The emergence of administrative harassment regarding Greece's Muslim minority in a new light: Confidential discourses and policies of inclusion and exclusion. *Nationalism and Ethnic Politics*, 19(4): 403–23.

Jodelet, D. 1991. *Madness and social representations*. Hemel Hempstead, UK: Harvester Wheatsheaf.

Jost, J.T. & Banaji, M.R. 1994. The role of stereotyping in system-justification and the production of false consciousness. *British Journal of Social Psychology*, 33: 1–27.

Kinder, D.R. & Sears, D. 1981. Prejudice and politics: Symbolic racism versus racial threats to the good life. *Journal of Personality and Social Psychology*, 40: 414–31.

Kokkali, I. 2010. Spatial proximity and social distance: Invisible forms of Albanian migrants' exclusion in the cityspace: evidence from Greece. Paper presented at the World Bank conference on poverty and social inclusion in the Western Balkans, Brussels, 14–15 December.

Larkey, L.K. 1996. Toward a theory of communicative interactions in culturally diverse workgroups. *Academy of Management Review*, 21: 463–91.

Major, B. & Schmader, T. 1998. Coping with stigma through psychological disengagement. In J.K. Swim & C. Stangor (Eds), *Prejudice: The target's perspective*. San Diego, CA: Academic Press, pp. 219–42.

Millett, K. 1970. *Sexual politics*. Garden City, NY: Doubleday.

Mills, A. & Tancred, P. 1992. *Gendering organizational analysis*. Newbury Park, CA: Sage.

Nahem, J. 1980. *Psychology and psychiatry today: A Marxist view*. New York: International Publishers.

Nelson, D.L. & Burke, R.J. 2000. Women executives: Health, stress and success. *Academy of Management Executive*, 14(2): 107–22.

Noels, K.A., Giles, H. & Le Poire, B. 2003. Language and communication processes. In M.A. Hogg & J. Cooper (Eds), *The Sage handbook of social psychology*. London: Sage, pp. 232–57.

Riordan, C.M. 2000. Relational demography within groups: Past developments, contradictions, and new directions. *Research in Personnel and Human Resource Management*, 19: 131–73.

Rogers, R.W. & Prentice-Dunn, S. 1981. Deindividuation and anger-mediated interracial aggression: Unmasking regressive racism. *Journal of Personality and Social Psychology*, 41: 63–73.

Rudman, L.A. & Glick, P. 2001. Prescriptive gender stereotypes and backlash against agentic women. *Journal of Social Issues*, 57: 743–62.

Sears, D.O. 1988. Symbolic racism. In P. Katz & D. Taylor (Eds), *Towards the elimination of racism: Profiles in controversy*. New York: Plenum, pp. 53–84.

Steele, C.M. & Aronson, J. 1995. Stereotype vulnerability and the intellectual test performance of African-Americans. *Journal of Personality and Social Psychology*, 69: 797–811.

Tajfel, H. & Turner, J.C. 1979. An integrative theory of intergroup conflict. In W.G. Austin & S. Worchel (Eds), *The social psychology of intergroup relations*. Monterey, CA: Brooks/Cole, pp. 33–47.

Taylor, D.M. & Moghaddam, F.M. 1994. *Theories of intergroup relations*. Westport, CT: Praeger.

Thomas, W.I. 1966. *W.I. Thomas on social organization and social personality*. University of Chicago Press.

Triandafyllidou, A. & Gropas, R. 2009. Constructing difference: The Mosque debates in Greece. *Journal of Ethnic and Migration Studies*, 35(6): 957–75.

Tsui, A.S., Egan, T.D. & O'Reilly, C.A. 1992. Being different: Relational demography and organizational attachment. *Administrative Science Quarterly*, 37: 547–79.

Tsui, A.S., Egan, T.D. & Xin, K.R. 1995. Diversity in organisations: Lessons from demography research. In M. Chemers, S. Oskamp & M. Costanzo (Eds), *Diversity in the workplace*. Thousand Oaks, CA: Sage, pp. 37–61.

Wright, S.C. & Taylor, D.M. 2003. The social psychology of cultural diversity: Social stereotyping, prejudice, and discrimination. In M.A. Hogg & J. Cooper (Eds), *The Sage handbook of social psychology*. London: Sage, pp. 432–57.

Young, J.L. & James, E.H. 2001. Token majority: The work attitudes of male flight attendants. *Sex Roles*, 45: 299–319.

Zanoni, P. & Janssens, M. 2003. Deconstructing difference: The rhetoric of human resources managers' diversity discourses. *Organization Studies*, 25(1): 55–74.

Leadership and diversity management in a global context

2

Clifford Lewis and Ahu Tatli

Intended learning outcomes

After reading this chapter, you will be able to:

- Identify different theoretical approaches to leadership
- Explain the role of leadership in diverse organisations in a global context
- Explain the challenges that practitioners face in developing leadership capacity in diverse organisations
- Understand the challenges that scholars face in theorising about leadership in diverse contexts

Introduction

Diversity management literature suggests that support from senior leadership of an organisation is key for the success of its diversity policies, programmes and initiatives (Fenwick et al., 2011; Kellough and Naff, 2004; Ng and Wyrick, 2011). A strong leadership commitment enhances the profile of diversity management, elevating it to a significant strategic priority. Furthermore, when leaders act as role models and diversity champions, they lend legitimacy to diversity goals and concerns in the eyes of other organisational actors including line managers and non-managerial employees (Tatli and Özbilgin, 2009). As a result, support from the top leadership cascades down to all levels and functions of the organisations, creating a sense of importance and urgency to achieve a culture of equality, diversity and inclusion in the organisation. However, research shows that leadership roles often lack diversity in terms of demographic diversity dimensions such as gender, race and ethnicity, social class and sexual orientation among others (Bebbington and Özbilgin, 2013; CEDA, 2013; Kang et al., 2007; Tatli et al., 2013). Furthermore, the meaning of leadership and expectations from a leader are not fixed universally, but vary across time and space depending on the specific geographical context under investigation. It is, therefore, important to understand the link between leadership and diversity management in its local and global contexts. Accordingly, this chapter aims to explore the interplay between diversity and leadership in its contextual specificity. In order to fulfil its aim, the chapter presents both theoretical and empirical insights. Theoretically, the chapter provides a critical review of the academic literature on leadership. We explore competing definitions of leadership; introduce three key approaches to leadership and discuss these approaches in relation to workforce diversity. In order to highlight the link between the theoretical debates and real-life situations, we present country-specific examples in the second half of the chapter. The examples are derived from the UK and South Africa. We have chosen case examples from the UK and South Africa as these two countries help us understand the breadth of contextual diversity challenges. The UK has a long-standing equality and diversity tradition, both in terms of the public debate around the issue as well as anti-discrimination legislation. South Africa, on the other hand, has a unique history of Apartheid, which was followed by a significant legal, political and economic push towards promoting equality, diversity and inclusion. Yet, both countries experience leadership challenges in terms of diversity of leadership, i.e. lack of diversity in corporate leadership as well as in relation to leadership for diversity, i.e. commitment to diversity from organisations' leaders. These two country examples help us to understand the convergence and divergence of diversity and leadership issues internationally. In order to contextualise these examples, we first provide background information on the societal and legal environment in these two countries. Following the contextual background, we present a sectoral example from the UK and a company example from South Africa. The UK example is based on a study of the arts and cultural sector, and explores the ways in which sectoral dynamics may create unique leadership challenges in terms of diversity. The South African example focuses on a retail company, which has invested significantly in its leadership diversity. The case study at the end of the chapter builds on the South African case example and further elaborates the use of a leadership development programme in order to increase diversity among organisational leaders. Table 2.1 provides definitions of key terms used in this chapter.

Table 2.1 Definitions of key terms

Term	Definition
Affirmative action	The act of providing special opportunities to a previously disadvantaged group in order to correct inequalities (Vermeulen and Coetzee, 2011).
Apartheid	An oppressive governmental regime in South Africa between the years 1948 and 1994. It involved complete racial segregation and the domination by the white minority population over the majority black population (Clark and Worger, 2004).
Broad-Based Black Economic Empowerment	A legislated industry practice in South Africa aimed at correcting unfairness and inequality in South African industry. It involves preferential treatment of organisations who are compliant in terms of equitable representation, regarding government procurement, funding opportunities, etc.
Diversity management	Organisational policies and practices to manage and promote workplace diversity in an effective manner.
Inclusion	An organisation's aspiration to improve the sense of belonging among all employees.
Leadership	A social process which uses power to create meaning in an organisation.
Meaning	An individual's experience of value of activity and membership of a collective (Podolny et al., 2010).
Power	The potential to affect outcomes (Wrong, 2009).
Workforce diversity	Demographic and job related differences among people within the organisational workforce.

Literature review: leadership and diversity

Diversity management initiatives are important, but not sufficient to address the management needs of growing diversity in modern workplaces (Combs, 2002). We propose effective leadership as a complement to existing diversity management efforts. In fact, diversity management literature emphasises the significant role that organisational leaders could play in promoting diversity (Cox, 1991). As a result, organisations need to have not only diversity managers or practitioners who are responsible for the design and implementation of diversity management policies, but also leaders from different organisational functions who are committed to diversity goals. Research also shows that diversity initiatives are more likely to succeed if the leadership of the organisation is diverse (Day and Greene, 2008). However, the credibility of this commitment to diversity goals among the organisational leadership is under threat if one considers national employment equity statistics. Bebbington and Özbilgin (2013) express concern over what they call the *diversity paradox*, a situation where a non-diverse leadership is tasked with promoting diversity. This chapter draws on contextual data from the UK and South Africa to demonstrate how diversity dynamics and leadership interact in organisations. Therefore, let us briefly consider some of the aforementioned statistics from these regions. In the UK women account for just under half of the economically active population (ONS, 2014), but according to a recent survey a mere 15.6 per cent of directors in FTSE 250 companies were women (BIS, 2011). Similar to this imbalance in gender representation in the UK, in South Africa white people account for 11.3 per cent of the economically active population, but fill a staggering 72.6 per cent of top management roles (Commission for Employment Equity, 2013).

Two important themes seem to emerge here. Firstly, organisations need to be aware of the seemingly systematic under-representation of certain groups in leadership positions and identify and remove processes that maintain these inequalities. Secondly, in establishing a more representative upper echelon of management, organisations should also aim to foster a legitimate and credible appreciation for diversity among its leadership. In so doing, organisations may avoid the creation of a *diversity paradox*. At this point it is necessary to explore the possible differences between management and leadership, because diversity from a managerial perspective can be very different from diversity from a leadership perspective. For the purpose of this discussion some clear conceptual distinctions need to be made, although in the day-to-day setting of organisations you may find that the processes of management and leadership are inextricably intertwined.

Although management and leadership are two concepts with many overlaps, they are two distinguishable organisational activities both using power in some way. Zaleznik (1977) differentiated these two concepts on the basis of the nature of the relationship between managers and their subordinates and that between leaders and their followers. According to Gabriel (2011) the differences in these relationships can be examined on four levels. These differences are juxtaposed in Table 2.2.

Albeit somewhat rigid, the distinction between management and leadership is useful as we can deduce both a functional and relational difference. Managers focus on boundaries and compliance and as a result need to maintain a somewhat clinical relationship with subordinates. Leaders on the other hand focus on vision and innovation and therefore need to establish and maintain relationships based in emotion which would sustain those relationships. Although it is hard to completely separate management from leadership, the emphasis on establishing and sustaining relationships in leadership is particularly important in understanding the leaders' role in

Table 2.2   Differences between managers and leaders

Managers	Leaders
Consider logic and rationality	Consider emotions and intuition
Focus on details and eliminate uncertainty	Focus on a broad and general future
Value efficiency and reducing waste	Allow waste for the sake of change
Seek order and regularity	Seek change and improvement

Adapted from Gabriel (2011).

championing diversity management. As opposed to simply ensuring diversity targets or quotas are met, diversity leaders need to ensure that diversity becomes part and parcel of organisational life. In other words, leading diversity requires going beyond managing top-down diversity initiatives towards a legitimate belief in the value of diversity which trickles down the organisational hierarchy.

Numerous definitions of leadership cite an influence on the behaviour of followers towards a common organisational goal (e.g. Bolden et al., 2011; Stogdill, 1997). However, the assumption that followers share an organisation's goals or objectives might not necessarily always be correct. With contemporary organisations comprising of people from different generations, cultures, socio-economic backgrounds, ethnic groups, genders – and the list goes on – it becomes difficult to imagine that this diverse group of people would all value and work towards a common set of organisational goals. Therefore, it is suggested that leaders should be seen as meaning makers, which in turn gives purpose to efforts through shared values, priorities and beliefs (Andreski, 1983). Meaning here refers to the extent to which an activity holds value and also affirms membership of a certain group – such as a work team or organisation. In essence, leaders create order and a compelling vision for the future of an organisation through the creation of meaning (Morrill, 2007).

Top management that is able to lead in diverse contexts will therefore first and foremost be representative of that specific context. Arguably, it is unlikely that an individual will find meaning through her membership of an organisation if she sees no representation of the demographic group to which she belongs. This lack of membership affirmation could be the result of various influences including, but not limited to, a lack of role models, exclusion from informal networks, perceived stereotyping and a lack of work–life balance support (Kilian et al., 2005). Similarly, one could argue that employees in organisational and social environments that foster diversity are more likely to find meaning and value in diversity. In this chapter we therefore frame leadership as a vehicle for this meaning creation around the significance of diversity management. Leaders, in the context of diversity management, use relational power in order to create a meaning and a common organisational goal that promotes workforce diversity.

Power is multi-dimensional, can be used in different ways and is responded to in different ways. The issue of gender differences serves as a good opportunity to illustrate the role of power in organisations. Bradley (2007) explains that the concept of gender, for example, is linked to the struggle over power between men and women. This imbalance of power between genders in society can then be used politically to maintain inequalities (Connell, 1987) including the glass ceiling to women's advancement into leadership roles (Pichler et al., 2008). Power is also contextual (Hardy and Clegg, 1996). Therefore, within the context of leading diverse organisational workforces, the power held by leaders is afforded to them through social norms and organisational practices. This would mean that leaders can only exercise power which would be deemed socially acceptable in any one particular national or regional context and also within the mandate of company policy. Furthermore, this power should be used by leaders to establish and maintain relationships with followers, as this would be necessary for the leader to act as an influential meaning-maker in an organisation.

Theoretical approaches to leadership

Leadership entered into scientific study early in the twentieth century and since then has evolved into many diverging theories and applications. It is possible to identify three broad approaches to leadership: the individual approach, the relationship approach and the social process approach. The core premises and assumptions of these approaches in the leadership literature are explored below.

Leadership as a property of the leader

The individual approach is the most widely used approach in leadership research. The assumption is that leadership is the result of one or many attributes, behaviours or actions by the individual leader. In organisational studies it is assumed that a leader with certain characteristics or abilities to perform certain tasks or behaviour would be able to effect desirable organisational outcomes. This approach assumes that certain inherent psychological traits, like personality for example, will influence a person's ability to be a leader. There is wide debate around this issue. Some scholars feel that certain psychological traits make for more suitable candidates in recruiting leaders, whereas others have shown that little evidence exists of inherent traits distinguishing leaders from non-leaders. The most well-known account of 'disproving' trait theory is that of Stogdill (1948). As the oldest approach to the studying of leadership, this approach is still used in contemporary research, which is problematic with regards to diversity. The majority of leader-centric approaches are positioned as culturally, racially, gender, class (etc.) neutral. If we consider, for example, the psychological approach to studying leadership it becomes clear that this is not the case. Psychological approaches to studying leadership often use psychometric instruments to measure constructs such as personality, intelligence and values. The constructs themselves are often informed by Western notions of culture, race, gender and class. For instance, organisational conceptions of the 'ideal leader' are often coloured by implicit assumptions around behavioural and appearance-based expectations. The ideal leader is often depicted as a white, middle/upper class man, who displays behaviours and characteristics that are historically associated with masculinity and the West (Acker, 2006). To mitigate this effect, instruments go through a rigorous process of testing for bias and unfairness before being available for use. Additionally, some instruments are also normed for different regions and groups of people so that diversity factors do not distort results. The same answer on the same personality test in the UK would therefore give a different result for someone being tested in South Africa. Cultural and contextual specificity of leadership poses a challenge for scholars and practitioners who wish to use the trait approach to studying leadership. An over-reliance on Western notions of leader-specific attributes can compromise the leader's ability to create meaning in diverse contexts. As the very constructs and measuring instruments are loaded with hidden Western ideals, the individual approach to leadership may potentially work against diversity by indirectly discriminating against certain groups and by inadvertently reproducing biases and stereotypes.

Relationship approach to leadership

In this approach, the focus is on the nature of the relationship between the appointed leader and his or her followers. It is asserted that leadership manifests as a relationship and that leaders can accomplish desirable organisational outcomes if they establish and maintain these relationships. Much of the leadership literature that conceives of leadership as a relational process between leader and follower also falls prey to the influence of Western conceptualisations of leadership, such as a hierarchical relationship between leader and follower. Although these types of leadership theory are not explicitly based on gendered, racialised and often culturally informed leader attributes, they still lack the ability to acknowledge complex diversity issues and in so doing could inadvertently work against diversity initiatives. This challenge to leadership as a relational process can be illustrated by using Leader–Member Exchange (LMX) theory as an example.

The LMX theory suggests that leaders establish exchange relationships with individual followers which result in in-groups and out-groups. In-groups comprise of followers who experience some form of emotional response to the leader, either in the way of inspiration, motivation or simply just being able to relate to the leader in a personal way. Out-groups are those individuals who are assigned to the leader as followers by virtue of their organisational position, but who do not experience an emotional response to the leader (Graen and Uhl-Bien, 1995). The discourse on how in- and out-groups develop is a key critique of LMX theory which also illustrates how a relational conceptualisation of leadership poses major challenges in diverse settings. As mentioned earlier in this chapter, contemporary workplaces are sites for various power struggles between groups – if we think specifically about gender and race. Additionally, workplaces are also often an eclectic combination of different value systems – if we think for example about culture and religion. If exchange relationships lead to the constitution of an in-group and an out-group, dominant values held by the in-group influence which individuals the leader is able to establish a relationship with. By extension, it is also plausible that this effect could also spill over into some exclusionary or even oppressive practices in diverse contexts.

For example, let's assume that a large portion of an organisation's board of directors has an individualistic value system that values individual excellence. If one of these directors were to be directly involved in the development of leadership talent, in- and out-group relationships could be established if some candidates ascribe to a more collectivistic value system. This might happen because more collectivistic candidates could be perceived as weak and lazy, while the individualistic director could be perceived as inconsiderate or selfish. As a result, the collectivistic out-group candidates might then have access to fewer developmental opportunities which will then further reinforce preconceived judgements on the part of the in-group and the individualistic leader. The failure to recognise such complex in-group/out-group diversity dynamics will constrain the leader's ability to create meaning and could also reinforce power structures that exclude certain groups from accessing leadership roles.

Social process approach to leadership

This approach affords significant attention to macro social processes when theorising about leadership. Leadership is seen as a social process, which is embedded into larger social processes. Leadership theories that consider social processes are those which look at national culture, race or gender. Arguably the most well-known of the cultural leadership theories is that presented by the GLOBE study (House et al., 2004). This framework presents the world as a collection of different cultural clusters. Each cluster holds a specific orientation towards leadership and would value certain traits and behaviours more than others. This implies that leaders who have followers in different cultural clusters would have to be sensitive to the social dynamics in each cluster in order to affect desirable organisational outcomes. Other leadership theories that incorporate certain identity elements such as gender or race are able to take into account macro social processes that become invisible, but which have an impact on fairness and equality in the workplace. Some examples include studies on what is known as *Female Leadership* (Eagly, 2007) and *African Leadership* (Jones et al., 1996; Nkomo, 2006; Byrd, 2008; Bertsch, 2012). These leadership theories typically focus on power, specifically power imbalances across different groups, which become evident when representation at organisational leadership level is considered. Leadership theories that consider social identity might ask questions such as 'why are black people under-represented in organisational leadership?' (e.g. Ospina and Su, 2009) or 'do women have a leadership advantage?' (e.g. Eagly, 2007). Such an approach to theorising about leadership is, however, not without its limitations. Firstly, in an attempt to address the inequalities brought on by imbalances of power in society, certain social approaches to leadership inadvertently legitimise Western and masculine notions of leadership (Parker, 2005). This type of *prefix-theorising* is a typical critique of some mainstream management concepts such as *Female Leadership* or *African Leadership*. Whenever a prefix like this is added to the concept of leadership it implies that the group in question does not adhere to the 'norm', and needs special consideration or needs to adapt (Acker, 2006).

Furthermore, although it allows for the incorporation of complex social processes such as power relations and competing value systems, this approach takes the focus away from the people facilitating the leadership process, namely the individual leaders. A major challenge when considering leadership as a socially embedded process is mindfulness of leaders' scope of influence. Leaders, although in many cases they are agents of change, do not necessarily hold the power or ability to effect mass social change in terms of equality in the society. The three different views of how one should theorise leadership afford priority to one or several factors of the phenomenon that is leadership. However, these theories may be used in a way to complement each other. For instance, individual leader-focused and relationship-focused theories of leadership are used in conjunction with social-process-focused theories to allow for a more nuanced account of the interplay between leadership and diversity.

Discussion activity 2.1

Discuss the role of leaders in diverse contemporary organisations. How might an organisation's leadership spearhead diversity initiatives? At the same time, discuss in your groups how mainstream leadership theory might in fact hinder human resource professionals from enabling organisational leadership in fulfilling their role as far as diversity is concerned.

Leadership and diversity in context: examples from the UK and South Africa

The review of the literature in the previous section demonstrates that understanding the impact of leadership on diversity as well as the diversity within the leadership itself requires us to take a multidimensional approach that accounts for individual-level factors as well as relational and contextual factors. In this section, the issues of leadership and diversity will be explored in their immediate social, sectoral and organisational context. The section will offer practical examples of leadership and diversity from the UK and South Africa. However, before we present these practical examples, we first provide contextual information for these two countries.

The UK context

The UK has been one of the pioneers in Europe in terms of adoption of the US-originated diversity management approach (see Kandola and Fullerton, 1994). The focus of the diversity management approach on voluntarism, the business case and difference echoed well with the Anglo-Saxon belief in free market ideology and individualism (Barmes and Ashtiany, 2003). In the late 1990s when diversity management had entered the public discourse, it was equated with a dual commitment on the one hand to a pro-business agenda and on the other hand to multiculturalism (Healy et al., 2010; Tatli et al., 2012). Although the proponents of diversity management place an overwhelming emphasis on voluntary action and the business case, qualitative and quantitative studies show that equality legislation is the most important factor driving the diversity agenda in both public and private sector organisations (Tatli et al., 2008; Tatli, 2011).

The UK has well-developed employment equality legislation tackling discrimination on the grounds of age, disability, gender, gender reassignment, pregnancy and maternity, race and ethnicity, religion or belief, and sexual orientation (Equality Act, 2010). The earliest anti-discrimination laws were in the area of gender equality: the Equal Pay Act of 1970 and the Sex Discrimination Act of 1975. In the 1970s, the Race Relations Act of 1976 was also passed. The next piece of key equality legislation was introduced in 1995 in order to address discrimination on the grounds of disabilities: the Disability Discrimination Act. These Acts were followed in the 2000s by laws that aim to tackle discrimination on the grounds of sexual orientation, religion and belief, and age. More recently, these separate pieces of anti-discrimination legislation were brought together in the Equality Act of 2010.

In that context, the Equality and Human Rights Commission (EHRC) was established in 2007 as a statutory body to oversee the implementation of the equality legislation. The EHRC is responsible for providing information on and support for legislation. The Commission does this by publishing statutory codes of practice for public sector organisations as well as non-statutory guidance for employers in both public and private sectors. In addition, the EHRC has powers to carry out investigations of organisations and take them to court in relation to unlawful discrimination. However, the enforcement powers of the Commission vary considerably between the public and private sectors due to the much stronger secondary legislation for the public organisations, and as a result the public sector fares better than the private sector in terms of managing workforce diversity (Klarsfeld et al., 2012). The public equality duties require public sector organisations to set equality and diversity objectives and monitor their progress across these objectives. As a result, diversity activities are better resourced in the public sector, and these activities have a greater breadth and coverage compared to the private sector (Tatli et al., 2008). These diversity activities include positive action programmes, equal pay audits, work–life balance programmes, accessibility initiatives, anti-harassment policies, inclusive service delivery activities, among others, and they target a range of equality strands including gender, race and ethnicity, age, disability and social class background.

The UK labour market is very diverse thanks to historical as well as more recent trends including the legacy of the slave trade and colonialism, international migration, rising female participation in the workforce and an ageing population (Oikelome, 2010;

Klarsfeld, 2012). Despite this diversity, the labour market continues to be characterised by unfair discrimination, pay gaps, and vertical and horizontal segregation along diversity faultlines such as gender, race and ethnicity, age, sexual orientation and disability, among others (EHRC, 2011). The top leadership in companies continues to be white men predominantly. For instance, Lord Davies' 2011 inquiry into women on boards in the UK showed that only 12.5 per cent of directors of FTSE 100 companies and 7.8 per cent of directors of FTSE 250 companies were women (BIS, 2011). Since then gender representation on boards has improved, with women accounting for 20.7 per cent of the FTSE 100 boards, and 15.6 per cent of the FTSE 250 boards in 2014. However, male dominance of company boards still persists with severe under-representation of women among executive directors, which stands as low as 6.9 per cent in the FTSE 100 boards and 5.7 per cent in the FTSE 250 boards (BIS, 2014). This shows that there is a significant diversity gap in the leadership of UK organisations. Considering that the current leadership serve as the gatekeepers of future leadership roles, it is imperative for organisations to address the lack of diversity in senior roles as well as in their overall workforce. Furthermore, as we highlighted earlier, leadership diversity, is not only a significant diversity target in itself, but also an instrumental one for promoting diversity at other levels and in different areas. Leaders can champion diversity, helping to increase the belief in and commitment to diversity by all organisational members. Leaders from diverse backgrounds can act not only as effective diversity champions but also as inspirational role models and mentors. Therefore, UK organisations in both public and private sectors need to consider the interplay between leadership and diversity as one of the core dimensions of their diversity approach.

The South African context

Arguably, one of the things South Africa is most famous for is its history of Apartheid. Following the National Party's (NP) election to power in 1948, new legislation classified South Africans into four racial groups, namely 'White', 'Native', 'Coloured' and 'Asian' (Baldwin-Ragaven et al., 1999). The 'White' category was reserved for Caucasian or European people, 'Native' referred to those individuals of African descent, the 'Asian' category included people who were of Asian (Asia continent) heritage, and those from a mixed-race background were classified as 'Coloured' (Watson, 2007). During the Apartheid regime, residential areas, education, medical care and public services were segregated, with inferior services provided to the non-white areas; political representation by non-white candidates was prohibited; and from 1970 black people were even deprived of their South African citizenship (Beck, 2000). These racial categories are still being used widely by South Africans to self-identify; organisations still use these categories for statistical and employment equity survey purposes and the National Statistics Authority still uses these racial categorisations in the national census (StatsSA, 2012b).

Apartheid legislation instituted geographic segregation and forced non-white South Africans into certain geographic areas. Due to 'pass-laws', which required the black population to carry pass-books regulating movement between geographic areas, black or 'Native' South Africans were severely limited in terms of where they could go, which in turn affected their ability to earn an income (Johnstone, 1979). In addition to restrictions imposed by pass-laws, the NP-led government established 'labour bureaux' where African men between the ages of 16 and 64 were required to register with a local employment officer. Being stuck in geographic areas without employment opportunities and with no legal right to move, job seekers were at the mercy of employment offices which notified them of job opportunities and then required them to sign a legally binding contract to take up said employment. The majority of these jobs were for manual, unskilled and minimum wage labour, while other positions like management jobs were reserved for white workers (Clark and Worger, 2004). These restrictions on movement in addition to poor education and development opportunities essentially meant that the non-white population in South Africa remained impoverished and without opportunities to change their circumstances.

In an attempt to correct these injustices of the past (pre-1994), at least in an employment context, affirmative action is utilised in South African industry, in both the private and public sectors. Affirmative action is not an original South African concept/practice. It was first cited in the Wagner Act of 1935 in the United States (Bacchi, 1996). In a modern context the concept refers to various practices that involve organisations taking positive steps towards a more inclusive, fair and equitable employment situation. Specifically, it involves ensuring that equal employment opportunities exist for individuals who have the same ability to compete for a position (Rossouw, 1994), and in South Africa it also includes remedial 'reverse discrimination' which is applied to lend more opportunities to those groups who have previously been denied them (Gamson and Modigliani, 1994). These ideals are all crystallised in South African legislation such as the Employment Equity (EE) Act of 1998 and the Broad-Based Black Economic Empowerment (BBBEE) Act of 2003. The EE Act is primarily concerned with the promotion of equality at work, the elimination of unfair discrimination, the achievement of a diverse workforce, the promotion of economic development and diverse representation. The BBBEE Act, in turn, is primarily intended to address a change in the racial composition of the South African workforce, but also to have an impact on business ownership, to address the issue of women in business and also to allow more opportunities for rural communities.

Since the abolition of Apartheid and the introduction of affirmative action policies the major changes seem to have taken place first in the public sector, and this has remained the situation to date (Scott et al., 1998; Sing, 2011; StatsSA 2012a; Commission for Employment Equity, 2013). Somehow, while still appearing to remain within the boundaries of legislation, the South African private sector is lagging far behind in achieving equality and inclusion targets in comparison to the public sector, especially at the higher influential levels of organisations. Tables 2.3 and 2.4 clearly indicate this equality challenge in South African industry. Pilot studies and opinion surveys have indicated that research is needed on the experiences and perceptions of the public and those who administer affirmative action (Amos and Scott, 1996; Vermeulen and Coetzee, 2011).

Table 2.3 South Africa's economically active population by gender and race

	Men (%)	Women (%)
Black	40.7	34.2
Coloured	5.8	5.0
Indian	1.9	1.1
White	6.4	4.9
Total	54.8	45.2

Adapted from Commission for Employment Equity (2013).

Table 2.4 South Africa's industry leadership by gender and race

	Top management (%)		Senior management (%)	
Black	12.4		18.4	
Coloured	4.7		7.1	
Indian	7.3		9.5	
White	72.6		62.4	
Foreign national	3.1		2.5	
Gender	Men: 80.2	Women: 19.9	Men: 69.2	Women: 30.7

Adapted from Commission for Employment Equity (2013).

Practical example: leadership and diversity in the arts sector in the UK

The UK and particularly London is well known for its vibrant arts and culture industry. Many universities which offer degrees in the field have work placement programmes in place to help their students gain industry experience and hence improve their employability upon graduation. Work placement is seen as an important source of networking, and of getting to know the sector and potential employers. However, research shows that students' demographic backgrounds have an impact on the quality and outcomes of the work placement experience as well as its positive impact (Smith et al., 2001; Tatli and Özbilgin, 2012).

Tatli and Özbilgin (2012) conducted research on the work placement practices in arts and culture departments of universities in London. The research included 26 interviews with three key stakeholders, university work placement directors, students and host organisations. The research showed that the lack of leadership diversity across certain strands had a negative impact on the inclusiveness of the sector. The sectoral leaders from the universities and host organisations believed that the arts and culture sector was inclusive, diverse and open, and hence ahead of other sectors in terms of diversity. The examples used to showcase the diversity in the sector were related particularly to gender and sexual orientation. As a result, there was a common belief that there was not much need for formal diversity programmes and policies in a sector that was already diverse. Interestingly, students who participated in the study told a very different story with regards to the diversity in the sector. Although all students thought that work placement could have served them well potentially by increasing their employability, this was not the outcome for many of them due to the inattention to equality and diversity issues among the sectoral leaders. This inattention was particularly acute in relation to social class and race and ethnicity diversity. For instance, although leaders from universities and host organisations accepted that the sector lacked diversity in terms of class and ethnicity, they failed to recognise this as an area of concern in organising and delivering work placement programmes. Conversely, interviews with the students demonstrated the significant role of social class background, and race and ethnicity in shaping the work placement experiences and outcomes. Below are the words of some students:

> You know but they're not making it very attractive to ethnic minorities. In the education department as well! They reckon they want to increase diversity, but they're all like 'why?' The local community are all like really posh; well, it's all really patronizing.

> They would take people from Tower Hamlets and Hackney and we were, you know all but one of us, she was an English white girl and the others, there was me and three Asians. And then an opportunity came up for a job … I didn't apply for it because I didn't feel it was my sort of thing and I know one of the Asian girls tried for it and the white girl got it. It just makes me question the organization.

> They need to move away from the middle class. It needs changing and you know, we are in a very diverse community. And the bigger institutions, these upper class places, they need to embrace that. And the problem is the art sector, you know I'm talking about the big organizations don't reflect the community we are living in. And when you see organizations in areas that are quite deprived, they're not doing anything to employ the local

people. And I think there needs to be more education to make them more aware of the people that are around them. Not tunnel vision. A recommendation would be not just more education but to just be culturally aware. Get away from this white, middle class attitude. It's not a very attractive industry for ethnic minorities.

(Excerpts taken from Tatli and Özbilgin, 2012)

To summarise, the ideal worker in the arts and culture industry is implicitly depicted as white and middle/upper class. Students from non-white and working class backgrounds felt unwelcome in the sector. Interestingly, the sectoral leaders resisted the idea that the sector might be excluding certain groups. The leaders both in universities and employing organisations were blind to the privilege of the white middle class, which they themselves also belonged to. Change in the sector towards greater equality, diversity and inclusion requires increasing the class, ethnic and racial diversity of the leadership as well as raising existing leaders' awareness of the class and ethnicity bias in the sector.

Practical example: a company example from South Africa

This example is from a large retail group in South Africa. The group operates in various cities and towns across the nation and sells food, groceries, household non-food products and clothing, and also provides some financial services such as money transfers. The company positions itself as an equal opportunity employer and as a result reflects South Africa's diverse population. For this example we will be looking specifically at the retail group's management development programme.

In order to manage thousands of employees across all nine of South Africa's provinces, this retail group needs a sufficiently large and competent supply of management. Both micro and macro influences create the situation where a member of the management team needs to be trained in various technical competencies as well as behavioural competencies. As a result, the company needs to maintain a steady management talent pipeline. In an effort to have a standardised framework to develop such managers for its retail outlets, the retail group has designed and developed, amongst others, an entry level programme for the systematic enrolment and development of leadership talent. A participant enrols in this programme for a standard 12-month period in any one of the group's operational divisions. This training programme aims to prepare participants for their role as assistant managers, which is the first level of junior management in the group's structure. Figure 2.1 is a graphical depiction of the management hierarchy and indicates where the programme participant will be appointed after successful completion of the programme.

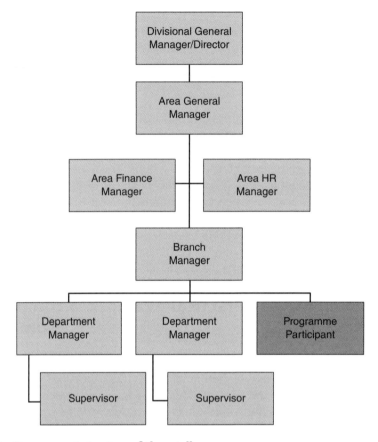

Figure 2.1   Management structure of the retail group

The programme is aimed at equipping the participant with the necessary foundational retail knowledge, retail-group-specific knowledge and practical skills, as well as leadership skills. No one walks into the organisation and immediately becomes a branch manager. One enrols in the programme and after successful completion is appointed as assistant manager, specialising in one department (e.g. administration, groceries, fresh foods, etc.). From assistant manager one will get the opportunity to be promoted to branch manager, from branch manager to area manager and so forth. This process implies an emphasis on development of skills in an effort to feed into the talent pipeline. Entry into this programme has two options. Either a candidate is recruited externally into this development role, or an employee at staff or supervisor level could be promoted into this position.

This programme has various benefits. It provides a standardised guideline for development and assessment activities and therefore minimises the chances of unfair discrimination. It also ensures that the organisation is continuously supplied with a stream of leadership talent. Finally, the programme also provides competitive advantage by way of attracting young leadership talent. Since the course is accredited by national quality assurance bodies, candidates earn a nationally recognised qualification after completion. This has proved to significantly increase the calibre of applicants into management roles at this organisation.

In addition to this in-house management development programme, which is designed especially for junior management, the group also makes regular use of leadership development schemes run by independent service providers. Enrolment into these programmes is time consuming and costly, and to ensure return on investment participants are carefully selected. Generally, participants for external leadership development programmes are selected based on merit, i.e. tenure with the organisation, existing management experience, performance track record and manager recommendations. No formal policy regulating gender, race or disability representation is currently in place.

As a large stakeholder in South African industry this organisation participates in affirmative action and BBBEE. Unfortunately, its representation at management level mirrors that of national trends in terms of gender and race. There is an active effort to recruit and select equitably into junior management and development schemes, but representation becomes skewed towards white men when moving up the management hierarchy. To date, no official policy has been implemented to correct for this trend.

Discussion activity 2.2

Think about the case of the retail group. They seem to invest a lot of resources into the development of management and leadership talent; however, their representation statistics still mirror those of the national trends that skew towards white men. Provide a detailed recommendation as to how they could improve their development initiatives in the hope of having a better representative management structure at all levels.

Summary and recommendations

This chapter has identified the key approaches to leadership and explored the relationship between leadership and diversity in a global context. As we have seen, the three key theoretical approaches to leadership can be differentiated on the basis of the level they locate leadership: individual leader level, at the level of the relationship between the leader and followers, or at the level of wider societal processes. All of these different views of how one should theorise leadership afford priority to one or several factors of the phenomenon that is leadership. However, the approaches that solely focus on the person of the individual leader or the relationship between the leader and followers overlook competing value systems and invisible power struggles that are the key characteristics of the multicultural and diverse organisations of today. As Barnard (1997) insists, leadership exists as a function of at least the interaction between leader, followers and conditions – the condition of diverse organisations being of particular concern here. Therefore, what seems to be lacking from several conceptualisations of leadership – especially those positioning leadership in the individual leader – is due consideration of the conditions within which these supposed individual and group processes are embedded. This makes the study of leadership from a diversity management perspective complex, as these 'conditions' could include various social dynamics at team, organisational and societal level. It is therefore important to reiterate our previous assertion that leadership is a process of meaning making.

The value of relating leadership in diversity management to the creation of meaning for followers becomes evident when one considers the two main components of meaningful action. First, an action can be considered meaningful when it supports an ultimate end which the individual performing the act values. Second, an action would be considered meaningful if it affirms the individual's connection to the community they feel a part of (Podolny et al., 2010). Leaders need to ensure both meaningful group interactions and that work assignments are perceived as meaningful. These components clearly resonate with the ethos of diversity management which advocates for equality, fairness and inclusion (Kilian et al., 2005; Eagly and Chin, 2010). The diversity of values, norms and expectations from leaders is a particularly prominent feature of organisations that operate in a global business environment (Syed and Özbilgin, 2009). Therefore, leaders should be able to identify and navigate through invisible power relations and conflicting value systems that are present in the organisational context. In that sense, formal diversity management policies are not enough. Organisations require leaders who relate to followers in an effort to create a strong meaning in relation to the importance and urgency of a diverse and inclusive organisational culture. As the practical example from the UK shows, the leaders, who are also often the gate keepers, need to recognise the power imbalances, privilege and disadvantage structures that stem from diversity categories such as gender, race and ethnicity, disability, sexual orientation, age and so on. They then need to act upon this recognition in order to redress the existing imbalances in order to promote inclusion, fairness and equality of opportunity. Furthermore, as our South African practical example shows, investment into training and development interventions may not be enough to ensure equitable representation at all management levels because organisations are embedded in a societal context that is characterised by structural inequalities and discrimination. For that reason, organisational leaders have a role to play in promoting equality, diversity and inclusion beyond their companies, in the wider society.

Discussion questions

1. What are the three theoretical approaches to studying leadership in organisations? Comment on their value as well as their limitations within the context of diversity management.
2. Explain the role of leadership in diverse organisations. Please provide evidence-based support for your position.
3. What challenges might practitioners face in developing leadership capacity in diverse organisations? Where applicable, provide real-life examples.
4. Explain the challenges that scholars might face is theorising about leadership in diverse contexts. Elaborate and comment on these challenges by drawing on the different theoretical bases for studying leadership.
5. Critically evaluate the role of leadership in diverse organisational contexts. Is leadership necessary or is management enough? Your answer should include a discussion of the broad approaches to leadership and their related limitations. Support your argument with relevant literature and illustrate it with real-life examples.

CASE STUDY

Implementing a leadership development programme in a South African company

This case study continues from the practical example in South Africa provided earlier.

(Continued)

(Continued)

A retail group in South Africa runs various development programmes to ensure that they have the necessary leadership talent for their rapidly expanding organisation. Despite a carefully designed in-house programme targeting junior management and specialised external development pro-grammes, run by experienced experts, the group still observes poor represen-tation of women and people of colour at top management level.

This poor representation of women and people of colour in top manage-ment has several negative consequences for the organisation. In addition to the obvious inequality, these consequences also pose certain tangible busi-ness threats in the South African context. These include a poor score on their BBBEE rating, a negative public image, as well as restricted access to certain public funds and licensing.

In an effort to become more representative at all levels of management the retail group has hired your consulting firm to get to the root of the prob-lem and suggest a solution for them. After receiving the assignment from your director, you start making arrangements with your client to conduct some research in the organisation. You decide to approach this problem from a group-level perspective, as it is the opinion of various stakeholders that this is a group-level problem. You subsequently request a series of focus groups, which include participants enrolled in a leadership development programme, to be held. Since the most striking under-representation relates to gender and race, you divide your focus group participants into white women, black women, black men and white men.

During your focus group sessions you receive very interesting responses from all the participants. You transcribe the responses from your digital voice recorder and sit down to analyse the content. Some of the most interesting responses were as follows:

White women group

I just thought that a coach would be more actively involved than what there was.

I think exactly what she said, like we trained in the departments our-selves which is fine, we know how to bake a bread, mould the dough, but there was never a specific time when you worked with the specific

(Continued)

(Continued)

manager of that department to show me what management skills are supposed to go with that.

I expected to learn about how to handle the people.

I expected to learn more about managing instead of doing the job itself.

A lot of times I've gone to my managers and said, 'this is what I've noticed, please explain it to me or help me', only to hear that they don't have time.

Yes, I also get along with the guys way better than with the girls.

Yes, this week is already going better than last week. But I still think that skin colour does have an effect.

They always say, 'if you want to know ask', but how are you supposed to ask something you don't know about? So it's good to go to the class to get guides and stuff so you can know what to ask.

Black women group

When I started here, I expected to be, like, a manager. Doing the job like a manager, not being used to do the job like a staff member.

I was expecting myself sitting in the office the whole day.

With me, um, the on-the-job training is there, the classroom training is marvellous, the mentoring is lacking.

We were not trained as a person. We had to take information. We had to train ourselves.

We have to help each other. It doesn't matter whether you are a junior manager or if you are a branch manager, sometimes you need help.

(Continued)

(Continued)

I just feel that men, they can open up to me. I can ask questions and you know we can communicate better, but now with women, I don't know. We have this thing where we are looking at each other like no, she thinks she is better.

Sometimes when a customer comes to you and explains a problem then they say they want to talk to a manager, and I say I am the manager and when the white junior manager walks past, then they will explain to them.

I expected to know the technical skills first, you know, then after that, you know, you have to learn the management skills. But I didn't expect to be on the technical part all the time.

[Facilitator] Do you feel that there is a perception among some people that black females do not have authority?

[Majority of respondents] Yes.

Black men group

Basically I thought it was going to be a six months training, we will be getting experience from people who have that previous experience in retail and then the others they don't have the experience on that. And then secondly I thought there was going to be an execution of on-the-job training. Same as like the mentors. Maybe they will be coming into the stores and then see you when you are doing the job.

What I expected to learn, I think I'm getting it. Leadership skills like communicating with staff and being assertive.

I wasn't expecting working like long hours.

I disagree with some things that happen in some branches. It's just a matter of like, at branch level, the managers' style that they are using.

Most of the stuff that I was given to instruct, or to delegate to the staff or to motivate the staff, was very easy for me.

(Continued)

(Continued)

If we see like someone is not coping, we try to help that person to build to the same level as the rest of us. So that's why you won't see a difference because we are always helping each other to build the same level.

Even in our store, we are treated like brothers and sisters.

My experience with ladies is no problem. I was the only guy in my group of this programme.

To be on my experience somebody to give you respect, actually we don't just demand respect from the staff, we earn the respect from the staff, by respecting them.

I think it's the manner of giving instruction. Each person has their own way of giving instruction, so the language that they are using, that is where the problem comes.

I think treatment of the managers is fair to me.

The skill that I grew in most is to function well under pressure. On this programme, you get exposed to working long hours, and you are under real pressure, you are required to work under those circumstances. So now I know I can work as a manager and handle that pressure.

White men group

I expected like, in the department, there should be a dedicated trainer for us.

I'm not happy with the sequence of the training, because one day they need you in a stocktake and one day they need you in the deli and you can't finish something.

[Facilitator] How has the content of the formal programme assisted you in dealing with challenges?

[Respondent] Not a lot.

(Continued)

(Continued)

Our area manager is very strict about our training. He wants to know how you are doing, what's your progress and stuff like that.

In the beginning my black colleagues were more helpful than the white ones.

It also depends on how you stamp down your authority because you don't really have that big authority. Also, I agree it will depend from different people if how you, um, approach the people or get information. Tell them listen what's your problem?

We did experience with some of the guys in the programme we worked with is that their attitude was a big problem. Their attitude towards other participants. You make difficult for yourself, because that is the people who is going to help you in the future, so that can be like career suicide also.

Um, I can also add to that, um, I don't think it's just authority, I think it's also a problem with race, because I've witnessed in my store there's been some black trainee managers and some white trainee managers. Then there are staff members who have been working for many years and they don't like sharing knowledge with a young white boy or young white girl.

Sometimes you are the only one from a certain race group and then you might get excluded from the group.

I think overall we've been treated good.

Questions — in the context of South Africa

1. Based on these responses and your knowledge of leadership in diverse contexts, suggest a few possible reasons for the retail group's current dilemma. Try to explain why there is sufficiently equitable representation in terms of gender and race at junior management level, but not at top management level. Make sure you consider the different themes and levels of responses from participants. Try to identify both similarities

(Continued)

(Continued)

and differences across groups. Also be careful not to focus only on the participants. There might be some indications of environmental, structural or social factors at play as well.

2. Finally, offer recommendations and possible solutions that the group might implement. Your recommendations should involve company-wide policy changes, but also include practical intervention recommendations as well. Provide your solutions in a detailed report with your findings, with a practical time-line and roll-out plan for the implementation of your solution(s).

Questions – in the context of the UK

The arts industry is often represented as one that is diverse as it is has a high visibility of women and homosexual people. However, from the case study it is evident that the industry does not have an equitable representation of individuals from a working class and ethnic minority backgrounds. How might an active campaign to recruit more people from working class and ethnic minority backgrounds into the arts affect what it means to be an artist? How might industry leaders facilitate this process to avoid backlash against the initiative?

Equality and diversity initiatives need to take place at multiple levels to be successful. In answering the case study questions, students need to pay attention to what policies and practices can be developed at three levels, i.e. societal, sectoral and organisational, and individual levels, in order to promote inclusion of people with diverse ethnic/racial and class backgrounds and to prevent potential backlash from the dominant groups in the arts sector. Examples of societal-level interventions include legal equality measures and awareness campaigns to change the existing perceptions of arts and artists. Similarly, sectoral and organisational-level initiatives such as industry-level equality and inclusion benchmarking, targeted recruitment by organisations, and sectoral and organisational leadership development programmes are of significant value. In addition, sectoral equality and diversity champions, and senior level organisational commitment to diversity, are important to effect cultural change and overcome backlash. Finally, at an individual level, careers of artists from under-represented class and ethnicity backgrounds can be promoted through role models, mentoring and networking, among others.

Further reading

Psychology and leadership

Buford, B.A., 2002. Management effectiveness, personality, leadership, and emotional intelligence: a study of the validity evidence of the Emotional Quotient Inventory. *Dissertation Abstracts International: Section B: The Sciences and Engineering*, 62(12), 6006.

Chiu, K.H. & Chen, T., 2011. Leadership as situational factor on personality–performance relationship: an empirical study of the Taiwan' s office machinery sales force. *International Journal of Business and Social Science*, 5(1), 11–31.

Harms, P.D., Spain, S.M. & Hannah, S.T., 2011. Leader development and the dark side of personality. *The Leadership Quarterly*, 22(3), 495–509.

Rubin, R.S., Munz, D.C. & Bommer, W.H., 2005. Leading from within: the effects of emotion recognition and personality on transformational leadership behavior. *Academy of Management Journal*, 48(5), 845–58.

Stein, S.J., Papadogiannis, P., Yip, J.A. & Sitarenios, G., 2009. Emotional intelligence of leaders: a profile of top executives. *Leadership & Organization Development Journal*, 30(1), 87–101.

Race and leadership

Littrell, R. & Nkomo, S.M., 2005. Gender and race differences in leader behaviour preferences in South Africa. *Women in Management Review*, 20(8), 562–80.

Logan, N., 2011. The white leader prototype: a critical analysis of race in public relations. *Journal of Public Relations Research*, 23(4), 442–57.

Nkomo, S.M., 1992. The Emperor has no clothes: rewriting 'race in organizations.' *Academy of Management Review*, 17(3), 487–515.

Nkomo, S.M., 2011. A postcolonial and anti-colonial reading of 'African' leadership and management in organization studies: tensions, contradictions and possibilities. *Organization*, 18(3), 365–86.

Rosette, A.S., Leonardelli, G.J. & Phillips, K.W., 2008. The white standard: racial bias in leader categorization. *The Journal of Applied Psychology*, 93(4), 758–77.

Gender and leadership

Bell, E. & Nkomo, S.M. 2001. *Our Separate Ways: Black and White Women and the Struggle for Professional Identity*. Boston: Harvard Business School Press.

Carless, S.A., 1998. Gender differences in transformational leadership: an examination of superior, leader, and subordinate perspectives. *Sex Roles*, 39(11), 887–902.

Eagly, A.H., 2003. Finding gender advantage and disadvantage: systematic research integration is the solution. *The Leadership Quarterly*, 14(6), 851–9.

Eagly, A.H. & Carli, L., 2003. The female leadership advantage: an evaluation of the evidence. *The Leadership Quarterly*, 14(6), 807–34.

Eagly, A.H. & Karau, S.J., 2002. Role congruity theory of prejudice toward female leaders. *Psychological Review*, 109, 573–98.

Ely, R.J., Ibarra, H. & Kolb, D.M., 2011. Taking gender into account: theory and design for women's leadership development programs. *Academy of Management Learning & Education*, 10(3), 474–93.

Johnson, D.G., 2011. The effect of sex and gender on perceptions of leaders: does situation make a difference? *Advancing Women in Leadership*, 31, 40–4.

Livingston, R.W., Rosette, A.S. & Washington, E.F., 2012. Can an agentic black woman get ahead? The impact of race and interpersonal dominance on perceptions of female leaders. *Psychological Science*, 23(4), 354–8.

Okimoto, T.G. & Brescoll, V.L., 2010. The price of power: power-seeking and backlash against female politicians. *Personality and Social Psychology Bulletin*, 36, 923–36.

Vecchio, R.P., 2002. Leadership and gender advantage. *The Leadership Quarterly*, 13(6), 643–71.

Vecchio, R.P., 2003. In search of gender advantage. *The Leadership Quarterly*, 14(6), 835–50.

Culture and leadership

Lok, P. & Crawford, J., 1999. The relationship between commitment and organizational culture, subculture, leadership style and job satisfaction in organizational change and development. *Leadership & Organization Development Journal*, 20(7), 365–74.

Lok, P. & Crawford, J., 2004. The effect of organisational culture and leadership style on job satisfaction and organisational commitment: a cross-national comparison. *Journal of Management Development*, 23(4), 321–38.

Schein, E.H., 2010. *Organizational Culture and Leadership*. San Francisco: John Wiley & Sons Inc.

References

Acker, J., 2006. Inequality regimes: gender, class, and race in organizations. *Gender & Society*, 20(4), 441–64.

Amos, T. & Scott, C.R., 1996. Perceptions of affirmative action: an empirical study. *South African Journal of Business Management*, 27(3), 1–13.

Andreski, S., 1983. *Max Weber on Capitalism, Bureaucracy and Religion*. London: George Allen & Unwin.

Bacchi, C.L., 1996. *The Politics of Affirmative Action: Women, Equality and Category Politics*. London: Sage.

Baldwin-Ragaven, L., London, L. & De Gruchy, J., 1999. *An Ambulance of the Wrong Colour: Health Professionals, Human Rights and Ethics in South Africa*. Cape Town: Juta & Co.

Barmes, L. & Ashtiany, S., 2003. The diversity approach to achieving equality: problems and pitfalls. *International Law Journal*, 32(4), 274–96.

Barnard, C., 1997. The nature of leadership. In K. Grint, ed. *Leadership*. Oxford: Oxford University Press, pp. 89–111.

Bebbington, D. & Özbilgin, M., 2013. The paradox of diversity in leadership and leadership for diversity. *Management International/International Management/Gestiòn Internacional*, 17, 14–24.

Beck, R.B., 2000. *The History of South Africa*. Westport: Greenwood.

Bertsch, A., 2012. Updating American Leadership Practices by Exploring the African Philosophy of Ubuntu. *Journal of Leadership, Accountability and Ethics*, 9(1), 81–97.

BIS, 2011. *Women on Boards*. Available at https://www.gov.uk/government/publications/women-on-boards-review [Accessed 18 August 2014].

BIS, 2014. *Women on Boards, Davies Review Annual Report 2014*. Available at https://www.gov.uk/government/publications/women-on-boards-2014-third-annual-review [Accessed 18 August 2014].

Bolden, R., Hawkins, B., Gosling, J. & Taylor, S., 2011. *Exploring Leadership*. Oxford: Oxford University Press.

Bradley, H., 2007. *Gender*. Malden: Polity Press.

Byrd, M., 2008. Negotiating new meanings of 'leader' and envisioning culturally informed theories for developing African-American women in leadership roles: an interview with Patricia S. Parker. *Human Resource Development International*, 11(1), 101–7.

CEDA, 2013. *Women in Leadership: Understanding the Gender Gap*, Committee for Economic Development of Australia (CEDA), Australia. Available at: http://ceda.com.au/media/310731/cedawiljune%202013final.pdf [Accessed 20 January 2014].

Clark, N.L. & Worger, W.H., 2004. *South Africa: The Rise and Fall of Apartheid*. Harlow, UK: Pearson.

Combs, G.M., 2002. Meeting the leadership challenge of a diverse and pluralistic workplace: implications of self-efficacy for diversity training. *Journal of Leadership & Organizational Studies*, 8(4), 1–16.

Commission for Employment Equity, 2013. *Thirteenth Commission of Employment Equity Annual Report*, Pretoria.

Connell, R.W., 1987. *Gender and Power*. Cambridge: Polity Press.

Cox, T.H., 1991. The multicultural organization. *Academy of Management Executive*, 5, 45–56.

Day, N.E. & Greene, P.G., 2008. A case for sexual orientation diversity management in small and large organizations. *Human Resource Management*, 47(3), 637–54.

Eagly, A.H., 2007. Female leadership advantage and disadvantage: resolving the contradictions. *Psychology of Women Quarterly*, 31(1), 1–12. Available at: http://pwq.sagepub.com/lookup/doi/10.1111/j.1471-6402.2007.00326.x [Accessed 8 November 2012].

Eagly, A.H. & Chin, J.L., 2010. Diversity and leadership in a changing world. *The American Psychologist*, 65(3), 216–24. Available at: www.ncbi.nlm.nih.gov/pubmed/20350020 [Accessed 7 November 2012].

EHRC, 2011. *Equality and Human Rights Commission Triennial Review 2010: How Fair is Britain?* www.equalityhumanrights.com/uploaded_files/triennial_review/how_fair_is_britain_-_complete_report.pdf [Accessed 20 February 2014].

Equality Act, 2010. www.legislation.gov.uk/ukpga/2010/15/pdfs/ukpga_20100015_en.pdf [Accessed 20 February 2014].

Fenwick, M., Costa, C., Sohal, A.S. & D'Netto, B., 2011. Cultural diversity management in Australian manufacturing organisations. *Asia Pacific Journal of Human Resources*, 49(4), 494–507.

Gabriel, Y., 2011. Psychoanalytic approaches to leadership. In A. Bryman et al., Eds. *The SAGE Handbook of Leadership*. London: Sage, pp. 393–404.

Gamson, W.A. & Modigliani, A., 1994. The changing culture of affirmative action. In P. Burnstein, ed. *Equal Employment Opportunity: Labor Market Discrimination and Public Policy*. New York: Aldine de Gruyter.

Graen, G.B. & Uhl-Bien, M., 1995. The relationship-based approach to leadership: development of LMX theory of leadership over 25 years: applying a multi-level, multi-domain perspective. *Leadership Quarterly*, 6(2), 219–47.

Hardy, C. & Clegg, S.R., 1996. Some dare call it power. In S. Clegg, C. Hardy & W.R. Nord, Eds. *Handbook of Organization Studies*. London: Sage, pp. 622–41.

Healy, G., Kirton, G. & Noon, M., 2010. Inequalities, intersectionality and equality and diversity initiatives. In G. Healy, G. Kirton and M. Noon, Eds. *Equality, Inequalities and Diversity*. Basingstoke: Palgrave, pp. 1–17.

House, R.J., Hanges, P.J., Javidan, M., Dorfman, P.W. and Gupta, V., 2004. *Culture, Leadership, and Organizations*. London: Sage.

Johnstone, F.A., 1979. *Class, Race & Gold: A Study of Class Relations and Racial Discrimination in South Africa*. London: Routledge.

Jones, J., Blunt, P. & Sharma, K.C., 1996. Managerial perceptions of leadership and management in an African public service organization. *Public Administration and Development*, 16, 456–67.

Kandola, R. & Fullerton, J., 1994. *Diversity in Action: Managing the Mosaic*. London: IPD.

Kang, H., Cheng, M. & Gray, S.J., 2007. Corporate governance and board composition: diversity and independence of Australian boards. *Corporate Governance: An International Review*, 15(2), 194–207.

Kellough, J.E. & Naff, K.C., 2004. Responding to a wake-up call: an examination of federal agency diversity management programs. *Administration & Society*, 36(1), 62–90.

Kilian, C.C., Hukai, D. & McCarty, C.E., 2005. Building diversity in the pipeline to corporate leadership. *Journal of Management Development*, 24(2), 155–168. Available at: www.emeraldinsight.com/10.1108/02621710510579518 [Accessed 15 October 2012].

Klarsfeld, A., Ng, E. & Tatli, A., 2012. Social regulation and diversity management: findings from France, Canada, and the UK. *European Journal of Industrial Relations*, 18(4), 309–27.

Morrill, R.L., 2007. *Strategic Leadership*. Maryland: Rowman & Littlefield.

Ng, E.S.W. & Wyrick, C.R., 2011. Motivational bases for managing diversity: a model of leadership commitment. *Human Resource Management Review*, 21(4), 368–76.

Nkomo, S.M., 2006. Images of African leadership and management in organisation studies: Tensions, contradictions and re-visions. In *Inaugural Lecture* (pp. 1–28). Pretoria: Unisa.

Oikelome, F., 2010. Relevance of US and UK national histories in the understanding of racism and inequality in work and career. In G. Healy, G. Kirton And M. Noon, Eds. *Equality, Inequalities and Diversity*. Basingstoke: Palgrave, pp. 195–211.

ONS, 2014. People in Work, Office for National Statistics. Available at: http://www.ons.gov.uk/ons/taxonomy/index.html?nscl=People+in+Work [Accessed 17 November 2014].

Ospina, S. & Su, C., 2009. Weaving color lines: race, ethnicity, and the work of leadership in social change organizations. *Leadership*, 5(2), 131–70. Available at: http://lea.sagepub.com/cgi/doi/10.1177/1742715009102927 [Accessed 15 October 2012].

Parker, P.S., 2005. *Race, Gender and Leadership*. Mahwah: Lawrence Erlbaum.

Pichler, S., Simpson, P.A. & Stroh, L.K., 2008. The glass ceiling in human resources: exploring the link between women's representations in management and the practices of strategic human resource management and employee involvement. *Human Resource Management*, 47(3), 463–79.

Podolny, J.M., Khurana, R. & Besharov, M.L., 2010. Revisiting the meaning of leadership. In N. Nohria and R. Khurana, Eds. *Handbook of Leadership Theory and Practice*. Boston: Harvard University Press, pp. 65–105.

Rossouw, D., 1994. *Business Ethics: A Southern African Perspective*. Halfway House: Southern Books.

Scott, C.R., Amos, T. & Scott, J., 1998. Affirmative action as seen by business majors in the U.S. and South Africa. *SAM Advanced Management Journal*, Summer, 28–38.

Sing, D., 2011. Promoting and auditing affirmative action in the South African public service. *Public Personnel Management*, 40(4), 349–58.

Smith, S.M., Edwards, H.E., Courtney, M.D. & Finlayson, K.J., 2001. Factors influencing student nurses in their choice of a rural clinical placement site. *Rural and Remote Health*, 1(89). Available at: www.rrh.org.au [Accessed 17 November 2014].

StatsSA, 2012a. *Quarterly Labour Force Survey*.

StatsSA, 2012b. *South African Census Results 2011*.

Stogdill, R.M., 1948. Personal factors associated with leadership: a survey of the literature. *The Journal of Psychology*, 25(1), 35–71.

Syed, J. & Özbilgin, M., 2009. A relational framework for international transfer of diversity management practices. *The International Journal of Human Resource Management*, 20(12), 2435–53.

Tatli, A., 2011. A multi-layered exploration of the diversity management field: diversity discourses, practices and practitioners in the UK. *British Journal of Management*, 22(2), 238–53.

Tatli, A. & Özbilgin, M.F., 2009. Understanding diversity managers' role in organizational change: towards a conceptual framework. *Canadian Journal of Administrative Sciences*, 26: 244–58.

Tatli, A. & Özbilgin, M., 2012. Surprising intersectionalities of inequality and privilege: the case of the arts and cultural sector. *Equality, Diversity and Inclusion: An International Journal*, 31(3), 249–65.

Tatli, A., Özbilgin, M., Worman, D. & Price, E., 2008. *State of the Nation, Diversity in Business: a Focus for Progress*. London: CIPD.

Tatli, A., Vassilopoulou, J., Al Ariss, A. & Özbilgin, M., 2012. The role of regulatory and temporal context in the construction of diversity discourses: the case of the UK, France and Germany. *European Journal of Industrial Relations*, 18(4), 293–308.

Tatli, A., Vassilopoulou, J. & Özbilgin, M., 2013. An unrequited affinity between talent shortages and untapped female potential: the relevance of gender quotas for talent management in high growth potential economies of the Asia Pacific region. *International Business Review*, 22(3), 539–53.

Vermeulen, L.P. & Coetzee, M., 2011. Perceptions of the dimensions of the fairness of affirmative action: a pilot study. *South African Journal of Business Management*, 37(2), 53–64.

Watson, W., 2007. *Brick by Brick: An Informal Guide to the History of South Africa*. Claremont: New Africa Books.

Wrong, D.H., 2009. *Power: Its Forms, Bases, and Uses*, New Jersey: Transaction Publishers.

Zaleznik, A., 1977. Managers and leaders: are they different? *Harvard Business Review*, 55 (May–June), 47–60.

Policy and practice of diversity management in the workplace

3

Darren T. Baker and Elisabeth K. Kelan

 Intended learning outcomes

After completing this chapter, you should have a firm understanding of the policy and practice of diversity management in the workplace, and how this has changed over space and time.

You should be able to:

- Outline temporal changes in the meaning of diversity management
- Explain the business case for diversity management
- Explain how different approaches have influenced the policy and practice of diversity management in organisations
- Discuss the arguments against diversity management
- Explain some of the complexities faced when implementing diversity initiatives
- Outline the development and impact of European Union (EU) equality legislation on one specific strand of diversity

Introduction

Picture this: in a large, sterile executive office, the CEO of a London-based multinational corporation grills a female candidate for a senior post in his organisation.

Referring to the applicant's two children, the CEO asks: 'How's life going to be if I say to you … "right, you're down in London. You've got to move your family, move your location"'. The candidate responds: 'I'm not making a decision without having the courtesy to speak to the people who care for my children. It's a risk, it's a discourtesy to my parents'. The CEO furiously responds: 'I haven't got time to wait for you to make a phone call'. Was it fair for the CEO to ask the candidate about her family and child-care commitments in an interview? The UK Equality Act 2010 protects job applicants from less favourable treatment. In this case, the fact that the candidate had family commitments was used as a potential reason not to hire. What is interesting about this interview is that it was aired on television to millions in the 2007 UK series of *The Apprentice*. In this series, aspiring businessmen and women competed for a £100,000 role to work with the CEO of a multinational. The episode was widely condemned by trade unions and equality groups for violating UK sex discrimination laws.

Despite widespread criticism, the fact that a clear case of discrimination can be positioned as fair and effective business on national television, does beg the question: how far have we *really* come in diversity management? On the one hand, it is seen as an integral part of an organisation's strategy, while on the other, newspapers and scholarly discourses reflect persistent discrimination, 'glass ceilings', racism, homophobia and sexism in the workplace. In this chapter, we explore some of these tensions. In doing so, we attempt to define diversity management by situating it in a fluid, highly contested and often contradictory discourse. We also discuss how different approaches to diversity management have influenced non-discrimination legislation in the European Union and US, and organisational policies and practice, and how these have changed over space and time. At the end of the chapter, we critically examine the successes and lessons learnt from diversity management at the 2012 London Organising Committee of the Olympic and Paralympic Games (LOCOG).

The term 'diversity management'

The term 'diversity management' is both multi-faceted and fluid. It is, therefore, widely contested (Kossek et al., 2006; Prasad et al., 2006) and criticised by scholars for its broad and often inconsistent meaning (Wrench, 2002). Traditionally, diversity was defined as demographic differences (McGrath et al., 1995), such as race, class, or gender between individuals and minority groups. It is now recognised as encompassing 'deeper' or unobservable attributes (Milliken and Martins, 1996) including cultural (Wrench, 2002), technical and cognitive differences. The *Oxford Dictionary of Human Resource Management* also reflects this broadness, defining diversity management as 'valuing an individual's qualities – personality, skill, knowledge and competences – and their unique contribution to an organisation' (Heery and Noon, 2001). Organisations must create an inclusive culture to leverage the 'unique' power and potential of diversity (Miller and Katz, 2002).

Temporal changes in the meaning of diversity management

The term 'diversity management' becomes even more problematic when considered in relation to other terms, such as 'affirmative action' and 'equal opportunity'. In this section, we clarify the meaning of diversity management by situating it in an ever evolving, and often contradictory, discourse. Diversity management emerged in the 1960s in the US from the civil rights movement. Title VII of the 1964 Civil Rights Act made it an unlawful employment practice for organisations to discriminate on the basis of race, colour, religion, sex or origin. President Johnson then went one step further in 1965 by prohibiting discriminatory behaviour by organisations in employment matters, including recruitment (SHRM, 2008). This was founded on moral and ethical principles of equal opportunities and compensatory justice for groups that had historically been discriminated against (Kellough, 2006). This formed the case for affirmative action, which refers to artificial efforts to assure that minority groups receive equal opportunities (Thomas, 1992). Organisations were thus forced to seek demographic variation in their workforce through increasing opportunities for under-represented minority groups (Acker, 2006).

Affirmative action informed the 'discrimination-and-fairness' paradigm which guided diversity initiatives during this time (Thomas and Ely, 1996). This measured diversity progress based on how well an organisation recruited and retained minority groups. However, the discrimination-and-fairness paradigm went one step further than affirmative action as organisations sometimes provided support structures for minority employees through, for example, mentoring and development (ibid.). This paradigm was organised around the assimilation of diverse groups into a homogenous or monolithic organisational culture (Gottfredson, 1992), which treats all members of a demographically diverse workforce the same (Thomas and Ely, 1996). However, this can be problematic or even impossible as diverse groups must assume the values and interests of the dominant group (Thomas, 1992), typically white males. This can result in resistance and increased conflict, and diminished cultural cohesiveness between different groups (ibid.).

Organisations then began shifting their diversity focus from legal compliance and 'sameness' to one emphasising difference. The influential *Workforce 2000* report predicted that the US workforce would become increasingly diverse and segmented (Johnston and Packer, 1987). In parallel, there were changes in consumer demographics (Jackson and Alvarez, 1992). De-industrialisation, the move towards a service sector economy, and globalisation helped to drive these changes (ibid.). Leaders started taking note and integrating diversity into their corporate strategy (Wentling and Palma-Rivas, 1997). In this increasingly global and competitive context, the 'access-and-legitimacy' paradigm that emerged predicated on differentiation and matching demographic characteristics with, for example, specific geographical markets (Thomas and Ely, 1996). In other words, organisations began to leverage diversity as a way to drive their business, tap into new markets and clients, and ultimately to impact their bottom line. In the access–legitimacy paradigm, employees are typically trained to accept diversity. However, these initiatives are often basic and are not embedded within the structure of the organisation (e.g. into performance, promotion and reward frameworks), and are, therefore, unsuccessful at creating long-term behaviour change across the organisation.

This interest in changing workforce demographics sparked a new debate about how diversity should be managed in organisations in the 1990s. Thomas (1990) proposed a new paradigm shift in diversity management called 'learning-and-effectiveness'. This is where organisations leverage workforce pluralism in all aspects of business strategy and process (Thomas and Ely, 1996). He concluded that organisations must create equitable organisational cultures and manage diversity in order to yield a similar, or perhaps, better performance as homogenous groups (Thomas, 1990). In the access–legitimacy paradigm, there is a genuine attempt by organisations to help learn from conflict generated from diversity and difference, rather than simply glossing over it using ineffective training initiatives. Rather than just focusing on how diversity impacts the bottom line of a business, diversity and equality are embedded into the very fabric of the organisation (for example, business practices, products and culture), with the aim of problematising traditional ways of working. In the learning-and-effectiveness paradigm, progress on diversity is measured more effectively in contrast to the other two paradigms, and is measured across a number of important organisational metrics including diversity demographics, retention, attrition, performance frameworks, promotion, and team or group effectiveness. Overall, this paradigm can help with remodelling work processes and effectiveness.

This aligns with the multi-cultural model for social integration of diverse groups as proposed by Cox (1991). Multi-cultural organisations are characterised by 'pluralism, full integration of minority-cultural members both formally and informally, an absence of prejudice and discrimination, and low levels of inter-group conflict' (pp. 46–7). The Mission and value; Objective and fair process; Skilled workforce; Active flexibility; Individual focus and Culture Model (MOSAIC) also highlighted the transition from a monolithic to a multi-cultural organisation (Kandola and Fullerton, 1998). Unlike prior paradigms, the 'learning-and-effectiveness' paradigm promotes equitable behaviours whilst recognising difference (Thomas and Ely, 1996). This allows everyone to contribute and reach their full potential (Cox, 1991).

Inclusion enables a multi-cultural organisation to be achieved. Inclusion is a change process focusing on engaging, integrating and valuing individual employees. The study by Roberson (2006) to disentangle the meaning of diversity and inclusion found that diversity was related to the establishment of a heterogeneous, bio-demographically varied workforce, whereas inclusion focused on employee engagement and cultural integration. Miller and Katz (2002) outline a conceptual framework for how inclusion can support an organisation to move towards a more equitable and productive workplace. Firstly, organisations need to 'lift the playing field' to eliminate differences between dominant and non-dominant groups and obstacles to effective performance; secondly, organisations must 'lift the *entire* playing field' to leverage everyone as 'irreplaceable assets in an organisation' (ibid., italics added).

Section synopsis

- Affirmative action concerns providing specific opportunities and favouring minority groups who have historically been discriminated against
- Affirmative action is linked to the discrimination-and-fairness paradigm where organisations recruit, retain and provide support structures for minority groups
- The access-and-legitimacy paradigm looks at how organisations can leverage diversity in order to increase business profitability by matching certain groups with clients, products and markets
- The learning-and-effectiveness paradigm leverages workforce pluralism in all aspects of business strategy and process
- The contemporary approach to diversity management espouses a focus on inclusion in which all aspects of an organisation's pluralism are leveraged to generate business outcomes including increased innovation, creativity and more effective decision making

Inclusion and the business case for diversity

As Thomas (1990) suggests, for organisations to realise the business benefits of diversity, they must espouse a focus on inclusion. Whereas affirmative action was a force external to an organisation, diversity management at present concerns how inclusive practices can leverage diversity and generate tangible business returns. As discussed, whereas diversity focuses on increasing representation of minorities, different skills and experiences in an organisation, inclusion concerns how diverse individuals and groups can be engaged, valued and harnessed to increase the effectiveness of an organisation's human capital. This is what Lorbiecki and Jack (2000) call the 'economic turn' in diversity management. This suggests that monolithic organisational cultures are not as competitive in a highly dynamic, global marketplace (ibid.). Diversity management has now become a voluntary programme (Gilbert and Ivancevich, 2001) in which priorities have become organisationally specific and reflect the realities of an organisation's strategic aims and workforce (Wallace and Pillans, 2011). Cox (1991) suggests that there are a number of areas that effective diversity management could impact: cost; resource acquisition; marketing; creativity; problem solving and system flexibility. In this section, we highlight research supporting this.

Cost

Ineffective diversity management can have both direct and indirect cost implications for an organisation. There are many examples of high profile and costly litigation cases, for example, in the UK. In the recent equal pay compensation case brought against Birmingham City Council, the compensation bill totalled £1.1 billion, leaving the council no choice but to sell off important public assets (Elkes, 2013). The number of cases brought to tribunal courts continues to increase, and between 2012 and 2013 increased by 3 per cent according to the Ministry of Justice (Ministry of Justice, 2013). However, most discrimination cases are settled before reaching court and although the amounts remain confidential, they can be substantial (Wallace and Pillans, 2011). Employment lawyers are also expensive and the average cost for a business in the UK is £90,000 per case (Shah, 2012). Indirect costs to organisations of ineffective diversity management include minority employee turnover and absenteeism. The Corporate Leavers Survey by Korn/Ferry International puts the cost of replacing professionals and managers due to ineffective diversity management for US employers at US$64 billion in 2006 (Korn/Ferry International, 2007). Other associated costs include exit interviews and loss of productivity due to unfilled posts (Bell, 2007).

Resource acquisition

Organisations are under increased pressure to tap into diverse talent pools as workforce demographics and labour supply change (Prasad and Mills, 1997). For example, in Europe, the numbers of highly qualified workers continue to decline (Desvaux et al., 2007). According to McKinsey, increasing the participation of women in the workforce may be one way for organisations to plug this skills gap. This also has implications for organisations wishing to tap into other diverse talent pools. Therefore, in an era of increased competition for talent, organisations known for effective diversity management are more likely to attract highly skilled workers from diverse 'talent pools' (Cox and Blake, 1991).

Marketing

In a globalised marketplace, organisations must compete for consumers across multiple geographies and cultures (Jackson and Alvarez, 1992). A diverse workforce can bring its rich cultural knowledge to bear when designing products and marketing strategies, which appeal to various tastes and preferences (Bell, 2007). For example, global organisations often form 'transnational innovation teams' (Bouncken and Winkler, 2009). Team members come from diverse backgrounds and this is integrated into product design (ibid.), helping organisations to access different markets.

Creativity and problem solving

Different ideas, perspectives and competences increase the potential for innovation (Triandis et al., 1965) and solutions to organisational problems (Bachmann, 2006). For example, Gratton et al. (2007) studied whether gender proportion impacts a team's ability to be innovative. It was discovered that greater gender diversity impacts innovation by increasing a team's: psychological safety; willingness to experiment and take risks; and efficiency (ibid.). The report points towards an optimal gender balance in teams of 50 per cent women and 50 per cent men. However, if women were in the majority (approximately 60 per cent), it was found this positively impacted a team's self-confidence (ibid.). Horwitz and Horwitz (2007) also studied the impact of team diversity on group-level outcomes. The study found that there was a positive relationship between task-related diversity and team performance. However, they found no relationship between bio-demographic diversity and team performance.

System flexibility

Cox (1991) suggested that organisations will become more fluid and adaptable as diversity increases, and organisational structures, policies and operating models broaden. Organisations, thus, open up to new ideas (ibid.) and ways of working. For example, there has been much research showing the permeability between people's lives at work and outside of work; this is called 'spillover effect' and indicates a positive or negative relationship between the two spheres (Gratton et al., 2007). When spillover is positive at either home or work, there is an enriching effect; however, when one is more negative than the other, there is a depleting effect, including: decreased passion; reduced commitment; reduced team participation; and reduced innovation (ibid.).

Workplace flexibility is one approach by organisations to ameliorate the conflict between these two spheres. Hill et al. (2001), for example, compared the productivity levels of employees who were given control over where and when they worked and those who worked standard office hours and days. The study concluded that those with flexible schedules experienced reduced work–life conflict and worked longer hours per week than those on non-flexible schedules (ibid.). Gratton et al. (2007), who studied the impact of gender diversity on team innovation, showed that despite working longer hours and suffering more from negative spillover, men do not take up flexible working options as much as women. Research shows that inadequate work–life flexibility and long working hours have impacts on employees, including increased stress (Almeida and Davis, 2011) and health problems such as coronary heart disease (Virtanen et al., 2010).

Diversity management: a double-edged sword

However, diversity management is often seen as a double-edged sword. As discussed in the previous section, despite the plethora of scholarship on the positive impacts of diversity, there are a number of scholars who remain sceptical (Tsui et al., 1992; Rothman et al., 2003). Critics of diversity management cite sub-optimal performance of teams including ineffective communication, discrimination, and lower attachment, commitment and satisfaction, as reasons against diversity (Bell, 2007; Horwitz and Horwitz, 2007). The prevalence of stereotypes and power imbalances between different groups and individuals in the workplace, and associated 'dysfunctional behaviours', are understood to be 'defensive reactions' to the 'threat' of difference (Ely and Morgan Roberts, 2008). For example, Tsui et al. (1992) found that levels of group cohesion diminished with increased gender and racial diversity for dominant groups. This can result in increased absenteeism and turnover (ibid.). Wharton and Baron (1991, 1987) found similar asymmetrical results. However, Gilbert and Ivancevich (2001) found that leadership was important to the success of diversity initiatives; when leadership commitment was low, diversity strategies were poorly implemented which resulted in higher female attrition from organisations, absenteeism and resentment by dominant groups towards women and ethnic minorities (ibid.). Leadership can play a pivotal role in monitoring dysfunctional behaviour, facilitating communications and challenging stereotypes between dominant and non-dominant groups (Bell, 2007).

Liberal, radical and relational approaches to diversity management

In the previous sections, we have explored how discourses on diversity management have changed through time. At present, diversity management concerns leveraging the value of diversity and generating tangible business outcomes by driving inclusive organisational cultures. In this section, we explain the three main theories that have influenced legislation and organisational policies and practices regarding diversity and equality: firstly, Jewson and Mason's (1986) equality model has been particularly influential and contrasts both liberal and radical approaches to corporate diversity management; and secondly, the transformational approach is based on Cockburn's (1991) and Fraser's (1997) models of equality of redistribution and recognition.

Liberal approach

This is based on equal access to opportunities such as services, rewards and positions. It is grounded in theories of neo-classical economics and free market competition where reward is based on merit. Discrimination is, thus, at odds with a rational marketplace. The liberal approach focuses on 'positive action' – which is different from 'affirmative action' – where organisations remove obstacles to a meritocratic culture (Jewson and Mason, 1986). For example, organisations may carry out diversity recruitment campaigns (Kirton and Greene, 2005). The business case argument is fundamental to the rhetoric of the liberal approach (Özbilgin, 2000). The study by Herring (2009), for example, indirectly advocates a liberal approach to diversity management; the study strongly supports the business case for diversity by showing how group heterogeneity is linked to an increase in sales revenues, customers and greater market share for organisations.

Despite the successes of the liberal approach in increasing the representation of, for example, women in the workforce (Webb, 1997), Collinson et al. (1990) show how employees are sometimes able to evade legislation and organisational procedures on a daily basis. It is shown how managing diversity alone is not effective in ensuring unbiased decisions by managers and leaders who have challenges in disentangling, for example, role competences from gender stereotypes, which can have significant implications for recruitment, promotion and performance practices (ibid.). These behaviours often mask direct forms of discrimination. Liberal approaches it seems cannot guarantee equitable outcomes within organisations, and fail to redress the causes of discrimination (Rees, 1998).

Radical approach

The radical approach is more interventionist than the liberal approach, as it seeks to achieve equitable outcomes rather than simply equitable policies and procedures. This is because, as Gatrell and Swan (2008) explain, equal access alone is not effective enough to challenge the structures that have privileged dominant groups. The radical approach purports that discrimination can only be identified at the group level, and therefore, change is focused on groups rather than individuals. Noon (2007) explains that the challenge with the liberal approach is that it identifies and individualises personal traits as more important than group attributes. Thus, by dissolving differences between groups, it renders the inequities associated with gender or ethnicity unimportant with regards to employment opportunities (ibid.). There is considerable evidence to show how a focus on group-level discrimination has significant impacts on equality in organisations. In their study of the effects of the gender quota requiring 40 per cent females on boards and among CEOs in Norway, Wang and Kelan (2013) showed how radical legislative pressures have not only increased gender equality in the boardroom, but have also had a spillover effect on top leadership positions. Therefore, their study raises considerable doubts over the voluntary or liberal approaches to gender diversity in organisations. It is clearly shown in the study that mandatory quotas are able to bring about effective top-down changes in gender diversity in organisations (ibid.).

Transformational approach

There are many critics of both the liberal and radical approaches to diversity and management. They argue that these approaches have failed to challenge the structures and underlying causes of discrimination in the workplace (Özbilgin, 2000), and have resulted in resentment by dominant groups in organisations (Cockburn, 1989). A new, 'transformational approach' to diversity management has emerged out of these criticisms. This approach seeks to challenge the structural and cultural inequities within organisations. This encompasses the business practices of an organisation, such as procurement, decision making, recruitment, training and career planning, through to cultural and behavioural transformations, particularly around understanding biases and understanding multiple, diverse perspectives, conflict resolution and critical thinking. For a transformational approach, Cockburn (1991) suggests developing short- and long-term agendas for diversity management. Short-term agendas focus on tackling unconscious biases, for example, in day-to-day activities; and long-term agendas are more profound and focus on placing non-dominant groups in positions of power and influence within an organisation. The study by Kochan et al. (2003) also highlights the importance of 'sensitive managerial strategies and culture change initiatives in addition to organisational policies and practices to diversity management' (p. 16). In their study, Kochan et al. (ibid.) looked at large organisations with long-standing diversity practices and policies, and highlighted how increased race and gender diversity neither positively nor negatively impacted organisational performance. Kochan et al. (ibid.) conclude that leaders must, therefore, focus on creating a culture change for diversity in order to move beyond just the business case and to maximise organisational effectiveness.

The study by Kalev et al. (2006) also supports a transformational approach to diversity management. In their study of federal workforce data and employment practices between 1971 and 2002, they found that diversity initiatives to eliminate managerial biases and reduce the isolation of diverse groups, such as mentoring and networking, showed the least impact on increasing diversity at managerial levels. However, they found a clear pattern between establishing structures that embed accountability, such as affirmative action plans, committees and diversity managers, and increasing diversity at the manager level in organisations. It was also found that changing structures, in turn, catalysed the effectiveness of other initiatives, such as training, mentoring and network initiatives (ibid.).

The transformational approach to diversity management has emerged partly from the social justice model proposed by Fraser (1997). Fraser advocates integrating two approaches to justice – the redistribution of resources and cultural recognition. In other words, arguments are often polarised between, for example, social democracy and multiculturalism or class politics and identity politics, when neither is sufficient for justice. Justice, according to Fraser, must have two fronts: firstly, it requires practices that preclude social arrangements that institutionalise deprivation, exploitation, and disparities in wealth, time and income, which work to prevent individuals from interacting with their peers; secondly, it requires respect and recognition for achieving social esteem and, therefore, precludes the 'othering' or significant differentiation of people. With regards to gender parity, Fraser (2007) argues that this model of justice broadens out traditional conceptions of parity to combine both class and status in understanding and assessing justice and gender order. In other words, society institutionalises 'sexist maldistribution' by denying women the resources and support, for example, to progress in their careers; and, in tandem (as the status order of society institutionalises 'sexist misrecognition') as less than full partners in interaction (ibid.: 28). Thus, by tackling both the structural and cultural barriers to equality, organisations can more effectively manage diversity.

However, the management of diversity is arguably more complex than academic and practitioner work reflects. Roberson (2006) attempted to show this by highlighting the similarities and differences in the practice and outcome of both 'diversity', and its successive paradigm, 'inclusion' in organisations. The study found that organisations clearly defined the attributes of diversity and inclusion: firstly, diversity related to the establishment of a heterogeneous, bio-demographically varied workforce; whereas, secondly, inclusion focused on employee engagement and cultural and structural integration (ibid.). However, Roberson (ibid.) found that the terms themselves did not always represent separate types of work environments, but, rather, different approaches to diversity management. Thus, diversity management is more complex than a simple two-category approach as either 'diversity' or 'inclusion'. For example, this could include practices that manage 'fair treatment issues, increasing stakeholder diversity and leadership commitment to diversity, whilst inclusion may include the integration of diversity into organisational systems and processes in order to increase engagement' (ibid.: 25). This may help organisations to understand fully their approach to diversity management, and therefore maximise their approach by identifying strategies to increase diversity and/or inclusion (ibid.)

Section synopsis

- Liberal approaches focus on access to opportunities such as services, rewards and positions, and the business case for diversity
- Radical approaches seek to achieve equitable outcomes through initiatives such as quotas for boards
- Transformational approaches focus on changing the structures and underlying culture of organisations

Understanding intersectionality in inequality

Transformational approaches to diversity management may consider how individuals can be represented by different categories, and can in turn be disadvantaged and oppressed in multiple ways within an organisational setting. Intersectionality was central in Joan Acker's 2006 seminal article 'Inequality regimes: gender, class, and race in organizations'. In this paper, she directs scholarship to 'pay attention to the *intersection* of, at least, race/ethnicity, gender and class' to comprehend the complex, fluid nature of 'inequality, dominance and oppression' (p. 442, italics added). Acker (ibid.) employs the notion of an 'inequality regime' to reflect how formal, informal and inter-related processes, actions and meanings, perpetuate, reconfigure and contradict class, gender and racial inequalities within specific organisational contexts (ibid.) through:

- *Organising the general requirements of work:* these are based on the ideal white man, who typically has fewer responsibilities outside of work. Women, on the other hand, normally have more responsibilities including child caring and domestic obligations. Work requirements can be problematic for women and others and, thus, work requirements reinforce gender inequality within organisations.
- *Organising class hierarchies:* job tasks and responsibilities are linked to organisational hierarchy and remuneration. Roles occupied by women are sometimes poorly defined in comparison to men's roles, and linked to lower rankings and wages.
- *Recruiting and hiring:* to Acker (ibid.) 'competence involves judgement'. Competences are neither gender nor racially neutral and are constructed in the image of the white, male worker. Therefore, recruitment and hiring processes position white males as more suitable for job roles and effective work in organisations.
- *Informal interactions whilst doing work:* similar to the above, employees typically use gender, race and class assumptions when interacting with others. Minority individuals might be devalued in the workplace through, for example: sexual harassment, exclusion in meetings and job performance reviews.

Organisational controls that maintain these processes are both direct and indirect: direct controls include bureaucratic rules and reward and remuneration; indirect controls include technological controls such as monitoring of telephone calls and internet-usage.

Acker's work has been pivotal in opening up research on the intersection of inequality across class, gender and race in organisations. However, Tatli and Özbilgin (2012) argue that scholars need to question the salience of these in understanding inequality in organisations. They argue 'when considering the inclusion of a demographic category such as gender, ethnicity, class or sexual orientation in intersectional analysis, we need to examine the extent to which the chosen demographic category produces disadvantage in its situated context' (p. 250). Context is, therefore, fundamental in understanding the interplay of different aspects of inequality.

Diversity legislation in the EU

In the previous section, we explained the different theoretical approaches to diversity management. In this section, we show how some of these theoretical approaches have informed non-discrimination law in the EU. Despite related global issues of power, dominance and discrimination, in this section we highlight how different approaches to diversity management have resulted in different legislative practices in different geographies. We contrast EU law with that of the US.

EU labour and non-discrimination law

The EU is made up of 28 economic and political 'Member States' or countries. They give powers to the EU to provide European Directives; Member States have an agreed time-line within which to implement these laws (Equality and Diversity Forum, 2008). The original purpose of the EU was to stimulate economic growth through the free movement of capital and labour (European Union Agency for Fundamental Rights, 2010). However, The Treaty of Rome 1957, which founded the European Economic Community (EEC), also prohibited discrimination on the basis of sex to ensure 'a level playing field between Member States' (ibid.). The EU's legal structure has increasingly become more complex as further EU treaties have been added. The prohibition of discrimination is arguably one of the most important EU laws affecting Member States (Whittle, 2002). We outline the chronology of key EU non-discrimination directives below (Ius Laboris, 2011):

- 1975 – directive for the right to equal pay by employees,
- 1976 – Directive 76/707 prohibiting gender discrimination in terms of access to employment, training, promotion and working conditions,
- 1980s and 1990s – extension of gender discrimination directives to include social security,
- 1997 Treaty of Amsterdam – gave the European Council authority to prohibit discrimination based on more than just gender.

In 2002, two directives were introduced: the Racial Equality Directive (Directive 2000/43/EC) and the Employment Equality Directive (Directive 2000/78/EC). They prohibited discrimination based on race, ethnicity, religion or belief, disability, age and sexual orientation (Chopin and Gounari, 2010). The directives advocate a principle of 'fair treatment' which means that there will be no direct or indirect forms of discrimination irrespective of diversity (Euro Info Centre, 2006). The directives do not, however, define what the assumed attributes are of each strand of diversity, which poses challenges when discrimination occurs (Chopin and Gounari, 2010). In other words, if individuals are subjected to direct forms of discrimination pertaining to their race, how can they advocate that this was an infringement of their human rights when the attributes of their race are not identified in legislation?

The purpose of the 2002 Directives was to improve the opportunities for certain groups of people, but they do not advocate any form of positive discrimination (Whittle, 2002). They, thus, support a meritocratic framework and, therefore, demand that employers act fairly in all employment matters (ibid.). EU non-discrimination law, therefore, upholds liberal approaches to diversity management, as it pursues equality of opportunity for all individuals.

A comparison with non-discrimination labour laws in the US

However, unlike the more liberal approaches that have influenced EU labour laws, more radical approaches have influenced laws in the US. Affirmative action has been arguably one of the most effective ways to redress employment injustices suffered by diverse groups throughout history in the US (American Civil Liberties Union, 2000). The Civil Rights Act in 1964 sought to eliminate discrimination and also set up the Equal Employment Opportunity Commission (EEOC) to administer the act (ibid.). The EEOC is an independent federal agency that promotes equal opportunities in employment through administrative and judicial enforcement of federal civil rights laws and through education and technical assistance. One aspect of affirmative action, for example, requires employers who contract with the government or who otherwise receive federal funds, to document and present their affirmative action practices and metrics (United States Department of Labor, 2002). Although this has increased minority group representation in the workplace, once within the organisation, however, minority groups were often excluded from the dominant organisational culture (Wrench, 2002); thus, organisations began introducing support structures, such as mentoring and network groups, to address diversity-related challenges such as higher turnover rates amongst minority groups.

In addition to the Civil Rights Act, discussed above, there are a number of other federal laws that protect individuals from discrimination in the US, including (US Equal Employment Opportunity Commission, 2014):

- The Equal Pay Act of 1963 – this prohibits unequal pay between genders when they perform equal work,
- The Age Discrimination in Employment Act of 1967 – this prohibits discrimination against those who are 40 years old and above,
- Title I of the Americans with Disabilities Act of 1990 – this prohibits discrimination against qualified individuals with disabilities in the private sector, and state and local governments.

The US has a relatively stronger history of anti-discrimination law, compliance and affirmative action than the EU (Wrench, 2002). The US also has a far greater number of large, global organisations, where diversity is more likely to be welcomed, than in Europe, where businesses tend to be smaller to medium sized and focus on specific geographical markets (ibid.).

Section synopsis

- The 2002 Racial Equality Directive (Directive 2000/43/EC) and the Employment Equality Directive (Directive 2000/78/EC) prohibited discrimination based on race, ethnicity, religion or belief, disability, age and sexual orientation in the EU
- The US Civil Rights Act in 1964 prohibited unlawful employment practices for organisations to discriminate on the basis of race, colour, religion, sex or origin
- EU legislation has been influenced more by liberal approaches to diversity management, based on equality of opportunity, whereas US law has been influenced more by radical approaches such as affirmative action, based on equality of outcome

Summary and recommendations

This chapter has sought to highlight some of the key tensions and paradoxes in the management of diversity in organisations overtime and across different geographies. We have identified three prevalent organisational models or paradigms to diversity management for organisations. The discrimination-and-fairness paradigm, linked to the Civil Rights Movement in the US, ensures equitable recruitment, retention and support structures for minority groups. The access-and-legitimacy paradigm focused on how organisations can increase business profitability through effectively leveraging and aligning minority demographics with clients, products and markets. The contemporary learning-and-effectiveness paradigm focuses on integrating diversity into all aspects of business performance, and measuring progress against multiple organisational metrics.

In this chapter, we have also identified two approaches to diversity management and linked these to legislative demands at the national and supra-national level. The liberal approach to diversity is recognised for increasing the representation of certain minority groups in the workforce, particularly further down within the organisational hierarchy. EU non-discrimination law, for example, upholds liberal approaches to diversity management as it supports a meritocratic culture and, therefore, demands that employers act fairly in all employment issues. However, we have argued that, despite best practice policies and procedures, the liberal approach fails to contend with the underlying processes of discrimination and bias within organisational cultures. On the other hand, we argue that a radical approach, which focuses on targets and quotas, provides better equality outcomes, specifically in the representation of minority groups in senior positions, which can have a positive spillover effect further down within organisations. The US has more radical legislation in place than in the EU to deal with discrimination. Affirmative action has arguably been one of the most effective ways to redress employment injustices suffered by minority groups. An independent federal agency promotes equal opportunities in employment through administrative and judicial enforcement of federal civil rights laws, education and technical assistance. Although it has increased the representation of minority groups in the workplace, diverse groups often face exclusion from the dominant organisational culture. Thus, radical approaches help organisations to achieve equality outcomes but do not seek to change the underlying organisational culture.

However, we recommend that organisations pursue a transformational approach to diversity management. The transformational approach aims to embed, firstly, diversity into the organisational structure, including its procurement practices, decision making and recruitment, and secondly, ensure an equitable organisational culture through the implementation of behaviour change initiatives, such as unconscious bias training, conflict resolution and the promotion of critical thinking and challenge. We have sought to bring this approach to life with the use of the LOCOG diversity case study (see pp. 94–101). This is a good example of how organisations can bring together both structural and cultural change to ensure organisational justice. The diversity and inclusion team at LOCOG designed a robust change framework, 'understand', 'lead' and 'deliver', with three areas for intervention, workforce, procurement and service delivery, to inspire and drive change across the organisation. However, we have also highlighted the lessons learnt from the programme, including examples of non-compliance, which organisations can consider as potential risks in the design of their own diversity change strategies.

Key terms

Bio-demographic diversity: this refers to the physical attributes of an individual or group which can include gender, race and ethnicity

Inclusion: practices that leverage diversity and generate tangible business returns

Liberal approach: liberal approaches focus on access to opportunities such as services, rewards and positions, and the business case for diversity

Radical approach: seeks to achieve equitable outcomes, through affirmative action, rather than just equitable policies and procedures

Transformational approach: this approach seeks to challenge both structural and cultural inequities within organisations.

Discrimination-and-fairness paradigm: this is where organisations attempt to recruit, retain and provide support structures for minority groups

Access-and-legitimacy paradigm: this is predicated on differentiation and leveraging diversity as ways to grow a business, for example, by matching the demographic characteristics of one group with a geographical market

Learning-and-effectiveness paradigm: this leverages workforce pluralism in all aspects of business strategy and process

Discussion questions

1. 'We see diversity as more than just policies and practices. It is an integral part of who we are as a company, how we operate and how we see our future' (Coca-Cola: Global Diversity Mission). Define the meaning of the term 'diversity management' in relation to this statement.
2. 'The question is, how do you integrate diversity into what you do and how your business makes money?' (Gil Casellas: attorney at Mintz Levin in Washington, DC). Write a hypothetical business case for diversity to be presented to the CEO of a multinational.
3. 'Liberal approaches to diversity management are nothing more than warm and fuzzy'. Discuss in relation to non-discrimination legislation and organisational policies and practices.
4. Transformational diversity approaches concern embedding diversity structurally into the daily activities of a business and culturally, including training and educating employees on biases and diversity. Consider the work of the diversity and inclusion team at LOCOG (see case study below). Compare the transformational approach with the liberal and radical approaches to diversity management.

CASE STUDY

Diversity and inclusion at LOCOG

From the vibrant opening ceremony to the montage of Jessica Ennis in the heptathlon, Katherine Copeland and Sophie Hosking in the double skulls, and Zoe Smith in the weight lifting – to name but a few – the London 2012 Games represented a significant step change for equality in women's sports. It also heralded a breakthrough for Paralympic sports with record-breaking ticket sales, widespread global media coverage and public interest, appreciation and awareness. The London 2012 Games drove equality in ways never previously imagined.

Previously in this chapter, we outlined the different theoretical approaches to diversity and inclusion (D&I) that organisations can adopt. In this final section, we analyse how LOCOG adopted a transformational approach to D&I leading

(Continued)

(Continued)

up to and during the 2012 London Games. As we have already outlined, the transformational approach to diversity seeks to challenge both structural and cultural inequities within organisations. This is often done by embedding diversity into everyday business practices, such as procurement, decision making, recruitment, training and career planning, and through cultural and behavioural change initiatives focused on tackling unconscious biases, and understanding multiple, diverse perspectives, conflict resolution and critical thinking.

In this section, we analyse the key elements of the transformational approach by LOCOG.

Structural

- Partnering with the key stakeholders in each function to empower them to drive D&I change across the business
- Creating a compelling business case
- Reporting clear D&I workforce metrics to leaders and executives
- Benchmarking departments on D&I metrics

Cultural

- Breaking down siloed working and harnessing a more collaborative culture
- Training on unconscious bias

We explore the details of the interventions and lessons learnt at LOCOG.

Structure, workforce and culture of LOCOG

LOCOG was a temporary organisation that was set up to deliver the 2012 London Olympic and Paralympic Games. Delivering this monumental event would require both technical skills and hard work. This was important in light of the challenges at previous Olympic Games which included: venue readiness at Athens 2004; terrorist threats at Munich 1972 and Atlanta 1996; and boycotts in Moscow 1980 and Los Angeles 1984. When LOCOG was set up in 2005, there were just 50 employees but by 2012, there were 200,000. It was the first time that both the Olympic and Paralympic Games were organised and delivered by the same organisation and workforce. The scale of

(Continued)

(Continued)

delivering the Olympics was monumental, consisting of: 19 competition days; 26 world championships; 34 venues; 8.8 million tickets; 10,490 athletes; 303 medal events; 21,000 media representatives and broadcasters; 2,961 technical officials; 5,770 team officials; and 5,000 doping samples. It was, therefore, understandable that there was an emphasis on technical skills.

However, the backdrop to this was as equally challenging. There were a diverse range of stakeholders and clients with which to engage. Each stakeholder had their own individual perspectives and opinions on what 'success' meant for the London 2012 Games. This resulted in tensions between different stakeholders. Although LOCOG was set up as a private company, it was still bound by the social responsibilities of a public sector organisation. Some of the executive and leadership had come from banking, professional services and the law and wanted to steer the organisation like a private sector business; however, those from public and not-for-profit organisations, such as civil servants, charity personnel and government secondees, wanted to focus on the ethical and social responsibilities of the organisation. There were those in-between such as 'Game Junkies' who had helped with the operational delivery of prior Games. It was this rich tapestry of perspectives, experiences and cultures that sometimes led to tensions and contestation.

However, no one, single voice triumphed. Everyone agreed that technical skills were a prerequisite but there was also a significant push to produce more than *just* a successful Games; LOCOG wanted to inspire change. Firstly, there was a need to engage in adaptive work, where problems and solutions are unclear and highly complex; and secondly, a focus on the legacy of the Games to inspire societal change. This was arguably the perfect environment to develop diversity and inclusion.

Although people were clear on the meaning and importance of 'technical skills' to a successful Games, they sometimes found the term 'inclusion' challenging. The first objective of the D&I team was, therefore, to define clearly the term inclusion and educate people regarding its value. This was challenging, as people had different preconceptions of its meaning, often from their previous organisations. Added to this, budgets were tight and resources were stretched. The D&I budget was only £1.3 million for four years. Coupled with an irremovable deadline, would the D&I team be able to define the term and educate people regarding its value?

(Continued)

(Continued)

The business case

As part of re-defining 'inclusion', the D&I team set about creating a compelling business case. Firstly, they defined a mission statement for D&I. There was a need to design an inclusion programme that would add value both for the organisation and for wider society. Building on the overarching mission of the Games 'to inspire change', they came up with 'Everyone's 2012'. This meant that everyone was welcome to come and participate in the Games. The D&I team then underpinned this with a set of objectives for the workforce and procurement. One of the outcomes of the business case was that LOCOG achieved exceptional employee engagement scores for minorities.

Structure of the D&I team

The business case was set. However, individual departments defined what success meant. This was complex at LOCOG as many departments worked in a siloed or uncollaborative way and were often very competitive with one another. However, the D&I team was cross-functional, consulting and engaging with individual departments. The D&I team, therefore, was pivotal in challenging the siloed nature of the organisation. This put significant pressure on the D&I team, as practitioners had to build strong relationships with key stakeholders in each area of the business. This enabled the team to benchmark different departments against one another regarding progress on D&I. This carried a potential reputation risk for executives as they did not want to be viewed as failing in comparison with their peers.

Tensions and innovation

LOCOG was a culturally rich organisation with many competing perspectives. Adaptive working was required in such environments. For example, employees who had worked only in the sports sector, worked alongside consultants and bankers. They had both been socialised in very different ways. It was not unusual for individuals to be challenged, perhaps for the first time in their careers. However, everyone was talented and experienced. Employees had to learn to appreciate each other's talents and strengths, and think harder about how to persuade one another of the merits of their proposed

(Continued)

(Continued)

actions. This constant negotiation drove innovation and creativity that played a huge part in the success of the Games.

The D&I change framework

The D&I team designed a change framework. This started with 'understand', then 'lead' and 'deliver'. The three areas for intervention were: workforce, procurement and service delivery. The framework was designed as a feedback loop in which information on successes and failures would be fed back to leadership in real time. D&I change became quickly embedded in the change process.

D&I change activities

Understand

The D&I team had to educate employees on what was meant by 'diversity and inclusion', and what was not. Otherwise, the D&I programme would be potentially threatened by people assuming what it meant and challenging the initiatives without due cause. The programme, therefore, had to be communicated in a compelling and palatable way that would deliver the change required.

One of the key ways this was done was through the definition and communication of the D&I business case, which focused on: customers, employees, growth and the economics of D&I. Different people in the organisation, therefore, connected with different parts of the business case, and through these, created actionable change in their departments.

Lead

Each person had to take responsibility for the D&I programme, regardless of level. The programme metrics had to be sympathetic to those under pressure. The D&I team developed a toolkit which would be adapted by each individual to support them to achieve the agreed D&I targets in their function. This was a technique employed not to burden but to empower and inspire the change in diversity at LOCOG. In other words, D&I was positioned as an enabler for each department rather than an inhibitor.

The LOCOG D&I team found that partnering with others and building relationships, based on shared values, helped to drive the change forward.

(Continued)

(Continued)

Externally, for example, LOCOG did not know from where to source disabled drivers, but Mobilie, a small charity, did. These were two different organisations but they needed each other in order to achieve their goals. Internally, the D&I practitioners built alliances with stakeholders to get them on board the change programme.

Deliver

Leadership was accountable for the success of diversity and inclusion at LOCOG. However, individuals were accountable for the delivery of D&I. The D&I team, therefore, benchmarked each department against one another, which proved to be a healthy way of generating competition around the implementation of D&I goals.

Workforce

As previously discussed, technical skills and workforce numbers would be incredibly important to the successful delivery of the Games. The workforce would eventually total 200,000. It would, therefore, become the face of the Games. However, applications tended to come from candidates who were already well networked and had prior experience at the Games. The aim was to create as diverse and inclusive workforce as possible.

- Recruitment action plans: this was one way of getting others to lead on work that would add value rather than waste time. It strengthened the purpose of partnerships through collaboration and directed efforts towards the right, diverse talent pools.
- Access now: this was a guaranteed interview scheme that meant that those with disabilities who met the job specification were guaranteed interviews.
- Efficient use of the recruitment system: LOCOG built talent pools of diverse skill sets and diverse communities. This was also helpful when looking for talent quickly.
- Leadership pledge: leaders had to opt in or out and, therefore, this drove a sense of personal commitment towards D&I.
- Group interviews: LOCOG used more than one interviewer to counteract any potential implicit biases. They also used group interviews that showed the different skills that each candidate had in relation to others. Here,

(Continued)

(Continued)

demographic characteristics become less important and their skills take precedent. This also reduces cost and time.

- Benchmarking: rather than quotas, recruitment teams can be benchmarked against one another. This means that recruiters are rated based on their success at attracting diverse talent with the right skills to the organisation. This creates a competitive dynamic and a market for diverse talent. This approach can also be used for external recruitment agencies.

Procurement

- One approach taken by LOCOG was to put contract opportunities, worth £1.7 billion, online. This encouraged open competition and potentially tapped into smaller businesses. This was good value for both LOCOG and small suppliers. The D&I team also established a procurement report to assess the diversity status of each supplier.
- Legacy evaluation group: this focused on applying LOCOG standards at all stages of the procurement process across all areas of the business.

Talent

- D&I statistics were published every month and distributed to all directors, heads of departments and the diversity board. One of the objectives of doing this was to inspire success and empower individuals to change. The statistics covered 22 'Everyone's 2012' projects and focused on the three main areas for interventions. This included a further breakdown with the following information: recruitment cycle; applications; interviews; job offers; and offers accepted. This was broken down further by department. Inclusion measurements were also included from a 'YourSay' survey.

Service delivery

- The D&I team implemented a service delivery report that identified the successes and failures of each of the 22 projects using a simple red, amber and green system. It allowed senior leaders and directors to evaluate quickly the status of their departments and teams. The team later included a National Governing Body progress report in the Equality Standard for Sport. The reports were succinct and, therefore, could be digested quickly, helping to

(Continued)

(Continued)

position diversity and inclusion as an enabler rather than a bureaucratic process.

- Immovable deadline: the deadlines forced adaptive ways of working and forced the quick resolution of conflicts.
- Sponsors forum and diversity board: diversity was openly discussed and debated on boards and this gave opportunities to persuade sceptics of the business and ethical cases.

Lessons learnt

Procurement: Non-compliant suppliers – the online diversity assessment and the guaranteed interview for candidates with disabilities were sometimes hard to follow up. Despite good workforce D&I data, the data were less complete for procurement. People often did not know how to respond to the diversity questions online and, therefore, would leave this part incomplete. However, mid-way through the programme, completing this section became obligatory.

Service delivery: Ticketing – there could have been a further limitation on the number of tickets that an individual could apply for. This might have enabled more people to each access a smaller number of tickets.

Knowledge management: The Olympic Games knowledge management programme captures Games learning and transfers it to the next Games.

The information for this case study was taken from: Frost, S. (2014) *The Inclusion Imperative: How Real Inclusion Creates Better Business and Builds Better Societies.* London: Kogan Page Limited.

Many thanks to Stephen Frost – Head of D&I at LOCOG 2007–2012 – for his support in completing this case study: @frostincluded, stephen@frostincluded.com, www.frostincluded.com.

Questions

1. What challenges did the D&I team face?
2. How and with what success were the D&I team able to resolve these challenges?
3. You are working in the D&I team for the forthcoming 2016 Rio Olympic Games in Brazil. What can you learn from the team from the London 2012 Games?

Further reading

Acker, J. 2006. Inequality regimes: gender, class and race in organisations. *Gender and Society*, 20, 441–64.

Cockburn, C. 1989. Equal opportunities: the long and short agenda. *Industrial Relations Journal*, 20, 213–25.

European Union Agency for Fundamental Rights 2010. *Handbook on European Non-discrimination Law*. Vienna: European Court of Human Rights and the FRA.

Kalev, A., Kelly, E. & Dobbin, F. 2006. Best practice or best guesses? Assessing the efficacy of corporate affirmative action and diversity policies. *American Sociological Review*, 71, 589–617.

Roberson, Q.M. 2006. Disentangling the meanings of diversity and inclusion in organizations. *Group and Organization Management*, 31, 212.

Wrench, J. 2002. Diversity management, discrimination and ethnic minorities in Europe: clarifications, critiques and research agenda. *Occasional Papers and Reprints on Ethnic Studies*, 19, 1–179.

References

Acker, J. 2006. Inequality regimes: gender, class and race in organizations. *Gender and Society*, 20, 441–64.

Almeida, D.M. & Davis, K.D. 2011. Workplace flexibility and daily stress processes in hotel employees and their children. *The Annals of the American Academy of Political and Social Science*, 683, 123–40.

American Civil Liberties Union (ACLU) 2000. *Affirmative Action*. New York: ACLU.

Bachmann, A.S. 2006. Melting pot or tossed salad? Implications for designing effective multi-cultural workgroups. *Management International Review*, 46, 721–47.

Bell, M.P. 2007. *Diversity in Organizations*. Mason OH: Cengage.

Bouncken, R.B. & Winkler, V.A. 2009. National and cultural diversity in transnational innovation teams. *Technology Analysis & Strategic Management*, 22, 133–51.

Chopin, I. & Gounari, E.M. 2010. *Developing Anti-Discrimination Law in Europe: The 27 EU Member States Compared*. Luxembourg: Publications Office of the European Union.

Cockburn, C. 1989. Equal opportunities: the long and short agenda. *Industrial Relations Journal*, 20, 213–25.

Cockburn, C. 1991. *In the Way of Women: Men's Resistance to Sex Equality in Organisations*. Basingstoke: Macmillan.

Collinson, D., Knights, D. & Collinson, M. 1990. *Managing to Discriminate*. London: Routledge.

Cox, T. 1991. The multi-cultural organization. *Academy of Management Executive*, 5, 34–47.

Cox, T.H. & Blake, S. 1991. Managing cultural diversity: implications for organizational competitiveness. *Academy of Management*, 5, 45–56.

Desvaux, G., Devillard-Hoellinger, S. & Baumgarten, P. 2007. Gender diversity, a corporate performance driver. *Women Matter*. McKinsey & Company.

Elkes, N. 2013. Birmingham taxpayer's equal pay bill passes £1bn. *Birmingham Post*.

Ely, R.J. & Morgan Roberts, L. 2008. Shifting frames in team-diversity research: from difference to relationships. In: Brief, A.P. (ed.) *Diversity at Work*. New York: Cambridge University Press.

Equality and Diversity Forum. 2008. *European Law and Equality: An Introduction*. London: Equality and Diversity Forum.

Euro Info Centre. 2006. *EU Employment Law*. Euro Info Centre, London Chamber of Commerce and Industry.

European Union Agency for Fundamental Rights 2010. *Handbook on European Non-discrimination Law*. Vienna: European Court of Human Rights and the FRA.

Fraser, N. 1997. *Justice Interruptus: Critical Reflections on the 'Postsocialist' Condition*. London: Routledge.

Fraser, N. 2007. Feminist politics in the age of recognition: a two-dimensional approach to gender justice. *Studies in Social Justice*, 1, 23–35.

Frost, S. 2014. *The Inclusion Imperative: How Real Inclusion Creates Better Business and Builds Better Societies*. London: Kogan Page Limited.

Gatrell, C.J. & Swan, S.E. 2008. *Gender and Diversity in Management: A Concise Introduction*. London: Sage.

Gilbert, J.A. & Ivancevich, J.M. 2001. Effects of diversity management on attachment. *Journal of Applied Social Psychology*, 31, 1331–49.

Gottfredson, L.S. 1992. Dilemmas in developing diversity programs. In: Jackson, S.E. (ed.) *Diversity in the Workplace*. New York: Guilford Press.

Gratton, L., Kelan, E., Voigt, A., Walker, L. & Wolfram, H. 2007. *Innovative Potential: Men and Women in Teams*. The Lehman Brothers Centre for Women in Business, London Business School.

Heery, E. & Noon, M. 2001. *A Dictionary of Human Resource Management*. Oxford: Oxford University Press.

Herring, C. 2009. Does diversity pay? Race, gender, and the business case for diversity. *American Sociological Review*, 74, 208.

Hill, E.J., Hawkins, A.J., Ferris, M. & Weitzman, M. 2001. Finding an extra day a week: the positive influence of perceived job flexibility on work and family life balance. *Family Relations*, 50, 49–58.

Horwitz, S.K. & Horwitz, I.R. 2007. The effects of team diversity on team outcomes: a meta-analytic review of team demography. *Journal of Management*, 33, 987–1015.

Ius Laboris 2011. *Employment Discrimination Law: A European Guide*. Brussels: Ius Laboris.

Jackson, S.E. & Alvarez, E.B. 1992. Working through diversity as a strategic imperative. In: Jackson, S.E. (ed.) *Diversity in the Workplace*. New York: Guilford Press.

Jewson, N. & Mason, D. 1986. The theory and practice of equal opportunities policies: liberal and radical approaches. *The Sociological Review*, 34, 307–34.

Johnston, W. & Packer, A. 1987. *Workforce 2000: Work and Workers for the 21st Century*. Indianapolis: Hudson Institute.

Kalev, A., Kelly, E. & Dobbin, F. 2006. Best practice or best guesses? Assessing the efficacy of corporate affirmative action and diversity policies. *American Sociological Review*, 71, 589–617.

Kandola, R. & Fullerton, J. 1998. *Diversity in Action: Managing the Mosaic*. London: Chartered Institute of Personnel and Development.

Kellough, J.E. 2006. *Understanding Affirmative Action: Politics, Discrimination, and the Search for Justice*. Washington, DC: Georgetown University Press.

Kirton, G. & Greene, A.M. 2005. *The Dynamics of Managing Diversity: A Critical Approach*. Boston, MA: Elsevier Butterworth-Heinemann.

Kochan, T., Berzrukova, K., Ely, R., Jackson, S., Joshi, A., Jehn, K., Leonard, J., Levine, D. & Thomas, D. 2003. The effects of diversity on business performance: report of the Diversity Research Network. *Human Resource Management*, 42, 3–21.

Korn/Ferry International 2007. The cost of employee turnover due to failed diversity initiatives in the workplace. *The Corporate Leavers Survey 2007.* Korn/Ferry International.

Kossek, E.E., Lobel, S.A. & Brown, J. 2006. Human resource strategies to manage workforce diversity: examining the business case. In: Konrad, A., Prasad, P. & Pringle, J. (eds) *Handbook of Workplace Diversity.* London: Sage.

Lorbiecki, A. & Jack, G. 2000. Critical turns in the evolution of diversity management. *British Journal of Management,* 11, 17–31.

McGrath, J.E., Berdahl, J.L. & Arrow, H. 1995. Traits, expectations, culture and clout: the dynamics of diversity in work groups. In: Jackson, S.E. & Ruderman, M.N. (eds) *Diversity in Work Teams.* Washington, DC: American Psychological Association.

Miller, F.A. & Katz, J.H. 2002. *The Inclusion Breakthrough: Unleashing the Real Power of Diversity.* San Francisco: Berrett-Koehler Publishers.

Milliken, F. & Martins, L. 1996. Searching for common threads: understanding the multiple effects of diversity in organizational groups. *Academy of Management Review,* 21, 402–33.

Ministry of Justice 2013. *Tribunals Statistics Quarterly,* 1 January to 31 March 2013. London: Ministry of Justice.

Noon, M. 2007. The fatal flaws of diversity and the business case for ethnic minorities. *Work, Employment and Society,* 21, 773–84.

Özbilgin, M.F. 2000. Is the practice of equal opportunities management keeping pace with theory? Management of sex equality in the financial services sector in Britain and Turkey. *Human Resource Development International,* 3, 43–67.

Prasad, P. & Mills, A.J. 1997. From showcase to shadow: understanding the dilemmas of managing workplace diversity. In: Prasad, P., Mills, A.J., Elmes, M. & Prasad, A. (eds) *Managing the Organizational Melting Pot: Dilemmas of Workplace Diversity.* Thousand Oaks, CA: Sage Publications, Inc.

Prasad, P., Konrad, A.M. & Pringle, J.K. 2006. Examining workplace diversity. In: Konrad, A.M., Prasad, P. & Pringle, J.K. (eds) *Handbook of Workplace Diversity.* London: Sage.

Rees, T. 1998. Social exclusion and equal opportunities. *International Planning Studies,* 3, 15–34.

Roberson, Q.M. 2006. Disentangling the meanings of diversity and inclusion in organizations. *Group and Organization Management,* 31, 212.

Rothman, S., Lipset, S.M. & Nevitte, N. 2003. Does enrollment diversity improve university education? *International Journal of Public Opinion Research,* 15, 8–26.

Shah, A.K. 2012. The costs of discrimination. *Equality and Diversity at LSE: Redefining Difference.* http://blogs.lse.ac.uk/diversity/2012/03/the-costs-of-discrimination/, The London School of Economics and Political Science.

SHRM 2008. *2007 State of Workplace Diversity Management: A Survey Report by the Society for Human Resource Management.* Alexandria, VA: Society for Human Resource Management.

Tatli, A. & Özbilgin, M.F. 2012. Surprising intersectionalities of inequality and privilege: the case of the arts and cultural sector. *Equality, Diversity and Inclusion: An International Journal,* 31, 249–65.

Thomas, D.A. & Ely, R.J. 1996. Making differences matter: a new paradigm for managing diversity. *Harvard Business Review,* 74, 79–90.

Thomas, R. 1990. From affirmative action to affirming diversity. *Harvard Business Review,* 68, 107–17.

Thomas, R.R. 1992. Managing diversity: a conceptual framework. In: Jackson, S.E. (ed.) *Diversity in the Workplace.* New York: Guilford Press.

Triandis, H.C., Hall, E.R. & Ewen, R.B. 1965. Member heterogeneity and dyadic creativity. *Human Relations,* 18, 33–55.

Tsui, A.S., Egan, T.D. & O'Reilly, C.A. 1992. Being different: relational demography and organizational attachment. *Administrative Science Quarterly*, 37, 549–79.

United States Department of Labor 2002. *Office of Federal Contract Compliance Programs (OFCCP)*, www.dol.gov/ofccp/regs/compliance/aa.htm.

US Equal Employment Opportunity Commission 2014. *Laws Enforced by EEOC*, www.eeoc.gov/laws/statutes/.

Virtanen, M., Ferrie, J.E., Singh-Manoux, A., Shipley, M.J., Vahtera, J., Marmot, M.G. & Kivimaki, M. 2010. Overtime work and incident coronary heart disease: the Whitehall II prospective cohort study. *European Heart Journal*, 31, 1737–44.

Wallace, W.T. & Pillans, G. 2011. *Diversity and business performance*. CRF Research: Corporate Social Forum.

Wang, M. & Kelan, E.K. 2013. The gender quota and female leadership: effects of Norwegian gender quota on board chairs and CEOs. *Journal of Business Ethics*, 117, 449–66.

Webb, J. 1997. The politics of equal opportunity. *Gender, Work and Organization*, 4, 159–69.

Wentling, R.M. & Palma-Rivas, N. 1997. Diversity in the workforce: a literature review. *Diversity in the Workforce Series Report No.1*. University of California at Berkeley: National Centre for Research in Vocational Education.

Wharton, A.S. & Baron, J.N. 1987. So happy together? The impact of gender segregation at work. *American Sociological Review*, 52, 574–87.

Wharton, A.S. & Baron, J.N. 1991. Satisfaction? The psychological impact of gender segregation on women at work. *The Sociological Quarterly*, 32, 365–87.

Whittle, R. 2002. The framework directive for equal treatment in employment and occupation: an analysis from a disability rights perspective. *European Law Review*, 27, 303–26.

Wrench, J. 2002. Diversity management, discrimination and ethnic minorities in Europe: clarifications, critiques and research agenda. *Occasional Papers and Reprints on Ethnic Studies*, 19, 1–179.

PART II

DIMENSIONS OF DIVERSITY

Part II Contents

Gender equality in the workplace

4

Faiza Ali[1]

Intended learning outcomes

After reading this chapter you will be able to understand:

- The concepts of gender equality and gender segregation at work
- Key issues of gender equality such as pay gap, gender stereotyping and the glass ceiling
- Various theories explaining gender segregation and inequalities at work
- Approaches to achieving gender equality at work
- Contextual and organisational influences on approaches to gender equality

Introduction

This chapter discusses and critically evaluates theories of gender segregation at work and the related ideologies of gender equality. It examines how these theories approach employed and unemployed workers, men and women, in a society. The role of prevailing

[1]The author would like to thank her students of diversity course, Ms Shannon Wong and Ms Charlotte Sexstone, for identifying helpful and interesting examples for inclusion in this chapter.

employment norms in a society (see the case study of Pakistan) and gender segregation of the labour force arising from those norms is discussed in particular. The chapter starts with an examination of the Marxist and radical feminist theories, followed by an analysis of dual system theory. Following this, the post-structuralist and human capitalist critiques of the earlier theories are offered. Human capital theory tries to explain the sex segregation of the labour market on purely economic grounds. Traditionally the interpretations of the labour market segregation process drew heavily on the capitalist system and its needs. Some of the concepts economists used have been borrowed and adapted by sociologists (Bradley, 1989), which justifies the theory's inclusion in this theoretical background to this work. The chapter also discusses the change ideologies related to the issues of gender equality within employment contexts.

Key concepts of gender equality

Gender equality at work refers to the equal rights, responsibilities and opportunities of women and men in employment (UN, 2013). Equality does not mean that women and men will become the same but that women's and men's rights, responsibilities and opportunities will not depend on whether they are born male or female. Gender equality implies that the interests, needs and priorities of both women and men are taken into consideration, recognising the diversity of different groups of women and men. Equality between women and men is seen both as a human rights issue and as a precondition for, and indicator of, sustainable people-centred development (an approach to international development that focuses on improving local communities' self-reliance, social justice and participatory decision-making).

Gender segregation in occupations relates to the different work that women and men do as a consequence of their patterns of socialisation, identifying tasks traditionally seen as 'women's work' or 'men's work'. Gender segregation in occupations is the tendency for men and women to be employed in different occupations across the entire spectrum of jobs. Two kinds of gender segregation have been identified: horizontal segregation and vertical segregation. Horizontal segregation is where the workforce of a specific industry or sector is mostly made up of one particular gender. An example of horizontal segregation can be found in construction where men make up the majority of the industry's workforce, whereas childcare is predominantly a female occupation. Vertical segregation is where opportunities for career progression within a company or sector for a particular gender are narrowed. Vertical segregation affects women far more than men. For example, women are less likely to work as managers or senior officials than men (Hakim, 1979).

Gender stereotypes that have been enforced regarding the role of women over the years, and the actions of others who have an influence on women's progression in the workplace, have led to problems such as the glass ceiling and the gender pay gap. The *glass ceiling* refers to an 'invisible barrier' which inhibits progression to higher levels of an organisation's hierarchy for women and other disadvantaged minority groups (Weyer, 2007). It is where women are fixed at lower levels of an organisation and there is very little or no opportunity for development and advancement. Heilman (2001) argues that the glass ceiling is an inevitable result of gender stereotypes which shape beliefs about how each gender should behave. Gender stereotypes also emphasise areas where one sex may be deficient in comparison to the other sex. Despite a woman's competence to fulfil the needs of their job and progress further within an organisation, they are often disregarded when considered against men.

The *gender pay gap* refers to the difference in earnings between men and women in the workplace (Kirton and Greene, 2005). According to the Office for National Statistics (ONS) (Bovill, 2013), the mean average pay gap between men and women for both full- and part-time employees fell from 19.6 per cent to 18.6 per cent from 2011 to 2012, which does show positive improvements. However, despite the narrowing of the gender pay gap over time, its existence is still an issue, especially in cases where men and women are paid differently for completing tasks which are of similar value and require comparable skill.

Resilience to gender inequality has been shown particularly as the female labour market has increased, including the number of mothers working. According to the ONS (ONS, 2011), there has been a significant narrowing of the gap in employment rates between women with children and women without children from 1996 to 2010. In 1996 there was a difference of 5.8 per cent and in 2010 there was a difference of 0.8 per cent, which indicates that women are showing greater willingness to work, even when they are mothers. The statistics show more consistent results for mothers working part-time; however, from 1996 to 2010 there was also a percentage increase of 5.9 per cent in mothers working full-time (ONS, 2011). Therefore, these statistics show that women are aiming towards achieving more responsibility in the workplace through showing more commitment to their careers, and as a result it being recognised that women are capable of meeting the requirements of top management positions (Syed and Murray, 2009).

Classical theories of gender segregation in the workplace

In this section, different theories of gender segregation will be discussed, explaining reasons for gender inequality at work.

Marxist theory

The key characteristics of Marxism in philosophy are its materialism and its commitment to political practice as the end goal of all thought. With respect to gender relations, the main focus of Marxist theory is to analyse the impact of the capitalist system on segregation of the labour force. Marxist feminism seeks to dismantle capitalism in order to achieve women's liberation. This method has two major contributions. First, it provides a class analysis, which is important for the study of power. The exercise of power is a main element in generating and perpetuating inequality. Second, it proposes a historical dialectic materialist method to analyse patriarchal relations (Eisenstein, 1983: 6–7). The Marxist feminist method was originally used to explain the relationship between production and reproduction. The concept was subsequently expanded to extend our knowledge of gender segregation in the labour market (O'Brien, 1982).

Marxist theorists argue that women comprise a 'reserve army of labour' (Bruegel, 1979). They argue that women can enter into paid jobs when there is a shortage of male labour. But they are also expected to leave formal employment when they are no longer required. Marxist theorists question the conventional notion of creating surplus value by demonstrating how gender inequalities are exploited by capitalists to achieve their greater economic advantage (Lockwood, 1986). In the words of Gardiner:

> At a time of economic crisis … when the major requirement for capital is to hold down the level of wages, domestic labour performs a vital economic function and further socialisation of housework and childcare would be detrimental from a capitalist point of view. However, other pressures (e.g. the need for women wage workers or the need to expand markets for workers' consumption) might lead to further socialisation of housework and childcare in a period of capitalist expansion. (Gardiner, 1979: 188)

Gardiner's analysis explains how capitalistic systems benefit from sustaining current inequalities in the distribution of domestic duties between women and men. However, the analysis has been challenged by some feminist scholars who argue for a holistic approach towards gender equality within socio-political and economic spheres, both at work and at home (Smith, 1982; Foster, 1990; Lips, 1993). The holistic view includes other reasons for gender inequality, such as socio-cultural, religious and economic factors.

According to Marxist labour segmentation theorists, conflict between labour and capital is the main cause of inequality of labour in organisations (Wright, 1989; Braverman, 1974). Instead of identifying class conflict as the only cause of gender segregation, these theorists argue that employer strategies to use cheap labour and to deter worker resistance tend to uphold gender segregation in employment (Beechey, 1978). Though Marxist theory does not treat women as a class, it treats gender inequality as a result of class conflict. For that reason, radical feminists have criticised Marxist theory for 'trivialising' the issues of gender segregation. Some feminist scholars argue that gender relations and the related issues of gender segregation in employment have been mainly ignored by Marxist writers (Walby, 1990). Some are more emphatic, and argue that the Marxist approach tends to reduce women's issues to a sub-category of 'malestream' articulation of class conflict (Daly, 1978).

Marxist theory has also been criticised because of its supposed neglect of childcare. According to Chodorow (1994), childcare and mothering are integrated with women's work life in industrialised countries. Chodorow argues that women all over the world are mainly responsible for childcare. The capitalist system has been largely ineffective in providing new ways of enabling parents to combine childcare with employment. Chodorow suggests that radical political feminist theory addresses the issue of childcare and women's employment whereas Marxist theory alone cannot deal with effective proposals for the reorganisation of parenting, employment and childcare.

Furthermore, the Marxist perspective on gender segregation seems to have a limited relevance and applicability within non-capitalistic societies such as Islamic society. Islamic countries today, such as Pakistan, Iran and Saudi Arabia, represent a society that may be described as a blend of three major socio-economic systems (i.e. Islamic values, capitalistic market structures and socialistic preferences). Interest-free banking is an example offered by some banks in Pakistan, Iran and Saudi Arabia. The Islamic values' system prohibits 'Riba' (interest on 'idle' wealth) and instead promotes the Islamic institution of 'Zakat', forcing the rich to share a portion of their wealth with the needy and the destitute. The Marxist critique on gender segregation may perhaps not be attributed to class and capitalistic structures in Islamic society. Yet, the role of patriarchy and its 'collusion' with local feudal structures in maintaining and perpetuating the female disadvantage within societal and employment contexts cannot be denied (Syed et al., 2005).

Radical feminist theory

Radical feminism originated in the 1970s in the US (Echols and Willis, 1990). Historically, radical feminism started with the assumption that the sexes are adversarially poised, that men have power over women, and that society and its various social relationships can be best understood in terms of their relationship to that situation (Eisenstein, 1983). Radical feminists argue that all kinds of oppression are derived from a system of patriarchal relations (Walby, 1990). For Marxists, capitalism is the main influence on the relationship between capital and labour. In contrast, radical feminists treat gender segregation as the core concept. Radical feminists consider the concept of patriarchy as the basis of oppression in employment. Formerly, patriarchy was known as the power of the father (head of the family) over his family members including females and younger men (Lockwood, 1986). Today, patriarchy refers to the systems and structures that accommodate the power of men over women (Walby, 1990). In its present form, patriarchy recognises women as a class and refers to a system where men are privileged and women are not, suggesting that inequality is legitimately professed.

Radical feminists argue that men benefit from domestic labour as a dominant task completed by women in their families. They treat this gender division of labour as the root of patriarchal social relations giving advantages to men over women in employment. Radical feminists argue that patriarchy enforces the lower status of women socially and economically. However, some scholars have challenged the concept of patriarchy as an explanation of the contemporary disadvantaged status of women in the labour force.

For example, Colgan and Ledwith (1996) criticise the idea which implies that only males exercise patriarchy. According to Wilson (1995), patriarchy is old and it refers to only one kind of male supremacy. Likewise, Lockwood (1986) contends that this idea of patriarchy is not applicable to modern societies since it refers to a specific historical form of domestic relationships; contemporary gender segregation in societies is more complex. In addition to this, patriarchy does not explain other fields of oppression such as race, ethnicity, gender orientation and religion.

The domain of radical feminism within Islamic society is not an easy terrain. Religion is a sensitive subject and people of faith have a special affiliation towards and respect for their religious beliefs and practices. Yet, the issues of Islamic principles (such as those enshrined in the Qur'an) need to be differentiated from contemporary Islamic practices. Some scholars such as Mernissi (1996) and Hassan (2001) have argued for un-reading patriarchy from the fundamental sources of Islamic principles. These scholars argue that a gender egalitarian ideal of Islamic society can be achieved only when Islamic teachings are liberated from male-dominated (i.e. patriarchal) influences and interpretations. Yet, there is some scope to reinterpret but not to challenge the Qur'anic ideals of a perfect man and a perfect woman.

Dual systems theory

Some scholars argue that Marxist and radical feminist theories alone are unable to explain the status of women in employment. These scholars have proposed joining these two mutually exclusive theoretical propositions in a progressive socialist feminist theory of capitalist patriarchy. This new theory endeavours to explain the dual role of the capitalist system and patriarchy in producing and sustaining gender segregation in the labour force. It treats the two apparently independent systems as actually interlinked and theorises them together to demonstrate the patriarchal relations, which would otherwise be obscured by the capitalist system (Hearn, 1987). The idea of capitalist patriarchy can be seen as an advance in the study of gender inequalities in employment. In the words of Walby (1986: 31): 'A considerable advance over the "capitalism alone" and "patriarchy alone" approaches to explaining gender inequality can be found in the conception of one system of capitalist patriarchy'.

Socialist-feminist analysis seems to address the criticism faced by Marxist and radical feminists regarding the status of women in employment and domestic life (Hartmann, 1979). According to Hartmann, Marxist theory ignores the role of patriarchy in excluding women from employment on social and historical grounds, seeing the exclusion of women from the labour force as a result of capitalist desires to employ the cheapest possible labour. Similarly, radical feminist theory overemphasises the idea of patriarchy and fails to mention the role of the capitalist system in sustaining and further exploiting the inequalities existing in the workplace and society. Hartmann explains job segregation by gender in terms of the intersection of the two systems of capitalism and patriarchy, from which the dominant groups of each system, capitalists and men, benefit.

Supporters of dual systems theory differ in the theorisation of the relationship between capitalism and patriarchy. For example, Walby (1986) argues that both capitalists and patriarchs might have different or similar reasons for maintaining the suppressed status of women in society and employment. However, Eisenstein (1983) and Hartmann (1979) argue that both capitalism and patriarchy are independent systems that blend with each other and both promote the same interests.

Although Hartmann's dual systems approach advances our understanding of gender segregation at work, her work has not escaped criticism. The main issue is whether she was able to maintain an analytic separation between capitalism and patriarchy. Young (1981) argues that either dual systems theorists give capitalism and patriarchy the same base where both are analytically inseparable, or on the other hand, they may have separate bases where each cannot explain the full range of features of both capitalism and patriarchy. Walby (1986) also points out that Hartmann's analysis of capitalism and patriarchy overstates the degree of harmony between the two systems. Walby suggests a more developed formulation of the dual systems theory. Dual systems theory has also been criticised by post-structuralists, who argue that structural theories ignore the diverse experiences of women and men at work.

Post-structuralist theory

Feminist post-structuralism looks philosophically at the ways in which women are treated in the world and attempts to break down barriers by identifying how societal influences have led to the status quo. In contrast with the Marxist approach of treating class as the root cause of segmentation, post-structuralist theorists identify the dominant discourse and the systems of representation as the basis of gender segregation. Their main focus is, for example, the representation of males and females in employment. They argue that, depending on who controls the dominant discourses of representation, women and men can be included or excluded from employment and other societal contexts. Post-structuralist feminism argues that by referring to the head teacher as 'headmaster', students are encouraged to believe that he is dominant through his gender; and that the other female teachers are less important due only to the fact that they are not male. The work of the French post-structuralist philosopher, Foucault (1979), is largely mentioned by the supporters of post-structuralist feminism. They argue that gender roles and identities are no more than social performances determined by the dominant discourses, which vary between different cultures and communities. According to this approach, theorisation based on structural issues is an oversimplification of experiences faced by women in employment.

Scholars such as Collinson and Hearn (1996: 10) have also discussed the exclusive nature of structural analyses of gender relations that 'caricature men's power and women's subordination and ignore the analytical significance of the organisational practices through which these categories are constituted'. Post-structuralist feminist theory endeavours to recognise males' and females' diverse, complex, and in some ways, conflicting lifestyles within and outside the employment contexts. Collinson and Hearn mention the role of 'gender subjectivities and their ambiguous, fragmented, discontinuous and multiple characters within asymmetrical relations. In deconstructing and decentring the subject, some writers argue that all subjectivities are fragmentally non-rational and frequently contradictory' (1996: 10).

The post-structuralist theorists criticise the structural analysis of gender segregation. According to them, structural analysis of gender segregation tends to ignore the variety of experiences of women and men in the labour force, while enforcing basic gender stereotypes. Indeed, at least in the past few decades, the structural analysis of gender relations in employment has been used to explain the inferior status of women compared with men. In highlighting the changing gender roles of a small number of 'successful women' within employment contexts, particularly in the industrialised nations, post-structuralist theorists tend to ignore the fact that the majority of women within industrialised nations as well as non-Western contexts (such as those in Islamic society) remain restricted to lower levels of 'employment class' when compared to their male counterparts. For instance, in Pakistan, although the proportion of working women in the formal sectors of employment has somewhat increased in the past few decades (Ali, 2013; Syed, 2008), little change in the status and quality of women's employment experiences has been noted. Consequently, life choices for most women remain constrained by poverty and a lack of economic and social capabilities.

Though post-structuralist analysis of segregation at work is of use when it is taken from an individual perspective, it has however some general difficulties. It ignores the maintenance and reproduction of inequality and discrimination at workplaces experienced by most female workers. Because of its predominant focus on the diversity of experiences, the post-structuralist analysis ignores the real-life discrimination faced by a larger proportion of the workforce. Instead, the concept seems to produce a seamless web of pure description that ignores the material reality and history of patriarchy and capitalism (Witz, 1994: 25).

Human capital theory

Neo-classical economists suggest that a worker's education, training and natural capability determine the rewards they get from their job. They argue that organisations base their recruitment decisions on the market value of each individual's human capital. This school of thought is known as 'human capital theory'. Human capital theorists explain the position of women in paid jobs in terms of their lesser human capital, arguing that women have fewer skills and qualifications and less labour market experience than men (Bradley, 1989). They argue that because of the traditional gender division of labour involving women's engagement with house chores and rearing children, women tend to possess inferior skills (i.e. human capital) compared to men. The human capital gap widens as men spend more time in paid jobs.

Other scholars (such as Mincer, 1962) argue that domestic work is similar to paid work and women voluntarily choose to work at home. Some argue that women choose occupations involving less skill and greater flexibility so that they are penalised less for their irregular pattern of work (Polachek, 1976, 1981). According to this perspective, human capital decreases when the worker is out of the labour market for some time, which results in low wages on re-entry after maternity leave. Women workers try to enter occupations which are usually low paid where the evidence of human capital decline is less observable. However, Polachek's approach has some empirical difficulties. For example, England (1984) found that although there was a decline in women's earnings resulting from their temporary exit from the labour force, this did not suggest large differences between male and female occupations.

Human capital theory faces much criticism from sociologists. According to Lonsdale (1985), when males and females leave school, opportunities in the labour market are not equal. Walby (1986) argues that employment rewards and benefits cannot be solely determined by labour demand and labour supply. Walby further argues that the concepts of patriarchy and domestic power relationships are missing from the analysis of human capital theory. Furthermore, women who are equal with men in terms of their human capital still do not enjoy the same high income (Tan, 2014; Bradley, 1989). According to Large and Saunders (1995), career imbalance starts between male and female graduates with more or less the same qualifications. For example, international comparisons show that females with similar qualifications, at least within the same occupations, earn less and enjoy less mobility of labour compared with males.

Table 4.1 gives an overview of the above discussed theories of gender segregation at work, identifying the root causes of segregation at work. As illustrated, Marxist feminists purpose capitalism as the root cause of gender segregation in employment.

Table 4.1 An overview of theories of gender segregation at work

Theories	Studies	Causes of gender segregation at work
Marxist theory	Braverman, 1974; O'Brien, 1982; Wright, 1989	Capitalism
Radical theory	Daly, 1978; Eisenstein, 1983; Echols and Willis, 1990	Patriarchy
Dual-systems theory	Hartmann, 1979; Walby, 1986; Hearn, 1987	Capitalism and patriarchy
Post-structuralist theory	de Beauvoir, 1949; Foucault, 1979; Connell, 1987; Calas and Smircich, 1993	Dominant discourse and system of representation – gender subjectivity
Human capital theory	Mincer, 1962; Polachek, 1976, 1981; Bradley, 1989	Differences in human capital possessed by individuals

Radical theory considers patriarchy as the base of gender segregation. Dual systems theory argues that both capitalism and patriarchy are the grounds for segregation in employment. Post-structuralist theorists draw on gender subjectivity. Lastly, human capital theorists argue that gender segregation at work is dependent on the value of the human capital that individuals possess.

Discussion activity 4.1

Choose one of the theories discussed above and act as a proponent of that theory. List pros and cons of the theory along with at least one organisational example, and then compare your list with people or groups who are acting as proponents of a different theory.

Approaches to promote gender equality in the workplace

During the past few decades, an increasing trend within industrialised countries has been to promote equal opportunity in order to attract skilled women and at the same time to redress their public image (Cockburn, 1989). However, a number of different approaches have been used to achieve this goal. For example, Jewson and Mason (1986) discuss liberal and radical change ideologies to explain this wave of change. Cockburn (1989) proposes the concept of transformational change ideology. These three ideologies constitute the framework within which organisations operate. Each of these ideologies is examined below.

Liberal approaches

The liberal approach towards equal employment opportunity in organisations is aimed at achieving the removal of discriminatory policies and practices in employment. The approach endeavours to create equal terms and conditions of employment for women and men. The proponents of the liberal approach regard men and women as equal in terms of their current socio-economic positions and do not acknowledge any differences between them. They argue that employment practices and policies should be the same for both men and women (Jewson and Mason, 1986).

Straw's (1989) work on equal employment opportunities draws on the liberal approach. Straw defines equality at three levels in organisations: equal chances at the recruitment level, equal access to the selection level, and equal shares in the organisational hierarchy. Since the argument is founded on the assumption of gender neutrality, the liberal approach tends to discount or simply ignore the structural inequalities in employment, which are rooted in traditions, history and culture. For instance, the institution of patriarchy, deeply entrenched in the form of certain religious practices, is hardly acknowledged.

The liberal approach towards equal employment opportunity (EEO) has been in practice in the US, Australia and European contexts for the past few decades. The related business case for equal employment opportunities emerged in the 1990s in US businesses, introducing the liberal approach into mainstream capitalist ideology. The business case is focused on convincing managerial audiences that equality is profitable (Schwartz and Zimmerman, 1992), assuming that employers would make their decisions on recruitment, selection and career development on the basis of bottom-line considerations.

Radical approaches

In contrast to the liberal perspective of EEO, the radical approach differentiates between dominant groups, such as middle-class, white, able-bodied men, and subordinate groups, such as women, ethnic minorities and the disabled (in the context of the US and Australia for example). The radical approach challenges the existing organisational and social structures, in the quest for equality for such disadvantaged groups based on some ethical and moral principles (Jewson and Mason, 1986). Organisations that seek to implement EEO through radical approaches use affirmative action and positive discrimination as commonly adopted tools. The approach treats men and women as essentially different from each other in terms of their biological as well as social identities. Radical approaches ensure the noticeable attendance of both women and men at the workplace, and seek the eradication of the barriers to advancement faced by disadvantaged groups. The approach is usually adopted by organisations possessing strong political and ethical considerations and values.

Adler and Izraeli (1988: 6) identify three phases of a radical change strategy for women's employment: 1) identifying the distinctive contributions of both women and men, 2) creating enabling conditions for both kinds of contributions to be made and rewarded within organisations, and 3) finding ways in which both contributions can be combined for more powerful managerial procedures and solutions to the organisation's problems.

Since the radical approach is aimed at making women's position better to bring them in line with their male counterparts, Lowery (1995) argues that affirmative action becomes anathema to many white men. However, there is no evidence that women have deprived the male middle-class of power or have even begun to challenge their dominance in the workplace (Lowery, 1995). In contrast, Watson (1994: 211) argues that equal employment policy is usually 'a compromise which recognises women's differences from men, but tries to iron these out by finding ways to enable more women to join men's worlds'. Watson argues that the structure of organisations should be changed in a way that these differences can no longer serve as a barrier to women's employment.

Discrimination in hiring decisions is a complex phenomenon in organisational life. Members of discriminated groups experience different kinds and levels of discrimination because of several complex and intersectional attributes that they may possess. Improving one group's position does not necessarily translate into equal opportunities for others. According to Daly (1978), affirmative action is a 'reform tokenism', something that delays real change towards attaining equality. Some scholars argue that the radical approach is 'retrogressive in further dividing the already divided powerless groups' (Cockburn, 1989: 217). Cockburn argues that although the radical approach may improve the relative position of one disadvantaged group, it does not ensure improvement in the nature of the gendered organisation itself.

Organisational insight 4.1

North Yorkshire Police faces sex discrimination case

A female firearms officer sued the North Yorkshire Police for discrimination, claiming that she was not given the opportunity to be reassessed after she failed a training course, while evidence shows that other male officers who failed were reassessed.

The officer also claimed that she was constantly harassed and was told: 'female officers did not have loud enough voices to take part in operations', which caused her to leave one of the training exercises, as she felt humiliated by the male officers. She also claimed that a chief inspector asked if she wanted a 'pink gun', but later apologised for his remark. A male officer witness at the tribunal stated that: 'she was constantly singled out, accused of having an affair with an officer and generally belittled and humiliated in front of class mates by training staff' (BBC News, 2012a).

North Yorkshire Police authority has denied the claims of gender discrimination. Nevertheless the case represents a male-dominated work environment that stereotypically portrays women as unfit for that employment. This horizontal segregation between male and female officers is a barrier to achieving equality in the workplace.

Transformational approaches

Cockburn (1989) proposes the concept of transformational change towards equal employment opportunities as an alternate mechanism. Cockburn treats the liberal approach as being incapable of meeting its equality targets, and the radical approach, she argues, tends to boost the interests of some disadvantaged groups such as women, ethnic minorities and disabled workers, yet it does not challenge gendered hierarchal structures. Her proposed transformational change approach has a two-pronged agenda: short term and long term. The short-term agenda is aimed at 'combating day to day inequalities in organisational life' (Özbilgin, 2000: 45). The long-term agenda by comparison seeks to change the organisational structures and cultures to form a democratic organisation, where equality is sustained throughout the organisational system.

This ideal workforce profile proposed by the transformational approach is somewhat similar to the one that is identified by other scholars (such as Morrison et al., 1987) whose approaches towards EEO are informed by diversity theory. The approach argues that organisations benefit from diverse workforces including workers from disadvantaged groups of the society. However, the type of organisation assumed by transformational change is broader than the one offered by diversity theory (Özbilgin and Woodward, 2003). This means that the transformational approach seeks to alter current organisational structures rather than exclusively focus on a diverse workforce.

Diversity theory is predominantly focused on the business case. In contrast, the transformational approach is mainly concerned with moral and ethical cases for equality. Diversity theory is focused on the multi-cultural approach to promote equality in organisations, which assumes that women and ethnic minorities (under-represented groups) will provide organisations with new ideas and ways of working if they have greater representation in the workforce. The business case for diversity does not recognise the existence of gender and racial imbalance and power and culture in current organisational settings. The business case tends to discriminate legitimately against some disadvantaged groups who are under-skilled and cannot improve the competitive edge of the organisation (at least partially because of their marginal position in society). The diversity discourse's exclusive emphasis is on the diversity of the managerial elite where policies originate. Transformational change aims at changing organisational systems to promote diversity among its entire staff, not only as a business choice but also as a moral and ethical requirement. At least in the short term, transformational change relies on measures such as mainstreaming.

Mainstreaming can be the major organisational task for equal opportunity. It is an action that aims to amalgamate equal opportunities into the mainstream of organisational thinking, strategy, planning, resource allocation and decision making within organisations (Foster, 1990). Mainstreaming seems to support the short-term agenda of transformational ideology in aiming to ensure equality within organisational systems. But, for the long-term agenda, it is essential to alter the systems that have led to the present position of gender inequality, in order to establish an open systems democracy, where members of different groups enjoy equal representation and occupational benefits in employment. According to Buzzanell (1995), this transformation can be achieved if individuals are free of social gender stereotypes in their thinking, interacting and organising. Similarly, Ramsay and Parker (1992) proposed a model of bureaucracy which is beneficial to gender equality. Their proposed model can be located between classical bureaucracy and anti-bureaucracy, hence its name: neo-bureaucracy. 'Neo-bureaucratic organisations would be continually attempting to refuse the fixity of patriarchal and capitalist imperatives whilst recognising the power of organised labour to bring wider social benefits' (1992: 269).

The transformational approach, despite its advantages, has rarely been adopted for any practical applications in existing organisations. According to Cockburn (1989), there are two main reasons for this. Firstly, pressure groups such as women and ethnic groups do not exhibit strong co-operation and coordination with each other and secondly there is a lack of strong working relationships between these groups and the trade unions. With the redistribution of power to promote equality between members of an organisation, there can be conflicts that hinder the application of the transformational approach. Ramsay and Parker's (1992) work on neo-bureaucratic organisations is one of the ideal visions of transformation, but since it indicates real change in the distribution of power, the conflict between the existing holders of power and the one who lacks power is unavoidable. Organisational change involves two kinds of conflicts: one is between the powerful and powerless, and the other is between the members of the different disadvantaged groups themselves.

To achieve change in organisations, actions should be organised and alliances should be built with the members of the organisation who currently enjoy power and support equal opportunity initiatives, despite the fact that these policies will bring restrictions on their currently favoured positions.

Organisational insight 4.2

Discrimination in a school

A Larne Grammar School teacher – Julie Muldrew – was required to relinquish her position as the 'head of year' between 2008 and 2010, and again in 2011 because she had to change her employment type (from full-time employment to flexible working hours) for the purpose of childcare. However, she lodged a claim of indirect gender discrimination in 2011; the school's defence of the policy was that such important posts were usually held by staff employed full-time. However, the tribunal stated that it was an inappropriate way of 'achieving the legitimate objective of securing pastoral care for pupils at the school'. Hence, the teacher won the case as the tribunal declared it to be '... *unlawful discrimination against members of the teaching staff*' based on the fact that the teacher's reduced working hours should not be a barrier to performing her duties as 'head of year' (BBC News, 2012b). This case reveals indirect discrimination against gender, where the teacher's higher position was taken away because of her change in employment pattern.

Multi-level approaches

Previous research suggests that societal and institutional contexts may play a major role in shaping the status of disadvantaged groups, e.g. women in employment (Beller, 1982; Blau and Beller, 1988; Dickens, 2007). While, in the past few decades, there has been significant progress in many countries regarding legislation on equal opportunity (Kelly and Dobbin, 1999; Leonard, 1986), legislation per se is not sufficient to explain the progress (or lack of progress) on equal opportunity in a society. There are several other factors (discussed next) which need to be considered to develop a holistic view of equal opportunity.

In their theorisation of a multi-level approach to diversity management, Syed and Özbilgin (2009) propose a relational framework that bridges the divide between macro-societal, meso-organisational and micro-individual levels of analyses to arrive at a more comprehensive, realistic and context-specific framing of diversity management. The authors argue that a relational approach is imperative in order to fully capture individual choices, organisational processes and structural conditions – all of which collectively account for unrelenting power disparity and disadvantage within social and employment contexts. Previously, in their review of research on employment discrimination in the US, Hirsh and Cha (2008) identified factors at individual, workplace and societal levels that contribute to variation in sex and race discrimination across employment contexts. At each level, the authors were able to distinguish between factors that affect employers' sex and race biases, and factors that affect potential victims' capacity to identify discriminatory experiences at work.

There is evidence of the use of the multi-level approach in recent academic research. For example, drawing on a qualitative study of Lebanese skilled self-initiated expatriates in France, Al Ariss and Özbilgin (2010) adopted a multi-level approach as an alternative to theories of management that frame expatriate careers as either organisationally or individually driven. In doing so, the authors explicated how the international work experiences of self-initiated expatriates can be captured in ways true to their nature as multi-faceted and multi-level phenomena. Similarly, in their study of the English-language-related challenges facing migrant women, Syed and Murray (2009) took a multi-level perspective on the labour market issues and challenges facing migrant women from non-English-speaking backgrounds in Australia. The authors theorised their findings through a multi-level construct, examining the macro-societal, meso-organisational and micro-individual challenges facing migrant women in the Australian labour market.

Table 4.2 offers a summary of the ideologies and perspectives towards equal employment opportunities discussed thus far, with an account of their key propositions and the contexts in which these theories were proposed. As illustrated, the liberal and radical approaches towards EEO have been mainly adopted within Anglo-Western contexts such as the US, the UK and Australia. By contrast, the transformational approach is less observable in practice since (as Cockburn, 1989, proposed), there is a lack of cooperation between women and ethnic groups, and also between disadvantaged groups and the trade unions.

Table 4.2   An overview of approaches to gender equality

Ideology	Study	Proposition	Societal context
Liberal	Jewson and Mason, 1986; Straw, 1989	Treats men and women as equal; ensures equal terms and conditions for both sexes in employment; treats authority as gender neutral	US, UK and Australia
Radical	Adler and Izraeli, 1988; Jewson and Mason, 1986	Differentiates between dominant groups; demands equality based on ethical and moral values; affirmative action and positive discrimination as commonly used tools; seeks to remove barriers to employment faced by disadvantaged groups	US
Transformational	Cockburn, 1989; Ramsay and Parker, 1992	Short-term agenda (affirmative action and positive discrimination, mainstreaming); long-term agenda (alteration of organisational structure)	Not adopted practically
Relational perspective/ multi-level approach	Syed and Özbilgin, 2009	Investigation of gender equality issues at macro-national, meso-organisational and micro-individual level	Partially adopted in the Western countries

Country context: Pakistan

Compared to the extremely disadvantaged position of under-educated women from poor socio-economic backgrounds, skilled women in urban settings of Lahore, Karachi and Islamabad have relatively better access to employment opportunities. Yet, employment stereotypes based on gender are commonplace. The Pakistani public and private sectors rank EEO low on their list of priorities, as there is no substantive model for gender equality in Pakistani organisations. It is therefore unsurprising to find that female participation rates are low in Pakistan. According to the most recent Labour Force Survey (LFS, 2013), the overall labour force participation rate[2] in Pakistan is 47.06 per cent, which represents 70.03 per cent of males and a mere 22.79 per cent of females.

Although women comprise 49.1 per cent of the total population, the proportion of them in the labour force is 21.6 per cent, whereas their participation rate as a percentage of the total population of females, as of 2011, is only 22 per cent (World Bank, 2012).

In Pakistan, gender relations have historically been highly unequal, the sex ratio at 1.05 being even lower than that of India (CIA, 2013). Literacy, school enrolment and a persistently high fertility rate all point to the low status of women. Female primary

---

[2]The labour force participation rate is defined as the percentage of people in the labour force in respect to the total population.

school attendance is around 35 per cent, among the lowest in the world. Female labour force participation is very low and involves severe crowding into low-pay, low-skill occupations. The labour market is also highly segmented, especially in urban areas where there is also widespread segregation between sexes.

Other data suggest that the female participation rate was closer to 18 per cent for 2005–2006, increasing from 13.7 per cent in 1999–2000. Multiple factors are thought to have contributed to this increase in female participation, including: increased awareness of EEO, better educational opportunities and changing social attitudes (Ferdoos, 2005). Nevertheless, women's participation remains well below that of men and women's participation in economic activities is also likely to be low. Even though the average annual growth rate of female labour participation has increased slightly, 'the rate of growth has to go a long way to assume sustainable momentum' (LFS, 2013).

According to UNDP (2009), in Pakistan the female economic activity rate[3] for those aged above 15 years is 39 per cent of the male rate. The female labour force of age 15 years or above is 32.7 per cent. Out of this, total female employment in the formal sector is only 18 per cent. Female employment in industry as a percentage of total female employment is 16 per cent. However, the services sector accounts for 20 per cent of female employment. Women at professional level, such as legislators, senior officials and managers represent only two per cent. Out of total female employment, only 26 per cent of females are in professional and technical occupations. A miniscule percentage of women are clerks and plant and machine operators and assemblers. The female unemployment rate as a percentage of the total labour force is higher in Pakistan (i.e. 7.7 per cent) than in India and Bangladesh.

Critical analysis and discussion

The case study on the employment situation of Pakistani women at the end of this chapter demonstrates the application of the multi-level perspective framework. This relational perspective fills the gap identified earlier in the equal opportunity approach. Previous research has shown that decision-making and practices cannot be solely comprehended by evaluating organisational policies and the use of legislation. This multi-level perspective framework enables us to assess how societal factors such as gender, culture, religion, law and economic factors impact on the employment opportunities for women. These factors comprise the macro-national level and reflect how sociological and organisational forces interact in the way they influence workplace equality. Along with the introduction of meso-organisational and micro-individual levels, looking at the organisational rituals and individual identity and agency, respectively, a holistic understanding of the various factors affecting equal opportunity and gender inequality can be obtained.

---

[3]Economic activity rate is the percentage of the population in a given age group which is in the Labour force.

The study of the Australian model conducted by Syed and Özbilgin (2009) also supported the notion that the adoption of a multi-level framework can achieve better business outcomes and equity outcomes with a diverse workforce. By looking at three perspective levels, it has been found that the legislation in Australia puts little effort into enforcing that organisations manage cultural diversity. The present Australian model for diversity management does not adequately handle minority ethnic employees, especially migrants from non-English-speaking backgrounds.

However, even though it is possible that many benefits can be brought by the multi-level framework, there are limitations with this model. As the model aims at improving business outcomes as well as social outcomes through equal opportunity and social inclusion, it would take longer to achieve such outcomes, and the cost to government and organisations will also be higher. Some scholars argue that these social aspects do not help promote the proficiency of businesses, considering that there are particular institutions specifically intended to tackle those social factors. They also suggest that it is not necessary for organisations to operate beyond economic and legal responsibilities as supported by the liberal doctrine.

Summary and recommendations

The chapter has offered an overview of key theories of gender segregation in employment and their implications for gender equality. Marxist theory seems to treat the issues of female disadvantage as a by-product of the capitalistic class divide and treats gender equality as a result of the class conflict. Radical feminists trace female disadvantage within the patriarchal nature of social relations, which gives precedence to men over women in employment. Dual system theorists propose combining the Marxist and radical feminist theoretical propositions, in order to explain the dual role of capitalist systems and patriarchy in producing and sustaining gender segregation in the workforce. The dual system perspective has been criticised by post-structuralists, who argue that structural theories ignore the diverse experiences of women and men at work. The post-structuralist theorists identify the dominant discourses and systems of representation as the basis of gender segregation. Yet, because of its predominant focus on the diversity of experiences, the post-structuralist analysis ignores the real-life discriminations faced by a large proportion of the workforce. Neo-classical economists suggest that organisations base their recruitment decisions on the market value of each individual's human capital.

The chapter has also discussed the change ideologies related to the issues of gender equality within employment contexts. In particular, Jewson and Mason's (1986) notions of liberal and radical change ideologies and Cockburn's (1989) proposed concept of transformational approach have been discussed. These three ideologies constitute the framework within which organisations seem to operate and treat gender issues.

The chapter has also discussed the multi-level approach to achieving gender equality at the workplace. For working women to achieve their full potential, state and organisational policy makers need to recognise and address equal opportunity related issues facing women at multiple levels within and outside the workplace. When policies informed by multi-level insights are put in place to fight structural and social barriers, more women will be encouraged to pursue formal employment. States and organisations both need to play a role in achieving better equal opportunity outcomes in the workplace, also taking into account the internal heterogeneity of women based on their multiple forms of identity. Through increased awareness, cultural transformation and institutional monitoring at multiple levels, it will be possible to realise the lofty dream of equal opportunity in organisations.

Discussion questions

1. With the help of an organisational example/scenario, identify the different steps/levels you (as an HR consultant) would consider using in a multi-level approach to tackle the widespread issue of sexual harassment in an organisation in Egypt. Please provide a detailed yet critical analysis.
2. Review equality and diversity policies of four organisations – two each in a developed and a developing country. What are the key similarities and differences with regards to gender equality at work?
3. Is the Marxist approach to gender equality valid in the world today? Discuss.

CASE STUDY

Multi-level experiences of Pakistani women in the workplace

Considering the limitations of the equal opportunity approach, it can be argued that the approach ignores the significant societal- and individual-level factors that exist beyond the organisational level but at the same time impose imperative effects on organisational practices and the effectiveness of diversity management (Syed and Murray, 2009). As mentioned earlier in this chapter, the mainstream single level of diversity management with an emphasis on law and legislation fails to develop a comprehensive understanding of an array of factors influencing gender equality at the workplace. A multi-level framework as suggested by Syed and Özbilgin (2009) would be of paramount importance in filling this gap. This chapter will therefore explore Ali's (2013) paper as a case study for the discussion of a multi-level perspective on equal employment opportunity for women in organisations, and its presentation of the framework in Pakistan. Ali carried out

(Continued)

(Continued)

an empirical study with the aim of exploring multi-level experiences of Pakistani women in the workplace. Thirty highly qualified female employees working in banking, telecommunications and education were the interviewees.

First and foremost, there are three key components of the relational approach: the macro-national, meso-organisational and micro-individual levels of analyses. At the macro-national level, the relational framework considers the importance of structural and institutional conditions (e.g. law, religion, education, gender and race relations), as these factors can block or improve equality of opportunities. According to the narratives of the interviewees, Pakistani women have to deal with many socio-cultural challenges within organisations. Gender stereotypes are embedded in the culture of the workplace. Gender segregation reduces the occupational mobility and promotion of female workers. Socio-cultural issues such as modesty and inhibition seem to hugely affect the working lives of women (for example, Pakistani women tend to avoid complaining about or reporting sexual harassment issues at the workplace due to socio-cultural norms of inhibition). Sexual harassment becomes a common, implicit and subtle form of discrimination. Even though stress and discomfort are inflicted on the female victims, due to their embedded modesty, women are more likely to hide the incidents. Besides, it has been reported that women are not aware of their legal rights and any legal recourse available to rectify gender discrimination by their employers.

The meso-organisational level involves organisational norms, routinised behaviours and approaches to diversity. These develop the rules of the meso-level of gender and race relations and mediate job opportunities with a view to individual capabilities and contextual circumstances. As reported by the interviewees, the organisational policies on sexual harassment are weak and there is insufficient implementation or enforcement of those policies, and what makes matters even worse is the inadequate procedures for reporting the crimes. The glass ceiling is another challenge facing Pakistani women and their career prospects. With the family-oriented expectations of women, they are discouraged from participating in the senior levels of management. Therefore, many female employees acknowledge that there are many barriers preventing them from moving forward. Besides, Pakistani women face the highest income gap of South Asian countries (UNDP, 2009). It is commonplace to see that junior male employees are getting higher pay than senior female employees. Moreover, the interviewees raised some

(Continued)

(Continued)

structural issues, for instance, the significant importance of transport. Women would give up better employment opportunities and opt for lesser value jobs as long as the organisations provided pick-up and drop-off transportation facilities. Safety issues are of great concern to women. These findings suggest that social stereotypes have imperative implications at the workplace, and this will affect women's job experiences and the organisation's efficiency.

At the micro-individual level, individual issues such as family status, agency and identity are gendered. They have important influences on an individual's talents and opportunities. Intersectionality looks at the relationships between different forms of identity and, as suggested by the interviewees, there are some connections between their gender, marital status and the organisational practices. It was reported that single, unmarried women are more vulnerable to sexual harassment. Another important structural barrier facing married women is inadequate childcare support. Childcare centres are only available in big cities and the quality of those centres is not recognised or assured by the government. More importantly, these facilities are so expensive that low-income families are not able to afford them. Ultimately, some women have to leave their jobs due to these constraints and family responsibilities.

Having explained the employment conditions in Pakistan with the use of the multi-level framework, a more holistic understanding has been gained in order to formulate a better diversity management approach. For example, policies should be strengthened to tackle the socio-cultural factors, social identity and issues of sexual harassment, income inequality and the glass ceiling. To achieve a dynamic working environment, organisations should pay attention to helping women to balance both their job and family responsibilities. The government should provide better support in terms of childcare services and transport facilities.

Questions

1. What are some of the multi-level issues of gender equality facing women in Pakistani organisations?
2. How can such issues be addressed in the light of the relational framework?
3. How do you compare issues of gender equality at work in Pakistan with those in a Western country?
4. Critically discuss the multi-level approach to tackling gender-related issues in the workplace.

Further reading

Ali, F. 2013. A multi-level perspective on equal employment opportunity for women in Pakistan, *Equality, Diversity and Inclusion: An International Journal*, 32(3): 289–309.

Gimenez, M. and Vogel, L. 2005. Marxist-feminist thought today, *Science & Society*, 69(1): 5–10.

Özbilgin, M. 2000. Is the practice of equal opportunities management keeping pace with theory? Management of sex equality in the financial services sector in Britain and Turkey, *Human Resource Development International*, 3(1): 43–67.

References

Adler, N.J. and Izraeli, D.N. 1988. *Women in Management Worldwide*, Armonk, NY: M.E. Sharpe.

Al Ariss, A. and Özbilgin, M. 2010. Understanding self-initiated expatriates: career experiences of Lebanese self-initiated expatriates, *Thunderbird International Business Review*, 25(4): 275–85.

Ali, F. 2013. A multi-level perspective on equal employment opportunity for women in Pakistan, *Equality, Diversity and Inclusion: An International Journal*, 32(3): 289–309.

BBC News. 2012a. Gender Pay Gap at Risk of Worsening [Online]. Available from http://www.bbc.co.uk/news/business-20223264 [Accessed September 2014].

BBC News. 2012b. Larne Grammar teacher 'discriminated against' [Online]. Available from http://www.bbc.co.uk/news/uk-northern-ireland-17127871 [Accessed September 2014].

Beechey, V. 1978. Critical analysis of some sociological theories of women's work, in Kuhn, A. and Wolpe, A.M. (Eds), *Feminism and Materialism* , London: Routledge and Kegan Paul, pp. 155–97.

Beller, A.H. 1982. The impact of equal opportunity policy of sex differential on earnings and occupations, *American Economic Review*, 72: 171–5.

Blau, F.D. and Beller, A.H. 1988. Trends in earning differentials by gender, *Industrial and Labour Relations Review*, 41: 513–29.

Bovill, D. 2013. *Patterns of Pay: Results from the Annual Survey of Hours and Earnings, 1997 to 2012. Pay Differences between Men and Women*. Report. Office for National Statistics.

Bradley, H. 1989. *Men's Work, Women's Work: A Sociological History of the Division of Labour in Employment*, Oxford: Polity Press.

Braverman, H. 1974. *Labour and Monopoly Capital*, New York: Monthly Review Press.

Bruegel, I. 1979. Women as a reserve army of labour: a note on recent British experience, *Feminist Review*, 3: 12–23.

Buzzanell, P.M. 1995. Reframing the glass ceiling as a socially constructed process: implications for understanding and change, *Communication Monographs*, 62, 327–54.

Calas, M.B. and Smircich, L. 1993. Dangerous liaisons: the 'feminine-in-management' meets 'globalization', *Business Horizons*, 36: 71–83.

Chodorow, N.J. 1994. *Femininities, Masculinities, Sexualities: Freud and Beyond*, London: Free Association Books Ltd.

CIA. 2013. The World Fact Book: Pakistan. *Central Intelligence Agency of the USA*, [US government agency website]. Available from www.cia.gov/library/publications/the-world-factbook/geos/pk.html [Accessed April 2013].

Cockburn, C. 1989. Equal opportunities: the short and long agenda, *Industrial Relations Journal*, 20(3): 213–25.

Colgan, F. and Ledwith, S. 1996. Women as organisational change agents, in Ledwith, S. and Colgan, F. (Eds), *Women in Organisations: Challenging Gender Politics*, London: Macmillan Business.

Collinson, D.L. and Hearn, J. 1996. Breaking the silence: on men, masculinities and managements, in Collinson, D.L. and Hearn, J. (Eds), *Men as Managers, Managers as Men: Critical Perspectives on Men, Masculinity and Management*, London: Sage Publications, pp. 1–24.

Connell, R.W. 1987. *Gender and Power: Society, the Person and Sexual Politics*, Cambridge: Polity Press.

Daly, M. 1978. *Gyn/Ecology: The Metaethics of Radical Feminism*, Boston: Beacon.

de Beauvoir, S. 1989 [1949]. *The Second Sex*. New York: Vintage Books.

Dickens, L. 2007. The road is long: thirty years of equality legislation in Britain, *British Journal of Industrial Relations*, 45(3), 463–94.

Echols, A. and Willis, E. 1990. *Daring to Be Bad: Radical Feminism in America, 1967–1975*, Minneapolis: University of Minnesota Press.

Eisenstein, H. 1983. *Contemporary Feminist Thought*, Boston: G.K. Hall & Co.

England, P. 1984. Wage appreciation and deprecation: a test of neo-classical economic explanations of occupational sex segregation, *Social Forces*, 62: 726–49.

Ferdoos, A. 2005. Social Status of Urban and Non-Urban Working Women in Pakistan – A Comparative Study, unpublished Ph.D. dissertation, University of Osnabrueck, Germany.

Foster, J. 1990. Equality and the future, in Currie, E. et al. (Eds), *What Women Want*, London: Sidgwick and Jackson Ltd.

Foucault, M. 1979. *The History of Sexuality*, London: Allen Lane.

Gardiner, J. 1979. Women's domestic labour, in Eisenstein, Z.R. (Ed.), *Capitalist Patriarchy and the Case for Socialist Feminism*, London: Monthly Review Press.

Hakim, C. 1979. *Occupational Segregation: A Study of the Separation of Men and Women's Work in Britain, the United States and Other Countries*, Research Paper 9, London: Department of Employment.

Hartmann, H. 1979. Capitalism, patriarchy and job segregation by gender, in Eisenstein, Z.R. (Ed.), *Capitalist Patriarchy and the Case for Socialist Feminism*, London: Monthly Review Press.

Hassan, R. 2001. Challenging the stereotypes of fundamentalism: an Islamic feminist perspective, *Muslim World*, 91(1/2) 55–69.

Hearn, J. 1987. *The Gender of Oppression: Men, Masculinity and the Critique of Marxism*, Brighton: Wheatsheaf Books.

Heilman, M.E. 2001. Description and prescription: how gender stereotypes prevent women's ascent up the organizational ladder. *Journal of Social Issues*, 57(4): 657–74.

Hirsh, C.E. and Cha, Y. 2008. Understanding employment discrimination: a multilevel approach. *Sociology Compass*, 2(6), 1989–2007.

Jewson, N. and Mason, D. 1986. The theory and practice of equal opportunities policies: liberal and radical approaches, *Sociological Review*, 34(2): 307–34.

Kelly, E. and Dobbin, F. 1999. Civil Rights Law at Work: Sex Discrimination and the Rise of Maternity Leave Policies, *American Journal of Sociology*, 105, 455–92.

Kirton, G. and Greene, A-M. 2005. *The Dynamics of Managing Diversity: A Critical Approach* (2nd Edn). Oxford: Elsevier.

Labour Force Survey (LFS) Pakistan 2013. Pakistan Bureau of Statistics. www.pbs.gov.pk/content/labour-force-survey-2012-13-1st-quarter [Accessed March 2014].

Large, M. and Saunders, M.N.K. 1995. A decision-making model for analysing how the glass ceiling is maintained: unblocking equal opportunities, *The International Journal of Career Management*, 7(2): 21–8.

Leonard, J.F. 1986. The Effectiveness of Equal Employment Law and Affirmative Action Regulation, in R.G. Ehrenberg (Ed.), *Research in Labor Economies*, Vol. 8, Greenwich, CT: JAI Press, 319–350.

Lips, H. 1993. *Sex and Gender: An Introduction*, London: Mayfield Publishing Company.

Lockwood, D. 1986. Class, status and gender, in Crompton, R. and Mann, M. (Eds), *Gender and Stratification*, London: Polity Press.

Lonsdale, S. 1985. *Work and Inequality*, London: Longman.

Lowery, M. 1995. The war on equal opportunity, *Black Enterprise*, 25: 148–54.

Mernissi, F. 1996. *Women's Rebellion and Islamic Memory*, London: Zed Books Ltd.

Mincer, J. 1962. Labor force participation of married women: a study of labor supply, in National Bureau of Economics Research, *Aspects of Labor Economics*, Princeton, NJ: Princeton University Press.

Morrison, A.M., White, R.P., Van Velsor, E. and the Center for Creative Leadership. 1987. *Breaking the Glass Ceiling: Can Women Reach the Top of America's Largest Corporations?* Wokingham: Addison-Wesley.

O'Brien, M. 1982. Feminist theory and dialectic logic, in Keohane, N.O. (Ed), *Feminist Theory*, Brighton: Harvester Press.

Office for National Statistics (ONS) 2011. *Mothers in the Labour Market. More Mothers Working Now than Ever Before* [Online]. Available from: www.ons.gov.uk/ons/dcp171776_234036.pdf [Accessed April 2014].

Özbilgin, M. 2000. Is the practice of equal opportunities management keeping pace with theory? Management of sex equality in the financial services sector in Britain and Turkey, *Human Resource Development International*, 3(1): 43–67.

Özbilgin, M. and Woodward, D. 2003. *Banking and Gender: Sex Equality in the Financial Services Sector in Britain and Turkey*, London: IB Tauris & Company.

Polachek, S. 1976. Occupational segregation: an alternative hypothesis, *Journal of Contemporary Business*, Winter, 1–12.

Polachek, S. 1981. Occupation self-selection: a human capital approach to gender differences in occupational structure, *Review of Economics and Statistics*, February, 60–9.

Ramsay, K. & Parker, M. 1992. Gender, bureaucracy and organizational culture, in Savage, M. and Witz, A. (Eds), *Gender and Bureaucracy*. Oxford: Blackwell, pp. 253–76.

Schwartz, F.N. and Zimmerman, J. 1992. *Breaking with Tradition: Women and Work, the New Facts of Life*, New York: Warner Books.

Smith, D.J. 1982. Women in the local labour market: a case study with particular reference to the retail trades in Britain 1900–1930, in Day, G. with Coldwell, L., Jones, K, Robins, D. and Rose, G. (Eds), *Diversity and Decomposition in the Labour Market*, London: Gower.

Straw, J. 1989. *Equal Opportunities: The Way Ahead*, London: Institute of Personnel Management.

Syed, J. 2008. From transgression to submission: implications of moral values and societal norms on emotional labour, *Gender, Work and Organization*, 15(2): 182–201.

Syed, J. and Murray, P. 2009. Combating the English language deficit: the labor market experiences of migrant women in Australia, *Human Resource Management Journal*, 19(4): 413–32.

Syed, J. and Özbilgin, M. 2009. A relational framework for international transfer of diversity management practices, *International Journal of Human Resource Management*, 20(12): 2435–53.

Syed, J., Ali, F. and Winstanley, D. 2005. In pursuit of modesty: contextual emotional labour and the dilemma for working women in Islamic societies, *International Journal of Work, Organization and Emotion*, 1(2): 150–67.

Tan, E. 2014. Human capital theory: a holistic criticism, *Review of Educational Research*, doi: 10.3102/0034654314532696.

United Nations (UN) 2013. *Economic and Social Council: Gender Statistics* [Online]. Available at http://unstats.un.org/unsd/statcom/doc14/2014-18-GenderStats-E.pdf [Accessed January 2014].

Human Development Report (UNDP) 2009. Overcoming barriers: Human mobility and development [Online]. Available at http://hdr.undp.org/en/reports/global/hdr2009/ [Accessed March 2014].

Walby, S. 1986. *Patriarchy at Work: Patriarchal and Capitalist Relations in Employment*, London: Polity Press.

Walby, S. 1990. *Theorising Patriarchy*, Oxford: Blackwell Publishing.

Watson, S.D. 1994. Applying theory to practice: a prospective and prescriptive analysis of the implementation of the Americans with Disabilities Act, *Journal of Disability Policy Studies*, 5: 1–24.

Weyer, B. 2007. Twenty years later: explaining the persistence of the glass ceiling for women leaders. *Women in Management Review*, 22(6): 482–96.

Wilson, F.M. 1995. *Organizational Behaviour and Gender*, London: McGraw-Hill.

Witz, A. 1994. *Professions and Patriarchy*, London: Routledge.

World Bank. 2012. *World Development Indicators*, Washington, DC.

Wright, E.O. 1989. *The Debate on Classes*, London: Verso.

Young, I. 1981. Beyond the unhappy marriage: a critique of the dual systems theory, in Sargent, L. (Ed.), *Women and Revolution: The Unhappy Marriage of Marxism and Feminism*, London: Pluto.

Race and ethnicity in the workplace

Kurt April and Jawad Syed

5

Intended learning outcomes

After reading this chapter, you should be able to:

- Understand the notions of race and ethnicity and also their implications for diversity and inclusion management in organisations
- Understand why there is racial or ethnic discrimination, and how issues of racism and stereotypes affect equal opportunities at work
- Learn about issues of institutional racism, racialised organisations, intersectionality and migrant workers
- Understand how legislative, historical and demographic contexts in a specific country affect organisational approaches to race and ethnicity

Introduction

While race is generally believed to be a function of physical and biological variations, ethnicity may or may not be related to such variations (Rose, 2004). Racial categorisation, a social construct, refers to outside appearances, and is often associated with or identified by the colour of skin. Because of centuries of Western-dominated colonisation, modern economic power and industrialisation, racist ideologies of superiority exist and result in the differentiated treatment of people with varied racial origins (April & Shockley, 2007a; Torrington et al., 2008). Ethnicity, in contrast, pertains to cultural traits, such as language, religious belief and dress code. While there are certain differences between race and ethnicity, the two terms are at times conflated due to possible common heritage and expressions (Conley, 2003).

The use of 'race' as a category of evolution or a major division in the human species has no evidence in science. In fact, the very notion of genetically distinct sub-species is universally discredited (Müller-Wille & Rheineberger, 2008). Human beings inherit genes, not race, and all humans are 99.9 per cent identical in terms of their genes. There is thus no biological basis for racial differentiation and discrimination. However, it is a fact that external appearances, colour of skin in particular but also other traits including facial features, are often used to categorise and treat people differently on the basis of perceived racial identity.

According to Sue et al. (1992), race is related to the external appearance of an individual. Ethnicity, in contrast, denotes 'shared cultures, spirituality, values, language, beliefs and loci of control of a particular group of individuals' (Balcazar et al., 2010: 83). 'Racism', a blanket term generally used for discrimination on the grounds of race and ethnicity, can be defined as 'a belief that some races or ethnic groups are superior to others, used to devise and justify actions that create inequality between racial groups' (Mistry & Latoo, 2009: 20).

Racial and ethnic discrimination is closely related to ongoing stereotypes prevalent in a society. Stereotypes are defined as 'beliefs about the characteristics, behaviour and attributes of members of certain groups' (Hilton & von Hippel, 1996: 240). Societal stereotypical beliefs may also affect organisational life, and may even affect recruitment, promotion and other decisions in organisations (Jenkins, 1985). Adverse stereotypes may result in blatant or sophisticated discrimination in the workplace. Examples of adverse generalisations may be: 'Indian people have poor time management', 'Americans are domineering', 'Black Caribbeans are lazy', 'French people are obnoxious', 'Nigerians are aggressive', 'Singaporeans are uncreative', etc. These may influence employers or managers in making decisions that: (1) do not conform to the law or spirit of equal opportunity (Browaeys & Price, 2011), (2) prejudge individuals for recruitment, team assignment or career advancement (April & Shockley, 2007a), and (3) affect where to set up offices, plants and manufacturing sites.

Although stereotypes are generally negative, Kirton (2009) suggests that positive race stereotypes may also exist, such as some stereotypes which underpin that certain ethnic groups have a strong work ethic or quantitative capabilities. However, this type of stereotyping rarely results in preference for weaker economic minorities around the globe, although some exceptions exist.

Konrad et al. (2006) note that race affects individuals in the workplace in numerous ways. For example, this may result in disparities in rates of employment. This is evident within the UK with 13 per cent of ethnic minorities being unemployed compared with 8 per cent of the general population (DWP, 2012). A further way that race impacts on ethnic minority workers in the UK is through earnings. Research indicates that the pay gap between ethnic minority workers and white workers currently stands at £0.43p per hour in favour of the economically powerful whites (Re:locate, 2012). In South Africa, even though the number of ethnic majority people (African blacks are 79.2 per cent of the population) in employment has doubled since 1994, they remain an economic minority and therefore continue to be discriminated against. In 2005, the average monthly earnings for white people (whites are 8.9 per cent of the population) were more than five times more than the average monthly earnings for black people. In 2011, whites earned four times more. Additionally, while only 17 per cent of businesses are black-owned, 31 per cent of businesses listed on the Johannesburg Stock Exchange are foreign-owned (SAIRR, 2013). In Malaysia, the government introduced the Bumiputra policy in 1971 to raise the overall income levels of ethnic majority Malays, whose incomes were lower than those of ethnic minority Chinese. The race-based policy also provides a legal basis for giving preference to ethnic Malays in education and employment, among other fields. It is generally assumed that Chinese households earn, on average, 1.8 times what Bumiputra households earn (Malaysian Economic Planning Unit, 2014). The income gap has narrowed between the two ethnic groups over the years, but Chinese-Malaysians have suffered numerous consequences: they have only limited slots for university entrance, and they are rarely promoted to executive posts in government offices and state-affiliated companies (Yoshida, 2014). Even small businesses are affected, e.g. Malay-run food courts are administered by local municipalities and, in some cases, their monthly rents are held at 30 ringgit (about US$8.96). By contrast, ethnic-Chinese food courts are privately run and their rents stand at around 800 ringgit, roughly 25 times higher. Also, city-administered spaces openly favour Malay restaurant owners (Yoshida, 2014).

Around the globe, additional workplace factors such as measures of managerial competence, cognitive ability, learning agility, promotion and performance appraisal are also affected by racial and ethnic discrimination in organisations.

Racism and its types

Racism refers to the use of individual and institutional power to deny or grant people and groups of people rights, respect, representation and resources based on their skin colour (RDT, 2008). There are three main categories of racism: (1) systemic or structural racism (also known as institutional/organisational racism), (2) individual racism and (3) internalised oppression (Patychuk, 2011).

Structural racism refers to:

> a system in which public policies, institutional practices, cultural representations, and other norms work in ways which perpetuate racial group inequity. It identifies dimensions of

our history and culture that have allowed privileges associated with 'whiteness' and disadvantages associated with 'colour' to endure and adapt over time'. (Aspen Institute, 2009)

It occurs regardless of individual prejudices, beliefs or intentions and encompasses both individual and institutional forms of racism. According to Bhui and McKenzie (2007), public service choices or configurations, which result in disparities for black or economic/ethnic minority groups, are examples of institutional or structural racism. These include underfunding of translation services, and not recruiting community development workers, which affect access and outcomes. Other examples, cited in Patychuk (2011), include residential schools for Aboriginal children, immigration policies, racial profiling by police, employment, housing, banking, and media policies and practices, etc. Examples related to racialised groups who are immigrants include the location of the Canada Immigration offices across the globe systemically limiting access to people from Africa, selective (Patychuk, 2011: 22) immigration policies (requiring some visitors to apply for a visa before entering Canada), and selective detention of refugees from some countries/modes of travel. These are in addition to employment practices (requiring Canadian experience, English fluency), other employment (Oreopoulos, 2009), housing (Teixeria & Truelove, 2007; CERA, 2009) and discrimination in social assistance (Mirchandani & Chan, 2005) that newcomers and racialised groups disproportionately face. These are all distinguished from overt or individual forms of racism and discrimination that stem from conscious prejudice/racism and individual acts of discrimination (Henry & Tator, 2009; Tehera, 2010; Delgado & Stefancic, 2001; Barnes-Josiah, 2004).

Patychuk (2011) discusses how structural racism and white privilege create and perpetuate racialised health disparities. In reference to Canada, Handy (2010) claims that minorities within the Francophone group are left out when Francophone communities are treated as one single linguistic entity and where the needs of racial minorities are not effectively addressed – and this includes where communication, community engagement and governance structures operate without awareness of or attention to this diversity. Black Francophones experience triple marginalisation – as members of racialised groups, as a linguistic minority and as a racial minority within the Francophone language group (Patychuk, 2011: 15). Similar to studies of the marginalisation of racial minority Francophones in Quebec, Madibbo (2005, 2006) writes that in Ontario white Francophones, while struggling against their own oppression, have not fully integrated minority Francophones into planning, decision making and access to resources. Other communities such as Tamil, Spanish, Somali, Urdu and Punjabi speaking communities have large numbers of people who speak neither English nor French, live in precarious immigrant/refugee status, and also face multiple marginalisation, which is further multiplied by the lack of health service and health promotion that includes them. Gunderson and Cochrane (2012) write about the influence of language and race in South Africa in regard to the social determinants of public health.

Individual forms of racism are reflected in adverse stereotypes and discrimination that stem from conscious prejudice/racism and individual acts of discrimination (Henry & Tator, 2009; Barnes-Josiah, 2004). However, overt and visible forms of racism are the tip of the iceberg (Gee et al., 2009). Most racism is hidden – built into the fabric of law, ideology and institutions.

Internalisation (self-blaming) of recurring and systematic discrimination, and individual and community responses (coping, shame, guilt, anger/externalisation, community mobilisation, etc.) to the experience of discrimination are also important (Noh & Kaspar, 2003; Williams et al., 2003; April et al., 2012). This can mean being emotionally, physically, and spiritually battered to the point of believing that oppression is deserved, is one's lot in life, is natural and right, or that it does not even exist.

Psychological and sociological explanations

There are a number of psychological and sociological explanations for racial and ethnic discrimination. Psychological explanations suggest that stereotypes of ethnic minority groups lead to discrimination against them in the workplace. Additionally, the scapegoat theory portrays that some people, from majority or dominant racial groups, may displace their frustrations onto a 'scapegoat', which may happen to be a person or group of people from an ethnic minority or migrant background (Zawadzki, 1948). Another psychological explanation for race and ethnic discrimination is 'the authoritarian personality' (Adorno et al., 1950). An authoritarian personality is often correlated with prejudice and ethnocentrism. The authoritarian personality is inflexible and rigid, and people who hold this personality type have a low tolerance for diversity and uncertainty. They view members of minority ethnic groups as unconventional, degrade them and are likely to express authoritarianism through discrimination (Zastrow & Kirst-Ashman, 2010: 227).

There are also a number of sociological explanations of racial and ethnic discrimination. Ethnocentrism identifies how individuals judge another culture solely by the values and standards of their own culture (Sumner, 1940). We also notice a shift and erosion in the identities of individuals, which support their inclusion in groups of belonging, to identities which support institutional life (April & April, 2009). Up until recently, the dominant diversity discourse has been concerned mainly with socio-political and policy standpoints (Liff, 1996; Dandeker and Mason, 2001). However, an evolving workplace discourse is emerging, informed by a critical post-structuralist tradition which challenges the positive, empowering view of individuals with different capacities – in fact, it has focused our attention on how diversity operates in organisations (Zanoni & Janssens, 2004), economic efficiency (Litvin, 2002), the nature of professions (ibid.) and broader institutional settings (de los Reyes, 2000). These discourses, it would appear, serve mainly to control less-powerful employees, such as immigrant and foreign workers, and overlook the socio-material structure within which such discourse occurs (April & April, 2009).

Discrimination is also caused by group closure. This process involves groups maintaining boundaries and separating themselves from other groups. These boundaries are produced by means of exclusion devices, which amplify the division between one group and another, thereby enhancing discrimination on the grounds of race and ethnicity (Giddens, 2006: 496).

In the workplace this often involves settled zones of authority, constructed social spaces and legitimacy, credibility of histories and centres around which groups' hope(s) are being fostered through workplace interactions, leader behaviours and even organisational strategies. We also see evidence of this when religious leaders 'frequently lose their capacity to read the complex characteristics of human ecologies when they rigidly defend fixed articulations of their tradition' (Gunderson & Cochrane, 2012).

Prejudice, discrimination and exclusion

In general, prejudice is viewed as feeling (emotions), thinking (cognition) and holding negative attitudes (beliefs) about other individuals/groups, resulting in the manipulation of one's behaviour or interaction with others, and typically involves constructions of power and therefore dominant and subordinate individuals/groups. Ungerer and Ngokha (2006: 131) hold that prejudice and discrimination are closely related concepts, which have become 'nearly interchangeable in popular use'.

Exclusion, often a result of prejudice and discrimination, occurs when individuals and communities are denied the rights and opportunities that are available to others. Lopez-Rocha (2007: 12) links stereotypes and prejudice, while Loden and Rosener (1991) define stereotypes as rigid, distorted generalisations about all members of a particular group, and declare that these stereotypes are commonly used to reinforce an underlying prejudice about others. Hunsberger (1995: 114) uses the term 'prejudice' to denote 'a negative inter-group attitude, involving cognitive, affective, and behavioural components'. However, Reicher (2007: 831) holds the contrasting view that prejudice should be viewed as 'rooted in practices that are bound up with in-group identity and in-group power'. O'Bryan et al. (2004: 407) report that there is a common belief that 'children's and adolescents' prejudiced attitudes are simply reflections of their parents' attitudes'. However, O'Bryan, et al. (2004: 407–8) contrast this with the findings of some studies which indicate that 'prejudiced attitudes are moderately influenced by their parents' attitudes, while others have found no significant systematic relationship'.

Ultimately, these differences and the ensuing prejudice, discrimination and exclusion related to it, affect individuals psychologically – and ultimately affect their workplace motivation, their psychological presence in the workplace, their voice and willingness to speak up, their workplace relations, team collaborations and knowledge sharing, as well as their performance. Worryingly, we learn from Eisenberger et al. (2003) that such social pain is analogous, in its neurocognitive function, to physical pain – causing distress, dysfunctional electro-chemical releases in our body, and ultimately disease/impair functionality on the part of the individual.

Racialised organisation and institutional racism

'Racialised organisation' is a term used by scholars to refer to organisational structures and routines that mirror and perpetuate the racial inequalities and stereotypes in society. A racialised organisation has not only a discriminatory and/or harassing ambience for marginalised workers, it also often is characterised by disparate outcomes for different racial or ethnic groups. In such organisations, personal experiences and career trajectories of marginalised workers tend to mirror the ubiquity of racialised notions in society. For example, Alleyne (2004) refers to the personal cost of the racialised experience in her work on workplace stress. Her study reveals common patterns with respect to the psychological harm experienced by black professionals who are exposed to, and affected by, frequent race-related dilemmas and tensions in the workplace. Often such experiences are an outcome of racism which is hidden and refined, not visible and blatant. The hidden nature of racialised organisations contributes to creation of a culture of silence where black managers feel that they have little option but to remain mute about their racialised experiences (Bravette, 1996; cited in Jolliff, 2011).

Barker (2003: 220) defines institutional racism as 'policies, practices or procedures embedded in bureaucratic structures that systematically lead to unequal outcomes for people of colour'. This issue is widely researched and documented in the context of London Metropolitan Police in the UK. Institutional racism was evident within the Metropolitan Police following the racist murder of a young black male, Stephen Lawrence in London in 1993. Following the attack, police officers at the scene made no effort to provide Stephen with adequate first aid while he was lying on his chest, failed to manage the murder scene effectively and overlooked vital evidence. The police handling of this case was suspected to be a result of racism. After years of campaigning by Stephen's family, a high-level inquiry was announced by the government. Evidence was collected through police officers, witnesses and the family of the victim. The final report, released in 1999, summarised that the investigation into the murder of Stephen was flawed by a combination of professional incompetence and institutional racism (Dennis et al., 2000: 14). Following the findings, amendments were made to the Race Relations Act 1976. While the initial act outlawed direct and indirect discrimination in a number of areas, including employment, housing and provision of goods and services (Bourne, 2001: 10), the Macpherson inquiry ushered in amendments to this Act, referred to as the Race Relations Amendment Act (RRAA). This put all public bodies under the full force of the law and pushed them to actively promote racial equality (Bourne, 2001: 13). However, according to media reports, in 2012 there were 11 cases of alleged racism under investigation, involving 20 Metropolitan Police officers. This suggests that even with the introduction of the RRAA, institutional racism is still an ongoing issue and has not been fully eradicated (Lewis, 2012).

Research has shown that racism is not disappearing, but rather is being replaced by less overt forms (Deitch et al., 2003). Racism, in both its blatant and subtle forms, results in unequal employment outcomes for people of diverse racial backgrounds. For example, in the US, since the Bureau of Labor Statistics began monitoring unemployment data by race, the black unemployment rate has consistently been twice that of their white compatriots. In July 2013, the jobless rate among whites was 6.6 per cent; among blacks, 12.6 per cent (Desilver, 2013). In 1994 in South Africa, for every employed black person there were 4.9 unemployed (SAIRR, 2013). Today, there are 3.3. This is possible despite the rising unemployment rate, because total employment has increased and birth rates are dropping. White people are also better off in this regard; 1994 saw 2.2 jobless white people for every white person with a job, and now that is down to 1.4 (SAIRR, 2013).

Racial discrimination can also disadvantage certain minority groups in terms of their earning levels and progression opportunities. In 2012 in the US, the average weekly earnings of a black worker were US$606 compared with the national average of US$765 (Black Demographics, n.d.). Furthermore, in that same year, out of the 824,942 executive or senior level officials and managers, only 24,139 or 2.9 per cent were black (EEOC, 2012). By comparison, in South Africa, the white minority are still the wealthiest population group, with white-headed households earning an average annual income of R365,134, black-headed households R60,613, coloured/mixed race-headed households R112,172, and households headed by Indians or Asians R251,541 (SAIRR, 2013).

Intersectionality and ethnic minority women

A further issue that may affect the diversity of race and ethnicity within the workplace can be identified as intersectionality. Intersectionality relates to how two or more dimensions of diversity, such as gender and race, may result in multiple and intersecting layers of discrimination or disadvantage. An intersectional approach to diversity seeks to identify and understand the connections between numerous dimensions of social difference (Kirton & Greene, 2011: 75; Syed & Pio, 2010; Syed, 2007). Degele (2011) notes that intersectionality denominates reciprocities between race, class and gender; however, it also allows for the integration of other dimensions of diversity, such as nationality, sexuality or age.

The term 'intersectionality' comes from a critical legal theorist's (Kimberlé Williams Crenshaw) explanation in 1989 of how attempting to understand the causes of 'race' and gender oppression of black women is like attempting to piece together the causes of an injury that occurs in an intersection with traffic flowing in many directions (Carastathis, 2008). 'Intersectionality' means taking into consideration all the factors that structure identities and experiences of oppression (gender, race and ethnicity, religion, class and social status, sexuality, physical abilities, age, residency/nation/immigrant status, etc.).

Women, and in particular ethnic minority women, are frequently affected by multiple layers of discrimination in society and the workplace. Holvino (2001) describes how race, gender and class are shown to be simultaneous processes of identity, institutional and social practices; and the impact that this re-conceptualisation can have in supporting change efforts in organisations towards organisational health and justice. April and Shockley (2007b), as well as April and Soomar (2013), describe how black women in South Africa suffer multiple levels of discrimination – more so than white women – as a result of 'being a woman' as well as 'being black', and sometimes additional dimensions may add further levels of discriminatory complexity, e.g. if the black woman is also disabled, or seeks a career in an urban environment but grew up in a rural environment, or even when educated at tertiary institutions which do not form part of the 'ivy-league' group in South Africa. While diversity and equality policies in many countries and organisations focus on gender, more often than not beneficiaries of such initiatives are white women with little to no attention to unique issues and challenges facing other women, who continue to experience higher than average unemployment rates and slower than average career growth.

According to a recent high-level report (AAPG, 2012), minority ethnic women in the UK face discrimination at every stage of the recruitment process. The report revealed that unemployment rates of black, Pakistani and Bangladeshi heritage women have remained consistently higher than those of white women since the early 1980s. Pakistani and Bangladeshi women were the hardest hit with 20.5 per cent being unemployed, followed by 17.7 per cent of black women compared to just 6.8 per cent of white women being unemployed. The report uncovered the complex ways in which racial discrimination is played out, such as discrimination against names and accents, making it much harder for minority ethnic women to get responses to applications. Discrimination was still encountered during interviews, at recruitment agencies and in the workplace itself. The report concluded that 25 per cent of the unemployment rate for black and Asian men and women was because of 'prejudice'.

An example of how intersectionality affects diversity management is the legal case of Michalak v. Mid Yorkshire NHS Trust in the UK. The case involved the claimant Dr Eva Michalak, a Polish female doctor, being awarded almost £4.5 million in compensation after a tribunal uncovered she had been a victim of unfair dismissal in addition to discrimination against her two intersecting identities, sex and race (Judiciary, 2011: 1; Javaid, 2012). The employment tribunal upheld Michalak's sex and race discrimination claims, after it uncovered that she had been subjected to a discriminatory plan of action to end her employment with Mid Yorkshire NHS Trust. Evidence was presented of unjustified complaints about the doctor, continual references to her Polish origin and frequent questioning of her capability to carry out her job successfully due to her training being completed in Poland. She was also placed on unauthorised suspension and was subjected to a bogus disciplinary procedure resulting in her being dismissed for no justifiable reason. The tribunal heard that Mid Yorkshire Hospital NHS Trust had breached three different laws, these being: the

Employment Rights Act 1996, the Sex Discrimination Act 1975 and the Race Relations Act 1976 (Javaid, 2012; Judiciary, 2011: 8; Phillips & Scott, 2012: 113).

Race, ethnicity and diversity management

'Racial consciousness' is a step towards anti-racism. It should not be equated with racism. Being blind to racism is a type of racism. Some examples of this include: (1) passive toleration (failure to see evidence of racism, not looking for it, not monitoring it); (2) disregard (not making racial justice a priority, not doing anything about problems because they are seen as small/isolated incidents, not developing the necessary expertise to eliminate systemic racism); and (3) collusive toleration (operating norms encourage practices based on racialised standards) (CSROCJS, 1995: 54–5).

Although research and anecdotal evidence suggest that managing diversity efficiently could reduce racism and increase organisational success, certain critical race scholars suggest that racism is a normal part of society and cannot be completely eradicated by the law nor through organisational policies (Patrick & Kumar, 2012: 15; Delgado & Stefancic, 2001: 8).

However, the role of diversity management in alleviating racial and ethnic discrimination at work cannot be ignored. Studies have shown that there is a positive correlation between successful diversity management and increased organisational performance (Özbilgin & Tatli, 2008). This is also reflected in the research of Cox & Blake (1991) who uncovered that heterogeneous teams are more creative than homogeneous teams.

As an example of best practice, DiversityInc (2012) identified PricewaterhouseCoopers (PwC) as the world's leading company for diversity management. PwC has been described as an organisation that seeks to create innovative diversity-management strategies to find, engage and promote the best employees, with great emphasis placed on those from under-represented groups, as the company believes high levels of success are not attainable with a homogenous group. The company provides its employees with the opportunity to undergo cultural awareness training in order to successfully manage workplace diversity. PwC focus on increasing the proportion of individuals from ethnic backgrounds in senior grades within the organisation to better reflect the communities in which they live and operate (Churchman, 2011; DiversityInc, 2012).

In 2014, Novartis Pharmaceuticals Corporation (NPC) topped the same list (DiversityInc, 2014), which was a significant turnaround for a company which had settled a gender discrimination class action suit against it in 2010. The diversity and inclusion (D&I) department, and executive council, implemented a strategic planning process that included an organisational assessment and analysis of both the internal and external landscape. The executive leadership apparently insists on better metrics to assess demographic progress and accountability measures to ensure an inclusive workplace. Additionally, the annual performance-management goals include a 20 per cent weighting towards people-related objectives, which have specific diversity objectives. The company also introduced a centralised process to attract, monitor and verify veteran, disability and lesbian, gay, bisexual and transgender (LGBT) talent. In addition, the company aims to work on building its diversity-training curriculum to meet the needs of a flexible workplace, and has 15 employee resource groups (ERGs), including groups for working parents, caretakers and a group called Cancer Hope (DiversityInc, 2014).

Looking deeper: discrimination and discriminatory tendencies

'Stereotyping, prejudice, and discrimination reflect, respectively, people's cognitive, affective, and behavioural reactions to people from other groups' (Fiske, 1998, quoted in Fiske, 2002: 123). With reference to the prediction of discriminatory behaviour arising from prejudiced attitudes, scholars (Monteith et al., 1996; Tougas et al., 1995) note that the current broad social norm makes it socially unacceptable to espouse blatantly prejudiced attitudes or beliefs. 'However, despite this broad social norm, prejudice and discrimination have not been eliminated from society' (Masser & Moffat, 2006: 122).

Discriminatory tendencies can be considered under the following sub-constructs.

Stereotyping

'Young children are often perceived as being untainted by the negative social biases that characterize adults, but many studies reveal that stereotyping and prejudice exist by the age of 4' (Bigler & Liben, 2007: 162). While Bigler and Liben (2007: 166) argue that in the everyday world it is difficult to study what causes stereotypes due partly to the pervasiveness of messages about social groups, they do maintain that 'once categorization along some particular dimension occurs, stereotyping and prejudice are likely to follow'. Lipton et al. (1991: 129) examine occupational stereotypes and quote Shinar's (1975) definition of an occupational stereotype as 'a preconceived attitude about a particular occupation, about people who are employed in that occupation, or about one's own suitability for that occupation'. Lipton et al. (1991) highlight gender and culture as factors at play in the holding of occupational stereotypes. With regards to the negative impact of occupational stereotypes for both employers and employees, Lipton et al. (1991: 133) posit that 'potential job applicants may be inhibited from seeking particular jobs because of occupational stereotypes', and that 'employers may cut off segments of the population who would otherwise be viable employees because of how they advertise or describe jobs'.

Generalised inference and pre-judgement

'The generalization of information for decision-making is a major concern in social psychology' (Martin & Sell, 1985: 178). Martin and Sell refer to how characteristics such as race, sex and age factor into the contact between individuals. They argue that in the absence of any other basis of discrimination, characteristics that differentiate the individuals will be used, even if there is evidence of equating characteristics. 'On a daily basis, people make formal and informal judgements about their own personality traits and the traits of others that have various impacts on them' (Farah & Atoum, 2002: 150). Farah and Atoum warn of the potential for error when making such judgements, as these are made using limited information and also have the potential to be subject to bias and interpretation.

Negative labelling

'Labels play an important role in defining groups and individuals who belong to the groups' (Smith, 1992: 496). In examining the relationship between labelling and stigmatisation with specific reference to dyslexia, Riddick (2000: 653) cites Gallagher's (1974) description that one of the negative outcomes of labelling is 'a way of maintaining the status quo by keeping minority groups at the bottom of the social hierarchy'. With regards to some of the beliefs associated with labelling, Riddick (2000: 654) refers to arguments that 'labelling can lead to stigmatisation, and give the child and adults involved negative expectations'. Smith (1992: 512) reports on the changing of racial labels with specific reference to the name for blacks changing from 'coloured' to 'negro' to 'black' to 'African-American' and, observes that 'as long as blacks remain discriminated against and oppressed, any name eventually becomes tainted by the racial prejudice'. 'As long as a group is ostracised or otherwise demeaned, whatever name is used to designate that group will eventually take on the demeaning flavour and have to be replaced' (Raspberry, 1989, quoted in Smith, 1992: 512).

Intolerance of difference

'Intolerance may take the means of negative verbal opinions and/or the anticipation of prejudice and discrimination from members of the out-group (implied intolerance)' (Bannan, 1965: 22). Hightower (1997: 370) refers to the work of Gough and Bradley (1993) who argue that 'intolerance is an integral part of the way individuals express their feelings of incompleteness and inefficacy'. Gough and Bradley (1993) indicate that poor interpersonal skills and poor internal controls are some of the characteristics of intolerant individuals. April et al. (2013) assert that such intolerance often emanates from low levels of maturity within the perpetrating individuals.

Differential treatment

Stodolska (2006: 3) cites Driedger and Mezoff's (1981) classification of differential treatment as one of the four classes of discrimination, with the other classes being prejudicial treatment, denial of desire and disadvantaging treatment. Stodolska (2005: 2) presents evidence of differential treatment in the leisure industry and refers to the claim by (Philipp, 1999) that 'both whites and minority members are aware of tacit rules that determine where minorities "belong" and where they are not accepted'. 'White ethnic groups experience less discrimination in leisure settings than do easily recognizable racial minorities' (Stodolska & Jackson, 1998, quoted in Stodolska, 2005: 2). Gatewood and Field (2001) suggest that disparate treatment is said to occur when different standards are used for different groups. 'When individuals were given a business justification for racial discrimination their implicit racist attitudes were positively related to their discriminatory behaviour' (Ziegert & Hanges, 2005: 561). To endorse the view 'that individuals apply differential standards when evaluating applicants', Kraiger and Ford (1985) report that both black and white raters give higher ratings to members of their own race.

Racist feelings

'Whatever one's role in the race relations scenario, feelings naturally accompany that position – whether confusion, grief, guilt, indignation, relief, or simple annoyance' (Mulvey & Richards, 2007: 225). Mulvey and Richards (2007: 225) report on using group conversation and dialogue to facilitate race relations and, point out that:

> in contrast to the conventional antiracism model which tends to favour expressions of emotion primarily from participants of colour (and to silence expressions that border on 'offensive'), our experience tells us that it is critical that we accept and explore the thorny feelings of all participants.

Mulvey and Richards (2007: 225) state that the facilitation process they describe involves exploring feelings that are expressed or suggested, because 'facing the messiness of personal sentiments is the natural territory of a race dialogue – no matter who is doing the expressing'.

Racist remarks or jokes

'Most humour is verbal in nature and relies upon double meanings, ambiguities, degrees of insult, superiority, and one's level of empathy with the aggressor and victim to create amusement' (Gallois & Callan, 1985: 63). Percival (2005: 93) notes that we sometimes declare jokes to be not funny because we identify the message as being offensive. Guerin (2003: 35) associates the telling of racist jokes with an individual's image by revealing that 'while some people will try the strategy of presenting an image of not being prejudiced at all under these circumstances, and not make any racist jokes, others can gain status by risking the use of prohibited conversational material'.

Xenophobia and ethnocentrism

Xenophobia usually refers to fear and hatred of anyone or anything that is foreign or strange. Ethnocentrism refers to evaluation of other cultures according to one's own cultural perceptions and standards. Karakatsanis and Swarts (2007: 117) report on xenophobic attitudes displayed by the Greeks towards the Albanians and state that 'the presence of large numbers of foreigners in Greece, as elsewhere in Europe, has been met by many with apprehension and fear'. To illustrate their argument, Karakatsanis and Swarts (2007: 113; 117) cite actual xenophobic remarks made by a Greek Ministry of Public Order spokeswoman and an Archbishop: 'We did not sell any tickets to Albanians, only to Greeks'; 'For God's sake, are we going to turn Greece into Albania'. Karakatsanis and Swarts (2007: 122) argue that the attitudes towards migrants stem from views that 'migrants pose a significant threat to the security, cultural integrity, and overall well-being of their country'. April and Blass (2010: 187), while describing the changing European Union (EU), state that:

> the question of who is central and 'matters' in this newly defined dual labour market and who is 'marginal' raises issues around power, meaning, dignity, status, perceived and practiced justice, equity and democracy, living standards and virtues, and the value of all life in an allegedly free society.

'The wars, conflicts, violence, hostilities and animosities around the world today are to a large extent rooted in positions of strong universalism, which often seeks to erase cultural differences' (Khondker, 2006: 442). Khondker (2006) argues that one should not strive to eradicate the differences between the various cultures but rather to make peace with these differences. Lopez-Rocha (2007: 12) expresses similar views on how the differences between cultures give rise to conflicts and suggests that 'cultural conflicts arise from the lack of understanding or the insufficient knowledge of the differences that exist between cultural groups'. Lopez-Rocha (2007: 12) points out that holding the belief that one's culture is right and appropriate over other cultures reinforces stereotypes and prejudices about others: 'When prejudices are combined with institutional power they force others to a lower position, which often leads to discrimination'.

Blatant racist behaviour

'Direct cognitive discrimination occurs when a subject's beliefs are formed in a way that is biased towards certain people' (Lippert-Rasmussen, 2006: 171). In distinguishing between subtle and blatant biases, Fiske (2002) refers to subtle biases as being unconscious, and blatant biases as being more conscious.

Hightower (1997: 369) distinguishes between blatant and subtle racists and claims that 'blatant racists aggressively assert that members of [other] groups are inferior', while 'subtle racists blame social inequities on [other] group cultures and customs'. Fiske (2002: 127) also distinguishes between subtle and blatant bias, and observes that 'because of hot, direct, unambiguous prejudices, extremists advocate segregation, containment and even elimination of out-groups'. In examining the psychosocial characteristics of subtle and blatant racists as compared to tolerant individuals, Hightower (1997: 373) concludes that 'tolerant individuals are psychologically healthier than prejudiced individuals'.

Subtle discrimination

'In recent years, racist attitudes have evolved from being blatant and hostile in nature to being more subtle and ambivalent' (Brief et al., 2000, quoted in Ziegert & Hanges, 2005: 553). Meertens and Pettigrew (1997: 54) draw the distinction between blatant and subtle prejudice and explain that, while blatant prejudice is 'hot, close and direct', subtle prejudice is 'cool, distant and indirect'. Meertens and Pettigrew argue that subtle discrimination is often difficult to identify because of its covertness, and refer to it as the covert expression of socially acceptable minority views.

Country context: history of Apartheid in South Africa

South Africa was colonised by the English and Dutch in the seventeenth and nineteenth centuries. During this period, the seeds of discrimination against indigenous and migrant/imported people of colour were sown and entrenched. Following independence from the UK, an Afrikaner minority party, the National Party, came to power in 1948 and enacted a series of race segregationist laws favouring whites (the minority), known as Apartheid ('apartness'). These laws allowed for the formal, systematic discrimination against people of colour (the majority), and attempted to enforce general white supremacy by classifying all South African inhabitants into racial groups (white, black, coloured and Indian). All young white males were conscripted into mandatory military service (following school), ensuring that the white minority could defend themselves in case of an uprising. Political participation by people of colour was outlawed, black citizenship revoked, and the entire public sphere, including education, employment, housing, medical care and common areas such as public transportation, restaurants and beaches, was segregated. All blacks were required to carry 'passbooks' – a system that was initially put in place by the British, and served them well to control migrant miners during their rule. Failure to produce a passbook, during Apartheid, often resulted in arrest. In 1953, the government declared increased penalties for protesting against the Apartheid laws. Starting in the 1960s, a plan of

'Grand Apartheid' was executed, emphasising territorial separation ('independent homelands', most of which were infertile land in which black people were settled) and brutal police and military repression. Thousands of individuals died in custody, frequently after gruesome torture, or simply 'mysteriously disappeared' after being picked up or sought out at night during police/military raids. Those who were tried were sentenced to death, banished or imprisoned for life.

Apartheid was officially ended in 1990, with the unbanning of a number of 'underground struggle/revolutionary organisations', after widespread unrest within the country and a long international embargo against South Africa. The factual end to Apartheid, however, is widely regarded as 1994 when a multi-racial election was held, transitioning power from the Apartheid government to a tripartite alliance, comprising the African National Congress (ANC), the South African Communist Party (SACP) and the Congress of South African Trade Unions (COSATU) – with Nelson Mandela being the first democratically elected President of the country.

In the post-Apartheid era, mainly to guard against white wealth and skills flight from the country, the protection of minority rights, including those of whites and other non-black communities, became fundamental to the new 1996 Constitution of South Africa. The 1998 Employment Equity legislation allowed for positive action to encourage black (African black, Indian and coloured, and in 2008 the Chinese population who arrived before 1994 and were considered coloured during Apartheid) and white women (also considered oppressed under white male patriarchal rule) South Africans' employment preference to address the gaps and the disadvantages they have been historically facing. Gazetted in 2007, Black Economic Empowerment (BEE) Codes of Good Practice were instituted by the government to redress the ongoing economic disadvantage of the listed groups, and considered ownership, employment, training and skills development, socio-economic development, preferential procurement, and social responsibility initiatives.

South African context: social pain of prejudice, discrimination and exclusion

As the South African workplace has become increasingly diverse and democratic, there has been a tension between the promise and the reality of inclusion and diversity acceptance in the workplace – with the government being most aggressive in the public sector arena with respect to corrective measures and the democratisation of the workplace. However, there exists strong motivation to move away from a pessimistic view of diversity: in which quotas are viewed as devaluing all ethnic/racial groups, parts of the population assume reverse discrimination, social divisions are further embedded and economic inequality is enhanced, all resulting in superficial equity measures being blamed for creating negative performance outcomes in the workplace, specifically, and socially, in general. Much of the legislation and workplace practices do not address the psychological, physical and physiological effects of long-term and current-day discrimination.

Therefore, we next present brief findings from research involving responses of 257 individuals, working in junior- and middle-management roles across South Africa, who were asked to reflect (as self-reports) on experiences in which some aspect of their diversity/difference was not valued in the workplace. After analysis of the qualitative data and using software coding techniques, the following core themes were highlighted.

Alienation

Alienation can be considered from either a physical or psychological perspective, or both. Segregation, ostracism, exclusion and not being taken seriously reflect the physical elements of alienation, whilst withdrawal, disregard, lack of support and disrespect represent the psychological elements. Comments such as this one from a participant, 'Our relationship reached a turning point, which I was not particularly conscious of. From then on I somehow started to withdraw from my friends', highlight the unconscious processes at work that may result in alienation and distancing.

Avoiding tension: code of silence

This theme is related to the experience of stress and anxiety at work, how it may be caused by or result in racial discrimination at work and how one copes with such experiences. The sub-topics focus primarily on 'the how', i.e. the coping mechanisms and behaviours displayed in response to stressful situations. Examples of these are not doing anything, pretending, avoidance and remaining silent, which were prompted by comments, such as the following, cited by the participants: 'I honestly could not handle it. I could not say anything, do anything, or even think anything at the time'; 'I handled the situation by ignoring it completely. It did not change anything much for me'. A deeper understanding of why participants would choose to behave in this manner, i.e. the underlying belief systems and cognitive processes at play, is important to understanding the code of silence at work. The propensity to avoid tension may also be related to low self-esteem (Baumgardner et al., 1989, quoted in Hussain & Langer, 2003). The statement, 'Being a person of colour, and coming from a diverse background, there was no way that I could intervene or communicate my feelings', highlights the need to delve into the deep-seated concerns at the core of this response.

Conflicting thoughts

This theme relates to the role of cognitive dissonance in cognitive development, and the impact of being a victim, or target, of prejudice and discriminatory behaviour. The following comment from a participant highlights the importance of a deeper discussion of cognitive dissonance:

> In private we seethed. I burned, I agonized, I hated myself, and I separated myself from my white friends and my girlfriend at the time. Outside work, I retaliated wildly and physically to any racial taunts, almost getting my friends and I arrested ... although sending those racists to hospital, or home bleeding. At work, I quietly went about my work, my anger billowing within me like angry volcanic lava.

Also it is important to take into account the role of ambiguity in relation to individuals' experiences, in particular being subjected to prejudice and discrimination. This feedback from a participant makes reference to a 'missing link', something that deserves more research in the area of ambiguity: 'It was weird. I had the feeling there was something very wrong, but I could not object to the girl because at the same time many of her reasons somehow made sense. There was a missing link'. In addition, a review of the prevalence of conflicting thoughts in relation, perhaps, to an individual's level of self-esteem and self-efficacy may be useful in linking this to the effects of prejudice and discrimination. A participant makes reference to issues of this nature with the observation: 'I didn't feel secure enough to do much. I must frankly admit it that I didn't have the courage to stand up and try to rationalize with the "insulters"'.

Negative self-image

This theme pertains to the impact of stigma, and other such experiences, on an individual's self-belief. The literature shows how constructs such as internalisation, victimisation and self-doubt contribute to a devalued and negative self-image. An indication of the conditions or factors that lead to a greater tendency for individuals to internalise their experiences will add substance to the discussion, as would an indication of why individuals choose to accept or resonate with a negative stereotype, rather than the positive. Comments such as: 'Firstly I need to work on this negative self-image I have built up based on colour', or 'I reacted in a way that was new to me as well ... I became very uncertain, uncertain about my professional skills, social skills, I lost appetite in a lot of things', highlight the call for literature to delve, not only into the 'what' and 'why', but also into 'the road ahead' and 'how' to rescue one's self-image. From the perspective of self-doubt, the following response justifies the reasoning behind one's self-doubt:

> It is hard to confront situations like these, because it's not easy to pin-point what is happening, it's like the situation is happening in our minds, we know it but we are not prepared to discuss them. Anybody knows when they are being discriminated against, but to prove it is very hard to do and we end up not talking about the situation at all.

Therefore, it is important to take into account the difficulties associated with confronting situations of discrimination, adverse implications for self-image and how these may be remedied.

Discriminatory tendencies

Research in this area presents a range of perspectives, from the view that discriminatory tendencies are cognitive or the view that they are behavioural; that we are born knowing about stereotypes or that we are influenced by our environments and thereby learn about stereotypes. There is further distinction made between blatant and subtle racism, between overt and covert sexism, and between conscious and unconscious behaviour. Highlighting both the blatant and subtle nature of discrimination is this comment: 'What surprised me about it is that these obvious inequalities can happen in bright daylight, and that I had not been acutely aware of it'. Another participant responded: 'Discriminatory behaviour by the three guys was not obvious, but rather subliminal'. Some researchers attribute discriminatory behaviour to a lack of understanding and to intolerance, but one is left asking 'what else' is at the root of discriminatory tendencies? What does this mean for the future of diversity and inclusion, considering the statement by a participant that 'What is worth noting here is that if there is no tolerance when it comes to differing viewpoints, this can lead to a situation where society is homogenous'? The views presented throw light on the pervasiveness of discriminatory behaviour and experiences in society. There is almost a sense of needing to be forthright and do what needs to be done, having the difficult conversations that are necessary, and facing the messiness, as described by Mulvey and Richards (2007).

Empowerment

Empowerment may be described as having power and control over resources and decision making within and outside organisations. This is related to benefits related to empowerment, primarily the notion of feeling in control, and successful outcomes. For example, a participant remarked: 'I will not tolerate disrespect and racism. We often turn a blind eye to any form of disrespect. As long as it does not touch us, we are fine about it. This is unacceptable behaviour and should not be tolerated'. Likewise, in relation to proactive behaviours, feedback on the factors, such as trust, that play a role in making an environment conducive to proactive behaviour, would be useful in deepening one's understanding of empowerment. Also it is important to consider the key factors that play the determining role in individuals' attempts to solve problems, presumably elements such as one's self-assuredness and the nature of the problem, i.e. how critical it is. This comment from a participant gives an indication as to why they chose not to solve the problem: 'I did not intervene with the situation myself as I could not see an easy solution at first glance'.

Formal and informal support structures

This theme is related to coping in the context of a support mechanism. As coping can be viewed from a cognitive and behavioural perspective, a deeper discussion of support structures would require that this be carried out with reference to both cognitive and behavioural aspects. Researchers cite powerlessness as a reason for why individuals do not lodge complaints via formal structures. To take this further one could consider what other reasons exist for not lodging complaints and what the enablers are that drive individuals to use these formalised support structures. Take for example the response: 'As I am writing this I am wondering whether reporting such behaviour, which can be considered to be discriminatory … although initially not meant to be … to higher management would be an effective solution'. With regards to formal training, and diversity training in particular, it may be useful to examine the conditions under which these programmes are successful. The view expressed by a participant is that: 'The workplace has to train employees in new social behaviours to interact with the diverse group of workers'. The arguments reflect common experiences, issues and attitudes with regards to successful implementation.

Group consciousness

This term is related to social identity theory and the need to belong. The discussion also included feedback on the benefits of groups in the context of teamwork and team spirit. Taking into account the response, 'I think, it was just "uncool" to intervene and much easier to stick with the group than exposing oneself and go with the weaker, different person', or the comment, 'A group can be very powerful, so that others keep quiet and "die" in this group', consideration must be given to interpersonal relationships and how these affect or are affected by group dynamics. Views on in-group and out-group formation, and the drivers for determining an 'in' versus an 'out' group, would also enrich our understanding. The comment:

> What surprises me when I think of these kind of incidences is that it is all about setting yourself apart from the group, or the prevailing mentality. On all levels this is extremely powerful and even as I consider myself to be someone who is not scared to be different, how often the need to belong determines my behaviour.

prompts questions such as: Do individuals aspire to belong to groups with no further thought to whether the group is an 'in' or 'out' group, or does everyone want to belong to an 'in' group? Is there a fundamental human need to belong that is more powerful than other negative feelings we experience?

Negative organisational consequences

This themes highlights negative organisational consequences, such as loss of control, assigning blame, scapegoating and humiliation, which arise primarily due to diversity not being successfully accommodated in organisations, while some of these arise from other key factors not taken into consideration. The following responses from participants highlight their varying experiences, thoughts and feelings: 'From these experiences I could probably become hostile, and could change my attitude in general in a very wrong direction. This is always possible when people are pushed for some reason outside the circle'; 'This made me feel misunderstood and made me feel as if I am in a working environment I do not wish to be in'; 'Ultimately, I began resenting my group, and lost all interest in my work. Going into the office became something I hated, and I eventually resigned'.

Negative psychological and behavioural consequences

This theme is related to notions of impacted confidence, feeling like a failure, impacted sense of self and vulnerability as some examples of negative psychological and behavioural consequences. It is equally important to note the causes of these consequences and what specifically prompts these reactions in individuals. Comments such as: 'Most of these times we fail ourselves and most importantly we fail those who the comments are made against', 'It made me less confident and made me wonder why I had put in so much effort', and 'A reaction to the situation was out of character, as I would normally have said what needed to be said, even though I was angry. In hindsight I think I was more stunned about the perceptions that people had of me and this took me aback', leads one to ask if there is a 'lack of voice' in the experiences of the participants that causes them to react in this way. With regards to the issue, damage inflicted on impressionable children/young adults is long-lasting, and consideration should be given to the circumstances under which children/young adults are able to successfully overcome traumatic childhood/formative experiences, versus others who are not. This response reveals the importance of providing children/young adults with a positive, supportive environment, as well as inculcating positive, resilient responses from them: 'This situation highlighted how impressionable our children are and how much damage we can cause with inappropriate statements'.

Positive organisational consequences

Transformation is one of the positive organisational consequences highlighted in this study. While scholars such as Billet and Somerville (2004) describe workplace transformation as a result of individuals' transforming practices, due consideration should also be given to individual transformation with regards to beliefs, unlearning, emotional choices and cognitive processes. This is supported by the following comments from participants:

> Depending on what is the case, a public or personal conversation may help to give a clear signal about what is considered (in)appropriate and thus create a more constructive work environment.

> Dealing with diversity, which includes people with physical impairments, can evoke the best in us, heroic feelings and responses, humanity, compassion, respect, gratitude and humility. However, this is only possible when we are able to rise above our [often very primitive] fears, disgust, desire to rescue and discomfort with living with ambiguity.

The value and richness of diversity, as a positive organisational consequence, was also discussed in the context of its benefits. It is important to consider successful strategies for appreciating and realising the value of diversity and the richness which full inclusion illuminates. Comments from the participants reflect their learning in this area:

> I have learned that diversity is not only positive, but also important in many regards.

> My intention and my learning is that I have to [purposefully] create a space where contribution is valued.

> A truly diverse environment appreciates difference, values the difference, recognises the variety of perceptions involved and addresses fears and concerns, from whatever quarter. True diversity should not stifle comment or dissent, and it is a necessity to appreciate [and respect] the dignity of people as well as their values and norms.

Positive psychological and behavioural choices

Responses such as these pertain to psychological and behavioural choices in the workplace:

> Further, in view of my current intention to establish my own company, and having experienced such incidences, I will strive to create an environment in which diversity is understood and respected.

> I will welcome and leverage diversity better by making every employee feel comfortable and accepted and not feel alienated. I will also make all employees aware and sensitive to diversity by uncovering innate and hidden biases in officers and assist them to overcome [such biases].

This comment from a participant indicates the need to move beyond race as an explanation for conflict situations:

> I have no grand plan to deal with these situations in future. Racial tension is a reality in South Africa and each situation will have to be dealt with individually. Hopefully, through experience, education and training, South African's will, at some stage, learn to accept that not everything is racially motivated, even though the difference will always be there.

Power relationships

This theme relates to the influence of power from the perspective of authorities who seek to enforce social control (Grimes, 1978). The following comments from participants highlight the influence of power:

> I feel disempowered to confront the issues, because she is not doing it to me directly but to the new black colleagues who joined us.

Having grown up in an Indian culture, I have come across numerous statements that I did not do anything about. Naturally these were still the days when I was young … in high school … and I could basically not do anything, as it was my elders who made the comments.

I certainly felt that everyone had equal opportunity to express and be themselves. I questioned whether this was only in the eyes of the beholder, and that perhaps there was an implicit power differential between the majority of the group and the individual who perceived herself as being different.

The responses from participants reveal a need to examine informal positions of power:

The conclusion is that it is probably linked to some race or gender superiority underpinning. It is almost as if the person asking the question is merely being entertained, but no real value is assigned to acknowledging that person's presence.

The power of groups has always intrigued me. Groups can really make a person's life hell if s/he does not fit into what the group thinks is right or appropriate. Individuals start behaving differently in a group. However, there appears always to be some kind of informal hierarchy or ranking in a group.

Dividends of diversity management

In his examination of the relationships among racial diversity, business strategy and firm performance in the banking industry, Richard (2000) shows that racial diversity interacts with business strategy in determining firm performance measured in three different ways, i.e. productivity, return on equity and market performance. Richard's study shows that there are important dividends attached to effective management of racial or ethnic diversity at work, and that diversity adds value and, within the proper context, contributes to firms' competitive advantage. Werner and Roythorne-Jacobs (2006: 265) assert that 'The successful integration of diversity in the workplace leads to increased performance, well-adjusted employees and satisfied customers'. Lattimer (1998: 5) agrees, pointing out that 'differences in the workforce are increasingly being seen as powerful opportunities for strengthening organisational performance'. Kirby and Richard (2000: 370) refer to the observation by Cox (1991), and Cox and Blake (1991) that 'diversity can result in a competitive advantage via: (a) the resource-acquisition argument, (b) the marketing argument, (c) the system-flexibility argument, (d) the creativity argument, (e) the problem-solving argument and (f) the cost-reduction argument'. Dividends of diversity can be considered under the following key sub-constructs.

Transformation

'Transformations in the workplace are the product of individuals remaking or reconstituting (transforming) practice' (Billett & Somerville, 2004: 311). Rao and Stuart (1997: 10) contend that organisational transformation is more than just 'organisational development' or 'organisational change'. 'We want to move organisations in a direction that can accommodate, cherish, and foster the creativity and the productivity of women, men, young, old, people of colour, people of differing ability' (Rao & Stuart, 1997: 10–11). Billet and Somerville (2004: 311) argue that these transformations require active involvement and engagement. 'Cultural change such as that which occurs in workplaces will be a product of relational interactions between the socially-derived activities or technologies, and individuals who will deploy them' (Rogoff, 1990, quoted in Billett & Somerville, 2004: 311).

Restoration of confidence

With regards to confidence as a factor for success in work teams, Chowdhury et al. (2002: 349) report that 'members with strong self-efficacy of working in a team environment are those who are highly confident of being successful in tasks specific to a team environment'. Hollenbeck and Hall (2004: 255) describe self-confidence as 'our judgment of our capability to successfully accomplish something'. Hollenbeck and Hall (2004: 257) further argue that because self-confidence involves a judgement call, it can be accurate or inaccurate, influenced by any other judgement, by how well we make judgements, how accurate the data are on which we base the judgements, the data we choose to consider and how we process it. Describing the control individuals have over their self-confidence, Hollenbeck and Hall (2004: 258) suggest that 'our level of confidence results from our specific experiences, and it develops through a cognitive sense-making process that we can influence'.

Openness

'Individuals high on "openness to experiences" are described as creative, inquisitive, introspective, and attentive to inner feelings' (Costa & McCrae, 1992; Hofstee et al., 1992, quoted in Bono et al., 2002: 320). However, with respect to conflict, Bono et al. (2002: 320) refer to Blickle's (1995, 1997) conclusion that 'openness was positively correlated with the tendency to approach (vs. avoid) arguments'. In their study of the role of personality in task and relationship conflict, Bono et al. (2002) found that people who scored high on openness reported more conflict. In light of this, Bono et al. (2002) point out differing viewpoints in the literature about the role of such conflict. 'The position-oriented conflict of open individuals is the sort of conflict that has been found to be beneficial to work group performance' (Amason, 1996; Jehn, 1995, 1997, quoted in Bono et al., 2002: 338). On the negative side, Bono et al. (2002: 338) refer to Jehn's (1995, 1997) declaration that 'individuals who score high on "openness to experiences" also tended to attribute their conflicts to relationship concerns, which can have detrimental effects on both relationships and work group performance'.

Richness of diversity

Lattimer (1998) argues that while managing diversity includes race and gender, one should adopt an all-encompassing view:

> Managing diversity for strategic and competitive advantage is an ongoing process of addressing the full array of diverse issues that impact the business performance of an organisation, such issues as the changing workforce, shifting employee values, new and emerging markets, globalisation of the enterprise, mergers and acquisitions, the impact of technology, and information systems, to mention a few. (Lattimer, 1998: 4)

Freedom of expression

'Persons realize their potentialities when they can flourish autonomously, freely expressing their beliefs, concerns, dreams, and hopes' (Held, 1984: 52). However, for this to happen, Held (1984: 53) acknowledges that it is important that 'persons have rights to the means to express themselves, i.e., to the economic and cultural resources with which to develop the expression of self and community'. Lattimer (1998: 12) refers to positive experiences at a bank in Chicago which found that 'the diverse work team forces an individual to listen, to really pay attention'. Trevor Davis, an employee at the bank is quoted in Lattimer (1998: 12) as stating that, as a result, 'you get the whole range of different perspectives going back and forth, and that gets the diverse creative juices flowing toward the same thing'.

Inclusive culture

Nagda et al. (2006: 446) discuss social inclusion in the context of reducing prejudice, and comment that 'while prejudice reduction may be conceived of as involving individual-oriented outcomes, social inclusion broadens the sphere of outcome measurement to encourage positive changes at social and societal levels'. Werner and Roythorne-Jacobs (2006: 274) describe inclusion with respect to organisational socialisation, reporting that 'one of the principle features of effective socialisation programmes is the assigning of challenging work to new employees'. With reference to group cohesiveness and its benefits in the workplace, Cilliers (2006: 241) advises that 'the successful attainment of group goals, and the members' feelings of having been part of a successful unit, can serve to enhance the commitment of members'. According to Cox and Blake (1991), cited in Kirby and Richard (2000: 368), 'successfully implemented diversity programs result in a balance of organisational power, inclusion in decision-making and equal opportunity across all participants, which, in turn, may lead to a competitive advantage for the organisation'.

Justice

Kirby and Richard (2000: 368) comment on organisational justice, advising that 'much of the success or failure of diversity-management programs can be attributed to whether employees believe the programs to be fair and equitable'. Highlighting some positive consequences associated with organisational justice, Kirby and Richard (2000: 369) refer to observations regarding awarding of organisational benefits (Bies & Shapiro, 1987; Folger & Martin, 1986), and that 'if the allocation process is viewed as justifiable, it can lessen resentment'. 'Past researchers have shown that justification of managerial actions often encourages high levels of employee performance' (Greenberg, 1998, quoted in Kirby & Richard, 2000: 370).

Positive contribution

'The development of a strong community among a diverse workforce has positive implications for more effective productivity in the workplace' (Wiltz et al., 2005: 178). Describing the behavioural successes associated with being well-adjusted in a diverse environment, Werner and Roythorne-Jacobs (2006: 265) cite examples such as 'the learning and exhibition of social skills appropriate to a diverse environment'; 'the development of positive interpersonal relations with a broad range of diverse employees'; and 'the effective execution of tasks'. Wiltz et al. (2005: 173) explain 'diversity self-efficacy' as one of the stages in diversity training and management that 'involves the development of employees to acquire and utilize the resources necessary to act as change agents and promote a positive work environment'.

Summary and recommendations

To begin, managers may educate themselves about issues of race and diversity at work and consider, in a self-reflexive manner, their own approach to economic minorities, ethnic minorities (where appropriate) and migrant employees (marginalised groups). The idea is to acknowledge, welcome, value and respect racial, ethnic and cultural differences among individuals, as well as uphold their dignity as human beings. Managers may, in particular, review organisational structures, policies and routines to identify biases and discrimination, and address any key issues identified. Organisations that have used a proactive approach to diversity and inclusion have reported an increase in harmonious race relations in the workplace (Patrik & Kumar, 2012: 11; DiversityInc, 2014). If the acceptance of groups-of-difference is made and embedded into the organisational culture from the top level, it will enable them to lead by example and ensure greater employee engagement (April & Shockley, 2007a; Rodriquez, 2006).

Naturally, managers must make themselves aware of, and abide by, relevant diversity laws and regulations, to not only avoid legal repercussions but also to afford all members of the labour market an equal chance of employment and growth. For example, at the recruitment and selection stage, it is important to avoid judging individuals based on stereotypes, and only use their suitability for the job, regardless of race or ethnicity (Acas, 2013). Additionally, we also know that race and ethnicity differences have the potential to increase organisational innovation (Johansson, 2004), and thus being 'best in class' (known as welcoming and giving all races/ethnicities fair opportunities) as an employer, can serve to enhance an organisation's social capital with national and local governments.

To create a diverse and inclusive culture, managers may conduct awareness and training sessions to educate employees about the importance of a diverse workforce, and, more critically, what it means to be inclusive. Explicit policies may be laid out to monitor, record and redress any instances of discrimination in the workplace, particularly racial/ethnic discrimination. By doing so, individuals from marginalised backgrounds may feel more valued within the workplace. Additionally, employees may be encouraged to work together in diverse teams and also through socialisation. This may help in eliminating stereotypes and racism.

A final recommendation is to collect feedback from marginalised workers, including marginalised women who face multiple disadvantages due to intersectionality. This may enable organisations to identify issues and challenges facing individuals from marginalised groups during the recruitment/talent acquisition process and also during the course of their employment, and advancement, in the organisation. Such identification may also serve to raise the awareness of organisations as to their strengths and weaknesses, particularly in the human capital arena and its links to business/organisational performance.

In conclusion, it is evident that managing race and ethnic diversity within the workplace is a challenging task. Although individuals may hold visible or subtle stereotypical views, that lead them to discriminate against ethnic minorities, it is important for organisations to formulate and implement diversity and inclusion policies, to ensure there is no harassment or discrimination in the workplace. Ultimately, such policies and behaviours must be practised and disseminated from the top-level managers, in order to encourage buy-in, to inform mid- and low-level management that performance in such matters occupies the minds of top-level managers, and to signal that everyone will be held to account with regard to under-performance in the diversity and inclusion arena.

Discussion questions

1. Can you explain the difference between 'race' and 'ethnicity'? Explain what issues are at stake in the workplace, if we understand/prefer (and therefore act accordingly) one of these concepts, as opposed to the other.

(Continued)

(Continued)

2. From your own perspective, please identify potential and real issues/challenges faced by individuals from marginalised groups during: (a) the recruitment/talent acquisition process, (b) during the course of their employment, and (c) during their advancement or recruitment, in the organisation.

3. In your own words, describe what you understand by the term 'intersectionality'.

4. What is the role of power dynamics of organisations? Please list some instances, from you own life, in which you experienced 'good' and 'bad' power dynamics, and what the effects were on your self-esteem and self-confidence.

5. What are the costs to individuals (emotional, psychological and even economic/career and opportunities) if (a) the individuals themselves remain silent about feeling excluded and/or marginalised in the workplace, (b) if colleagues/team members remain silent about feeling excluded and/or marginalised in the workplace, and (c) if the organisation remains silent regarding employees feeling excluded and/or marginalised in the workplace?

6. Tabulate as many characteristics as you can list relating to workplace cultures in which people feel excluded (in a column), as well as that of inclusive cultures (in another column).

CASE STUDY 5.1

'What it means to be Muslim in South Africa' – by Idries Kahaar

I grew up in a coloured township (Gelvandale) in Port Elizabeth in the 1970s and 1980s. I grew up during the final part of the 'official' Apartheid era of our country's history. I mention 'official' since racism is still rife in South Africa, even though formal Apartheid has been dismantled since 1994. I attended the local public primary and secondary schools. I am Muslim. I grew up in a household with an emotionally abusive father and a submissive mother. My dad was mostly an angry person and I believe that his upbringing during Apartheid was one of the primary contributors towards his repressed anger. I am the eldest of four children. My dad owns a corner-shop café in a very poor coloured township in Port Elizabeth called 'Katanga' by its inhabitants. This is where I spent 90 per cent of my childhood, i.e. working in the shop. My life experiences as a coloured Muslim in South Africa and growing up in the household that I developed in, have largely shaped me into who I am

(Continued)

(Continued)

today. By the time I was 18 years old, I had an immense amount of repressed anger towards many people, including my parents. This was a very confusing time in my life. Attending my first year at the University of Cape Town compounded the anger and confusion, and brought Apartheid alive for me in a way that I did not know before leaving home for Cape Town. It was during 1989 that I realised, for the first time, the degree of social engineering that was achieved by the Apartheid regime and the impact that Apartheid had on all South Africans (black and white), especially me. I began to understand why I had such an immense 'inferiority complex' and why my dad was so angry (even though he tried to hide this from us). I began to understand that Apartheid was a significant contributor towards the judgements I held of others, especially people of other races and religions.

Until that year, I had led a very protected life and, in one year, my view of the world was changed radically. All these experiences shaped and still do shape my reality, i.e. my ever-evolving mental models are the result of my values, assumptions, beliefs and expectations. I inherited my father's stubbornness (and anger) and my mother's 'always pleasing everybody' approach. I made these traits my own. My traits are not exactly like those of my parents, i.e. they are a little more subtle in the way that I display them to the world around me. This was how I subconsciously learnt the art of controlling and manipulating those around me so that I could create a perfect world where nobody, especially I, would get into trouble. I subconsciously carried this desire to want to please people throughout my life – I had become a people pleaser. The thing with always pleasing other people is that I ended up confused about who I was as an individual because I, quite often, used to contradict how I felt in favour of another's wishes ... or so I though at the time, i.e. I was putting myself second and was resenting those people that I believed were responsible for my predicament. The other side-effect of pleasing was indecisiveness. I took extra long to make decisions, because I was always trying to please everybody but myself. The other thing with my indecisiveness was that, deep down, I was afraid of disappointing others, I was afraid of making mistakes. As a result, I became a procrastinator. My inner conflict kept on growing.

One morning (about six years ago now) I woke up and I was unusually aware that my life was characterised by an immense amount of indecisiveness and resentment. I was married and now living in Cape Town. I am not sure what awoke me from my life-long slumber but I became aware of how very frustrating

(Continued)

(Continued)

my life had become, and how much repressed anger I had bottled up inside of me. Until that point, I often blamed others, especially those closest to me, for my inability to deal with the challenges in my life. Decisions at home (including the social arrangements) were taken by my wife and decisions at work were spread amongst my colleagues. I was so afraid of making mistakes, of dealing with the consequences of making mistakes that I refined my ability to manipulate and became a master at manipulating others so that they would be held accountable instead of me. I took my wife, my family, my friends and my career for granted. I realised, for the first time, that my reaction to the world was somehow linked to my past experiences as well as my religion, my race, my schooling, my home environment, my social circles, my family, my culture and my ever-changing circumstances. I became aware of my mental models and the role that social networks have played in shaping me into the person that I am today. Somehow I was restricting reality through my structure of interpretation (a term borrowed from the coaching world), i.e. my mental models resulted in me only seeing what I wanted to see in every experience. It seemed as if my personality was the result of my mental models and that my social networks contributed towards the shaping of my mental model. I was not as in control as I believed I was.

At work, I was perceived as being in control of my life. Deep down inside, I really felt like a passenger in life and not in control. I felt that I was a victim. At the time I had a very strong, but subconscious, external locus of control. I unconsciously believed that the events in my life were attributable to actions/forces beyond my control. I did not feel good about myself and about my abilities. I suffered from very low self-esteem. I wanted approval from people, I wanted recognition and I wanted to belong. This proved to be a very frustrating and confusing time in my life. The manipulation/pretending was not working in the way I had planned and, as a result, people were constantly disappointing me, i.e. the expectations I had of others were not being met. Something was terribly wrong and I was unable to put my finger on it.

From my experiences at work I noticed that effective communication is something that is key in understanding myself as well as understanding others, and that I had to do some learning in this area. I realised that poor communication at work was resulting in inefficiencies and that this was one of the main contributors to many of my colleagues' frustrations (including myself). These frustrations were often due to the poor management of ambiguity that is perpetuated by poor communication, i.e. management had one idea of what the

(Continued)

(Continued)

problem was and the workforce had another, and we were talking past one another. Adding uncertainty to the recipe did not help either, i.e. where management displayed a lack of communication in certain matters, and this often resulted in alienation between workers and management. I was caught somewhere in between all of this and I realised, even more, the importance of clear and effective communication. I came to realise that the more I learn, the less uncertainty there is in my life and the more empowered I feel. I also realised that there was a connection between 'low self-esteem' and 'uncertainty', i.e. the more uncertainty I experienced, the lower the self-esteem I had. The reality is that life means uncertainty – a crystal ball does not exist that can accurately predict the future. I have come to realise the importance of self-awareness in dealing with uncertainty. The more empowered I am, the better I am able to deal with new situations.

The challenge, for me, is thus to spark the growth of self-awareness in every individual I encounter, i.e. to become conscious 'change agents' for personal and societal evolution.

In order to water the seeds of self-awareness, I consciously decided that coaching would be, and is today, a major part of how I lead my life. I have found that the more I pursue my purpose the more I automatically express my purpose in my daily life, i.e. the more I begin to live my purpose.

This means that I would need to choose a career that would allow me to live my purpose and a career that would foster my self-awareness. Being spiritual would also serve to be a core enabler of my growth. For me, spirituality is not the same as organised religion. The experience of spirituality is different for every person. Also, in my view, spirituality is something that you cannot separate out from work, it is there whether you consciously choose to express it or not, i.e. kindness, compassion, gratitude, friendship, sharing, smiling, laughing, crying, consoling, helping, doing your job, etc., are all forms of expressing your spirituality at work and at home. For me, attempting to define and therefore confine spirituality is the same as trying to define the concept of 'love', the altruistic type.

Our country was (and still is) divided for many decades through the social engineering of Apartheid. Most South Africans grew up in a world that encouraged separateness and that emphasised the power of individuality. I believe that our past has been a blessing in disguise since it has made us stronger and more resilient, and made us appreciate our common humanity so much more than before. Our country and much of the world is still divided by a host of

(Continued)

(Continued)

different discrimination criteria. Our recent past has shown us what we are not.

It is up to us, as the future leaders, to either follow the status quo or consciously decide to collectively work together towards a better, more inclusive society for all of humanity. It is nobody else's responsibility other than our own, and that responsibility starts with me.

Questions

1. What did you learn from this case study?
2. To what extent does racial and ethnic discrimination in society affect racial and ethnic discrimination in the workplace?
3. What are the personal effects of racial and ethnic discrimination on individuals, such as Idries?
4. How can individuals from racially or ethnically marginalised groups cope with the challenge of racism that they face in the course of employment?
5. To what extent is the eradication of workplace racism the responsibility of individuals?
6. What can organisations do to eradicate racism from the workplace?
7. What can individuals from economic and other dominant groups do to alleviate racism in organisations?
8. 'Racism is a thing of the past. Now there are robust laws and organisational policies in place, thus issues of racial or ethnic discrimination no longer exist.' Comment.

Idries Kahaar started in information technology (IT) in 1994 at Telkom's Regional Information Services. Since then, his career focus has shifted from being a technical expert to that of being a facilitator, business leader, manager, architect, coach and mentor. Today, he works at Cornastone Enterprise Management Systems (an IT service provider) as the Chief Operations Officer. Idries also serves as an independent board member at Apollo Brick, a national manufacturing concern, where he represents the Apollo Brick Employee Trust at board level. He holds an MBA from the Graduate School of Business at the University of Cape Town, Certificates in Coaching from the South African College of Applied Psychology and the University of Cape Town, a Bachelor of Science Degree in Mathematics and Computer Science from Nelson Mandela Metropolitan University, and a Diploma in electrical engineering from Port Elizabeth Technikon. Additionally, he was a Sainsbury Management Fellow at the University of Cambridge in the UK.

CASE STUDY 5.2

'Will I ever be fully accepted in India?' — by Jyot Chadha

> Your insecurity seems self-inflicted and you come across as immensely biased with little or no faith in India's democracy ... do take a trip abroad and if you like it there better than here, please exercise your right to choose where you live.

Many minutes went by as I typed and deleted responses to this Facebook posting, unable to decide if I wanted to retaliate or make light of this attack. In the end, my fear won. I typed out measured responses that questioned my friend, but did not reveal my stance. With the country embroiled in a nasty, polarising election, I knew my post on Facebook would open me up to snarky remarks. But I was unprepared for the ferocity of this statement on my wall. My brain raced as I tried to deal with a roar of conflicting emotions: How dare he judge the validity of my fears! What if my other friends *like* his comment? I refuse to be bullied! Since when are people with a different opinion unwelcome in this country? Am I crazy? Am I alone in my opinion?

My parents, brother and I moved back to India from Singapore when I was six. We lived in Delhi with my paternal grandparents. We are Sikhs. I remember waking up to find my mother and grandmother crying on the first day of my summer vacations when I was about ten. A suicide bomber had killed our former Prime Minister, Rajiv Gandhi. That day, the elders in the house were tense. There were hushed conversations that stopped when I entered the room. My parents' whispers scared me more than their anger. It was years before I understood their reaction that day. In November 1984, anti-Sikh riots had rocked India. The then Prime Minister, Indira Gandhi, had been fatally shot by her Sikh bodyguards. Thousands of Sikhs were pulled out of their homes and massacred. Men were made to drink kerosene and set light to. Women were tortured and killed, children brutally murdered. My family lived with the knowledge that our security was fragile.

I once asked my father what my family had done in 1984. My maternal grandparents hid in a hotel room for three days while my paternal grandparents found an alternate escape route after being refused shelter by their neighbours. There were stories of uncles caught by mobs and of families that cut their hair to pass as Hindu. After the riots, some cousins left India, unable to look their colleagues in the eye. Most kept their head down and tried to

(Continued)

(Continued)

manufacture a new peace with their neighbours. Growing up in India a decade after the anti-Sikh riots was disorienting for me. My family was adamant that we would not hide and would visibly present ourselves as Sikhs (for example, I was not allowed to cut my hair). But there was pressure from my friends, both Sikh and Hindu, to blend in. I was acutely aware of Bollywood's portrayal of the Sikh man as the idiotic but loyal bumpkin. Never the star, the Sikh man made people laugh and defended the heroine's honour. Sikh women were portrayed as beautiful and big hearted. As I grew older, I vacillated between rebelling against these stereotypes, which the other kids found boring ('you're too sensitive'), and propagating it by reciting jokes about Sardars. I became good at gauging the right amount of 'Sikh-ness' that was appropriate in different groups. But I was deeply unhappy in my final years in school. I became withdrawn and focused all my attention on leaving India to go to college in the US. At the time, I attributed my depression solely to the sexual abuse I had faced as a child at the hands of a relative. But as I realised years later, the weight of constantly wearing masks was exhausting. At 18 years old, my mind felt empty of any desire, excitement or ambition, other than to get out of the country.

Leaving India was a breath of fresh air. When I returned six years later, I found it difficult to remain quiet in the face of blatant and subtle bullying of religious minorities. When the newspapers glossed over yet another Sikh widow denied justice for the 1984 riots, I brought it up at dinner parties. I spoke up when people at work portrayed Sikhs and Punjabi-Hindus as being the same people. I voiced my deep discomfort at Muslims being portrayed as the 'other'. But I paid the price of being seen as volatile, radical, or even a bore, in work and social circles. I had a deep desire to be accepted by my country as from a religious minority with differing opinions, traditions and values. I did not want to be whitewashed as an extension of the majority in order to make me valid.

Fast forward to 2014. The leading contender in the Prime Ministerial race has spurred an acrimonious debate as to what we stand for as a nation. Charged (and acquitted) for inciting and condoning the anti-Muslim riots of 2002, this candidate is receiving majority support based on a perceived ability to revive the economy and refusal to 'appease minorities'. The very definition of secularism is being changed by a savvy political campaign. To be secular now is to be elite and intellectual at best, or not welcome in this new India at worst. Until last year, I felt safe speaking my mind and not forcing

(Continued)

(Continued)

myself to blend into the majority. This is the first time that I have truly felt like a minority in this country. I am aware of censoring myself again. I am cautious when people ask whom I will vote for. I do not engage in political discussions. I am unable to feel comfortable or close to colleagues. At times, I wonder if I am wrong, if I am blinded by the minority 'fear-mongering' media. I feel unsure of myself and worried for my parents who still speak their minds.

Questions

1. How do historical representations of groups of people affect individuals' sense of belonging?
2. Are there aspects of your own identity, which you feel are not fully accepted by others? Comment.
3. Would you be willing to shed or hide aspects of your identity if you were being discriminated against? Why?
4. Why do some people ferociously defend their own perspectives on reality, and why are they unable to entertain challenge or criticism of that reality?
5. What are the workplace implications of such close-mindedness?
6. Do you think that authenticity and honesty are related? Why? What does inauthenticity mean for workplace relations and team cohesion?
7. What stereotypes have you perpetuated or not objected to in conversations, or interactions, with friends, family or work colleagues?
8. What do you think the role is of forgiveness in the workplace?
9. What are some of the personal blocks you feel to speaking your mind?

Jyot Chadha has a keen interest in how access and mobility positively impact economic enhancement, thus enabling poverty reduction at a large scale. She works with EMBARQ to identify business models for the private sector to invest in infrastructure that solves urban India's mobility problems. In addition, Jyot is exploring the possibility of launching a transport-focused seed fund and incubator in India. Prior to EMBARQ, Jyot co-founded a US$0.5 million incubation fund to invest in businesses run by young people living in Delhi slums. She started her career with Langham Capital, an investment bank focused on cross-border mergers and acquisitions, and RogersCasey, an investment consulting firm. Jyot has an MBA from the Saïd Business School at the University of Oxford (UK). She is an Associate Fellow with the Skoll Centre for Social Entrepreneurship and a Shell Foundation Fellow. Jyot is a member of the External Diversity and Inclusion Advisory Council for Novartis International.

CASE STUDY 5.3

'When all hell breaks loose in Iraq' — by Hanafi Talib

Managing stakeholders from different nationalities, with different sets of beliefs and cultures, is very challenging for any leader. For example, when I was a Country Head for PETRONAS in Uzbekistan, the challenges were more around the language and leadership styles. So some of the diversity challenges were a result of the locals using the Russian language as their medium for business, instead of English. And one had to really make genuine efforts to truly understand the diversity of cultures between the indigenous/traditional Uzbekistanis and the more modern Russian influence (as Uzbekistan is part of the Commonwealth of Independent States (CIS) of former Soviet Republics). Other challenges included how to handle high-level meetings between yourself, as the senior representative of your company, and the country's Ministers who are very autocratic. But the essence of any business is still about having good relationships with others. As a result of my many years of work experience and expat life in multiple countries away from my home country of Malaysia, I have developed a guiding principle: 'Understand the locals and respect their cultures, to deliver!'.

This guiding principle has served me well for nearly all of my years of working, particularly when encountering other cultures and customs in foreign countries – however, while working in Iraq, I was to be reminded of how important cultural practices and symbols are to particular groups of people (and how they can lead to serious misunderstanding and wrong perceptions). The incident occurred at our Garraf Asset Operations (GAO), in the District of Rifa'I in Iraq. On 29 November 2012, we nearly got all of our Malaysian expats (approximately 300 of them) slaughtered by the locals, when they stormed our camp.

Some of the background

PETRONAS entered into a Development Production Sharing Contract (DPSC) with the Iraqi government in 2009 to develop the Garraf oil fields. Garraf is situated between Baghdad and Basrah, in the province of Thi Qar. PETRONAS built a camp to house all of their employees and some of the contractors in the Garraf Contract Area (GCA), and named it Garraf Base Camp (GBC). The camp can accommodate approximately 500 people easily at any one time, and the tenants came from all over the world. However, the

(Continued)

(Continued)

majority were Malaysian expats. Private security companies provide protection for us – these companies have mostly Westerners in their organisations, including South Africans, and they were all well trained as military men before arriving in Iraq. We also have local Iraqi hired staff in the camp, but mainly in the service areas, i.e. they work as gardeners, kitchen helpers, housekeepers,

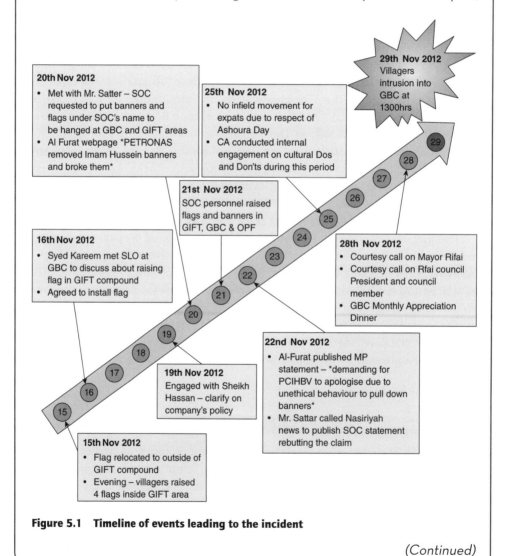

20th Nov 2012
- Met with Mr. Satter – SOC requested to put banners and flags under SOC's name to be hanged at GBC and GIFT areas
- Al Furat webpage *PETRONAS removed Imam Hussein banners and broke them*

25th Nov 2012
- No infield movement for expats due to respect of Ashoura Day
- CA conducted internal engagement on cultural Dos and Don'ts during this period

29th Nov 2012 Villagers intrusion into GBC at 1300hrs

21st Nov 2012
SOC personnel raised flags and banners in GIFT, GBC & OPF

16th Nov 2012
- Syed Kareem met SLO at GBC to discuss about raising flag in GIFT compound
- Agreed to install flag

28th Nov 2012
- Courtesy call on Mayor Rifai
- Courtesy call on Rfai council President and council member
- GBC Monthly Appreciation Dinner

22nd Nov 2012
- Al-Furat published MP statement – *demanding for PCIHBV to apologise due to unethical behaviour to pull down banners*
- Mr. Sattar called Nasiriyah news to publish SOC statement rebutting the claim

19th Nov 2012
Engaged with Sheikh Hassan – clarify on company's policy

15th Nov 2012
- Flag relocated to outside of GIFT compound
- Evening – villagers raised 4 flags inside GIFT area

Figure 5.1 Timeline of events leading to the incident

(Continued)

(Continued)

drivers and general clerks. Only a few of the Iraqis are hired at junior business/ technical levels. The GCA is generally flat with sandy/clay silts, shrubs and low vegetation, and the local villagers are poor, mainly due to wars.

The incident

The Shia (in Arabic, *Shī'ah*) represent the second largest denomination of Islam and constitute the majority sect in Iraq. The adherents of Shia Islam are called Shias or the Shi'a as a collective (in English we use the term Shi'ites). During Arbain (a religious ceremony whereby all the Shi'ites will mourn the death of Imam Hussein for 40 days), all in the land were expected to observe this ceremony by not having parties or celebrations during the period. Due to either ignorance of our food service providers' sensitivities or naivety, we continued our monthly birthday celebrations inside the camp. We put up balloons and held a celebratory birthday session as usual. The local staff informed the villagers about this and we were attacked. Figure 5.1 shows the timeline leading up to the incident.

The hanging of balloons on the day of mourning was seen as disrespectful. GCA staff then removed the balloons. Some locals misinterpreted what we were doing through the spread of rumours and we were accused of celebrating the 'death of Imam Hussein'. The attackers were initially asked to disperse. However, the crowd grew, and this ultimately led to the damage and destruction of buildings and infrastructure (structures dented, windows broken, doors smashed, broken surveillance cameras, broken blinds, broken fans, smashed TVs, damaged wash basins, damaged air conditioner units, damaged fire extinguishers, destroyed signage, smashed lights – street lights and internal to the buildings), damage to rental and staff cars (dents, broken windows, broken mirrors) and, regrettably, injuries to staff/personnel (body and head injuries, with a need for hospitalisation).

Questions

1. Who do you think has been discriminated against in the case study? Comment.
2. Is the truth always relevant in cases of discrimination?
3. In which circumstances is violence a potential channel for reaching a solution? Discuss.

(Continued)

(Continued)

4. How important are symbols and rituals in establishing and maintaining the identity of groups of people? How important are they to you? Name some of them, and discuss.

5. Is ignorance of the cultural practices in the regions in which you live or work a justifiable excuse for contravening local customs?

6. Can you think of any customs, rituals or even symbols, which you may be offended by? Or ones which you have contravened or offended? What are the consequences?

7. What is some of the information that needs to be shared with expat employees before they go off on assignments?

8. What services/processes need to be put in place in order to secure their safety, well-being and extraction?

9. If you were Hanafi – leading this site – what would be your next steps for re-establishing trust between your various employee groups, as well as between the company and locals/villagers?

10. Are there other stakeholders to consider in re-establishing engagement? What would you do to achieve such engagement?

Hanafi Talib has a keen interest in unleashing the potential of people from various countries and cultures wherever he works. Currently, he is working with a national oil company (PETRONAS) in Iraq, leading approximately 500 workers of various nationalities. Previously, he was in both Pakistan (as General Manager) and Uzbekistan (as Country Head) where he was involved in tough negotiations with the host authorities and government agencies. He started his career with an international oil company (ExxonMobil), where he acquired technical skills and insight into the oil and gas business. Hanafi has an engineering degree from Monash University, Australia, and Management Certificates from both Melbourne University and Duke Corporate Education, UK. He is also a motivational speaker for University Technology Mara (UiTM) and a member of the Malaysian Institute of Engineers.

 Further reading

Bourgois, P. 1989. *Ethnicity at work*. Maryland: The Johns Hopkins University Press.

Ely, R.J., & Thomas, D.A. 2001. Cultural diversity at work: The effects of diversity perspectives on work group processes and outcomes. *Administrative Science Quarterly*. 46(2), 229–273.

Hudson, M., Netto, G., Sosenko,F., Noon, M., de Lima, P., Gilchrist, A. & Kamenou-Aigbekaen, N. 2013. *In-work poverty, ethnicity and workplace cultures*. Joseph Rowntree Foundation. Available at: http://www.jrf.org.uk. [Last accessed 15th October 2013].

Kivel, P. 2002. *Uprooting racism: How white people can work for racial justice*. Gabriola Island, BC: New Society Publishers.

References

Acas 2013. *Acas-Equality.* Available at: www.acas.org.uk/index.aspx?articleid=1363. [Last accessed 17 April 2013.]

Adorno, T.W., Frenkel-Brunswik, E., Levinson, D.J. & Sanford, R.N. 1950. *The Authoritarian Personality*. New York: Harper and Row.

All Party Parliamentary Group on Race and Community (AAPG) 2012. *Ethnic minority female unemployment: Black, Pakistani and Bangladeshi heritage women*. Report prepared by the Runnymede Trust. Available at: www.runnymedetrust.org/publications/181/32.html. [Last accessed 30 April 2014.]

Alleyne, A. 2004. Race-specific workplace stress. *Counselling and Psychotherapy Journal*. 15(8), 30–3.

Amason, A. 1996. Distinguishing the effects of functional and dysfunctional conflict on strategic decision making: Resolving a paradox for top management. *Academy of Management Journal*. 39, 123–48.

April, K. & April, A. 2009. Reactions to discrimination: Exclusive identity of foreign workers in South Africa. In M.F. Özbilgin (Ed.), *Equality, Diversity and Inclusion at Work: A Research Companion*. Cheltenham: Edward Elgar Press, pp. 216–28.

April, K. & Blass, E. 2010. Ethical leadership required to lead a diverse Europe. In W. Matiaske, S. Costa & H. Brunkhorst (Eds), *Contemporary Perspectives on Justice*. München, Mering: Rainer Hampp Verlag, pp. 183–201.

April, K. & Shockley, M. (Eds) 2007a. *Diversity: New Realities in a Changing World*. Basingstoke: Palgrave Macmillan.

April, K. & Shockley, M. (Eds) 2007b. *Diversity in Africa: The Coming of Age of a Continent*. Basingstoke: Palgrave Macmillan.

April, K. & Soomar, Z. 2013. Female breadwinners: resultant guilt and shame. *Effective Executive*. 16(4), 32–47.

April, K., Ephraim, N. & Peters, K. 2012. Diversity management in South Africa: inclusion, identity, intention, power and expectations. *African Journal of Business Management*. 6(4), 1749–59.

April, K., Kukard, J. & Peters, K. 2013. *Steward Leadership: A Maturational Perspective*. Cape Town: UCT Press.

Aspen Institute 2009. *Roundtable on Community Change: Dismantling Structural Racism. Constructing a Racial Equity Theory of Change*. Available at: www.aspeninstitute.org/sites/default/files/content/images/Roundtable%20on%20Community%20Change%20RETOC.pdf. [Last accessed 10 May 2014.]

Balcazar, F.E., Balcazar, Y.S., Ritzler, T.T. & Keys, C.B. 2010. *Race, Culture and Disability*. London: Jones & Bartlett Publishers.

Bannan, R.S. 1965. The other side of the coin: Jewish student attitudes toward Catholics and Protestants. *Sociological Analysis*. 26(1), 21–9.

Barker, R.L. 2003. *The Social Work Dictionary* (5th edn). Washington, DC: NASW Press.

Barnes-Josiah, D.L. 2004. *Undoing Racism in Public Health: A Blueprint for Action in Urban MCH*. NE: CityMatCH at the University of Nebraska Medical Centre.

Baumgardner, A.H., Kaufman, C.M. & Levy, P.E. 1989. Regulating affect interpersonally: When low self-esteem leads to greater enhancement. *Journal of Personality and Social Psychology*. 56, 907–21.

Bhui, K.S. & McKenzie, K. 2007. Institutional racism in mental health care. *British Management Journal*. 334, 649–50.

Bies, R.J. & Shapiro, D.L. 1987. Interactional fairness judgments: The influence of causal accounts. *Social Justice Research*. 1, 199–218.

Bigler, R.S. & Liben, L.S. 2007. Developmental inter-group theory: Explaining and reducing children's social stereotyping and prejudice. *Current Directions in Psychological Science*. 16(3) 162–6.

Billett, S. & Somerville, M. 2004. Transformations at work: Identity and learning. *Studies in Continuing Education*. 26(2), 309–26.

Black Demographics n.d. *African-American Income*. Available from: http://blackdemographics.com/households/african-american-income/. [Last accessed 9 April 2014.]

Blickle, G. 1995. Conceptualization and measurement of argumentativeness: A decade later. *Psychological Reports*. 77, 99–110.

Blickle, G. 1997. Argumentativeness and the facets of the big five. *Psychological Reports*. 81, 1379–85.

Bono, J.E., Boles, T.L., Judge, T.A. & Lauver, K.J. 2002. The role of personality in task and relationship conflict. *Journal of Personality*. 70(3), 311–44.

Bourne, J. 2001. Race class. *The Life and Times of Institutional Racism*. 43(7), 10–14.

Bravette, G. 1996. Reflections on a black woman's management learning. *Women in Management Review*. 11(3), 3–11.

Brief, A.P., Dietz, J., Cohen, R.R., Pugh, S.D. & Vaslow, J.B. 2000. Just doing business: Modern racism and obedience to authority as explanations for employment discrimination. *Organizational Behavior and Human Decision Processes*. 81(1), 72–97.

Browaeys, M.J. & Price, R. 2011. *Understanding Cross Cultural Management* (2nd edn). Harlow, UK: Pearson Education Ltd.

Carastathis, A. 2008. *Intersectionality & Feminism*. Available at: www.kickaction.ca/node/1499. [Last accessed 1 May 2014.]

CERA (Centre for Equality Rights in Accommodation) 2009. *Measuring Discrimination in Toronto's Rental Housing Market*. Available at: www.equalityrights.org/cera/docs/CERAFinalReport.pdf. [Last accessed 21 January 2015.]

Chowdhury, S., Endres, M. & Lanis, T.W. 2002. Preparing students for success in team work environments: The importance of building confidence. *Journal of Managerial Issues*. 14(3), 346–59.

Churchman, S. 2011. *Making Anything Possible – Diversity*. Available at: www.pwc.co.uk/annualreport/diversity.jhtml. [Last accessed 17 April 2013.]

Cilliers, F. 2006. Group behaviour. In Z. Bergh & A. Theron (Eds). *Psychology in the work context*. Cape Town: Oxford University Press, pp. 229–49.

Commission on Systemic Racism in the Ontario Criminal Justice System (CSROCJS) 1995. *Final Report*. Queen's Printer for Ontario. Available at: www.archive.org/details/reportracismont00comm. [Last accessed 15 November 2014.]

Conley, D. 2003. *What is the Difference Between Race and Ethnicity? Race – The Power of an Illusion*. Available at: www.pbs.org/race/000_About/002_04-experts-03-02.htm. [Last accessed 27 March 2014.]

Costa, P.T. & McCrae, R.R. 1988. Personality in adulthood: A six-year longitudinal study of self-reports and spouse ratings on the NEO Personality Inventory. *Journal of Personality and Social Psychology*. 54, 853–63.

Costa, P.T. & McCrae, R.R. 1992. *Revised NEO Personality Inventory (NEO-PI-R) and NEO Five Factor Model (NEO-FFI) professional manual*. Odessa, FL: Psychological Assessment Resources.

Cox, T. 1991. The multicultural organization. *The Executive*. 5(2), 34–47.

Cox, T.H. & Blake, S. 1991. Managing cultural diversity: implications for organizational competitiveness. *Academy of Management Executive*. 5, 45–56.

Dandeker, C. & Mason, D. 2001. The British Armed Services and the participation of minority ethnic communities: from equal opportunities to diversity. *Sociological Review*. 49, 219–33.

Degele, N. 2011. Intersectionality as multi-level analysis: dealing with social inequality. *European Journal of Women's Studies*. 18(1), 51–6.

Deitch, E.A., Barsky, A., Butz, R.M., Chan, S., Brief, A.P. & Bradly, J.C. 2003. Subtle yet significant: the existence and impact of everyday racial discrimination in the workplace. *Human Relations*. 56(11), 1299–324.

Delgado, R. & Stefancic, J. 2001. *Critical Race Theory: An Introduction*. New York: New York University Press.

de los Reyes, P. 2000. Diversity at work: paradoxes, possibilities and problems in the Swedish discourse on diversity. *Economic and Industrial Democracy*. 21, 253–66.

Dennis, N., Erdos, G. & Al-Shahi, A. 2000. *Racist Murder and Pressure Group Politics*. London: The Cromwell Press.

Department for Work and Pensions (DWP) (2012). *Ethnic Minorities in the Labour Market*. Available at: http://webarchive.nationalarchives.gov.uk/20130128102031/http://www.dwp.gov.uk/emesg/what-we-do/background/ethnic-minorities-in-the-labour/. [Last accessed 17 April 2013.]

Desilver, D. 2013. *Black Unemployment Rate is Consistently Twice that of Whites*. Pew Research Center. Available from: www.pewresearch.org/fact-tank/2013/08/21/through-good-times-and-bad-black-unemployment-is-consistently-double-that-of-whites/. [Last accessed 9 April 2014.]

DiversityInc 2012. *PricewaterhouseCoopers (PwC)*. Available at: www.diversityinc.com/pricewaterhousecoopers/. [Last accessed 17 April 2013.]

DiversityInc 2014. *Novartis Pharmaceuticals Corporation: No. 1 in the DiversityInc Top 50*. Available at: www.diversityinc.com/novartis-pharmaceuticals-corporation/. [Last accessed 13 May 2014.]

Driedger, L. & Mezoff, R.A. 1981. Ethnic prejudice and discrimination in Winnipeg high schools. *Canadian Journal of Sociology*. 6, 1–17.

EEOC 2012. *2012 Job Patterns for Minorities and Women in Private Industry (EEO-1)*. Available from: www1.eeoc.gov/eeoc/statistics/employment/jobpat-eeo1/2012/index.cfm#select_label. [Last accessed: 9 April 2014.]

Eisenberger, N.I., Lieberman, M.D. & Williams, K.D. 2003. Does rejection hurt? An fMRI study of social exclusion. *Science*. 302, 290–2.

Farah, A. & Atoum, A. 2002. Personality traits as self-evaluated and as judged by others. *Social Behaviour & Personality: An International Journal.* 30(2), 149–56.

Fiske, S.T. 2002. What we know now about bias and inter-group conflict, the problem of the century. *Current Directions in Psychological Science.* 11(4), 123–8.

Folger, R. & Martin, C. 1986. Relative deprivation and referent cognitions: Distributive and procedural justice effects. *Journal of Experimental Social Psychology.* 22, 531–46.

Gallagher, J. & Burke, P.J. 1974. Scapegoating and leader behaviour. *Social Forces.* 52(4), 481–8.

Gallois, C. & Callan, V.J. 1985. The Influence of ethnocentrism and ethnic label on the appreciation of disparagement jokes. *International Journal of Psychology.* 20(1), 63–76.

Gatewood, R. & Field, H. 2001. *Human Resource Selection.* Orlando, FL: Harcourt Brace & Company.

Gee, G., Ro, A., Shariff-Marco, S. & Chae, D. 2009. Racial discrimination and health among Asian Americans: evidence, assessment, and directions for future research. *Epidemiologic Reviews.* 31, 130–51.

Giddens, A. 2006. *Sociology* (5th edn). Cambridge: Polity Press.

Gough, H.G. & Bradley, P. 1993. Personal attributes of people described by others as intolerant. In P.M. Sniderman P.E. Tetlock & E.G. Carmines (Eds). *Prejudice, Politics and the American Dilemma.* Stanford, CA: Stanford University Press, pp.60–85.

Grimes, A.J. 1978. Authority, power, influence and social control: A theoretical synthesis. *The Academy of Management Review.* 3(4), 724–35.

Guerin, B. 2003. Combating prejudice and racism: New interventions from a functional analysis of racist language. *Journal of Community & Applied Social Psychology.* 13(1), 29–45.

Gunderson, G.R. & Cochrane, J.R. 2012. *Religion and the Health of the Public: Shifting the Paradigm.* Basingstoke: Palgrave Macmillan.

Handy, R. 2010. *Three Key Issues with Health Promotion for the Francophone Racial Minorities.* Prepared for the Health Nexus/Health Equity Council, Building Capacity for Equity in Health Promotion for Racialized Groups Project.

Held, V. 1984. Free expression. *Society.* 21(6), 49–56.

Henry, F. & Tator, C. 2009. *The Colour of Democracy: Racism in Canadian Society.* Toronto: Nelson Thomson.

Hightower, E. 1997. Psychosocial Characteristics of subtle and blatant racists as compared to tolerant individuals. *Journal of Clinical Psychology.* 53(4), 369–74.

Hilton, J.L. & von Hippel, W. 1996. Stereotypes. *Annual Review of Psychology.* 47, 237–71.

Hollenbeck, G.P. & Hall, D.T. 2004. Self-confidence and leader performance. *Organizational Dynamics.* 33(3), 254–69.

Holvino, E. 2001. *Complicating Gender: The Simultaneity of Race, Gender, and Class in Organization Change(ing).* Center for Gender in Organizations, Simmons Graduate School of Management, Working Paper No. 14.

Hunsberger, B. 1995. Religion and prejudice: The role of religious fundamentalism, quest, and right-wing authoritarianism. *Journal of Social Issues.* 51(2), 113–29.

Hussain, M.S. & Langer, E. 2003. A cost of pretending. *Journal of Adult Development.* 10(4), 261–70.

Javaid, M. 2012. *Michalak v Mid Yorks NHS.* Available at: http://obiterj.blogspot.com/2011/12/employment-tribunal-award-huge.html. [Last accessed 13 April 2013.]

Jehn, K. 1995. A multi-method examination of the benefits and detriments of intragroup conflict. *Administrative Science Quarterly.* 42(2), 256–82.

Jehn, K. 1997. A qualitative analysis of conflict types and dimensions in organizational groups. *Administrative Science Quarterly.* 42, 530–57.

Jenkins, R. 1985. Black workers in the labour market: the price of recession. In P. Braham, A. Rattansi & R. Skellington (Eds). *Racism and Antiracism: Inequalities, Opportunities and Policies*. Milton Keynes: The Open University Press.

Johansson, F. 2004. *The Medici Effect: What Elephants and Epidemics Can Teach Us about Innovation*. Boston: Harvard Business School Publishing.

Jolliff, T. 2011. The racialized organisation: the experiences of black managers. In T. Wright & H. Conley (Eds), *Gower Handbook of Discrimination at Work*. Surrey: Gower Publishing, pp. 113–28.

Judiciary 2011. *Employment Tribunals*. Available at: www.judiciary.gov.uk/judgement-jurisdiction/tribunals. [Last accessed 16 April 2013.]

Karakatsanis, N.M. & Swarts, J. 2007. Attitudes toward the Xeno: Greece in comparative perspective. *Mediterranean Quarterly*. 18(1), 113–34.

Khondker, H.H. 2006. Cultural conflicts, fundamentalisms, and globalization. *Globalizations*. 3(3), 441–8.

Kirby, S.L. & Richard, O.C. 2000. Impact of marketing work-place diversity on employee job involvement and organizational commitment. *Journal of Social Psychology*. 140(3), 367–77.

Kirton, G. 2009. Career plans and aspirations of recent black and minority ethnic business graduates. *Work, Employment and Society*. 23(1), 12–29.

Kirton, G. & Greene, A.M. 2011. *The Dynamics of Managing Diversity: A Critical Approach* (3rd edn). Oxford: Elsevier.

Konrad, A.M., Prasad, P. & Pringle, J.K. 2006. *Handbook of Workplace Diversity*. London: Sage Publications.

Kraiger, K. & Ford, J.K. 1985. A meta-analysis of ratee race effects in performance ratings. *Journal of Applied Psychology*. 70, 56–65.

Lattimer, R.L. 1998. The case for diversity in global business, and the impact of diversity on team performance. *Competitiveness Review*. 8(2), 3–17.

Lewis, P. 2012. *Eleven Met Police Cases of Alleged Racism*. Available at: www.guardian.co.uk/uk/2012/apr/16/met-police-cases-alleged-racism. [Last accessed 14 April 2013.]

Liff, S. 1996. Two routes to managing diversity: individual differences or social group characteristics. *Employee Relations*. 19, 11–26.

Lippert-Rasmussen, K. 2006. The badness of discrimination. *Ethical Theory & Moral Practice*. 9(2), 167–85.

Lipton, J.P., O'Connor, M., Terry, C. & Bellamy, E. 1991. Neutral job titles and occupational stereotypes: When legal and psychological realities conflict. *Journal of Psychology*. 125(2), 129–31.

Litvin, D. 2002. The business case for diversity and the 'iron cage'. In B. Czarniawska & H. Hopfl (Eds). *Casting the Other: The Production and Maintenance of Inequalities in Work Organizations*. London: Routledge, pp. 160–84.

Lopez-Rocha, S. 2007. Diversity in the Workplace. *International Journal of Diversity in Organisations, Communities & Nations*. 5(5), 11–18.

Madibbo, A. 2005. *Immigration, Race, and Language: Black Francophones in Ontario and the Challenges of Integration, Racism, and Language Discrimination*. CERIS Metropolis Centre. Working Paper No. 38.

Madibbo, A. 2006. *Minority within a Minority: Black Francophone Immigrants and the Dynamics of Power and Resistance*. London & New York: Routledge.

Malaysian Economic Planning Unit 2014. *Mid-term Review*. Available at: www.epu.gov.my/en/mid-term-review-ninth-malaysia-plan. [Last accessed 11 May 2014.]

Martin, M.W. & Sell, J. 1985. The effect of equating status characteristics on the generalization process. *Social Psychology Quarterly*. 48(2), 178–81.

Masser, B. & Moffat, K.B. 2006. With friends like these…the role of prejudice and situational norms on discriminatory helping behaviour. *Journal of Homosexuality*. 51(2), 121–38.

Meertens, R.W. & Pettigrew, T.F. 1997. Is subtle prejudice really prejudice? *Public Opinion Quarterly*. 61(1), 54–71.

Mirchandani, K & Chan W. 2005. *Racialized impact of welfare fraud control in British Columbia and Ontario*. Canadian Race Relations Foundation. Available at: www.crr.ca/divers-files/en/publications/reports/pubRacialized_Impact_Welfare.pdf. [Last accessed 21 January 2015.]

Mistry, M. & Latoo, J. 2009. Uncovering the face of racism in the workplace. *British Journal of Medical Practitioners*. 2(2), 20–4.

Monteith, M.J., Deneen, N.E., & Tooman, G. 1996. The effect of social norm activation on the expression of opinions concerning gay men and Blacks. *Basic and Applied Social Psychology*. 18, 267–88.

Müller-Wille, S. & Rheineberger, H.J. 2008. Race and genomics. Old wine in new bottles? Documents from an interdisciplinary discussion. *Journal of the History of Science, Technology and Medicine*. 16(3), 363–86.

Mulvey, L.L. & Richards, S.M. 2007. Thoughts on a conversational approach to race relations. *Sociological Forum*. 22(2), 220–6.

Nagda, B.A., Tropp, L.R. & Paluck, E.L. 2006. Looking back as we look ahead: Integrating research, theory, and practice on inter-group relations. *Journal of Social Issues*. 62(3), 439–51.

Noh, S. & Kaspar, V. 2003. Perceived discrimination and depression: moderating effects of coping, acculturation, and ethnic support. *American Journal of Public Health*. 93(2), 232–8.

O'Bryan, M., Fishbein, H.D. & Harold, P.N. 2004. Intergenerational Transmission of Prejudice, Sex Role Stereotyping, and Intolerance. *Adolescence*. 39(155), 407–26.

Oreopoulos, P. 2009. Why Do Skilled Immigrants Struggle in the Labour Market? A Field Experiment with Six Thousand Résumés. *Metropolic British Columbia, Working Paper Series*. 9(3). Available at: http://mbc.metropolis.net/assets/uploads/files/wp/2009/WP09-03.pdf. [Last accessed 21 January 2015.]

Özbilgin, M. & Tatli, A. 2008. *Global Diversity Management: An Evidence-Based Approach*. London: Palgrave.

Patrick, H.A. & Kumar, V.R. 2012. Managing workplace diversity: issues and challenges. *Sage Open*. 2(2), 1–16.

Patychuk, D. 2011. *Racialized Groups: A Literature Review*. Toronto: Health Nexus, and Health Equity Council. Available at: http://en.healthnexus.ca/sites/en.healthnexus.ca/files/resources/healthequityracializedgrps_literature_review.pdf. [Last accessed 15 June 2013.]

Percival, P. 2005. Comic normativity and the ethics of humour. *Monist*. 88(1), 93–120.

Philipp, S. 1999. Are we welcome? African American racial acceptance in leisure activities and the importance given to children's leisure. *Journal of Leisure Research*. 31(4), 385–403.

Phillips, G. & Scott, K. 2012. *Employment Law*. Guildford: College of Law Publishing.

Rao, A. & Stuart, R. 1997. Rethinking organisations: A feminist perspective. *Gender & Development*. 5(1), 10–16.

Regional Diversity Roundtable (RDT) 2008. *Developing the Diversity-competent Organization: A Resource Manual for Non-profit Human Service Agencies in Peel and Halton*. Available at: www.regionaldiversityroundtable.org/?q=node/96. [Last accessed 20 April 2014.]

Re:locate 2012. *UK's Ethnic Pay Gap on Increase*. Available at: www.jrf.org.uk/sites/files/jrf/JRF_Roundup_Tacking%20poverty_3022_aw.pdf. [Last accessed 17 April 2013.]

Reicher, S. 2007. Rethinking the Paradigm of Prejudice. *South African Journal of Psychology*. 37(4) 820–34.

Riddick, B. 2000. An examination of the relationship between labelling and stigmatisation with special reference to dyslexia. *Disability & Society*.15(4), 653–67.

Richard, O. 2000. Racial diversity, business strategy, and firm performance: a resource-based view. *Academy of Management Journal*. 42(2), 164–79.

Rodriguez, R. 2006. HR's new breed. *HR Magazine*. 51(4), 66–71.

Rogoff, B. 1990. *Apprenticeship in thinking: Cognitive development in social context*. New York: Oxford University Press.

Rose, E. 2004. *Discrimination and Diversity within the Employment Relationship*. *Employment Relations* (2nd edn). Harlow, UK: Pearson Education Ltd, Chapter 12, pp. 555–618.

SAIRR 2013. *Racial Transformation Not 'Complete Failure'*. Available at: www.sairr.org.za/media/media-releases/PRESS%20RELEASE%20-%20Racial%20transformation%20not%20complete%20failure.pdf/view. [Last accessed 11 May 2014.]

Shinar, E.H. 1975. Sexual stereotypes of occupations. *Journal of Vocational Behavior*. 7, 99–111.

Smith, T.W. 1992. Changing racial labels. *Public Opinion Quarterly*.56(4), 496–514.

Stodolska, M. 2006. A conditioned attitude model of individual discriminatory behaviour. *Leisure Sciences*. 27(1), 1–20.

Stodolska, M. & Jackson, E.L. 1998. Discrimination in leisure and work experienced by a white ethnic minority group. *Journal of Leisure Research*. 30, 23–46.

Sue, D.W., Arredondo, P. & McDavis, R.J. 1992. Multicultural counseling competencies and standards: a call to the profession. *Journal of Counseling and Development*. 20(2), 64–88.

Sumner, W.G. 1940. *Folkways: A Study of the Sociological Importance of Usages, Manners, Customs, Mores and Morals*. New York: New American Library.

Syed, J. 2007. 'The other woman' and the question of equal opportunity in Australian organisations. *International Journal of Human Resource Management*. 18(11), 1954–78.

Syed, J. & Pio, E. 2010. Veiled diversity: workplace experiences of Muslim women in Australia. *Asia Pacific Journal of Management*. 27(1), 115–37.

Tehera A.K. 2010. *Approaches to People of Colour and Food Bank Use in the City of Toronto, Peel Region and York Region*. Masters Program in Planning, University of Toronto.

Teixeira, C., Lo, L. and Truelove, M. 2007. Immigrant entrepreneurship, institutional discrimination and implications for public policy: A case study in Toronto. *Environment and Planning C: Government and Policy*. 25(2):176–93.

Torrington, D., Hall, L. & Taylor, S. 2008. *Human Resource Management* (7th edn). Harlow, UK: Pearson Education Ltd.

Tougas, F., Brown, R., Beaton, A.M. & Joly, S. 1995. Neosexism: Plus ça change, plus c'est pareil. *Personality and Social Psychology Bulletin*. 21(8), 842–9.

Ungerer, L. & Ngokha, G. 2006. Perception. In Z. Bergh & A. Theron (Ed.). *Psychology in the Work Context* (3rd edn). Oxford University Press: Cape Town., pp.116–34.

Werner, A. & Roythorne-Jacobs, H. 2006. Social processes in organizations. In Z. Bergh & A. Theron (Eds). *Psychology in the work context*. New York, NY: Oxford University Press, pp. 262–75.

Williams, D., Neighbours, H. & Jackson, J. 2003. Racial/ethnic discrimination and health: findings from community studies. *American Journal of Public Health*. 93(2), 200–8.

Wiltz, F., Venter, P. & Porter, V. 2005. A workplace diversity training and management model. *International Journal of Diversity in Organisations, Communities & Nations*. 5(3), 171–9.

Yoshida, W. 2014. *Malaysia's Ethnic Tensions Rise as its Economy Declines*. Available at: http://asia.nikkei.com/Politics-Economy/Policy-Politics/Malaysias-ethnic-tensions-rise-as-its-economy-declines. [Last accessed 2 February 2014.]

Zanoni, P. & Janssens, M. 2004. Deconstructing difference: the rhetoric of HR managers' diversity discourses. *Organization Studies*. 25, 55–74.

Zastrow, C. & Kirst-Ashman, K.K. 2010. *Understanding Human Behaviour and the Social Environment*. Boston: Cengage Learning.

Zawadzki, B. 1948. Limitations of the scapegoat theory of prejudice. *The Journal of Abnormal and Social Psychology*. 43(2), 127–41.

Ziegert, J.C. & Hanges, P.J. 2005. Employment discrimination: The role of implicit attitudes, motivation, and a climate for racial bias. *Journal of Applied Psychology*. 90(3), 553–62.

Age diversity in the workplace

6

Hélène Mountford and Peter A. Murray

Intended learning outcomes

After reading this chapter, you should be able to:

- Acquire critical knowledge related to managing age diversity in the workplace
- Distinguish between classical approaches to age diversity and more contemporary approaches adopted in modern organisations
- Relate to various socio-economic, legal and demographic factors in determining age diversity policies
- Explore cross-cultural comparisons between age diversity approaches and how these influence diversity practices
- Reflect on institutional power and on social forces of constraint in formulating diversity policy
- Analyse and apply age diversity principles to practical case problems
- Specify how to develop age diversity practices in contemporary settings

Introduction

This chapter outlines a number of facts and key reflections relating to the importance of older workers (those aged 45 years or more) in the overall labour market. Here, the focus is largely on Australia with world-wide implications noted. Cross-cultural issues are also outlined within the context of research on ageing and the importance of policy debates and strategies for ageing. There is little theory in the older worker literature but the authors have proposed that an adaptation of the Resource Based View (RBV) is appropriate (Mountford & Murray, 2011). The basis of the RBV is that all workers have intrinsic value and that economic, social and intellectual investments lead to increased organisational capital which in time leads to higher strategic returns. But the RBV can also recognise the value added by older workers' skills, abilities and experience (Quiggin, 2001), their individual productivity (Munnell et al., 2006) or their further contribution to productivity by being part of an age-diverse team (Feyrer, 2007). This value can be additionally increased by appropriate HR practices (Wright et al., 2001) to enhance this human capital, such as appropriate training and education, recruitment and selection.

The 'baby boomers', the largest generation ever, born between 1946 and 1964, are now by definition older workers. Australia is one of only four countries to benefit from a 'true' baby boom (together with the US, Canada and New Zealand) as major post World War II migration countries. The baby boom resulted in a disproportionate number of births over a longer period (Jackson, 2007). Although other developed countries experienced lower post war 'spikes' of peak birth rates, they were generally for shorter lengths of time – five

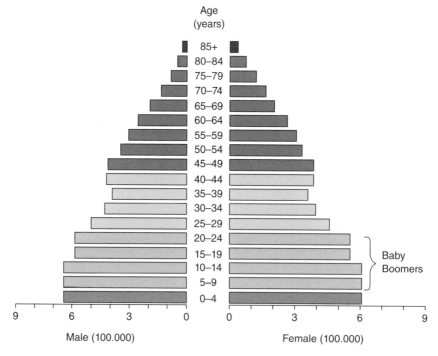

Figure 6.1   Australia's 1971 census pyramid showing a preponderance of people in the working ages

Source: Australian Bureau of Statistics, 2012, cat. no. 2071.0.

to six years compared with Australia's 19 year cohort. The baby boom generation is an anomaly in structural ageing – a hiccup in the steady decline in fertility from the late 1800s (Jackson, 2007). Lower birth rates, lower death rates and longer life expectancy (more than 20 years in the past century and still growing) have combined to increase the average age of the population leading to the ageing effect. The ageing effect on the workforce has been compounded by the longer amount of time that younger age groups spend in education (school and university) before joining the workforce, and the ageing baby boomers, combining to increase the workforce's median age. With ever increasing female education, there is no expectation that fertility will rise. Over the 10 years to 2011 the number of people aged 50 to 69 grew roughly twice as quickly as the population aged 15 to 49 (Productivity Commission, 2013). The traditional demographic pyramid is becoming squarer and in the next 20 years could almost become inverted. Compare Figures 6.1 and 6.2 to see the movement of the baby boomers through the age cohorts.

Baby boomers have been and are still the single largest cohort in the population. In Australia 4.2 million people were born into this generation but statistics usually include

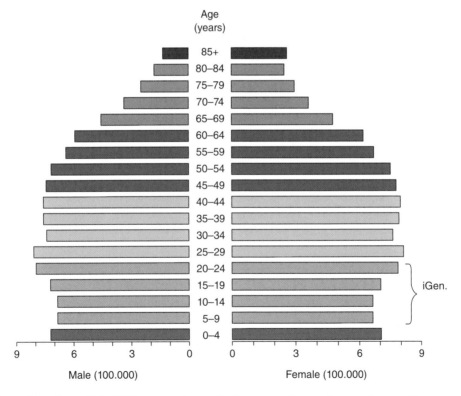

Figure 6.2 Australia's 2011 census demonstrates population ageing and longer life expectancy is increasing the elderly numbers

Source: Australian Bureau of Statistics, 2012, cat. no. 2071.0.

migrants born overseas during the same years, bringing the total to about 5 million people – almost a quarter of the total population and more than a third of the workforce.

But older workers are not a homogenous group. Demographers are now distinguishing two components – those born between 1946 and 1956, the older baby boomers, and those born between 1957 and 1966, the younger baby boomers. This pattern reflects all countries although specific demographic features will change depending on socio-economic, socio-legal and political goals. In 2013, the older group was aged between 57 and 67 years and had life and work experiences which differed from those of the younger group, which was aged between 47 and 56 years. The older group of baby boomers experienced major social change and entered the workforce when there were high rates of employment and burgeoning economic conditions. They can remember the Vietnam War – the first war to be broadcast nightly on television news. They changed many social institutions – from schools to pop music, from youth culture to share investment and housing prices. The younger members of this generation have not had the same employment opportunities throughout their lives, with many affected by the recessions of the late 1980s and early 1990s. Many baby boomers do not feel 'old' and most are healthy and active. They are generally healthier and more active than their predecessors at the same age. The popular press has resulted in believable narratives: 50 is the new 40; as the baby boomers age, we are hearing 70 is the new 60!

Generally, there is no fixed age for becoming an older worker. Being older or younger is often subjective. For example a 1998 survey in Australia found 62 per cent of employers considered 55-year-old employees were older workers, compared with only 32 per cent of employees who thought this (Steinberg et al., 1998). In the UK, research found the mean age of those considered 'older' was 48 years for women and 51 for men (McGoldrick & Arrowsmith, 2001). As a consequence, studies use different classifications in reports, some using 45 years, others preferring 50 or 55 years. Throughout this chapter we use the Australian Bureau of Statistics' (ABS) definition of older worker, that is, employed people aged 45 to 64 years (ABS, 2004), although since 2004 the ABS has been tracking workers older than 64.

Key concepts and context

Older workers and their continued employment are important because reproduction rates fell dramatically with the introduction of 'the pill'. Instead of an average of more than three births per woman before the mid-1960s, fertility has steadily fallen since then until it was fewer than two births per woman most recently. This is below population replacement level so that even if demand for workers does not continue to grow (which it is) there are not enough workers to replace the baby boom generation as they retire.

Organisational insight 6.1

Westpac Bank

The Westpac Group was one of the first Australian organisations to deliberately recruit older workers and has increased its focus on extending the mean retirement age and creating a better quality of life for older staff. Westpac, one of Australia's 'big four' banks, first began trading as the Bank of New South Wales in 1817, making it the first bank established in Australia. Currently it employs about 36,000 people throughout Australia, New Zealand and the near Pacific and has offices in key financial centres around the world. Westpac's recruitment policies have led to an increase of staff aged 50 years or more in the past three years, from 18 per cent in 2010 to 24 per cent currently. Workplace flexibility has been available at Westpac for many years and as the workforce ages, flexibility demands are increasing so that it now accounts for 62 per cent of all employees. This has included reduced working hours and more convenient locations.

To support its employees, the company runs a biennial Diversity and Flexibility Survey to gather feedback on age and flexibility. The 2012 survey found, for example, more focus was needed to support greater access to development opportunities, and gradual transitions to retirement. As well as the survey, Westpac has an employee action group known as Sage, which represents older workers. The Sage network provides regular input into diversity initiatives to help improve understanding of the expectations of older employees.

In 2013 a 'Prime of Life' programme was piloted with older workers and their supervisors. The programme included sessions on career, money, health and future planning, while supervisors learnt about the needs of the ageing workforce, why it was a business priority and how they could support older staff in lifestyle transition planning. The programme achieved outstanding positive feedback as participants felt valued and empowered to take action after the programme to set late career goals, undertake health and financial checks, and establish ways of transferring their knowledge to others. The success of the pilot has encouraged Westpac to develop and roll out a broader Prime of Life programme across the group. It is also creating updated resources for employees and supervisors on flexible working including toolkits to support carers. The company believes that focused strategies to engage and retain its older workforce will contribute to its overall business success, and better support the financial and personal well-being of its older employees.

The Australian economy has grown consistently for more than 20 years, which has also led to increased immigration. While this occurred, substantial structural change in the labour market led to manufacturing employment declining and service work becoming the major source of jobs (Figure 6.3). The move away from manufacturing employment and the large growth in service work is reflected in a corresponding change in the proportion of blue and white collar employees. Simultaneously, a large increase of female workers has added to white collar employment, as this term also includes growth occupations for what is sometimes called 'pink collar' workers – part-time, low paid, predominantly female (Kouzmin et al., 1999) – such as those in hospitality, child and aged care.

Less reliance on the physical capabilities often required for manufacturing jobs offers greater opportunities for older workers to remain employed. Leading up to the year 2000, early retirement was the norm (Henkens & van Dalen, 2003) with early retirement schemes growing as a social trend in developed countries over the previous 30 years. Simultaneously, many employers offered early retirement incentives to manage the size and composition of their labour force with an abundance of workers easily 'replenishing' their workforce with younger and cheaper employees (Hedge et al., 2006). Against this background, policy makers needed to convince workers and employers that baby boomers should stay in the workforce longer than previous generations.

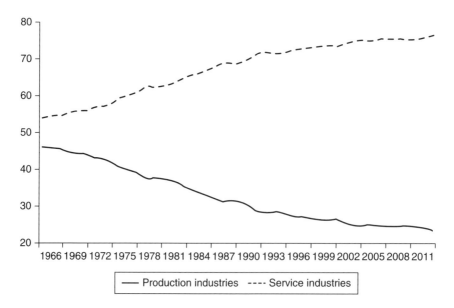

Figure 6.3   Proportion of employed people in the production and service industries – 1966–2011

Source: Australian Bureau of Statistics, 2011, *Labour Force Historical Timeseries, Australia*, cat. no. 6204.-0.55.001, *Labour Force, Australia, Detailed, Quarterly*, cat. no. 6291.0.55.003.

From the early 2000s onwards a limited number of employee studies and surveys indicated that some mature employees wanted to remain working for a variety of reasons. But there was little evidence that business identified with the need to retain or employ older workers, nor that it had taken action to capitalise on the growth of the '50 years plus' demographic. A clear lack of age diversity policies was evident among employers with little overall increase in older worker participation levels. However, policy makers regarded older worker participation and retention as an absolute necessity (Intergenerational Report, 2002).

Discussion activity 6.1

Jalna Industries, a conglomerate organisation, employs more than 500 workers in three separate strategic business units comprising spare parts, tyre manufacturing and supply, and ignition electronics. Most of the staff are located in the electronics division (250) with a ratio of one supervisor to every 20 workers. This ratio of supervisors to staff is similar in other divisions. In addition, there are three separate General Managers (GMs), one for each division, as well as a Factory Manager and a Warehouse Manager. As recently as 2014, managers have not used a formal HR department, preferring to use outsourcing for recruitment, selection and performance management systems. While the latter arrangement has saved costs, training and retention strategies have not allowed staff to grow apart from the normal on-the-job training. Additionally, a classic view of letting staff go at age 55 has been common. Since about 40 per cent of the staff are aged 45 or more and with supervisors and GMs currently aged 50 or more, this raised alarm in a recent management meeting. Supervisors have been struggling to meet shift deadlines with staff turnover in the 18–25 age group forming 25 per cent of Jalna's total workforce. According to one supervisor, staff turnover in the 35 plus age group is only 2 per cent.

What kind of age diversity policies would you say Jalna Industries follows? How would you describe the current pattern of staff development? And what kind of new age diversity policies might be relevant to reverse the current trend of worker displacement?

Policy concerns

Similar to most developed countries, Australia has been concerned for some time that the population was ageing, that the baby boom generation was approaching (historically) early retirement. The principal concern was that the cost of social security and health and aged care provisions would be more than the economy (i.e. the remaining taxpayers) could afford. The economic gap between spending and revenue by 2042 is estimated at 5 per cent of gross domestic product in the absence of major change (Intergenerational Report, 2002). It was estimated that in 2007 for each older person, there were five working-age people. In 2056 when the number of people aged 65 to 84 years is projected to reach 6.4 million, there will be fewer than three working-age people to provide taxation revenue for each retiree (ABS, 2009b).

The more recent concern was that a smaller source of labour supply would create labour and skills shortages, inhibiting Australia's economic growth. Australian government authorities began anticipating the economic cost of losing a large number of retiring workers 20 years ago. Numerous policy documents recommended that the baby boomers needed to be encouraged to remain in or re-enter the workforce; there were not sufficient numbers in the subsequent generations to replace them if they left, and an orderly transfer of corporate knowledge was vital to organisations.

The idea of encouraging older employees to stay at work was particularly encouraged by the Federal Government's first Intergenerational Report (IGR1) published in 2002 when Australia was said to be facing an 'ageing crisis'. At the time of the report, workforce participation by those aged more than 55 years was low, and the report assumed that the baby boom generation would replicate the older generations' 'traditionally' lower labour market attachment. It projected that the total participation rate would fall from 64 per cent in 2007–8 to 56 per cent participation 25 years later. Critics of this projection believed The Treasury should have taken into consideration baby boomers' greater levels of education than earlier generations. For instance, in most developed countries such as Australia, the UK and the US, classical workforce ageing models show that men started work at age 15, often working in heavy manual labour and retiring early. Forward projections of ageing also needed to consider retraining, greater experience in changing jobs, the probability of having children later in life and the need to support dependants through higher education. Baby boomers were healthier and would live longer than earlier cohorts.

The criticisms of IGR1 caused some revision of calculations when the Federal Government issued IGR2 five years later with new participation projections (Intergenerational Report, 2007). The new report was again based on conservative historical data, projecting a participation rate of 57.1 per cent. It also recognised substantially increased participation in all working age groups, particularly women. The IGR3 (Intergenerational Report, 2010) again increased the projected total participation rate to 60.06 per cent in recognition of increased migration and participation.

Socio-economic forces

When concerns were first raised about the ageing workforce, the Australian economy was booming, producing its lowest unemployment rate (4 per cent in March 2008) and highest skilled immigration in more than 30 years (Mountford, 2011). Prior to the global financial crisis (GFC) in late 2008, the older worker debate was cast more in the light of concern over labour and skills shortages and the loss of corporate memory. Industries with the largest number of older employees were predicted to suffer the most if retirement followed historical patterns. The education industry employed the highest number of mature workers in 2003–4 with 47 per cent of people in education aged 45–64 years (ABS, 2005). The health and community services industry employed the next highest proportion of older workers (42 per cent) followed by the electricity, gas and water supply industries; government administration and defence; and agriculture, forestry and fishing industries each with 41 per cent of workers aged between 45 and 64 years (ibid.). As well, there were some estimates that more than half the Australian baby boomers intending to retire early were concentrated in only six white collar occupations in which they were over-represented as a proportion of the workforce. These included occupations relating to specialist managers; science, building and engineering professionals and associate professionals; education professionals; business administration associate professionals; and secretaries and personal assistants (Jackson & Walter, 2009). This meant that these occupations would suffer significant numeric and informational losses unless older workers were encouraged to postpone early retirement while at the same time passing on their knowledge to younger workers.

Before the GFC the national participation rate (the proportion of people working in a particular age group) increased to 65 per cent in 2007, reflecting three significant developments: 1) continued growth in the female workforce aged between 25 and 54 years (largely in part-time employment), 2) levelling of the decline in male participation and 3) a rise in participation of people aged more than 55 years (Betts et al., 2007). Table 6.1 shows the substantial increases in female participation in the 20 years to 2005–6, particularly among the 45–65 age groups and the decline in male participation in all age groups except those aged 55 and older.

Table 6.1 Australian labour force participation rates by age (per cent)

	Males		Females	
Age group	1985–6	2005–6	1985–6	2005–6
15–19	61.4	58.8	60	61.3
20–24	90.4	85.5	74.9	77.9
25–34	94.8	91.4	59.3	72.5
35–44	94.7	91.4	63.1	73.6
45–54	89.9	88.1	52.2	75.9
55–64	62.0	67.0	20.8	46.1
65 +	8.9	11.9	2.4	4.2
Total	75.9	72.1	47.4	57.2

Source: Australian Bureau of Statistics, 2007, *2007 Year Book Australia*, cat. no. 1301.0.

Fearing employer pressure, the Federal Government at the time introduced a number of policy changes aimed at stimulating the labour market. It increased the age at which women could receive the age pension to the same as men (gradually from 60 to 65 years), reduced access to the Disability Support Pension and brought in 'welfare to work' programmes to encourage disabled, long-term unemployed, mature workers and single parents into the workforce. It also introduced a Mature Age Worker Tax Offset in 2004, and, from 2007, tax-free access to individual superannuation accounts after the age of 60 to make employment more attractive to intending retirees. In the past there has been little emphasis on age diversity policies such as retaining, retraining and rehiring older employees. But IGR3 (Intergenerational Report, 2010) placed greater emphasis on the availability of retraining and support services, while recognising improved older participation rates required an 'ongoing policy effort to identify and remove the barriers' for those who want to stay at work (p. 30). These included cultural (including employer) attitudes, workplace flexibility, educational attainment and parts of the tax and transfer system. Alongside IGR3, the Federal Treasurer, Wayne Swan, announced an A$43 million Productive Ageing Package comprising funding for training packages, support services and a consultative forum on mature age participation (Swan, 2010). From 2013 the then Federal Government started rolling out an A$25.8 million 'Experience + Work Ready' package to assist job seekers aged more than 50 years who were registered for work and not in the labour force. This included an annual bonus for employers of A$1,000 for each of three years and up to A$20,000 worth of resources and services for employers to recruit and retain older workers over an 18 month period. It also appointed an Advisory Panel on Positive Ageing. However, the new Liberal (conservative) Federal Government, which won power in September 2013 scrapped the Panel in late 2013 even though it had almost finished its *Blueprint for Ageing* which was to outline practical ways for Australia to take advantage of its ageing demography (Crompton and Millane, 2014). In the Government's 2014 Budget A$10,000 assistance is provided to employers who hire a registered job seeker aged 50 years or more. The amount is paid in stages over two years and the cost is estimated at A$524.8 million over four years (Restart Wage Subsidy, n.d.). The Federal Government also announced its intention to increase the pension age incrementally from 65 to 70 years by 2035. The previous Labor Government had already increased the pension age to be 67 years by 2023.

Discussion activity 6.2

Pradeep Dempassa is an Indian national, aged 52 from a rural area, who was familiar with quite serious age discrimination. As a worker from the country, he noted that urban employees were often favoured over country workers and that one's age played a key part in this. Recently, in his factory in Mumbai, his multinational

(Continued)

(Continued)

company had used its own laws for hiring and wage classifications as the Indian government allowed the company virtually 'free rein' in workplace arrangements. As long as the company was employing up to 80 per cent of Indian nationals, the State turned a blind eye to internal company matters. Since the company was mainly in the IT service industry where most staff worked up to 12 hours a day, six days a week, in long shifts, staff were already under pressure from the long hours. Coupled with this, the company decided quite suddenly to dismiss all workers who were aged 45 or more to increase productivity. Pradeep's family is entirely dependent on his income, having previously been classed as very poor. Pradeep moved to the city to take advantage of the opportunities for his family but now is facing the prospect of no income with bleak prospects for the future.

What cultural factors exist in this case, and what does that suggest about how age diversity is context specific? What role could the State play in relation to this, and what things could be done at the company level?

Retirement forces and workforce demographics

It is surprising that workforce participation among older men is lower than it was 50 years ago. The male employment rate for 45–65 year olds fell from almost 100 per cent in the 1950s to almost 50 per cent in 2000 (Kerr et al., 2002). By the early twenty-first century, early retirement had become almost standard practice for workers in the industrialised world (Henkens & van Dalen, 2003). In Australia the average age of retirement (for the pre-baby boom generation) in 1997 was 48 years, while in 2005 it was 52 years (Jackson et al., 2006).

Historically, early retirement was more common for those with the means to retire, those with poor health or laid-off workers who, often after longer than average unemployment, stopped seeking work. But early indications were that retirement patterns for the baby boomers may not follow historic patterns. Of the total number of people in the workforce aged 45 years or more in 2006, 90 per cent of them indicated in an ABS survey that they intended to retire some time, although more than 384,000 people said they would never give up work (ABS, 2006). However, almost half (47 per cent) did not know at what age they would retire. The largest group of those who did estimate their retirement age (39 per cent) planned to do so when they were aged between 65 and 69 years. Thirty-one per cent planned to retire aged 60–64 years and only 19 per cent when they were aged 55–59 years. A similar, more recent, study found that of those aged 45 years or more in the workforce, 17 per cent intended to retire at 70 years or older, 49 per cent between 65 and 69, 25 per cent between 60 and 64 years, and only 9 per cent intended to retire between 45 and

59 years (ABS, 2013) (see Table 6.2). These figures reflect the changing attitude towards earlier retirement and an intention to keep working.

Table 6.2   Retirement intentions of Australian workers aged 45 years or more in 2006 and 2013

Ages	55–59	60–64	65–69	70+
2006	19%	31%	39%	11%
2013	9%	25%	45%	17%

Source: Australian Bureau of Statistics, *Retirement and Retirement Intentions 2006 and 2013*, cat. no. 6238.0.

Estimates of future intentions are not necessarily reliable, but studies reflect a different attitude towards work and life. No definitive reasons for this apparent change of view were highlighted by various reports. However, key facts evident within the Australian Bureau of Statistics and other sources suggest that a lack of financial resources, the need to maintain an identity through work and the availability of flexible employment were possible reasons. Within these broad parameters, the amount of higher education attained, and whether partners are in work or non-work are also strongly influential (Ho & Raymo, 2009; Warren, 2008). Interestingly, one study found that 40 per cent of respondents did not want to retire until their 70s, 80s or at all (Australian Psychological Society, 2007), while another found that retirement was repugnant to baby boomers because it represented old age, disempowerment and inactivity – the antithesis of the youth culture which the boomers created (Hamilton & Hamilton, 2006). But the vast majority (90 per cent) of workers older than 45 intend to retire 'at some time'; 70 per cent of them between 60 and 69 years. The influences on retirement are grouped into individual push and pull factors listed in no particular order in Table 6.3.

Table 6.3   Factors which encourage baby boomers to stay in work

Pull factors	Push factors
Identity derived from work	Growth in the economy encouraging retention of needed staff
Abolition of a retirement age	
Improved health and fitness	Lack of restructuring and redundancies which force retirement
Satisfaction from work	
Increased age women can receive the age pension	Changing employer attitudes towards older workers
Better educated	Availability of flexible employment
Reduced access to Disability Support Pension, 'welfare to work' programmes	Mature Age Worker Tax Offset
	Superannuation 'transition to retirement' option
Family responsibilities	Simpler and tax-free superannuation access for over 60s
Need to finance current lifestyle	
Lack of financial preparedness for a comfortable retirement	

Adapted from Bartlett, 2003; Kennedy and Hedley, 2003; Murray and Syed, 2005; Kennedy and Da Costa, 2006; and Lundberg and Marshallsay, 2007.

Since 2000, older worker participation has begun a gradual upward trend which is particularly pronounced among female part-time workers. While there was only a marginal increase of older men in the Australian workforce from 1970 to 2004 (2 per cent), the number of older working women increased by 13 per cent to 52 per cent of the cohort over the same period (OECD, 2006). People aged 45–64 comprised a third of the labour force compared with 24 per cent a decade earlier.

While the indications began to mount that baby boomers wanted to stay in work, evidence suggests that it 'should be on their terms'. Retirees want to have a meaningful transition from work to retirement by (among other things): staying with their current employer; regular part-time work; casual work; work flexibility; or less-demanding jobs with a reduced range of tasks (Jackson et al., 2006). But the most important factor influencing the decision to stay at work is to pass on their knowledge to younger staff (82 per cent) (Jackson et al., 2006). Further inducements to stay working could be related to government policies such as improved taxation or superannuation (Felmingham et al., 2008), flexible work (Productivity Commission, 2005), and reduced hours or contract employment. But it is important for older workers to feel 'truly needed' for an assignment which can delay retirement by up to two years (Helman et al., 2008). The overwhelming majority of older workers want a 'phased withdrawal' from the labour market. While work flexibility generally is the single most important factor for them, more than half (61 per cent), want to work regular part-time hours ideally with their current employers (ABS, 2009c). And there needs to be greater understanding of identity, status and gender differences which influence the decision to stay at work or retire (Shacklock et al., 2009). Employers play a vital role in contributing to the retirement decision by offering or more commonly, not offering, suitable employment options.

Discussion activity 6.3

Read this statement by a senior executive:

We believe that if you are serious about diversity in practice, you have to allow people of all ages to excel. So we seem serious about policies that encourage workers to progress mostly, as training and professional development is a part of who we are. People can work right up to 65 years now and older if they want ... Having said that, I see that most new senior managers are in their 30s or early 40s ... Umm, what does that say? I guess as some of the older managers leave we are bringing in a new stock of managers. But the more I talk about it to you, the more I realise that this isn't considering a number of older worker skills, for

(Continued)

(Continued)

instance 'such and such' is an outstanding individual in her 50s but was recently overlooked by someone in her 30s.

What does this statement indicate about the level of diversity in this organisation? What contradictions exist (if any), or is the organisation simply being pragmatic?

Employers are slowly realising that changes to work structures are needed to retain staff and that baby boomers could force that change. Flexible hours are the major attraction to staying in the workforce followed by a raft of other options such as teleworking, fewer hours, job sharing, mentoring, contracting, consulting, phased retirement and a variety of leaves – some of which, such as grandparents' leave are being implemented by Australia's largest corporations (Shaw, 2007). But business consultants' surveys have consistently demonstrated that Australian employers were not prepared for the needs of an ageing workforce. Increasingly in many countries, this reflects an inadequate understanding of the potential business impact that retirements have. The literature on employers' attitudes towards retaining or hiring older workers indicates that most are not prepared for baby boomers to retire. A lack of preparedness is possibly due to a lack of interest in ageing issues or not enough immediate concern. Some scholars suggest that the business case for the retention of older workers has not been sufficiently made (Vickerstaff et al., 2007); or similarly, that employers do not want older workers (Jorgensen & Taylor, 2008a), preferring to source new hires from other sources such as poaching from competitors or skilled migration (McKeown & Teicher, 2006). Many employers exhibit short-term, ad hoc approaches to resourcing combined with a sense of complacency when not faced with an immediate staffing problem. This means that employers increasingly rely on casual labour and intensification of work. Some studies indicate that older workers are not cost effective, inflexible, slow to learn and IT illiterate compared with younger workers, and too cautious and lacking creativity. Age discrimination at work is thought not only to be common but deeply embedded and systematic even in countries such as Australia, which has had anti-discrimination legislation since 1975.

A typical example is a study of 55 US restaurant managers which indicates the value of older workers. The study found that older workers were self-motivated, disciplined and respectful of authority, had superior communication skills and credibility with customers, were dependable and loyal, created a positive image for the organisation, had an equal ability to learn skills and performed work of higher quality (Strate & Di Pietro, 2006). However, only a quarter of the managers indicated that they would prefer older workers. The researchers commented that 'This result implies that despite the fact that older workers possess characteristics that are viewed positively for management, there are perceived barriers in the organisational culture, policies and procedures when it comes to actually hiring older workers' (p. 140). Scholars believe that governments need to encourage employers to overcome stereotypes in order to retain or hire older workers (e.g. Jorgensen & Taylor, 2008b; van Dalen et al., 2010). Diversity management scholars (e.g. Ridgeway, 2009; Ely et al., 2012; Ely & Thomas, 2001) enunciate the value of learning from experiences such as the learning and integration paradigm (Thomas & Ely, 1996). Here, age diversity will be positively moderated by worker experience gained over years of employment. However, when legitimate policies in organisations reinforce inequality in age diversity policies, traditional approaches to hiring, laying-off and retirement are more likely to prevail. In any organisation, normative beliefs and expectations about diversity and its role in the workgroup (Ely & Thomas, 2001: 234) are influenced by status ranking. That is, when ageing is regarded as a status by which agents and agencies in the organisation – including human resources (HR) policies – rank performance based on age as a barrier, then age diversity will be perceived as having a negative contribution to performance. Age diversity seen in this light does little to enhance the value of older worker contributions, reinforcing barriers and stereotypes.

The generally negative view of older workers holds sway despite numerous studies illustrating advantages, including greater reliability (Patrickson & Hartmann, 1995), dependability (Taylor & Walker, 1998), loyalty (Steinberg et al., 1996) and dedication (Bennington & Tharenou, 1996), commitment (Gallie et al., 2001) and lower absenteeism (Gringart et al., 2005). Similarly, others have found that older workers have fewer accidents, a greater work ethic, lower job turnover and greater knowledge (Steinberg et al., 1998). Older workers are also considered to be more presentable, punctual, responsible and wiser (Gringart et al., 2005), to be more positive about their work, to have higher morale (Bennington & Tharenou, 1996) and to offer a good return on expenditure (Brooke, 2003; Hayward et al., 1997). Other empirical studies have found that innovation does not decline with age and that older workers have greater levels of engagement with their employer's business through job satisfaction, organisational commitment and intention to stay (Brunetto et al., 2013). Maturity improves the performance of emotional labour (Dahling & Perez, 2010) and social reasoning (sometimes called wisdom) so that it could be beneficial to assign older workers to key social roles such as legal decisions, counselling and intergroup negotiations (Grossman et al., 2010). On the other side of the coin, younger workers are seen as more flexible, IT literate and with an ability to learn more quickly. Younger workers however manage their careers by more frequently moving between organisations (Sheehan et al., 2006). Age stereotypes based on historical cultural views are largely incorrect or outdated (Ng & Feldman, 2010) and need to be challenged by effective management practices before they become self-fulfilling prophecies, with negative and damaging effects on both workers and the organisation (Buyens et al., 2009). Recently a growing number of organisations have recognised that teams or autonomous groups comprising employees of different ages have advantages over homogenous age groups (e.g. Thun et al., 2007). They can be seen as complementary or synergistic and the degree of complementarity can affect the optimum age mix of the workforce or team (Guest & Shacklock, 2005).

Organisational insight 6.2

Queensland Urban Utilities

Queensland Urban Utilities (QUU) was established in 2010 as an amalgam of water utility functions from nine local authorities. As the fourth largest water utility company in Australia, it employs about 1,171 people across south-east Queensland with half its workforce aged 45 years or more. The company decided that it needed to be proactive in retaining its older workers' skills and experience and focus on well-being and injury prevention. Given its demographics, QUU had a need to reskill its older workers, to maintain knowledge continuity, health and safety, and workforce planning. The company focused on four areas from the former Australian Government's Corporate Champions programme. They were:

1. Better understanding of its workforce demographics,
2. Supporting employees in the transition to retirement or alternative roles,
3. Being proactive in retaining staff, and
4. Providing a safe working environment.

Guided by these aims, QUU identified where its older workers were filling pivotal roles across the organisation and developed measures to safeguard their expertise. QUU implemented a number of strategies including: a well-being strategy; reviewing its injury and return-to-work policy; and building partnerships with superannuation and pension agencies to provide employees with access and support. Its programme helped it to: engage staff and management; undertake specialised analysis into its demographics and workers' compensation data; review policies and practices; develop an internal capability to think and act on the issues; develop a strategy and action plan; access specialist consulting advice; and improve outcomes for older workers. The company developed four strategies relating to its people, intellectual capital, costs and the way in which it structured work. Using its new knowledge, QUU is taking a strategic approach to its ageing workforce while simultaneously safeguarding the company's future, ensuring it does not lose invaluable corporate knowledge and experience.

Training for mature workers

Too many Australian organisations, particularly small to medium enterprises (SMEs) are said to rely on poaching talent through initial attractive salaries, rather than engaging and retaining existing workers through such methods as career planning and development, job redesign, flexible work and training (McKeown & Teicher, 2006). Career development needs to be revitalised for all age groups including baby boomers, to maintain their satisfying psychological connection with work. Organisations traditionally presumed workers over the age of 40 did not want career development assistance. However, considering the health and life expectancy of baby boomers, organisations needed to be prepared to supply career development assistance for at least a further 20 years (Callanan & Greenhaus, 2008). Organisations also need to subscribe to lifelong learning and training. In the knowledge economy, Australia has had a poor record of training, with more than a decade of funding cuts to universities and technical colleges. The country has not kept up with the level and quality of training provided by most advanced economies For example, employer training has remained static at 1.3 per cent of payroll since 1996 while the number of hours of training fell by a third over the same period (Hancock, 2006; Watson et al., 2003: 158). An Australian Institute of Management (2007) survey also showed that just over half (52.3 per cent) of large companies and less than half (45.1 per cent) of small companies had dedicated training budgets. With continuous change in technology and labour conditions and the need for lifelong learning where employees move in and out of formal and informal training beyond their first 25 years of life, training is essential to the supply of skilled, engaged and more productive employees. Organisations world-wide need to see training as an investment not a cost.

Economic change and comparative countries

In the financial year 2008–9, Australia was one of only two of the 30 OECD countries not to be in a recession; the other was Poland (OECD, 2010b). The GFC had a substantially greater impact in the US and Europe than it did in Australia. In those countries unemployment rapidly increased to almost 10 per cent whereas Australia's peaked at 5.8 per cent (ABS, 2009a). It gradually declined to 5 per cent by the end of 2010 (ABS, 2011a) compared with an OECD average of 8.3 per cent (OECD, 2010a). During recessions a common organisational response is to lay-off workers and to enter restructuring programmes to reduce overheads. Consequently, economic downturns are typically characterised by falling employment, rising unemployment and a decline in the participation rate. Older workers are often at the forefront of lay-offs and long-term unemployment, leading to 'early retirement'. In the US and Europe, the GFC (called the 'great recession' in the US – Elsby et al., 2010) caused this typical pattern, but in Australia, there was only a small rise in unemployment and an unexpected increase in the labour force participation of older workers.

The GFC also brought about an unexpected change in parts of the Australian labour market by opening up flexible opportunities by employers from which baby boomers benefited. Employers were slow to lay-off workers, believing that to reduce staff would put them at a competitive disadvantage when the economy improved. Many employers had experienced labour and skills shortages in previous years so that it was common to see 'labour hoarding' by utilising different work practices to retain skilled employees. 'Different work practices' relate to the type of flexible working conditions motivating older workers to remain in the labour market. Employers reportedly negotiated a variety of non-standard work arrangements during the GFC to reduce overheads but retain strong connections with staff. These arrangements, including reduced hours, leave taking, more part-time work and increased casualisation, were reflected in a growth in part-time jobs and reduced hours (ABS, 2011b). Throughout 2009–10 the labour participation rate for the 45–64 year age group continued to grow, particularly for the older baby boomers whose retirement savings were severely reduced by the GFC. Participation grew strongly in the 55–64 age group from 2007 to 2010, by 11.3 per cent compared with a steady rate for the middle age groups, and during the same period, a decline of 6.5 per cent for the 15–24 year age groups (ABS, 2011b). Table 6.4 shows an overall increase of more than 30 per cent in workers older than 45 years in the decade to 2013. The largest increases of 49 per cent and 34 per cent are in the 60 plus age groups, nearer the conventional retirement age. The new employment conditions such as shorter hours, job sharing and contract or block

Table 6.4   Total older worker employment in Australia 2003–13 (thousands)

December	45–54	55–59	60–64	65 +
2003	2221.6	941.2	699.4	1917.9
2004	2232.7	979.8	743.9	1981.6
2005	2287.5	1010.1	766.5	2042.8
2006	2370.0	1025.1	828.5	2104.8
2007	2409.5	1058.9	899.2	2091.9
2008	2470.4	1069.1	928.0	2111.4
2009	2413.4	1048.1	943.2	2139.0
2010	2531.4	1114.6	1010.8	2342.7
2011	2530.5	1115.3	1009.3	2404.7
2012	2574.6	1134.9	1022.1	2500.5
2013	2547.1	1144.4	1045.2	2581.0
Increase over 10 years	14.65%	21.59%	49.44%	34.57%

Source: Calculated from Australian Bureau of Statistics, 2014, *Gross Flows by State, Age, Sex, Table 1 by month and sex.*

employment, introduced by organisations to restrain costs while retaining workplace skills, were, coincidentally, preferred by older workers and were utilised by both baby boomers and employers to mutually beneficial effect.

In addition to the GFC savaging their retirement funds, many baby boomers are now forced to wait longer to access the age pension. In the 2009 budget, the Federal Government gradually increased the pension access age from 65 years to 67 years. This means that anyone born after 1957 (which includes the younger baby boomer cohort), will have to wait the additional two years before accessing a pension. This follows the US, Germany, Iceland, Norway and Denmark, which are increasing their pension age to 67, and the UK, which is increasing it to 68 years. Developed countries are responding to the need to keep their older employees in the workforce, principally for national economic reasons, but with an awareness of anticipated skills shortages.

HR management

According to older worker research, the conditions sought by employees to remain at work comprise a range of flexible work options and other supportive work practices. Flexible work options are an important work condition for retention (Mountford, 2013a; Skinner et al., 2011) but other HR practices also contribute to staff retention. Previous research has not found consistent priorities among these HR practices but studies of workers find a number of consistent practices. They are: 1) the need for a supportive working environment, 2) recognition of skills, 3) availability of training with career paths, and 4) the opportunity to pass on knowledge to younger workers (Mountford, 2013b).

The need for flexible work is particularly important for older women sandwiched as they are with their care-giving between ageing parents and their adult children (many of whom still live at home) and grandchildren. The combination of baby boomers delaying childbirth, the delayed financial independence of their children and increased life expectancy of the older generation has seen the emergence of the multi-generational household. To balance these demands, flexible work is seen as the logical option. A US study of baby boomer employees confirmed earlier studies by finding that the top five flexible work options are: taking breaks, taking time off, regular scheduled shifts, moving work location (e.g. telecommuting vs the office) and modifying starting/finishing times (Pitt-Catsouphes et al., 2009). These work options appear to fit with the new working conditions recently introduced by some Australian employers.

Cross-cultural comparisons: China and Australia

The contrast between Australia and China is extreme. Australia has a population of only 23 million people. China has a population of 1.35 billion. Not surprisingly, the labour market contrast in each country is significant – 11.5 million of working age in

Australia, 767 million in China – which was a decline of 3.45 million in 2012 over 2011, the first time that the Chinese working age population has decreased (China Labour Bulletin, 2013). As well, the Chinese population is ageing. Figures from China's 2010 Census indicate that the number of people aged 60 years and more has grown from 10.3 per cent of the total population in 2000 to 13.3 per cent, while the future workforce (those aged 14 years or less) has dropped from 23 per cent of the population to 16.6 per cent (Giles et al., 2012). By the end of 2050, one-fifth to one-third of China's population will be aged 65 and over. The demographic dividend is expected to continue in the next 10 to 20 years depending on future fertility, which, in turn, is determined by changes in China's one-child policy (Mai et al., 2013).

Not only is there a significant difference in labour market size, but culturally, there is little similarity between the two countries. Australia is a typical Western nation with social security, unemployment benefits, age pensions and other forms of welfare. China's social welfare, especially for the elderly was based on two pillars – the state-owned enterprises which provided employment, health care and pensions, and the traditional belief of parents that their children would care for them as they aged. But the reform of state-owned enterprises and the rise of the private economy whereby life-time employment was replaced with labour contracts, plus the enforcement of a strict family planning policy reducing the number of children, has brought about immense societal change. Traditionally, older people were a 'treasure of the family' and could expect to be cared for, but China's one-child policy has left many couples with responsibility for four parents and eight grandparents.

The change in employment conditions is particularly highlighted in differences between urban and rural workers. Those in the formal, urban, employment sector can expect to receive a pension when they retire at the mandatory age of 55 for women and 60 for men (Giles et al., 2012). China's rural workforce is much more likely to be employed in agricultural production into old age as they are unlikely to have pensions. Chinese urban employment also sees higher rates of exit from the workforce in the 40s and 50s. Age discrimination is deeply ingrained in the Chinese workplace and the unskilled and low skilled particularly find it difficult to find work after the age of 40. Labour shortages in urban east-coast factories have caused improved wages and working conditions, or relocation to cheaper labour cost centres in South East Asia for large factories, but smaller businesses are struggling to attract migrant workers and have little option but to take on older workers to fill the gap (China Labour Bulletin, 2013).

While Chinese policy makers are aware of the country's changing demographics and are loosening its one-child policy, they have yet to actively encourage the retention of older workers.

Summary and recommendations

Traditional human resource practices, often characterised by generic programmes, are giving way to more sophisticated, individual methods of talent management. This type of management particularly suits older workers. Enlightened employers will recognise that baby boomers want to work, or have to do so, and that they have other priorities as well. The availability of more flexible work options suits older workers' lifestyles. It also increases their work motivation (Stead, 2009). At the same time, flexible work provides employers with, on the one hand, skill retention and cost containment, and on the other, employees with attributes they value, such as job-specific skills, experience, loyalty, reliability, productivity and corporate memory, which will be willingly passed on.

The benefits of flexible ageing policies in organisations coupled with the reality of socio-economic planning, including micro-economic interventions by governments, requires an integrated approach from one country to the next. While Australia has addressed many ageing strategies and policies as the population ages, there is much work to be done at the institutional or macro level, the meso or organisational level, and the micro or community level (Syed & Özbilgin, 2009). At the institutional level particularly, governments, and state and Federal agencies need to work to ensure that fiscal policies uniformly assist the long-term unemployed (which comprises a majority of older workers) and that return-to-work schemes encourage recruitment by employers. Across countries in Europe, the US and China for instance, populations are getting older, meaning that the ratio of younger workers supporting a large percentage of older workers will have implications for policy settings. Similar to the intergenerational support described in this chapter, countries need to start to predict the demographic constraints and implications of losing key skills together with the earlier retirement of older workers. Organisations will need to work in concert with governments to ensure that diversity policies are increasingly flexible. This means the introduction (and intervention) of flexible work practices such as those outlined. Following increases of the retirement age in many countries, organisational policies need to close the gap between structural change and workforce reality. The truth is that every country cannot turn a blind eye to an increasingly ageing workforce and the benefits they bring.

Discussion questions

1. In Table 6.1, the labour force participation rate has increased for women as a cohort in the 55-64 age group from 20.8 per cent in 1985-6 to 46.1 per cent in 2005-6. What does this indicate about age diversity? What kind of change(s) has occurred in company policies to allow this to occur and why?

2. Government fiscal policy in developed countries at least appears to counter the 'pull' factors that leave countries vulnerable to skill deficiencies as baby boomers leave the workforce in greater numbers than new workers enter. What kind of 'push' factors provides answers for policy makers? For organisations? For individuals?

(Continued)

(Continued)

3. Some popular narratives often heard on radio stations talk in ways that denigrate older or mature workers with phrases such as 'that old dude', he is 'so old' and 'all older workers are slow'. Since narrative is very much about strategy to create a believable plot, what social forces need to change towards older workers in society? In schools? In organisations?

4. Go online and find a Fortune 500 company. Now, check out their website. Look for the company's diversity management policy – search as many companies as you need until you find one. What does the site say about diversity? What does it say about age diversity? If it doesn't say anything much about age diversity, what does this indicate about diversity management practices within the company? Contact the company to see how much they are prepared to send you. Discuss what this exercise suggests to you about diversity management.

CASE STUDY

Sydney nursing homes

A recent case study of Sydney aged care facilities (ACFs) (nursing homes) has found that most are providing human resource practices and procedures that studies have shown older workers want, probably because they are staffed by a high proportion of older workers. The provision of these working conditions leads to long-term staff retention in a generally low-paid occupation. Many of the practices could be adopted by other industries.

In a qualitative study of ACFs comprising interviews with 20 Facility Managers (FMs) and 20 Personal Carers (PCs), it was evident that ACFs provided their mainly permanent, part-time, female workforce with flexible work options and a range of supportive work practices. ACFs operate 24/7/365 and provide long-term residential nursing care. In Australia, like most developed countries, aged care is a growing industry with a shortage of labour – demand for which, as a share of the working population, is set to increase by 140 per cent by 2050 as the population ages (OECD, 2011). In 2007 about 60 per cent of care staff in ACFs were aged more than 45 years compared with 37 per cent of the Australian workforce.

(Continued)

(Continued)

This study (Mountford, 2013a, 2013b) is believed to be the first qualitative research into human resource practices in ACFs and found that despite poor pay and what is seen as 'dirty work', many ACFs retained their staff for many years through a combination of flexible work, lack of age discrimination in hiring, modifications to work methods and equipment, and education, in a supportive workplace environment. Flexible work options are becoming recognised as a significant strategy for attracting and retaining older workers, although they are also attractive to all staff. In a multi-generational study of more than 2,000 people, Pitt-Catsouphes et al. (2009) categorised flexible work options into five major groups:

1. The number of hours worked (including part-time, part-year, job share, phased retirement and input into overtime),
2. Flexible schedules (shift choices, changes in start or quitting times),
3. Flexible place (location options, such as working from home),
4. Options for time off (short or extended for personal reasons such as care responsibilities, study, volunteering), and
5. Other options (such as control over timing of breaks, transferring to a job with reduced responsibility and pay).

By the very nature of the work, care in ACFs needs to be undertaken on the premises – so the only workplace flexibility option not appropriate to this study was flexibility of place.

Specifically, the flexibilities here are divided into four groups:

1. Choice of which and the number of days worked,
2. Choice of length of shift (hours),
3. A supervisor's discretion to accommodate short-term changes, and
4. Phased retirement and recalls to return.

Two flexible work choices particularly attract employees to ACFs – the selection of which days to work and the length of the shift. Most direct care workers are employed on a permanent part-time (PPT) basis. The flexibility of selecting their own regular shifts is a major attraction for care staff who are predominantly female and have family responsibilities such as children, grandchildren or ageing relatives. Initially, new PCs are asked to work a variety of shifts as casuals, but after they have established themselves as

(Continued)

(Continued)

competent and reliable and become PPT, they can elect which days to work. ACFs are also attractive to Registered Nurses (RNs) because the shifts can be chosen and are fixed, unlike hospitals where shifts are rotated. Because ACFs operate 24/7, there are many different shifts at different times of the day or night. Few nursing homes now operate the formerly standard three, eight-hour shifts a day, and in this study, while the average number of different shifts available to PCs was seven, one home operated 20 different shifts. The larger facilities offered a greater variety of shift lengths – eight, six or four hours each. The shorter shifts particularly appeal to older workers. The shorter shifts also allowed employer flexibility, enabling extra staffing at peak times during the day.

Employee flexibility engenders loyalty and job satisfaction (Chou & Robert, 2008). The opportunity to change regular shift days, or the length of a shift, or pick up an additional shift is widespread and important to retention (Moskos & Martin, 2005). The need for change may be brought about by one-off occurrences or semi-permanent change. All PCs in this study confirmed the ease of changing or downsizing shifts either formally (with a form) or informally (verbal request).

Supervisor's flexibility

An important part of employee flexibility is the supervisor's attitude towards a worker's request to adjust work time for family needs (Katz et al., 2011). Research in hospitals has found immediate line managers play a crucial role in making flexible work available and the relationship with the supervisor impacts firstly on the subordinate's morale, which then impacts on a nurse's commitment to their institution and well-being. Supervisor flexibility is common in aged care facilities, with emphasis on informal family-friendly policies. The work flexibility culture appears industry wide and contributes to low sick leave and staff turnover, lower costs through the reduced need for temporary agency staff, recruitment and training, and greater retention, providing stability of care for the residents. All facilities in this study had low staff turnover and most claimed to have low sick leave. In 2007 national annual staff turnover was 25 per cent for PCs and 20 per cent for RNs (Martin & King, 2008). FMs in this study estimated international students on average stayed about two to three years. Nursing students would work as PCs for up to seven years, then

(Continued)

(Continued)

graduate, and PCs in the middle and older years were the long-term staff – 10 years plus. The longest serving PC interviewed in this study had been in aged care for 34 years while three others had worked in ACFs for 30 years and another for 28 years.

Forms of retirement

It is generally uncommon in business for employees and supervisors to discuss the former's retirement plans in advance, making workforce planning difficult. Research on the topic is very limited and this was reflected in this study, with FMs waiting for direct care workers to announce their retirement. The PCs based this decision on a number of factors such as family demands, financial needs and their physical capabilities. Every PC in this study thought they would determine their own retirement age, commonly in their 60s, but often at an indeterminate time when their health was inadequate to continue.

Phased retirement is a strongly desired option by older workers and in the AFCs this was accommodated by a reduction in the number of shifts (days) and/or shorter shifts. It was common practice. Notice of the need to change was often lengthy – weeks, months or a year. FMs welcomed lengthy notice as it allowed for easier workforce planning and maintained morale. None of the FM interviewees would replace a direct care worker who had said they planned to retire, until they retired. They saw little point in replacing an experienced, competent worker with a new PC who would need training. Such a move would also affect morale. A lengthy notice of retirement also provided the opportunity for an experienced staff member to mentor others before they left.

Research indicates that many retired staff would welcome the opportunity to return to their work place, often on a casual or project basis. Retired staff can be brought in for peak demand times or one-off needs without the 'on boarding' costs of a temporary or contract worker because they know the culture and operating procedures of the organisation (Cappelli & Novelli, 2010). FMs in this study considered staff members who were retiring as a future pool of employees. They actively encouraged retiring direct care workers to join the facility's casual staff list or tried to find other useful positions or mentoring roles for them.

(Continued)

(Continued)

Supportive work practices

A supportive work environment is key to many practices which attract and retain employees by making them feel valued and heard, but by also providing a sense of autonomy and independence. It contributes to a high level of satisfaction, performance and retention (Jeon et al., 2010). While increased work intensity in aged care can reduce job satisfaction, supervisor and co-worker support can help mitigate it. ACFs do give a supportive working environment organisationally through supervisor empathy and co-worker support, in addition to small 'appreciation' practices such as thank you cards or bought-in food for special days. As well, above-award wages, modified work methods and retirement planning contribute.

The principal support came from PCs' supervisors – mainly the FMs who managed day-to-day operations. FMs are usually registered nurses who have 'come up through the ranks' and manage a single facility. Because of their own experience (juggling work and family) they are sympathetic to staff needs. Consequently, they build relationships which lead to staff trust and loyalty. To encourage the relationships, all FMs had 'open-door' policies and encouraged staff to express their views whether personal or professional. According to Timmons et al. (2011) among others, open-door policies are critical to workplace policy development for older workers.

Among the interviewees, co-workers were often seen as friends or family. The work relationships helped sustain emotional well-being, which is particularly important for care work which involves high levels of emotional labour. They also enjoyed the way the work is carried out – usually in teams of two or more.

Another supportive practice instituted at ACFs is job redesign. As their labour force has aged, FMs have reviewed their work practices and designed shorter shifts, fewer shifts and alternative shifts with lighter loads. Mandatory, no-lift policies are widespread with residents being moved by 'people lifters' and two staff. Wind-up beds are being replaced with electric ones and are greatly appreciated. New door and chair sensors alert staff when residents move about unexpectedly and clinical reporting is becoming computerised to reduce paperwork. Some medication trolleys have been redesigned to be smaller and lighter, or motorised, and the size of deliveries of chemicals and paper products is being made smaller, but more frequent. Linen bags have been made smaller and lighter.

(Continued)

(Continued)

Appreciation and rewards, both formal and informal, are widespread. They range from awards nights to movie passes or a coffee voucher for work which was 'above and beyond' what was expected. Some rewards are formalised in HR policies, many are not and are at the discretion of the FMs who use them frequently. The informal group includes regular barbeques and bought-in meals, celebrations for special days, birthday flowers, chocolates or presents and cards, and a variety of small gifts as one-off recognition (see Table 6.5). The FMs are aware of the effect on morale and productivity of these small tokens of appreciation.

The rewards also facilitated the 'recognition and respect' and the need to feel valued that research has found older workers want (Armstrong-Stassen, 2008). As well, FMs recognised staff contributions through formal work committees and informal discussions and, for example, testing new equipment on the floor, before deciding to purchase it. As most staff are paid the basic award wage, above award payment for key individuals and one-off bonuses for a shift which is short staffed, are also utilised.

Training with career paths is often not available for older workers. But, by being able to update their skills, older workers gain greater organisational support and work satisfaction which contributes to their retention (Armstrong-Stassen & Ursel, 2009). In aged care, Federal Government subsidies have encouraged widespread training and lifted the entry level for PCs to a Certificate 3 in Aged Care, whereas these staff were previously considered 'unskilled'. Experienced PCs are commonly upgrading to Certificate 4, which allows them to distribute a restricted range of medications and dress wounds. Training is available to all staff regardless of age. A large increase in the availability of training has helped PCs' morale. All the FMs in this study were enthusiastic about the availability and level of education for all staff and also saw it as an important retention factor. As well as numerous optional topics, regular mandatory training is required. PCs are also encouraged to enrol in nursing degrees with shifts adjusted to the university timetable.

Many experienced personnel want to pass on their knowledge to others (Jackson et al., 2006) and to facilitate this need, ACFs often 'buddy' older with new staff to become mentors before they retire. They can also return on a casual basis on regular shifts or for a fixed term while other staff are on holidays.

(Continued)

(Continued)

Table 6.5   Staff benefits in ACFs

Formal	Informal
Above-award payments	Barbeques
Bonuses	Birthday cards, presents, cakes
Carer's leave	Café vouchers
Education: in-service and external	Children of staff allowed at work in school holidays
Education scholarships	Chinese tapping therapy
Extra week's leave for over 45 year olds	Chocolates
Grief counselling	Christmas day (all meals)
In charge, on call loadings	Christmas gift or shopping voucher
Length of service recognition	Christmas hamper
No-lift policy	Christmas in July parties
Packaged staff benefits plan including discounts for health fund, telecom, cable TV, computer purchase	Christmas parties
	Counselling (personal)
Paid maternity/paternity leave	Flexible shifts
Rostered day off (full-time staff)	Flexible hours
Salary packaging (charities only)	Flowers
Shift allowances	Free meals or at nominal cost
Staff awards night	Gift vouchers
Staff newsletter	International days' celebrations
Strict enforcement of OH&S rules	International Nurses' Day (all meals)
Uniforms	Job redesign
Vaccinations	Laughter therapy
	Management open-door policy
	Massage therapy
	Lottery tickets
	Meditation
	Melbourne Cup celebrations
	Movie tickets
	New Year parties
	Non-documented sick leave
	On-site café
	On-site gym, hydrotherapy pool
	One-off shift allowance
	Recognition gifts
	Relaxation therapy
	Short shifts
	Supply of takeaway meals
	Thank you notes, cards

Source: Mountford (2013b) *Asia Pacific Journal of Human Resources*, 51: 272–91 from author's interviews. This is a consolidated list from all ACFs in the study. None offered all of these staff benefits, but many offered a large number of them.

(Continued)

(Continued)

Conclusion

ACFs are a good example of what employers are able to do to attract and retain older workers. Most important is flexibility – both formal and informal – through a supervisor's discretion. A wide variety of supportive work practices are also important to attract, retain, increase loyalty, minimise sick days and reduce staff turnover – particularly in the face of low wages and 'dirty work'. Interestingly, all the working conditions mentioned above were available to all staff – not just older workers, although they particularly appreciated them.

Question

The case study reflects the best outcome of aged care needs in aged-care facilities with the pragmatic needs of older workers. The push–pull factors, formal and informal staff benefits also have to be considered in the light of the growing gap in future years of baby-boomer retirements and new entrant workers. Coupled with these facts is that most organisations, not only in Australia but around the world, do not possess strategic age-diversity practises, meaning that human resource policies inadequately reflect the importance of knowledge assets and people.

Given these realities, *do some research about life in your country of origin 50 years ago and life today.* In order to draw conclusions about age diversity, obtain facts about changing demographics then and now. How do these changes influence older worker policies? Then, draw a table of the push–pull factors/formal–informal staff benefits that were offered then and now. Compare these tables with similar tables outlined in the chapter case study. What did you find? What are the critical general demographic changes?

 Further reading

Bal, P.M., Kooij, D. and Rousseau, D. (eds) 2014, *Aging workers and the employee-employer relationship*, Springer, Cham, Switzerland.

Baruch, Y., Sayce, S. and Gregoriou, A. 2014, 'Retirement in a global labour market: a call for abolishing the fixed retirement age', *Personnel Review*, 43(3): 464–82.

Cheng, Z., Smyth, R. and Guo, F. 2014, 'The impact of China's new labour contract law on socioeconomic outcomes for migrant and urban workers', *Human Relations*, published online 27 October 2014, DOI: 10.1177/0018726714543480.

Crowne, K., Cochran, J. and Carpenter, C. 2014, 'Older-worker-friendly policies and affective organizational commitment', *Organization Management Journal*, 11(2): 62–73, DOI: 10.1080/15416518.2014.925389.

Eichhorst, W., Galasso, V., Boeri, T., Kendzia, M., de Con, A. and Steiber, N. 2013, *How to combine the entry of young people in the labour market with the retention of older workers?* Discussion Paper No. 7829, IZA, Bonn.

References

Armstrong-Stassen, M. 2008, 'Human resource practices for mature workers – and why aren't employers using them?', *Asia Pacific Journal of Human Resources*, 46: 334–52.

Armstrong-Stassen, M. & Ursel, N. 2009, 'Perceived organizational support, career satisfaction and the retention of older workers', *Journal of Occupational and Organizational Psychology*, 82: 201–220.

Australian Bureau of Statistics (ABS) 2004, *Australian Social Trends, 2004*, cat. no. 4102.0, ABS, Canberra.

Australian Bureau of Statistics (ABS) 2005, *Year Book, Australia, 2005*, cat. no. 1301.0, ABS, Canberra.

Australian Bureau of Statistics (ABS) 2006, *Retirement and Retirement Intentions Australia* cat. no. 6238.0, ABS, Canberra.

Australian Bureau of Statistics (ABS) 2009a, *ANZCO, Australian and New Zealand Standard Classification of Occupations*, first edition, revision 1, cat. no. 1220.0, ABS, Canberra.

Australian Bureau of Statistics (ABS) 2009b, *Australian Social Trends*, cat. no. 4102.0, ABS, Canberra.

Australian Bureau of Statistics (ABS) 2009c, *Australian Social Trends*, cat. no. 4102.0, ABS, Canberra.

Australian Bureau of Statistics (ABS) 2011a, *Labour Force, Australia, Dec 2010*, cat. no. 6202.0, ABS, Canberra.

Australian Bureau of Statistics (ABS) 2011b, *Fifty Years of Labour Force: Now and Then, Australian Labour Market Statistics, Oct 2011*, cat. no. 6105.0, ABS, Canberra.

Australian Bureau of Statistics (ABS) 2013, *Retirement and Retirement Intentions Australia 2006 and 2013*, cat. no. 6238.0, ABS, Canberra.

Australian Institute of Management 2007, *National Salary Survey*, viewed 11 April 2014, www.aim.com.au/publications/salarysurvey.html

Australian Psychological Society 2007, *Attitudes towards ageing: A survey conducted by the Australian Psychological Society*, viewed 23 April 2008, http://www.psychologyweek.com.au/

Bartlett, H. 2003, 'An ageing perspective', *Foresight*, 5(6): 26–33.

Bennington, L. & Tharenou, P. 1996, 'Older workers: myths, evidence and implications for Australian managers', *Asia Pacific Journal of Human Resources*, 34(3): 63–76.

Betts, T., Connolly, E. & Orsmond, D. 2007, 'Trends in employment and labour supply', *Reserve Bank of Australia Bulletin*, September: 1–7.

Brooke, L. 2003, 'Human resource costs and benefits of maintaining a mature-age workforce', *International Journal of Manpower*, 24(3): 260–83.

Brunetto, Y., Shriberg, A., Farr-Wharton, R., Shacklock, K., Newman, S. & Dienger, J. 2013, 'The importance of supervisor–nurse relationships, teamwork, wellbeing, affective commitment and retention of North American nurses', *Journal of Nursing Management*. http://dx.doi.org/10.1111/jonm.12111

Buyens, D., Van Dijk, H., Dewilde, T. & De Vos, A. 2009, 'The aging workforce: perceptions of career ending', *Journal of Managerial Psychology*, 24: 102–17.

Callanan, G. & Greenhaus, J. 2008, 'The baby boom generation and career management: a call to action', *Advances in Developing Human Resources*, 10(1): 70–85.

Cappelli, P. & Novelli, B. 2010, *Managing the Older Worker: How to Prepare for the New Organizational Order*, Harvard Business Press, Boston.

China Labour Bulletin 2013, viewed 29 January 2014, www.clb.org.hk/en/content/employment-china

Crompton, E. & Millane, E. 2014, 'Ageing blueprint back on track – panel re-formed outside govt', *Crikey*, 12 February 2014, viewed 10 April 2014, www.crikey.com.au/2014/02/12/ageing-blueprint-back-on-track-panel-reformed-outside-govt/

Dahling, J. & Perez, L. 2010, 'Older worker, different actor? Linking age and emotional labor strategies', *Personality and Individual Differences*, 48: 574–8.

Elsby, M., Hobijn, B. & Sahin, A. 2010, 'The labor market in the great recession', *Brookings Papers on Economic Activity*, Spring: 1–48.

Ely, R. & Thomas, D. 2001, 'Cultural diversity at work: the effects of diversity perspectives on work group processes and outcomes', *Administrative Science Quarterly*, 46: 229–73.

Ely, R., Padavic, I. & Thomas, D. 2012, 'Racial diversity, racial asymmetries, and team learning environment: effects on performance', *Organization Studies*, 33(3): 341–62.

Felmingham, B., Jackson, N., Walter, M. & Yan, H. 2008, 'Australian early retirement tax biases prior to July 2007 and the likely effects of tax reform on retirement plans', *Economic Papers*, 27: 250–64.

Feyrer, J. 2007, 'Demographics and productivity', *The Review of Economics and Statistics*, 89(1): 100–9.

Gallie, D., Felstead, A. & Green, F. 2001, 'Employer policies and organizational commitment in Britain 1992–97', *Journal of Management Studies*, 38: 1081–101.

Giles, J., Wang, D. & Cai, W. 2012, 'The labour supply and retirement behavior of China's older workers and elderly in comparative perspective' in J. Smith and M. Majmundar (eds) *Aging in Asia*, Committee on Population, Division of Behavioral and Social Sciences Education, The National Academic Press, Washington, DC.

Gringart, E., Helmes, E. & Speelman, C. 2005, 'Exploring attitudes toward older workers among Australian employers: an empirical study', *Journal of Aging and Social Policy*, 17(3): 85–103.

Grossman, I., Na, J., Varnum, M., Park, D., Kitayama, S. & Nisbett, R. 2010, 'Reasoning about social conflicts improves into old age', *PNAS*, 107: 7246–50.

Guest, R. & Shacklock, K. 2005, 'The impending shift to an older mix of workers: perspectives from the management and economics literature', *International Journal of Organisational Behaviour*, 10: 713–28.

Hamilton, M. & Hamilton, C. 2006, *Baby Boomers and Retirement: Dreams, Fears and Anxieties*, Discussion paper 89, The Australia Institute, Manuka, ACT.

Hancock, L. 2006, 'Mature workers, training and using TLM frameworks', *Australian Bulletin of Labour*, 32(30): 257–79.

Hayward, B., Taylor, S., Smith, N. & Davies, G. 1997, *Evaluation of the Campaign for Older Workers*, Her Majesty's Stationery Office, London (cited in Brooke & Taylor, 2005).

Hedge, J., Borman, W. & Lammlein, S. 2006, *The Aging Workforce: Realities, Myths and Implications for Organizations*, American Psychological Association, Washington, DC.

Helman, R., Copeland, C., VanDerhei, J. & Salisbury, D. 2008, 'Recent retirees' survey: report of findings', *EBRI Issue Brief 319*, Employee Benefit Research Institute, Washington, DC.

Henkens, K. & van Dalen, P. 2003, 'Early retirement systems and behaviour in an international perspective', in G. Adams and T. Beehr (eds), *Retirement: Reasons, Processes and Results*, Springer Publishing Company, New York.

Ho, J. & Raymo, J. 2009, 'Expectations and realization of joint retirement among dual-worker couples', *Research on Aging*, 31: 153–79.

Intergenerational Report (IGR1) 2002, 2002–03 Budget Paper number 5, Commonwealth of Australia, Canberra.

Intergenerational Report (IGR2) 2007, Commonwealth of Australia, Canberra.

Intergenerational Report (IGR3) 2010, Commonwealth of Australia, Canberra.

Jackson, N. 2007, 'Population ageing in a nutshell: a phenomenon in four dimensions', *People and Place*, 159(2): 12–21.

Jackson, N. & Walter, M. 2009, 'Retirement intentions of Australia's baby boomers: an occupational overview', *Australian Survey of Retirement Attitudes and Motivations, Research Project 4*, University of Tasmania, Hobart.

Jackson, N., Walter, M. & Felmingham, B. 2006, *Will Australia's Baby Boomers Change their Retirement Plans in Line with Government Thinking? Key Points from ASRAM*, Australian Survey of Retirement Attitudes and Motivations, Research Project 1, University of Tasmania, Hobart.

Jeon, Y., Merlyn, T. & Chenoweth, L. 2010, 'Leadership and management in the aged care sector: a narrative synthesis', *Australasian Journal on Ageing*, 29(2): 54–60.

Jorgensen, B. & Taylor, P. 2008a, 'Older workers, government and business: implications for ageing populations of a globalising economy', *Economic Affairs*, March: 17–22.

Jorgensen, B. & Taylor, P. 2008b, 'Employees, employers and the institutions of work: the global competition for terrain in the ageing workforce agenda', *Foresight*, 10: 22–36.

Katz, R., Lowenstein, A., Prilutzky, D. & Halperin, D. 2011, 'Employers' knowledge and attitudes regarding organizational policy toward workers caring for aging family members', *Journal of Aging & Social Policy*, 23: 159–81.

Kennedy, S. & Da Costa, A. 2006, 'Older men bounce back: the re-emergence of older male workers', *Economic Roundup*, Spring: 31–43.

Kennedy, S. & Hedley, D. 2003, 'Educational attainment and labour force participation in Australia', *Economic Roundup*, Winter: 27–41.

Kerr, L., Carson, E. & Goddard, J. 2002, 'Contractualism, employment services and mature-age job seekers: the tyranny of tangible outcomes', *The Drawing Board*, 3: 83–104.

Kouzmin, A., Korac-Kakabadse, N. & Korac-Kakabadse, A. 1999, 'Globalization and information technology: vanishing social contacts, the "pink collar" workforce and public policy challenges', *Women in Management Review*, 6(4): 230–51.

Lundberg, D. & Marshallsay, Z. 2007. *Older Workers' Perspective on Training and Retention of Older Workers*, National Centre for Vocational Education Research, Adelaide, SA.

Mai, Y., Peng, X. & Chen, W. 2013, 'How fast is the population ageing in China?', *Asian Population Studies*, 9(2): 216–39.

Martin, B. & King, D. 2008, *Who Cares for Older Australians? A Picture of the Residential and Community Based Aged Care Workforce 2007*, National Institute of Labour Studies, Adelaide, SA.

McGoldrick, A. & Arrowsmith, J. 2001, 'Discrimination by age: the organizational response', in I. Glover and M. Branine (eds), *Ageism in Work and Employment*, Ashgate, Aldershot.

McKeown, T. & Teicher, J. 2006, 'Human resource development in a deregulated environment' in P. Holland and H. De Cieri (eds), *Contemporary Issues in Human Resource Development*, Pearson Education, Frenchs Forest, NSW.

Moskos, M. & Martin, B. 2005, *What's Best, What's Worst? Direct Carers' Work in Their Own Words*, National Institute of Labour Studies, Adelaide, SA.

Mountford, H. 2011, 'Oh won't you stay just a little bit longer: changing employers' views of older workers', *Australian Bulletin of Labour*, 37: 164–90.

Mountford, H. 2013a, 'Let's hang on to what we've got: flexible work options and the retention of older workers in Australia', *Journal of Business and Management Research*, 2: 88–100. doi:10.5430/bmr.v2n4p88

Mountford, H. 2013b, 'I'll take care of you: the use of supportive work practices to retain older workers', *Asia Pacific Journal of Human Resources*, 51: 272–91. doi:10.1111/j.1744-7941.2012.00048.x

Mountford, H. & Murray, P. 2011, Theoretical perspectives of older workers: integrating human resource management practices with resource-based strategies, in R. Ennals and R. Salomon (eds), *Older Workers in a Sustainable Society*, Peter Lang, Frankfurt, pp. 43–55.

Munnell, A., Sass, S. & Soto, M. 2006. *Employer Attitudes towards Older Workers: Survey Results. Issue in Brief*, Center of Retirement Research at Boston College, Chestnut Hill, MA.

Murray, P. & Syed, J. 2005, 'Critical issues in managing age diversity in Australia', *Asia Pacific Journal of Human Resources*, 43(2): 210–24.

Ng, T. & Feldman, D. 2010, 'The relationship of age with job attitudes: a meta-analysis', *Personnel Psychology*, 63: 677–717.

OECD 2006, *Live Longer, Work Longer: Ageing and Employment Policies*, Organisation for Economic Co-operation and Development, Paris.

OECD 2010a, *OECD Economic Outlook No. 88*, Organisation for Economic Co-operation and Development, Paris.

OECD 2010b, 'Return to work after the crisis', *OECD Economic Outlook Volume 2010/1*, Organisation for Economic Co-operation and Development, Paris, pp. 251–92.

OECD 2011, *OECD Stat Extracts, Labour Force Statistics*, viewed 11 April 2014, http://stats.oecd.org/index.aspx?queryid=251

Patrickson, M. & Hartmann, L. 1995, 'Australia's ageing population: implications for human resource management', *International Journal of Manpower*, 16(5/6): 34–46.

Pitt-Catsouphes, M., Matz-Costa, C. & Besen, E. 2009, *Workplace Flexibility: Findings from the Age & Generations Study*, Sloan Center on Aging & Work at Boston College, Boston, MA.

Productivity Commission 2005, *Economic Implications of an Ageing Australia*, research report, Commonwealth of Australia, Canberra, ACT.

Productivity Commission 2013, *Forms of Work*, Staff Working Paper, Commonwealth of Australia, Canberra, ACT.

Quiggin, J. 2001, 'Demography and the new economy', *Journal of Population Research*, 18(2): 177–93.

Restart Wage Subsidy n.d., Department of Employment, viewed 7 August 2014, http://employment.gov.au/restart-wage-subsidy.

Ridgeway, C. 2009, 'Framed before we know it: How gender shapes social relations', *Gender & Society*, 23(2): 145–60.

Shacklock, K., Brunetto, Y. & Nelson, S. 2009, 'The different variables that affect older males' and females' intentions to continue working', *Asia Pacific Journal of Human Resources*, 47(1): 79–101.

Shaw, M. 2007, 'Bank offers grandparents leave', *The Sydney Morning Herald*, 8 June 2007: 3.

Sheehan, C., Holland, P. & De Cieri, H. 2006, 'Current developments in HRM in Australian organisations', *Asia Pacific Journal of Human Resources*, 44: 132–52.

Skinner, N., van Dijk, P., Elton, J. & Auer, J. 2011, 'An in-depth study of Australian nurses' and midwives' work–life interaction', *Asia Pacific Journal of Human Resources*, 49(2): 213–32.

Stead, N. 2009, 'The effect of age and gender on motivation to work', *Proceedings of the 8th Industrial and Organisational Psychology Conference*, 25–28 June, Sydney, NSW, pp. 129–33.

Steinberg, M., Donald, K., Najman, J. & Skerman, H. 1996, 'Attitudes of employees and employers towards older workers in a climate of anti-discrimination', *Australasian Journal on Ageing*, 15(4): 154–8.

Steinberg, M., Walley, L., Tyman, R. & Donald, K. 1998, 'Too old to work?', in M. Patrickson and L. Hartman (eds), *Managing an Ageing Workforce*, Business and Professional Publishing, Warriewood, NSW.

Strate, M. & Di Pietro, R. 2006, 'Management perceptions of older employees in America's restaurant industry', in T. Rocco and J. Thijssen (eds), *Older Workers, New Directions. Employment and Development in an Ageing Labor Market*, Center for Labor Research and Studies, Florida International University, Miami, FL.

Swan, W. 2010, 'Harnessing the skills and experience of older Australians: Rudd government launches $43.3 million productive ageing package', Media Release no. 011, viewed 1 February 2010, http://ministers.treasury.gov.au

Syed, J. & Özbilgin, M. 2009, 'A relational framework for international transfer of diversity management practices', *The International Journal of Human Resource Management*, 20(12): 2435–53.

Taylor, P. & Walker, A. 1998, 'Policies and practices towards older workers: a framework for comparative research', *Human Resource Management Journal*, 8(3): 61–76.

Thomas, D. & Ely, R. 1996, 'Making differences matter: a new paradigm for managing diversity', *Harvard Business Review*, 74: 79–90.

Thun, J.-H., Grobbler, A. & Miczka, S. 2007, 'The impact of demographic transition in manufacturing', *Journal of Manufacturing Technology*, 18: 985–99.

Timmons, J., Hall, A., Fesko, A. & Migliore, A. 2011, 'Retaining the older workforce: social policy considerations for the universally designed workplace', *Journal of Aging & Social Policy*, 23: 119–40.

van Dalen, H., Henkens, K. & Schippers, J. 2010, 'How do employers cope with an ageing workforce? Views from employers and employees', *Demographic Research*, 22(32): 1015–36.

Vickerstaff, S., Loretto, W. & White, P. 2007, 'The future for older workers: opportunities and constraints', in W. Loretto, S. Vickerstaff and P. White (eds), *The Future for Older Workers: New Perspective*, The Polity Press, Bristol.

Warren, D. 2008, *Retirement Expectations and Labour Force Transitions: The Experience of the Baby Boom Generation*, Working Paper 24/08, Melbourne Institute of Applied Economic and Social Research, Melbourne.

Watson, I., Buchanan, J., Campbell, I. & Briggs, C. 2003, *Fragmented Futures: New Challenges in Working Life*, Federation Press, Leichhardt, NSW.

Wright, P., Dunford, B. & Snell, S. 2001, 'Human resources and the resource based view of the firm', *Journal of Management*, 27: 701–21.

Disabled persons in the workplace

7

Charmine E.J. Härtel and Jennifer M. O'Connor

Intended learning outcomes

After reading this chapter you will be able to:

- Understand the classic theories and key concepts underpinning the study of disability in the workplace
- Identify the key obstacles that disabled individuals face when gaining and maintaining effective employment
- Understand summary data from several countries demonstrating the extent of the issue relating to disabled persons at work
- Appreciate real-world case examples of disabled persons at work
- Critically consider the current state of research and suggestions for future conceptualisations of disabled persons at work
- Recognise evidence-based practices that promote the inclusion of disabled persons at work
- Find additional learning resources relating to disabled persons in the workplace

Introduction

Unemployment continues to be a serious issue consuming the attention of policy makers and academic researchers alike. However, interventions directed at alleviating this issue tend to focus on how to gain employment, and ignore the factors that lead to, or impede, employment. Research suggests that this is because past 'initiatives' do not assist employers or employees in understanding discrimination and the obstacles that disadvantaged groups face (Agocs & Burr, 1996).

The disabled community, in particular, face significant barriers to obtaining employment. In societies around the world, they are more likely than other workers to be unemployed or underemployed and experience disproportionate inequality in the workplace, facing barriers that are beyond their perceived functional limitations (Barnes & Mercer, 2005). The World Report on Disability (WHO, 2011) estimates the employment rate for working-age people with disabilities is 53 per cent for men and 20 per cent for women, compared with 65 per cent of non-disabled men and 30 per cent of non-disabled women. Paid work has been recognised as fundamental to the social inclusion of individuals with disabilities, yet disabled people continue to be marginalised from meaningful employment (Hall & Wilton, 2011).

It is estimated that 15 per cent of the global population lives with a form of disability (WHO, 2011). Despite the advent of the Disabled People's Movement, legislation enforcing anti-discrimination laws, policy promoting employment equal opportunity, and the establishment of the UN Convention on the Rights of Persons with Disabilities (UNCRPD), evidence confirms that people with disabilities (PWD) continue to be marginalised and disadvantaged in the labour market (Hall & Wilton, 2011; Kirakosyan, 2013). Despite the importance of disability issues in the workplace there is a lack of research from managerial and organisational perspectives; however, a plethora of literature has been developed in other fields of law, sociology, economics, rehabilitation psychology and disability studies (Foster, 2007). The purpose of this chapter is to provide the reader with an overview of the research and practice relating to disabled persons in the workplace, with a view to promoting evidence-based understanding and practice as well as stimulating new thinking.

Overview of classical theories and key concepts

Traditionally, the employment gap for disabled persons was attributed to the impact of physical impairments or medical conditions on an individual's physical and/or psychological capacity (Oliver, 1986). This view, known as *the individual or medical model of disability* focuses on individual and medical problems, explaining disability as a consequence of individual deficit or impairment (Barnes, 2000). The failure of individual and medical models to acknowledge the fundamental social challenges that affect disabled people's lifestyles have resulted in their rejection by disabled people and professionals (Barnes, 2000).

A progressive shift in the conceptualisation of disability from a medical perspective (i.e. biological impairment of the body) to one that acknowledged how social structures and constraining environments impose limitations to inclusion gave rise to the *social model of disability* (Barnes, 1992). Research from a social model perspective is primarily concerned with how people with disabilities are institutionally discriminated against in accessing employment and in the workplace through the constructs of capitalism, materialism and social environments. From the social model perspective, disability is defined as the relationship between impairment and society (Shakespeare & Watson, 2001) and thus as an outcome of social oppression caused by a diverse system of social constraints, restrictive environments and disabling barriers (Barnes, 2000). According to the social model, the inequality gap and disproportionate representation of disabled people in the labour market is a social phenomenon that can be explained by means of institutional discrimination (Barnes & Mercer, 2005; Barnes, 1992). Disabling barriers exist by means of diverse socially constructed ideologies, environmental constraints and institutionalised boundaries that impose limitations for disabled people to attain equal opportunity, especially in the workplace (Abberley, 1987; Barnes & Mercer, 2005). Physical and social constraints inherent within environmental surroundings, institutional arrangements, restrictive policies, organisational practices and social value systems directly or indirectly impose limitations and structural barriers resulting in inequality between disabled people and non-disabled people (Barnes, 1992; Foster, 2007). The social model has been a catalyst for progressing political reform in disability and fuelling the disabled people's movement, influencing social change to advance legislation, policy and organisational practices (Barnes, 2000).

The theoretical underpinning of the social model provided the foundations for developing *economic and political perspectives of disability*. These materialist approaches account for the employment disparity and equality gap as disability discrimination, due to capitalist economic systems and social ideologies that undervalue people with disabilities (Barnes, 2000). Within capitalist societies, the meaning and value of work centres around principles of maximising profit, waged labour and competitive performance (Barnes, 2000). This explanation highlights that discrimination experienced by people labelled as 'disabled' stems from capitalist and ableist hegemony (Abberley, 1987). These ideologies equate functional limitations or impairments affecting a person's capacity or working capability as being less productive and of less value, subsequently placing disabled workers at a direct disadvantage in the labour market (Foster, 2007). Underlying notions of normalcy are embedded within capitalist ideologies with regard to the meaning of work, the organisation of work and beliefs about what constitutes an ideal worker. These materialist and normative belief systems encourage the commodification of human ability and values of ableism, generating negative assumptions regarding the capability and value of disabled workers that perpetuate discrimination in the workplace (Chadwick, 1996; Priestly, 1998).

The social model has been criticised for ignoring the personal experience of disabled people by reducing them to passive victims and for further ignoring the bodily aspects of disability, assuming disability is entirely socially constructed (Shakespeare & Watson, 2001). More recent conceptualisations of theory have developed an *embodied approach to disability*, evolving from the disabled community, feminists and phenomenological perspectives. Complementing the social model's neglect of bodily aspects that affect disabled people in organisational life, these approaches take into consideration how disabled people experience their impairments on a personal level (Shakespeare & Watson, 2001; Swain & French, 2000). They focus on people's embodied experiences of impairment and acknowledge that disability is experienced both through social barriers and bodily impairments (Shakespeare & Watson, 2001). The embodied ontology argues that impairment is inherent within the nature of humanity and everyone has limitations or impairments, not only disabled people. Furthermore, everyone is vulnerable to impairment as part of the human experience and validity of life (Shakespeare & Watson, 2001). This approach emphasises that disability is multi-faceted with dimensions that cannot be condensed to a single identity or encapsulated as a constant state (Shakespeare & Watson, 2001). From these perspectives emerged the *affirmative model*, which encourages positive identification with disability, challenging the presumptions of tragedy and normality. It builds on the social model by including experiences of being disabled and supporting a positive identity with disability culture (Swain & French, 2000). The affirmative model inspires a future vision of positive self-determination with full participation and equal rights for disabled people within a society that values and embraces difference (Swain & French, 2000).

Despite progressive theoretical developments, disabled people continue to face inequality and discrimination in society and particularly in the workplace. Stone and Colella (1996) developed a *stereotype model* of factors affecting perceptions and treatment of individuals with disabilities in the workplace. The model highlights how stereotypes of different disabilities influence assumptions about capabilities and traits, according to subtypes and categorisation of disabilities, e.g. physical versus intellectual disability (Stone & Colella, 1996). The type of disability a person has indirectly influences how disabled employees are accepted and treated by their colleagues in the workplace (McLaughlin et al., 2004). Dimensions of stigma relating to the severity and controllability of disability affect people's judgement, acceptance and attitudes toward disabled colleagues (McLaughlin et al., 2004). Stigmatisation that influences attitudes towards disabled individuals affects decision-making processes that can create bias regarding opportunities for recruitment, inclusion, accommodation, retention, career progression and equal opportunity in the workplace (Barnes & Mercer, 2005; Colella & Bruyère, 2010). People who are stigmatised are *socially* disabled and 'have limited opportunities and resources available to them and face barriers that result in poverty and exclusion' (Block et al., 2001: 24). Certain organisational cultures and practices play a significant role in perpetuating discrimination and inequality experienced by disabled employees in organisational life (Fujimoto et al., 2014).

Power relationships and inequity

One of the main barriers to equality that disabled people face can be attributed to effects of social–cultural belief systems and misconceptions of disability that perpetuate stereotypes and stigma of disabled people. Stigmatised attitudes form the basis to explain ways in which perceptions of disability are constructed, and the roles these attitudes play in sustaining inequalities and barriers to inclusion for disabled people (Priestley, 1998). Evidence suggests that stigmatised attitudes and negative stereotypes create social prejudices that discriminate against individuals with disabilities, and arguably act as the greatest social barriers to equal opportunity (Stone & Colella, 1996). Stigmatised beliefs contribute to how disabled people are treated and accepted in the workplace (McLaughlin et al., 2004). People with disabilities are half as likely to be hired compared to their non-disabled counterparts (Jones, 2006). Those who suffer from mental illness are commonly stereotyped as more limited in their ability to perform quality work and interact with other employees (Scheid, 2005).

'Ableism' pertains to valuing certain abilities and also features negative differentiation against 'less able' individuals, leading to inequality, particularly in relation to productivity and economic competitiveness (Wolbring, 2008). Negative differentiation reinforces assumptions associated with stereotypes and stigmas related to people who are perceived as 'less able', creating unequal power dynamics that influence control over opportunities for employment and career progression (Priestly, 1998). These notions influence people's attitudes, social processes and organisational practices by placing value on physical, mental and emotional capacity, which adversely impacts economic, social and ethical outcomes for disabled workers (Vickers, 2009).

The outcome of social devaluing can lead to reduced self-efficacy or confidence in the ability to make a contribution to the workforce, fear of resentment and discrimination, and lack of career direction (Galvin, 2004: 350). These obstacles often lead to an unfocused job search and difficulty finding the motivation to continue looking for a job 'especially when their efforts have been met with limited success' (Galvin, 2004: 350). It can even lead the disabled to stop trying to obtain employment (Barlow et al., 2002).

Discussion activity 7.1

What are the key obstacles that disabled individuals face when gaining and maintaining effective employment? In answering this question, refer to the content of this chapter and the Further reading provided at the end of the chapter as well as the concepts discussed in Chapters 2 and 5. Also consider the specific societal norms and laws relating to the country you are currently living in.

Disabled persons in Australia

In 2004, the Australian Institute of Health and Welfare (AIWH, 2004) found that 96.4 per cent of disabled unemployed individuals experienced employment restrictions. According to the Disability Rights Commission (2003), 86 per cent of disabled people aged between 16 and 24 believe it is more difficult for disabled people to obtain employment and 30 per cent expect to earn less than others their age because of their disability.

Despite Government attempts to address this issue (such as through Equal Employment Opportunity (EEO) legislation and Disability Discrimination Acts), previous disability policies in the US have actually *increased* dependence on the Government instead of encouraging independence and active participation in mainstream society (Galvin, 2004). This is supported by the fact that 74 per cent of disabled people believe that the Government rarely listens to their views (Disability Rights Commission, 2003). This issue is compounded by a myriad of external factors (including the Government), namely, how organisations and their employees behave towards the disabled, including perceptions and attitudes toward them. What society now realises is that it is not simply a matter of developing new policies and practices, but rather there is an urgent need to shift mainstream society's mindset about working with disabled people. Therefore, the issue becomes one of diversity and disability management.

An international picture

The UNCRPD represents the first legally binding international instrument to protect the human rights of PWD (Kirakosyan, 2013). Many developing countries have ratified the Convention; however, disparity exists between employment legislation and the experiences of PWD, with variations in official employment statistics and disability prevalence. India's estimated population disability prevalence varies between 2 per cent and 8 per cent, with 37.6 per cent employment of PWD (Mitra & Sambamoorthi, 2006). Russia's disability prevalence varies from 6 per cent to 9 per cent, with 15–30 per cent of PWD employed (Andreev, 2008). South Africa's prevalence varies from 3.7 per cent to 12.8 per cent, with 80 per cent of PWD unemployed (Mitra, 2008). Similarly, Brazil's disability prevalence varies from 14.5 per cent to 21 per cent; with 52 per cent of PWD unemployed (Mitra et al., 2013). In contrast, China boasts high employment of PWD, between 50 per cent and 83.9 per cent; with disability prevalence ranging from 3.6 per cent to 8.4 per cent within the population (Myer & Sai, 2013). The disabled population in the United Arab Emirates (UAE) is 10.8 per cent, but there are no official employment statistics for PWD (WHO, 2011).

Socio-cultural contexts influence beliefs about disabled people that affect how they are treated and their opportunities for employment. In India, inequality is perpetuated through neoliberal ideologies, complex dynamics of the caste system and Hindu beliefs of karma. Disabled people experience exclusion and adverse treatment although they often remain perpetually grateful for employment opportunities (Kumar et al., 2012). In China, disabling conditions are perceived as punishment for wrongs in the past, and people with disabilities are considered bad luck (Stein, 2010). Disabled people in Brazil are perceived as unproductive, unemployable and unworthy of equal rights, affecting access to employment and equality (Mitra et al., 2013). The Russian word for a person with a disability translates to 'invalid', with disability perceived as an illness. During the Soviet era, disabled people could not legally work and were segregated in closed institutions that are still currently operational (HWC, 2013). During Apartheid, PWD in South Africa experienced discrimination and lacked basic rights to employment and social services. Some African cultures believe disability is a social and economic curse burdening one's family (Naidoo et al., 2011). Social attitudes in the UAE perceive people with disabilities as 'needy', although Islamic teachings and the Quran declare it a human right and honourable duty to assist disabled people, influencing paternalistic and charitable treatment (Alborno & Gaad, 2012).

The governments of the aforementioned countries have all ratified the UN Convention and attempted to address injustice through policy reform and laws to promote employment inclusion. India's 'Persons with Disabilities Act' promotes inclusion, social security and mandatory 3 per cent employment quotas for government and public workforces (Kulkarni & Lengnick-Hall, 2011). China's Constitution incorporates the 'Protection of Disabled Persons' and employment rights under Labour Law, including mandatory 1.5 per cent quotas and affirmative action (Fritsch, 2008). Disabled people in China have low socio-economic status and employers prefer to pay fines rather than hiring them (Myer & Sai, 2013). Brazil's democratic government enacted the 'Quota Law' and a constitutional anti-discrimination clause with mandated access-to-work employment quotas. Disabled people remain marginalised and are more likely to live in poverty within Brazil's emerging economy (Mitra et al., 2013). South African's 'Employment Equity Act' and 'Integrated National Disability Strategy' promotes inclusion and 2 per cent statutory quotas for government workforces (Mitra, 2008). Under Russian Federal law, the 'Rights of Persons with Disabilities in the Russian Federation' and employment policies emphasise protection, state-sponsored benefits and quota systems, lacking commitment to equality and inclusion in the workplace (Martz, 2007). The UAE's Federal Law and initiatives address the rights of disabled PWD, promoting inclusive approaches to enable social equality and employment access (MSA, 2006). Generally, government policies in these countries encourage access, although they lack substantial commitment to inclusion and equality within the workplace. Table 7.1 provides a summary of this cross-national comparison, with additional information regarding the population and macroeconomic contexts of each country.

Table 7.1 Cross-national comparison of disability in the workplace

Contexts	India	China	South Africa	Brazil	Russia	UAE
Population	1.237 billion	1.351 billion	52.27 million	198.7 million	143.5 million	9.205 million
Disability prevalence	2–8%	3.6–8.4%	3.7–12.8%	14.5–21%	6–9%	10.8%
Employment of disabled people	37.60%	50–83.9%	20%	48%	15–30%	Lack of statistics
Socio-cultural (perception and influences)	• Past life 'karma' • Caste system • Hindu beliefs	• Past life 'punishment' • Considered bad luck	• Social curse • History of Apartheid: discrimination and lacked basic rights	• Disabled people are 'unproductive' • Unemployable and unworthy of equal rights	• Disability is an illness • Translation: 'invalid' • Soviet era: closed institutions	• Disabled people are 'needy' • Islamic: honourable to assist disabled people
Legislation	• Ratified UNCRPD • 'Persons with Disabilities Act'	• Ratified UNCRPD • 'Protection of Disabled Persons in China' • Labour Law	• Ratified UNCRPD • 'Employment Equity Act' • 'Integrated National Disability Strategy'	• Ratified UNCRPD • 'Quota Law' • Constitutional anti-discrimination clause	• Ratified UNCRPD • 'Rights of Persons with Disabilities in the Russian Federation'	• Ratified UNCRPD • 'Federal law no. 29 of 2006'
Institutions	• 3% quotas for government and public workforces	• 1.5% quota	• 2% quotas for government workforces and government education	• Employment quotas	• Employment quotas	• Inclusive approaches to equal employment
Macro economics	• Fourth largest economy • Significant growth and development	• Second largest economy • Rapid economic and social development	• Prudent macroeconomics • Dual economy – high poverty, inequality and exclusion	• Seventh largest economy • Solid macroeconomics • Stable growth • Improvements in social well-being	• Economic downturn • Lack of structural reform • Higher risk environment • Political uncertainty	• Strong economy • Continued growth and development
	• GDP US$1.859 trillion 2012 • GDP growth 4.7%	• GDP US$8.227 trillion 2012 • GDP growth 7.8%	• GDP US$384.3 billion 2012 • GDP growth 2.5%	• GDP US$2.253 trillion 2012 • GDP growth 0.9%	• GDP US$2.015 trillion 2012 • GDP growth 3.4%	• GDP US$358.1 billion 2011 • GDP growth 4.2%

Variance issues

Governments have generally lacked regulatory provisions to effectively advance policy initiatives that promote equal employment rights for PWD and there is limited systematic analysis of policy implementation. India has not signed the UN Optional Protocol to strengthen and monitor the Convention (Hiranandani et al., 2014). Inadequate policy measures are unlikely to bridge the gap regionally, with effects primarily only reaching urban sectors (Mitra & Sambamoorthi, 2008). In China, the lack of adequate policy implementation and practice has resulted in a disproportionate unemployed, untrained and impoverished disabled population (Fritsch, 2008). South Africa has experienced a decline in employment participation of PWD since 1998. The government has left the responsibility of implementing legislation and removing employment barriers to the discretion of employers, posing issues for ensuring the implementation of inclusive work practices (Wiggett-Barnard & Swartz, 2012). Russia's Federal Employment Service is responsible for monitoring compliance with policies and laws; however, there is inadequate enforcement or commitment to ensure inclusion and access to employment (HWC, 2013). Brazil's government has identified indicators to measure policy effects, although compliance with quota laws was only 55 per cent in 2010, indicating a lack of influence and regulation to create substantial change (dos Santos Rodrigues et al., 2013). UAE's Ministry of Social Affairs is responsible for progressing policy initiatives; however, a lack of government monitoring authorities and legally binding legislation poses issues for regulating public and private employers (Alborno & Gaad, 2012). Proactive implementation of legislation and assessment of factors that enable or hinder inclusive practices is required to ensure employment equality for PWD.

Disability rights activists and organisations have been instrumental in advancing equal employment policies for PWD. In India the National Centre for Promotion of Employment for Disabled People (NCPED), along with other networks, has successfully achieved measurable outcomes by directly engaging government, private sector and community services in employment and rights-based initiatives (Benshoff et al., 2014). Brazil's education, private and civil sectors have introduced employment initiatives. The Federation of Banks introduced a training for employment scheme. The Brazilian Academy of Sciences and American Institutes for Research coordinated Programa Integrando which was inaugurated by Centro de Vida, a disability support agency and employment broker, with the aim of providing customised employment and training programmes (dos Santos Rodrigues et al., 2013). The majority of South African employers have equal employment policies, although most fail to implement them. Some businesses have advanced measures to remove barriers through accommodation, integration and specialised recruitment services. Disabled People South Africa (DPSA), alongside other networks, promotes opportunities to access equal employment, education and training programmes (Wiggett-Barnard & Swartz, 2012). Initiatives in Russia have been industry-led by the Business Advisory Board on Disability (BABD)

Table 7.2 Cross-national comparison of diversity initiatives

	India	China	South Africa	Brazil	Russia	UAE
Regulatory measures	• Not signed the UN Optional Protocol • Inadequate policy measures to regulate legislation	• Lack of adequate policy implementation and practice	• Lack of regulatory measures • Responsibility of employers	• Government has identified indicators to measure policy effects • Lack of regulatory measures and influence • 55% compliance with quota laws	• Federal Employment Service • Lack of enforcement or commitment	• Ministry of Social Affairs • Lack of government monitoring or regulation
Diversity institutions	• The National Centre for Promotion of Employment for Disabled People (NCPED) • NASSCOM Foundation • Development and Inclusion Equal Opportunity Centre (DEOC) • Action for Ability • National Disability Network	• The Chinese Disabled Persons' Federation • China Disabled Persons' Service Network (CDPSN)	• Disabled People South Africa (DPSA) • National Accessibility Portal South Africa • Disability Employment Concern • Development Trust for Disabled People • Southern Africa Federation of the Disabled	• Centro de Vida Independence	• Perspektiva, The Regional Society of Disabled People • Russian Society of Disabled People	• Zayed Higher Organisation for Humanitarian Care and Special Needs (ZHO) • The Dubai Center for Special Needs
Organisational interventions	• The Employers' Federation of India (EFI) • Confederation of Indian Industry (CII) • Samarth Corporation	• More than 3000 employment service agencies for people with disabilities operate in China	• Some businesses have incorporated inclusive policies	• The Federation of Banks • Academy of Sciences and America Institutes for Research • Business Network for Social Inclusion, Brazil	• Business Advisory Board on Disability (BABD)	• National Project for Inclusion of People with Special Needs coordinated with public and private sectors

in conjunction with Perspektiva, the Regional Society of Disabled People, focusing on practical employment, training, support and awareness programmes (ILO, 2011). The UAE government initiated the 'National Project for Inclusion of People with Special Needs', inaugurated by the Zayed Higher Organisation for Humanitarian Care and Special Needs (ZHO), and with the purpose of coordinating the public and private sectors to provide inclusive employment for PWD. The Chinese Disabled Persons' Federation promotes awareness and employment services for PWD and employers. The Chinese government has introduced occupational therapy stations within communities for vocational training and work integration (Benshoff et al., 2014). Collaborative efforts and grassroots measures have created tangible outcomes for social change and advancing equal employment rights for PWD. Table 7.2 provides a summary of these actions, including additional diversity initiatives.

Discussion activity 7.2

Identify some of the differences in issues faced by younger versus older disabled persons, male versus female disabled persons, as well as the experiences of disabled persons varying in race, ethnicity, religion and sexual orientation. In formulating your answer, refer to this chapter and Chapters 4-6, 8, 9 and 11.

Two practical examples

Injustice in the skies

This case focuses on the unfair treatment and workplace bullying experienced by a disabled employee following her disclosure of her disability to her employer (Vickers, 2009). An airline stewardess, formerly employed by an undisclosed Australian flight company, began to experience adverse treatment from her managers and colleagues after disclosing she had multiple sclerosis (MS). These experiences included stigmatisation, improper advice, exclusion, excessive scrutiny, disruptions to her work routine, removal of responsibilities, continual pressure to prove her capabilities, and subsequently, medical retirement. During the initial onset of MS the employee took five months leave, initially being wrongly advised to take Long Service Leave rather than be placed on Temporary Incapacity Benefit. The employee did not give reasons for the absence or disclose her diagnosis to the company at this time, keeping her condition concealed for a number of years. On returning to work she reported no effects on her working capability, other than a slight limp. The employee continued to work unaffected by the concealed disability, which was unnoticed by her colleagues. After she disclosed her condition to a performance manager, she subsequently began experiencing changes in attitude and behaviour from her managers and colleagues. Following a work incident and disclosure of her illness, the company's senior management began receiving internal performance reports in the guise of 'concerns for welfare, as a duty of care', and subsequently grounded her from flight duties. After numerous reports, she consulted the company doctor who recommended an ergonomics test. During the consultation the employee learned of malicious company rumours relating to her health. It took a further two months before she received the results stating that she had passed the ergonomics test.

Disclosure appeared to have triggered adverse patterns of work behaviour and unfair managerial treatment. These behaviours undermined her professional reputation with subsequent removal of work responsibilities. Continuous unfair treatment escalated, with incidences of excessive scrutiny and constant requests to undertake further physical and performance tests, which were beyond regular employee assessments, even though she had passed all previous tests. The continual experience of being scrutinised, challenged and having to prove her capability led to intensified stress, anxiety and diminished confidence. Stress from being continuously exposed to harassment and pressure contributed to her deteriorating symptoms. After being grounded and having passed all tests, she was allowed back to flight duties. However, her rapid deterioration in health caused problems with balance that affected her ability to carry out her duties. This led to further work absence and the company offering medical retirement, rather than supporting requests for a job placement on the ground.

Discussion questions

1. Describe the management of the affected employee. What problems are evident in this case? What perspective on disability did the employer adopt?
2. What would have been a more effective way for the organisation to handle this situation?

AIM Network at KPMG

KPMG LLP provides an exemplary inclusive model in their commitment and approach to attracting, accommodating, engaging and advancing individuals with disabilities within their national workforce (Linkow et al., 2013). KPMG established the Abilities in Motion (AIM) Network to support employees with disabilities and carers of people with disabilities, as a central component of the firm's diversity strategy. AIM

Network is a dedicated resource group that focuses on continuously developing a mutually respectful culture of inclusion for individuals with disabilities. The foundation of AIM and its positive outcomes are attributed to five critical factors: commitment from top management, voice from the grassroots, communication, focus on disclosure and fit. AIM's primary goal is to promote a mutually respectful work environment that provides guidance, encouragement and support.

The key elements in KPMG's successful outcomes were a top-down executive-level approach and integrated diversity strategies within the organisational framework. KPMG's partners and managers have diversity goals built into their performance assessment. This process engenders a deep commitment to ensuring successful implementation of programmes and a sense of inclusivity promoted within the organisation. AIM was established with a formal advisory board consisting of company managers and employees, co-chaired by two KPMG executives who have personal experience with disability. Consisting of 12 chapters across the national offices, AIM's efforts are tailored to focus on meeting the needs within each location rather than a blanket approach. Monthly focus groups are run to determine improvements, issues and new initiatives. Feedback is presented to KPMG's Diversity Advisory Board (DAB) and reported directly to the CEO.

KPMG has created an inclusive culture that encourages individuals to feel safe in bringing their authentic selves to work and disclosing their disabilities. To assist in strengthening the inclusive culture, KPMG implemented streamlined processes for accommodation and inclusion in the workplace. They are committed to matching employees with disabilities to their jobs and roles within the organisation by focussing on individual passions, skills and competencies, providing further opportunities for mentoring programmes, training advancement and leadership roles. The use of communication and awareness strategies, streamlined processes and support networks have created an open-door approach and sense of trust within the organisation. Disability awareness training is provided to promote understanding, etiquette and to address stigmas. Network webinars are conducted and internal communication strategies are used to promote inclusion. AIM has a website embedded on the homepage of the intranet, disabled employees are included in staff news and a 'Success at KPMG Series' was introduced, profiling outstanding professionals who have disclosed their disabilities or other diverse qualities. KPMG has established a successful approach to supporting their disabled employees by creating an inclusive working environment supported by policy and practices that are collaborative, proactive and transparent. These initiatives recognise the values of developing integrative and accommodative approaches to enhance the experiences, talents and outcomes that empower individuals with disabilities. KPMG endeavours to share their approaches by encouraging cross-fertilisation of practices amongst their diversity networks and more broadly through industry events.

Discussion questions

1. What perspective on disability did KPMG adopt in this case? How does this perspective differ from the perspective adopted by the airline in the case above? How do perspectives on disability influence the likely courses of action that an employer is likely to take towards disabled persons in the workplace?
2. How did KMPG create an inclusive culture for disabled persons at work?

Discussion activity 7.3

Discuss evidence-based practices that promote the inclusion of disabled persons at work. It may be useful to refer to the issues raised in Chapter 3.

Critical analysis and discussion: issues for disabled workers

Disabled employees continue to be subjected to inequality and injustice in the workplace. They are more likely to hold lower status jobs, receive lower wages, experience discrimination and face barriers to career progression (Snyder et al., 2010). From a social model perspective, inequality exists due to institutional discrimination and disabling barriers (Barnes, 1992). Dominant materialistic and normative ideologies perpetuated through capitalist hegemony and constructs of ableism encourage the valuing and commodification of ability (Chadwick, 1996). These beliefs reinforce negative stereotypes of disability and perceptions of disabled people's capacity, creating social barriers that influence inequality and discrimination in the workplace (Priestley, 1998). Flawed stereotypes create prejudice about disabled people's capabilities, their value and productivity that manifest in various forms of inequality within the workplace (Foster, 2007). Evidence suggests that disabled employees experience more procedural injustice and discrimination compared with non-disabled employees. People with non-physical disabilities are more likely to perceive negative work experiences compared with individuals with physical disabilities (Snyder et al., 2010). Disabled employees are more likely to encounter obstacles in maintaining their positions and advancing their career through inadequate support and lack of opportunity (Wilson-Kovacs et al., 2008). Evidence suggests that unsupportive work cultures that stigmatise disabled employees are more prone to create a climate of injustice and inequality (Snyder et al., 2010).

Table 7.3   Recommendations for inclusive work practices

Governments	• Develop equal employment legislation that protects the rights of employees with disabilities
	• Promote inclusive organisational practices in policy and law
	• Ensure organisations adhere to policies and legislation
Organisations	• Modify hiring and training processes
	• Enhance inclusive organisational cultures
	• Ensure physical work settings are accessible
	• Adapt work environment
	• Implement reform work practices
	• Revise job designs
	• Endorse inclusion in the organisation
	• Create supportive disability networks
	• Support all employees equally
Policy managers	• Adopt affirmative inclusion and accommodation policies
	• Understand legislation
	• Develop management strategies
	• Ensure practices are operationalised
	• Build inclusive strategies into business frameworks
	• Modify hiring and training processes
	• Devise interconnected strategies
	• Implement disability awareness training
Managers	• Understand legislative requirements
	• Instil an inclusive organisational culture
	• Support disabled employees
	• Ensure measures for accommodating working arrangements
	• Create an environment of psychological safety and trust
	• Allow employees to disclose their circumstances and seek advice
	• Value all employees equally
	• Provide challenging work, training and advancement opportunities
	• Address adverse behaviours in the workplace
Co-workers	• Create inclusion amongst co-workers
	• Provide supportive working relationships
	• Assist co-workers to integrate
	• Support co-workers in their workplace adjustments
	• Encourage a positive work environment
	• Attend disability awareness training
Employers	• Discuss required adjustments for work requirements
	• Negotiate work arrangements
	• Understand legal rights
	• Participate in disability awareness training
	• Create supportive networks
	• Engage with the work environment and colleagues
	• Encourage positive work relationships

Procedural injustice and discrimination contributes to understanding how inequality manifests through power dynamics and bias in the workplace. Disabled employees are subjected to higher levels of overt discrimination, and are more prone to experience workplace bullying than any other 'minority' group (Foster, 2007). Misuse of power is evident through negative work practices and adverse decision-making processes surrounding disabled employees' work circumstances. These practices can manifest in unreasonable pressure to prove capability, removal of responsibility, lack of support for career advancement and bullying behaviours (Foster, 2007). Effects of conflict and rigid inequality can also surface in work adjustment negotiations with the refusal, inflexibility or lack of reasonable accommodation. This is more frequently experienced with requests for time and work allocation as opposed to physical workplace adjustments (Foster & Fosh, 2010). Conflicts arising from neglect of legitimate policies are linked to adverse treatment, bullying and harassment, causing adverse outcomes for disabled employees (Foster & Fosh, 2010; Vickers, 2009). Damaging behaviours are often perceived by disabled employees as tactics for removal from the workplace (Vickers, 2009). Incidences of prejudice and injustice are more prevalent in organisations that have unjust cultural environments (Snyder et al., 2010).

Organisational culture and perceived effects of treatment can influence individuals' decisions regarding disability disclosure and accommodation requests (Schur et al., 2009). These decisions are multi-faceted and further compounded by the nature of a person's disability. People with invisible or recently acquired disabilities are more likely to conceal conditions and less likely to request accommodation; concealment is a means of self-preservation to prevent injustice or differential treatment (Foster, 2007). Issues faced by disabled employees are complex and multidimensional; evidence suggests that organisations and supervisors play a significant role in supporting disabled employees or perpetuating patterns of discrimination within the workplace (Snyder et al., 2010).

Summary and recommendations

The social theory of disability, affirmative models of inclusion and reformed government legislations that acknowledge and protect the rights of individuals with disabilities has engendered a reconceptualisation of disability in the workplace. This has prompted governments and organisations globally to recognise that mainstream work settings and the organisation of work can be limiting and can create barriers for disabled employees (Barnes, 2000). This shift in thinking has stimulated equal employment legislation, more inclusive approaches, revised work practices and reconfiguration of work environments (Lysaght et al., 2012), which have progressed the agenda to create more equitable access to employment, inclusion and accommodation for people with disabilities (Lysaght et al., 2012). To progress inclusion in the workplace, important considerations for reforming work practices are necessary. These include revising job design, modifying hiring and training processes, adopting affirmative policy and management strategies, developing inclusive organisational cultures and adapting physical work settings (Härtel et al., 2013; Lysaght et al., 2012). To effectively implement processes of inclusion and accommodation, it is essential to develop affirmative policies and strategies with commitment to ensuring practices are operationalised (Fujimoto et al., 2013; Gates & Akabas, 2011). Disability training is recommended to create awareness, an understanding of legislative requirements and to address stigma. Accommodation processes promote inclusion in the workplace and should be viewed as a fluid social activity (Härtel & Panipucci, 2007; Panipucci & Härtel, 2006). This requires consideration of several components to assess an organisation's readiness to enable the appropriate fit between an individual's health conditions and work environments (Gates & Akabas, 2011). Collaborative and interconnected strategies that both consider physical settings and recognise the importance of social and cultural dynamics within work contexts are essential for positive outcomes (Gates & Akabas, 2011). Flexible work arrangements enhance the ability of disabled employees to experience more productive and successful work outcomes that in turn enhance job satisfaction (Kirsh & Gewurtz, 2011). It is therefore important for disabled employees to feel safe in disclosing their condition and to feel supported in requesting workplace accommodation (Foster, 2007).

Evidence suggests that positive experiences of disabled employees have been greatly influenced by inclusive organisational cultures (Kirsh & Gewurtz, 2011). It is also imperative to recognise the significant effects that organisational culture has and to manage social and cultural dynamics within work contexts (Gates & Akabas, 2011). An inclusive organisational culture has the potential to empower disabled employees by providing a sense of belonging, value and trust through supportive work relationships (Kirsh & Gewurtz, 2011). Co-workers play a key role in the inclusion and integration of employees with disabilities (Rollins et al., 2011). Encouraging positive work relationships, mentoring opportunities and inclusive practices amongst co-workers has the potential to create greater social connections and support networks, resulting in enhanced morale, loyalty and cohesion (Lysaght et al., 2012). Managers and supervisors have an essential function in supporting disabled employees, as their behaviour and practices greatly influence co-workers and organisational climate. Supervisors need to ensure adequate measures are taken to accommodate working arrangements, and to create an environment of psychological safety and trust that allows employees to disclose their circumstances, seek advice and feel valued (Kulkarni & Lengnick–Hall, 2011). At the same time, it is important to provide challenging work, training, advancement and leadership opportunities. Fostering a positive culture supported by affirmative policies, equal opportunity, effective accommodation and positive work practices can have influential effects company-wide (Härtel, 2008; Härtel et al., 2002). Organisations that adopt inclusive cultures will benefit from increased employee satisfaction, commitment and overall performance (Hartnett et al., 2011).

Organisational diversity management practices that are effective reflect a holistic and community perspective. Five areas identified as opportunities for improving organisational inclusiveness of disabled persons are: '(1) non-minority-specific activities; (2) listening to minority voices; (3) multidimensional accessibility; (4) organizational and natural champions; and (5) cross-boundary networks and collaborations, all of which are centred on common interest activities' (Fujimoto et al., 2014: 530). In brief, organisations need to provide non-disability-specific activities that create a common and shared identity and experience for disabled workers and their counterparts. Organisations also need to seek out feedback and provide opportunities for voice from disabled persons in the workplace so that organisational practices embrace them fully as participants. Creating a welcoming space for all workers, including disabled persons, facilitates inclusive social interactions, again promoting a sense of belonging by all. Importantly, this means considering the informal social activities that take place amongst employees outside the formal workplace. Accessibility is thus much more than physical access; it is also 'virtual, informational and attitudinal access' (Fujimoto et al., 2014: 531). Moreover, given the importance of social capital in the form of dense and varied social networks, it is essential that organisations facilitate boundary-crossing opportunities that bring diverse individuals together across diverse settings in common interest activities (Fujimoto et al., 2014). Natural champions or individuals who volunteer of their own accord (versus organisationally appointed champions) are also important elements of the environment (both organisational and extra-organisational) that facilitate the participation of disabled persons in work and their opportunities to be included in organisational life (Fujimoto et al., 2014).

Based on our prior work, it is anticipated that perceived dissimilarity by others and by self, organisational policies and practices, physical layout of the job and organisation, and co-worker and employer attitudes towards the disabled will influence the magnitude and frequency of obstacles disabled workers report experiencing (cf. Fujimoto et al., 2005) and, subsequently, work-related outcomes (cf. Fujimoto et al., 2004; Härtel, 2004).

A visible disability refers to 'both mental and physical conditions that are immediately noticeable by an observer' (Matthews & Harrington, 2000). Some medical disabilities such as paraplegia are highly visible, others such as cancer are less visible, and some have both visible and invisible components such as a head injury (Joachim & Acorn, 2000). The point to note is that people who have an invisible disability have the option of whether to disclose their condition to others or not, as well as to decide how much information they will give and to whom (Joachim & Acorn, 2000). This means that people with an invisible disability can try to avoid the social disability that is linked with medical disabilities. Currently, the notion that disability can be visible or invisible, and whether this impacts on the individual's experience of both a medical and social disability, has not been incorporated into models of disability. Further, little is known about disclosure and non-disclosure of medical disabilities.

Notwithstanding these issues, while the goal of increasing disabled people's participation in employment is healthy both for the target group and society at large, it has also been noted that it is unrealistic to expect that this group will be 'able to compete successfully in a "hostile labour market"' given that it has traditionally been confronted by much prejudice in the workforce (Galvin, 2004: 348). Therefore, the socially constructed disadvantage that disabled members of our community face needs to be challenged now to ensure the marginalisation of these groups does not continue to be justified and that their value to society does not remain unrecognised, marginalised and underutilised.

Key terms

The individual or medical models of disability focus on individual and medical problems, explaining disability as a consequence of individual deficit or impairment (Barnes, 2000).

The social model of disability explains disability as an outcome of social oppression caused by a diverse system of social constraints, restrictive environments and disabling barriers (Barnes, 2000).

Ableism pertains to valuing certain abilities and negative differentiation against 'less able' individuals (Wolbring, 2008).

Economic and political perspectives of disability. Within capitalist societies, the meaning and value of work centres around principles of maximising profit, waged labour and competitive performance (Barnes, 2000), leading to the commodification of human ability and values of ableism (Chadwick, 1996; Priestly, 1998). These ideologies equate functional limitations or impairments affecting a person's capacity or working capability to being less productive and of less value, consequently placing disabled workers at a direct disadvantage in the labour market (Foster, 2007).

The embodied approach to disability focuses on people's embodied experiences of impairment and acknowledges that disability is experienced both through social barriers and bodily impairments (Shakespeare and Watson, 2001). The embodied ontology argues that impairment is inherent within the nature of humanity and everyone has limitation or impairment, not only disabled people; furthermore, everyone is vulnerable to impairment as part of the human experience and validity of life (Shakespeare and Watson, 2001).

The affirmative model challenges the presumptions of tragedy and normality by including experiences of being disabled and supporting a positive identity with disability culture (Swain & French, 2000).

The stereotype model of disability highlights how stereotypes of different disabilities influence assumptions about capabilities and traits, according to subtypes and categorisation of disabilities, e.g. physical versus intellectual disability (Stone & Colella, 1996).

Discussion questions

1. How do the unemployment, underemployment and discrimination experiences of disabled persons compare to other segments of the workforce?
2. How do capitalistic notions of labour promote discrimination against disabled workers?
3. Discuss and debate possible interventions to address inequities facing disabled workers.

CASE STUDY

The Desert Group

The following case study illustrates a successful example of workplace integration for young adults with disabilities. This work integration programme was implemented by the Desert Group, a private national landscaping company in the UAE that became the platform of research-based evaluation carried out by the UAE Community Development Authority (CDA) in conjunction with the British University in Dubai (Alborno & Gaad, 2012). The research aimed to investigate the effectiveness of the initiative and to assess the impact of implementing the UAE's equal opportunity legislative policies within a company's business framework. The Desert Group's equal employment programme was in response to the UAE's constitution and enactment of Federal Law No. 29/2006 governing the rights of people with disabilities to have equal access to education and employment (MSA, 2006; Alborno & Gaad, 2012). The research assessed the effectiveness of the programme in regard to employee productivity, psychological behaviour, professional development and impact on organisational culture, and within the broader society. Evaluation included recruitment processes, equal opportunity practices, training and development, health and safety regulations, workplace accommodation, management processes, appraisals, professional development incentives and the social impact of the programme.

(Continued)

(Continued)

In the UAE, there is a growing awareness relating to individuals with disabilities, although social stigmatisation of disabilities continues to exist. Generally the UAE is a caring society with embedded belief systems in the Islamic tradition that encourage honourable and rigorous acts. The majority of UAE society continue to believe that people with disabilities are in need and regard helping them as a charitable act. Providing employment opportunities for people with disabilities is considered charitable rather than a basic civil right of equal opportunity. Despite the UAE establishing the foundations of equal employment opportunity in the Federal Law, further policies and procedures have not been formally established to bind employers to the legislation. The Desert Group took their own initiative to comply with the law and initiated the employment programme as part of their company's strategic vision and corporate social responsibility plan.

Commencing in 2006, The Desert Group recruited nine young adults from rehabilitation centres in Dubai and Sharjah. Over five years they successfully employed 36 workers, with varying degrees of physical and intellectual disabilities. They provided disabled individuals with equal opportunity to access sustainable employment, training programmes and career advancement opportunities within a supportive working environment. To date, employees from the programme have been placed in permanent positions based within the organisation's head office, horticultural, administrative and sales teams. The company's horticulture department employs 27 individuals from the programme as gardeners, comprising 40 per cent of the department's total employees. The head office employs nine people from the programme in various administrative-based roles, including typing, data entry, mail distribution, photography and public relations. Employment terms and conditions for people with disabilities are equal to those of all other staff with an additional provision of extra time off for medical reasons. All employees in the company receive the same benefits in terms of annual holidays, pension plans, health insurance and transportation assistance. The recruitment process was dependent on reports and interviews, and did not include any formal testing of abilities. The Desert Group's practices illustrate a proactive commitment to the inclusivity of workers with disabilities and equal treatment of all company employees. The vocational management team initially consisted of a team leader, a counsellor and three supervisors. With the employment programme's growing success, the company recognised the necessity to provide further provision with respect to psychological and behavioural support, with

(Continued)

(Continued)

a need to gauge the success and social impact of the programme. A special-ised counsellor was engaged whose main responsibilities involved planning and supporting the development of the behavioural, psychological and pro-fessional skills of the employees with disabilities.

On commencing employment, individuals were provided with on-the-job training. Within the head office, co-workers from designated departments provided induction training using modelling techniques for instruction, teaching required work skills through demonstration and observation. As skills became developed, further tasks and responsibilities were assigned until competency levels were reached and the new employees could carry out relevant duties independently. For certain skill sets, including public rela-tions and photography, professional training was conducted and further assistance provided to facilitate communication during public out-of-office assignments, if required. The company provided sign language workshops for employees within the administration department, to facilitate communica-tion with colleagues that have hearing impairments. Similar techniques were mirrored for training horticultural staff by providing teaching in stages, com-mencing with introducing daily tasks, gradually using individual instruction and modelling techniques with positive reinforcement. According to the physical and mental abilities of employees, assigned tasks were rotated to ensure individuals mastered various skills and had the opportunity to take on different responsibilities.

Positive reports were received from employees expressing their job satis-faction, enjoyment of learning new skills, and positive support received from peers within a friendly atmosphere. These positive outcomes were attributed to the supportive working environment, effective training programmes, help-ful management and colleagues, in addition to the general morale instilled within the company. Improvements in self-esteem and self-confidence were reported by employees with disabilities who also stated that they felt valued and respected by their colleagues. An open-door management policy allowed for trust to be further established by providing a voice and opportu-nity to discuss any concerns or issues arising in the workplace. Feedback from the human resources department confirmed the company's satisfaction with their employees' commitment, hard work and excellent attendance records. The head of the employer's special needs department confirmed that since the programme had commenced they had a high retention rate of

(Continued)

(Continued)

88 per cent, highlighting the commitment, dedication and loyalty shown by their employees.

As an incentive and recognition for hard work, the company runs an 'Employee of the Month' appraisal programme, recognising and rewarding high performers. As part of the inclusive strategies and proactive approaches, the Desert Group's employees are given the option to participate in specialised development programmes to enhance skills and knowledge in IT, administration, public relations and horticulture and also offer opportunities for further career progression. A dedicated training scheme called the 'The Outstanding Salesman Programme', was introduced for gardeners with speech issues to develop communication skills and specialised horticulture knowledge. The programme successfully prepared nine gardeners to become active members of the sales team, having full interaction with customers and the public in the nursery. An example of the effectiveness of the programme's approach is one employee who progressed from a gardening job to become a photographer within the public relations department in the head office. Future working groups were proposed to include flower arrangement, planting and maintenance of seeds and shrubs. Continuous training, active communication with management and training personnel, and after-work recreational activities have encouraged the socialisation of employees with disabilities to be fully accepted and integrated within the workplace as valued employees of the Desert Group. These approaches also inspired non-disabled employees through their active involvement in the socialisation and integration processes, by taking on mentoring and training roles, taking sign language courses and participation in socialising activities, which increased a sense of pride and loyalty company-wide within the Desert Group. Inclusive organisational practices contributed to a more diversified inclusive workforce and reduced the effects of stigma within the organisation, which has been achieved through committing resources, proactive management leadership, integrating employees and developing supportive incentive programmes within the workplace.

Broader positive social impacts of the initiative have been to raise awareness of the competence levels of people with disabilities and their capacity for being equally productive participants in an active workforce. A unique national social endeavour called 'Let's Plant the UAE Together' connects employees with disabilities to the broader society within the UAE through

(Continued)

(Continued)

visits to ministries, governmental bodies, universities and schools, where the gardeners help rulers, ministers, government officials and students to plant trees. Another successful project called 'Joining Hand' was established with the Dubai Police Department to assist their environmental campaign by jointly planting trees in residential areas and mosques. The Desert Group also encourages employees to participate in national festivities such as the National Day, International Environment Day and various other open days and events. Active participation resulted in capacity building, raising confidence levels of employees and creating awareness within the community of equal opportunity and social inclusion.

This case study illuminates a company's proactive vision and responsive commitment to their corporate social responsibility beliefs by successfully delivering equal access to employment opportunities for adults with various physical and intellectual disabilities. The Desert Group's management leadership styles, belief in their company's vision, engagement of existing staff and supportive networks were instrumental components to effectively eliminate stigmas relating to employees with disabilities within the organisation and create an inclusive organisational culture. Commitment from the management team and cooperation from colleagues resulted in effectively facilitating integration into the workplace and empowering people with disabilities to acquire new skills and knowledge, and take part in socially inclusive networks. These processes and practices resulted in instilling a sense of pride, loyalty and commitment amongst all company employees. The Desert Group has successfully implemented significant foundational steps in their commitment to equal employment opportunities by providing sustainable livelihoods for individuals with disabilities. Furthermore, intrinsic value has been created within the organisation by promoting an organisational culture of acceptance and an enriched diversified workforce.

Questions

1. Reflecting on this case, how does societal culture influence the issues that disabled persons are likely to face in the workplace?
2. What lessons can be drawn from this case for linking organisational practices relating to disabled persons in the workplace with broader community and societal practices?

Further reading

CIPD & Mind 2011. *Managing and Supporting Mental Health at Work: Disclosure Tools for Managers*. London: Chartered Institute of Personnel and Development. www.cipd.co.uk/publicpolicy/policy-reports/mental-health-work-disclosure-tools.aspx

Coleman, N., Sykes, W. & Groom, C. 2013. *Barriers to Employment and Unfair Treatment at Work: A Quantitative Analysis of Disabled People's Experience*, Research Report no. 88. Manchester: Equality and Human Rights Commission. www.equalityhumanrights.com/sites/default/files/documents/barriers_and_unfair_treatment_final.pdf

ILO 2010. *Disability in the Workplace: Company Practices*. Geneva: International Labour Office. www.ilo.org/wcmsp5/groups/public/@ed_emp/@ifp_skills/documents/publication/wcms_150658.pdf

KNA 2009. *Disabled Employment Networks – A Practical Guide*. London: Kate Nash Associates. www.katenashassociates.com

Konrad, A.M., Moore, M.E., Ng, E.S., Doherty, A.J. & Breward, K. 2013. Temporary work, under-employment and workplace accommodations: relationship to well-being for workers with disabilities. *British Journal of Management*, 24(3): 367–82.

Linkow, P., Barrington, L., Bruyère, S., Figueroa, Y. & Wright, M. 2013. *Levelling the Playing Field: Attracting, Engaging, and Advancing People with Disabilities*. New York: The Conference Board. http://digitalcommons.ilr.cornell.edu/edicollect/1292/

RADAR 2011. *Doing Seniority Differently (Final Report): A Study of High Fliers Living with Ill-Health, Injury or Disability*. Royal Association for Disability Rights. www.disabilityrightsuk.org/sites/default/files/pdf/DSD%20Exec%20Sum%20(high%20res).pdf

Roulstone, A. & Williams, J. 2014. Being disabled, being a manager: 'glass partitions' and conditional identities in the contemporary workplace. *Disability & Society*, 29(1): 1–14.

Santuzzi, A.M., Waltz, P.R., Finkelstein, L.M. & Rupp, D.E. 2014. Invisible disabilities: unique challenges for employees and organizations. *Industrial and Organizational Psychology*, 7(2): 204–19.

Shakespeare, T. 2011. It's the economy, stupid! The ironic absence of class analysis in British disability studies. *Creating a Society for All: Disability and Economy Forum*. Leeds: Disability Press, pp. 40–9. www.panusp.org/wp-content/uploads/2013/02/Disability-and-the-Economy-2011-Book.pdf

References

Abberley, P. 1987. The concept of oppression and the development of a social theory of disability. *Disability, Handicap & Society*, 2(1): 5–19.

Agocs, C. & Burr, C. 1996. Employment equity, affirmative action and managing diversity. *International Journal of Manpower*, 17(4/5): 30.

AIWH 2004. *Disability and Its Relationship to Health Conditions and Other Factors*. AIWH DIS 37. Canberra: AIWH (Disability Series).

Alborno, N. & Gaad, E. 2012. Employment of young adults with disabilities in Dubai – a case study. *Journal of Policy and Practice in Intellectual Disabilities*, 9(2): 103–11

Andreev, A.A. 2008. *To Work or Not to Work? Labor Supply Decisions of Russia's Disabled*. Unpublished doctoral dissertation, Duke University, New York.

Barlow, J., Wright, C. & Cullen, L. 2002. A job-seeking self-efficacy scale for people with physical disabilities, *British Journal of Guidance and Counselling*, 30(1): 37–53.

Barnes, C. 1992. Disability and employment. *Personnel Review*, 21(6): 55–73.

Barnes, C. 2000. A working social model? Disability, work and disability politics in the 21st century. *Critical Social Policy*, 20(4): 441–57.

Barnes, C. & Mercer, G. 2005. Disability, work, and welfare: challenging the social exclusion of disabled people. *Work, Employment & Society*, 19(3): 527–45.

Benshoff, L., Barrera, M. & Heymann, J. 2014. Disability rights advocacy and employment: a qualitative study of the National Centre for the Employment of Disabled People (NCPEDP) in India. *Work: A Journal of Prevention, Assessment and Rehabilitation,* 48(3): 453–64.

Block, P., Balcazar, F. & Keys, C. 2001. From pathology to power. *Journal of Disability Policy Studies*, 12(1): 18–27.

Chadwick, A. 1996. Knowledge, power and the Disability Discrimination Bill. *Disability & Society*, 11(1): 25–40.

CIPD & Mind 2011. *Managing and Supporting Mental Health at Work: Disclosure Tools for Managers*. London: Chartered Institute of Personnel and Development. www.cipd.co.uk/publicpolicy/policy-reports/mental-health-work-disclosure-tools.aspx

Colella, A. J. & Bruyère, S.M. 2010. Disability and employment: new directions for industrial and organizational psychology. In S. Zedeck (Ed.), *APA Handbook of Industrial and Organizational Psychology, Volume 1: Building and Developing the Organization*. Washington, DC: American Psychological Association, pp. 473–503.

Coleman, N., Sykes, W. & Groom, C. 2013. *Barriers to Employment and Unfair Treatment at Work: A Quantitative Analysis of Disabled People's Experience*, Research Report no. 88. Manchester: Equality and Human Rights Commission. www.equalityhumanrights.com/sites/default/files/documents/barriers_and_unfair_treatment_final.pdf

Disability Rights Commission 2003. *A Survey of the Views and Experiences of Young Disabled People in Great Britain*. Disability Rights Commission, UK.

dos Santos Rodrigues, P., Luecking, R.G., Glat, R. & Daquer, A.F.C. 2013. Improving workforce outcomes among persons with disabilities in Brazil through youth apprenticeships and customized employment. *Journal of Vocational Rehabilitation*, 38(3): 185–94

Foster, D. 2007. Legal obligation or personal lottery? Employee experiences of disability and the negotiation of adjustments in the public sector workplace. *Work, Employment & Society*, 21(1): 67–84.

Foster, D. & Fosh, P. 2010. Negotiating 'difference': representing disabled employees in the British workplace. *British Journal of Industrial Relations*, 48(3): 560–82.

Fritsch, C. 2008. Right to work – a comparative look at China and Japan's labor rights for disabled persons. *Loyola University Chicago International Law Review*, 6: 403–20.

Fujimoto, Y., Härtel, C.E.J., & Azmat, F. 2013. Towards a diversity justice management model: integrating organizational justice and diversity management. *Social Responsibility Journal*, 9(1): 148–66.

Fujimoto, Y., Härtel, C.E.J., & Härtel, G.F. 2004. A field test of the diversity-openness moderator model in newly formed groups: openness to diversity affects group decision effectiveness and interaction patterns. *Cross-Cultural Management: An International Journal*, 11(4): 4–16.

Fujimoto, Y., Härtel, C.E.J. & Panipucci, D. 2005. Emotional experience of individualist–collectivist workgroups: findings from a study of 14 multinationals located in Australia. In C.E.J. Härtel, W.J. Zerbe & N.M. Ashkanasy (Eds), *Emotions in Organizational Behavior*. Mahwah, NJ: Lawrence Erlbaum Associates, Inc., pp. 125–60.

Fujimoto, Y., Rentschler, R., Le, H., Edwards, D. & Härtel, C.E.J. 2014. Lessons learned from community organizations: inclusion of people with disabilities and others. *British Journal of Management*, 25, 518–37. doi: 10.1111/1467-8551.12034

Galvin, R. 2004. Can welfare reform make disability disappear? *Australian Journal of Social Issues*, 39(3): 343–55.

Gates, L.B. & Akabas, S.H. 2011. Inclusion of people with mental health disabilities into the workplace: accommodation as a social process. In I.Z. Schultz & E.S. Rogers (Eds), *Work Accommodation and Retention in Mental Health*. New York: Springer, pp. 375–91.

Hall, E. & Wilton, R. 2011. Alternative spaces of 'work' and inclusion for disabled people. *Disability & Society*, 26(7): 867–80.

Härtel, C.E.J. 2004. Towards a multicultural world: Identifying work systems, practices and employee attitudes that embrace diversity. *The Australian Journal of Management*, 29(2): 189–200.

Härtel, C.E.J. 2008. How to build a healthy emotional culture and avoid a toxic culture. In C.L. Cooper & N.M. Ashkanasy (Eds), *Research Companion to Emotion in Organization*, Cheltenham, UK: Edwin Elgar Publishing, pp. 575–88.

Härtel, C.E.J., Hsu, A.C.F. & Boyle, M. 2002. A conceptual examination of the causal sequences of emotional labor, emotional dissonance and emotional exhaustion: the argument for the role of contextual and provider characteristics. In N.M. Ashkanasy, W.J. Zerbe & C.E.J. Härtel (Eds), *Managing Emotions in the Workplace*. Armonk, New York: M.E Sharpe, pp. 251–75.

Härtel, C.E.J., Härtel, G.F., & Trumble, R.B. 2013. IDADA: the individual difference approach to assessing and developing diversity-awareness. *Journal of Management & Organization*, 19(1): 60–74.

Härtel, C.E.J. & Panipucci, D. 2007. How 'bad apples' spoil the bunch: faultlines, emotional levers and exclusion in the workplace. In C.E.J Härtel, N.M. Ashkanasy & W.J Zerbe (Eds). *Research on Emotion in Organizations: Functionality, Intentionality and Morality* (vol. 3). Oxford, UK: Elsevier/JAI Press, pp. 287–310.

Hartnett, H.P., Stuart, H., Thurman, H., Loy, B. & Batiste, L.C. 2011. Employers' perceptions of the benefits of workplace accommodations: reasons to hire, retain and promote people with disabilities. *Journal of Vocational Rehabilitation*, 34(1): 17–23.

Hiranandani, V., Kumar, A. & Sonpal, D. 2014. Making community inclusion work for persons with disabilities: drawing lessons from the field. *Community Development*, 45(2): 150–64.

HWC 2013. *Barriers Everywhere: Lack of Accessibility for People with Disabilities in Russia*. New York: Human Rights Watch. www.hrw.org/node/118528

ILO 2010. *Disability in the Workplace: Company Practices*, Geneva: International Labour Office. www.ilo.org/wcmsp5/groups/public/@ed_emp/@ifp_skills/documents/publication/wcms_150658.pdf

ILO 2011. *Disability in the Workplace: Employers' Organizations and Business Networks*. Geneva: International Labour Office. www.ilo.org/wcmsp5/groups/public/@ed_emp/@ifp_skills/documents/publication/wcms_167204.pdf

Joachim, G. & Acorn, S. 2000. Stigma of visible and invisible chronic conditions. *Journal of Advanced Nursing*, 32(1): 243–8.

Jones, M.K. 2006. Is there employment discrimination against the disabled? *Economics Letters*, 92(1): 32–7.

Kirakosyan, L. 2013. Linking disability rights and democracy: insights from Brazil. *Societies Without Borders*, 8(1): 29–52.

Kirsh, B. & Gewurtz, R. 2011. Organizational culture and work issues for individuals with mental health disabilities. In I.Z. Schultz & E.S. Rogers (Eds), *Work Accommodation and Retention in Mental Health*. New York: Springer, pp. 393–408.

KNA 2009. *Disabled Employment Networks – A Practical Guide*. London: Kate Nash Associates. www.katenashassociates.com

Konrad, A.M., Moore, M.E., Ng, E.S., Doherty, A.J. & Breward, K. 2013. Temporary work, under-employment and workplace accommodations: relationship to well-being for workers with disabilities. *British Journal of Management*, 24(3): 367–82.

Kulkarni, M. & Lengnick–Hall, M.L. 2011. Socialization of people with disabilities in the work-place. *Human Resource Management*, 50(4): 521–40.

Kumar, A., Sonpal, D. & Hiranandani, V. 2012. Trapped between ableism and neoliberalism: critical reflections on disability and employment in India. *Disability Studies Quarterly*, 32(3).

Linkow, P., Barrington, L., Bruyère, S., Figueroa, Y. & Wright, M. 2013. *Levelling the Playing Field: Attracting, Engaging, and Advancing People with Disabilities*. New York: The Conference Board. http://digitalcommons.ilr.cornell.edu/edicollect/1292/

Lysaght, R., Ouellette-Kuntz, H. & Lin, C.J. 2012. Untapped potential: perspectives on the employment of people with intellectual disability. *Work: A Journal of Prevention, Assessment and Rehabilitation*, 41(4): 409–22.

Martz, E. 2007. Facilitating inclusive employment: an examination of the accommodations for and the barriers to employment for Russians with disabilities. *International Journal of Rehabilitation Research*, 30(4): 321–6.

Matthews, C.K. & Harrington, N.G. 2000. Invisible disability. In D.O. Braithwaite & T.L. Thompson (Eds), *Handbook of Communication and People with Disabilities: Research and Application*. Mahwah, NJ: Erlbaum, pp. 405–21.

McLaughlin, M.E., Bell, M.P. & Stringer, D.Y. 2004. Stigma and acceptance of persons with dis-abilities: understudied aspects of workforce diversity. *Group & Organization Management*, 29(3): 302–33

Mitra, S. 2008. The recent decline in the employment of persons with disabilities in South Africa, 1998–2006. *South African Journal of Economics*, 76(3): 480–92.

Mitra, S. & Sambamoorthi, U. 2006. Employment of persons with disabilities: evidence from the National Sample Survey. *Economic and Political Weekly*, 14(3): 199–203.

Mitra, S. & Sambamoorthi, U. 2008. Disability and the rural labor market in India: evidence for males in Tamil Nadu. *World Development*, 36(5): 934–52

Mitra, S., Posarac, A. & Vick, B. 2013. Disability and poverty in developing countries: a multidi-mensional study. *World Development*, 41: 1–18.

MSA 2006. *Federal Law No. 29 of 2006 in Respect of the Rights of People with Special Needs*. Abu Dhabi: Ministry of Social Affairs. www.msa.gov.ae/MSA/EN/Documents/RulesAndPolicies/Federal%20Law%20in%20respect%20of%20The%20Rights%20of%20people%20with%20special%20needs.pdf

Myer, S. & Sai, D. 2013. The effects of disability on earnings in China and the United States. *Book and Media Reviews*, 9(4): 34.

Naidoo, P., Maja, P.A., Mann, W.M., Sing, D. & Steyn, A.J. 2011. Employing people with disabil-ities in South Africa. *South African Journal of Occupational Therapy*, 41(1): 24–33.

Oliver, M. 1986. Social policy and disability: some theoretical issues. *Disability, Handicap & Society*, 1(1): 5–17.

Panipucci, D. & Härtel, C.E.J. 2006. Positive disobedience: when norms prescribe the exclusion of dissimilar others. In A. Della Fave (Ed.), *Dimensions of Well-Being: Research and Intervention*. Milan, Italy: FrancoAngeli, pp. 241–53.

Priestley, M. 1998. Constructions and creations: idealism, materialism and disability theory. *Disability & Society*, 13(1): 75–94.

RADAR 2011. *Doing Seniority Differently (Final Report): A Study of High Fliers Living with Ill-Health, Injury or Disability*. Royal Association for Disability Rights. www.disabilityrightsuk.org/sites/default/files/pdf/DSD%20Exec%20Sum%20(high%20res).pdf

Rollins, A.L., Bond, G.R., Jones, A.M., Kukla, M. & Collins, L.A. 2011. Work-place social networks and their relationship with job outcomes and other employment characteristics for people with severe mental illness. *Journal of Vocational Rehabilitation*, 35: 243–52.

Roulstone, A. & Williams, J. 2014. Being disabled, being a manager: 'glass partitions' and conditional identities in the contemporary workplace. *Disability & Society*, 29(1): 1–14.

Santuzzi, A.M., Waltz, P.R., Finkelstein, L.M. & Rupp, D.E. 2014. Invisible disabilities: unique challenges for employees and organizations. *Industrial and Organizational Psychology*, 7(2): 204–19.

Scheid, T.L. 2005. Stigma as a barrier to employment: mental disability and the Americans with Disabilities Act. *International Journal of Law and Psychiatry*, 28(6): 670–90.

Schur, L., Kruse, D., Blasi, J. & Blanck, P. 2009. Is disability disabling in all workplaces? Disability, workplace disparities, and corporate culture. *Industrial Relations*, 48(3): 381–410.

Shakespeare, T. 2011. It's the economy, stupid! The ironic absence of class analysis in British disability studies. *Creating a Society for All: Disability and Economy Forum*. Leeds: Disability Press, pp. 40–9. www.panusp.org/wp-content/uploads/2013/02/Disability-and-the-Economy-2011-Book.pdf

Shakespeare, T. & Watson, N. 2001. The social model of disability: an outdated ideology? *Research in Social Science and Disability*, 2: 9–28.

Snyder, L.A., Carmichael, J.S., Blackwell, L.V., Cleveland, J.N. & Thornton III, G.C. 2010. Perceptions of discrimination and justice among employees with disabilities. *Employee Responsibilities and Rights Journal*, 22(1): 5–19.

Stein, M.A. 2010. China and disability rights. *Loyola of Los Angeles International and Comparative Law Review*, 33: 7–27.

Stone, D.L. & Colella, A. 1996. A model of factors affecting the treatment of disabled individuals in organizations. *Academy of Management Review*, 21: 352–401.

Swain, J. & French, S. 2000. Towards an affirmation model of disability. *Disability & Society*, 15(4): 569–82.

Vickers, M.H. 2009. Bullying, disability and work: a case study of workplace bullying. *Qualitative Research in Organizations and Management: An International Journal*, 4(3): 255–72.

WHO 2011. *World Report on Disability*. Geneva: World Health Organization.

Wiggett-Barnard, C. & Swartz, L. 2012. What facilitates the entry of persons with disabilities into South African companies? *Disability and Rehabilitation*, 34(12): 1016–23.

Wilson-Kovacs, D., Ryan, M.K., Haslam, S.A. & Rabinovich, A. 2008. 'Just because you can get a wheelchair in the building doesn't necessarily mean that you can still participate': barriers to the career advancement of disabled professionals. *Disability & Society*, 23(7): 705–17.

Wolbring, G. 2008. The politics of ableism. *Development*, 51(2): 252–8.

Religious diversity in the workplace

8

Selçuk Uygur and Erhan Aydin

Intended learning outcomes

After completing this chapter, readers will have a clear understanding of religious aspects of diversity in the workplace, both state and private sector. In particular, they will be able to:

- Understand the concept of religious diversity
- Discuss religious and related concepts such as spirituality in the workplace
- Understand legislation related to religion and freedom of religion
- Compare the relationships between religious diversity and the workplace in different country contexts
- Discuss discrimination against religious beliefs in the workplace within different country contexts

Introduction

This chapter will enable students and readers to understand religion as a dimension of diversity. Religion in the context of diversity has been neglected by many scholars in terms of theoretical and empirical studies (Schaefer and Mattis, 2012). However, some scholars (e.g. Kelly, 1995; Dubow et al., 2000; Richards and Bergin, 2000) have considered the contribution of religion, together with the concept of spirituality, towards the global identity construction of diverse individuals. Thus, this chapter provides a brief under-standing of diversity through the logic of discrimination in diverse environments, and a discussion of religion, spirituality and the workplace in theoretical and research studies. In order to understand religious diversity and discrimination against religious beliefs or lack of belief, Turkey and the UK have been used as specific cases, looking at religion, religious diversity and overcoming discrimination in legislative-based approaches. The value of making such a comparison between these countries is due to the differences between the state and legislative structures of the countries. The chapter also examines secular conservative thought in Turkey and non-secular liberal thought in the UK through analysis of the legislations of both countries, European Court of Human Rights Factsheets, Equality and Human Rights Commission Reports and international research centre reports on religious minorities in both countries. While comparing Turky and the UK in terms of religious diversity, the main difference appears to be the type of workplaces where discrimination occurs. In Turky, religious discrimination is mostly observed in the public sector workplaces, while it is generally noticed in the private business sector in the UK. In the following sections, we will identify the key concepts in religious diversity and discrimination, and discuss the differences between Turky and the UK.

Understanding diversity and discrimination

The term *diversity* has been described as 'taken-for-granted' by Harrison and Klein (2007). In general, diversity has been used as a term that is employed in parallel to multiculturalism. Multiculturalism is associated with visible differences such as race and ethnicity (Wing-Sue and Sue, 2008; Mendoza-Denton and Espana, 2010). However, the discourse of cultural variation and individual difference constitutes diversity as an umbrella term that encompasses such differences as age, ability status, national origin, immigration status, sexual preference, and spiritual and religious identity (Hicks, 2003; Herring, 2009). Another perspective with regard to diversity has been visible and invis-ible social identity groups, as discussed by Schaeffer and Mattis (2012). Thus, they emphasise social identities (e.g. race, ethnicity, sexuality, class, religious identity and immigration status). They claim that identities impact on: 1) the representation of indi-viduals in the public and private spheres, 2) accessing opportunities and resources by individuals, and 3) their intellectual, social, economic, physical or socio-political welfare (Schaeffer and Mattis, 2012: 320). On the other hand, Loden and Rosener (1991) have a different approach to classifying diversity. They emphasise primary dimensions (e.g. age, ethnicity, sexual orientation and physical abilities) and secondary dimensions (e.g. edu-cational background, income, marital status and belief) of diversity. The definitions and classifications of diversity are important data in helping organisations to control the dimensions of diversity; therefore, managers of human resources in organisations should be aware of the potential advantages of diversity in order to minimise the disadvantages, such as creating conflict among organisation members (Cox, 1993). Diversity is a requirement for organisational survival (Morrison, 1996; Fleury, 2000). Thus, the concept has been evaluated as one of the management tools used to remove invisible barriers in an organisational context (Ditomaso et al., 2007; Reeves et al., 2013; Konrad, 2003). Having summarised diversity at the conceptual and dimensional level, the next term reviewed will be *discrimination*; because discrimination is seen in diverse populations.

Discrimination has been defined as 'adverse actions toward employees or applicants on the basis of race, colour, religion, national origin, age, sex or disability' (Wendell, 2003: 113). In the studies by Lawler and Bae (1998), and Regmi et al. (2009), discrimination has been used in relation to *inequality*, which encompasses exclusion of some specific groups with regard to power, income and utility, or other forms of some treatment (Ataov, 2002). As is widely accepted, the outcomes of modernity together with organisations which have an important position in the capitalist system have played an important role in the existence of discrimination (Özcan et al., 2011). According to Acker (2006), economic and social inequalities are increased within the organisational workplace through discrimination, and 'inequality regimes' are created. Inequalities based on gender, class, ethnicity and religion can be very obvious in the practices of organisations. Thus, differentiating between salaries or creating matches between some jobs and some religions can be called 'discriminatory behaviour' in an unequal workplace environment (Özcan et al., 2011).

One of the common discriminations has been on the basis of faith/religion-related differences in multicultural countries (Fox, 2000). Especially in the post-9/11 era, religious discrimination is an important issue for organisations, and after 9/11, some US-origin organisations have followed a discriminatory approach towards Muslims (Kuran and McCaffrey, 2008). In this chapter, two different case studies in the UK and Turkey will indicate biases which are the main reasons for discrimination in terms of religious diversity.

Organisational insight   8.1

Religious discrimination case at Tesco

Restrictions on an on-site prayer room led to Tesco losing a religious-discrimination case brought by two Muslim men. The Bedford Employment Tribunal found that Tesco had indirectly discriminated against Abdirisak Aden and Mahamed Hasan at Tesco's Crick depot after restrictions were placed on the use of the prayer room. The room was provided after lobbying by devout Muslims in 2008. In 2012 new 'prayer time guidelines' were introduced. Staff had to inform managers if they were going to pray and ask for a key. They had to fill in a book when they used the room and were only allowed to pray individually rather than as a group. The Tribunal decided against Tesco and awarded the men an undisclosed sum for 'injury to their feelings'.

Özcan et al. (2011) carried out research into health care employees in public hospitals in Afyonkarahisar, a Turkish city with a population of 171,000. Many discrimination areas and dynamics were considered in this research, such as ethnicity, religion, disability and physical appearance. However, when the mean values of the dimensions of ethnicity, religion and disability were examined, the results indicated that there was no discriminatory behaviour against employees. The results were similar for the other dimensions studied. Indeed, the dimension of religion is an important part of the study, as understanding of religion might vary and different interpretations could occur at the same time. Muslims are in the majority in Turkey, therefore research related to Muslims as a broad category will find that there is no discrimination against them. The main reason for this is the macro level approach to religion. In the research by Özcan et al. (2011), this approach was taken into consideration, and Alewism, which has a different interpretation from the orthodox Islam and has nearly 12 million followers in Turkey, was considered as a different religion. Nevertheless, the research indicated that perceived discrimination is notably low regarding religion. On the other hand, research by Poole (2000) based on 6,507 newspaper articles, found a common view that Islam is a threat to British society. In addition to this perception, another study found that Muslims are regarded as deviant, irrational and different from British society, and Islam is seen as an antiquated religion (Revell, 2010: 208). The research based on interviews with primary school students in their fourth year in primary school, shows that there are some stereotypes with regard to Muslims. These are (Revell, 2010: 210):

- Muslims are needy and other people are wealthy.
- Muslims do not have standard jobs.
- Their families are very intolerant.
- They have lots of children and big families.
- They cannot go to the same places as us; they are not allowed to go out at night.

It is obvious that perceptions with regard to Islam and Muslims in childhood are a base point for predicting the perceptions of business owners as adults; for that reason, these perceptions may create religion-based discrimination in workplaces in the UK.

Discussion activity 8.1

Discuss the concepts of discrimination, diversity, equality and inequality. Identify a developed and underdeveloped country and compare them with regard to diversity policies.

Religion, spirituality and the workplace

This section looks at religion, spirituality and the workplace. The concept of *spirituality* will be introduced to illustrate the conflicts among scholars in terminological discussion. The definitions and perspectives with regard to religion will also contribute to understanding religion in workplaces and religious diversity.

The world can be considered as a global town where individuals are mobile and work in virtual teams (Adler and Gundersen, 2008; Conlin, 1999). So, individuals are affected by many factors such as 'religious beliefs, norms and practices of others and need to develop awareness of the issues, and processes to manage religion at work' (Rao, 2011: 232). The word religion comes from the Latin word 'ligare' which means to join or to link (Hinnels, 1997). The main function of religion is to give power to individuals to control their destiny (Johnson, 1997). According to Cromwell (1997: 169) religion can be problematic, because religion is not like other characteristics (e.g. disability, gender, disability, etc.), it is 'an acquired property consisting of a set of beliefs that can be dynamic in nature'. Even if the concept of religion is clear, various areas of discussion have been noted by some authors. For instance, Harvey (2001) examines how the concept of religion in the scientific field has been avoided by many authors. Instead of this term, authors prefer using 'spirit' and 'community' as less-contested concepts. Hicks (2002: 380) indicates that most academicians claim 'public spheres like politics and workplaces are secular'. Thus, Hicks (2002) asserts that the roles of religion and spiritually in the workplace are neglected because of secular thought. Many authors (Bailey and Eastmen, 1994; Milbank, 1990; Mitroff and Denton, 1999a, b) criticise the framework of secular thought in the workplace and emphasise conceptual differences between religion and spirituality. However, the concept of spirituality is confused and is examined with negative connotations. It is seen like organised religion in terms of having particular beliefs, moral rules and traditions (Cacioppe, 2000). In their conceptual paper, Mitroff and Denton (1999b) emphasise that spirituality is informal, unstructured and unorganised. On the other hand, religion mentions salvation as a major aim (Cacioppe, 2000). Hicks (2002: 380) integrates the distinctions between these concepts by these authors as 'religion is institutional, dogmatic and rigid; spirituality is personal, emotional and adaptable to an individual's needs'. Due to the differences in the nature of the concepts, while spirituality is accepted in the secular structure, it is not possible to accept religion-related talk and action in that structure (Hicks, 2002). In parallel with the perspectives of authors (academics), religion is a topic that most managers avoid discussing (Rao, 2012).

It is common practice for individuals to have personal views on religion and spiritual matters in the workplace (Morgan, 2004). This desire has created some difficulties for today's managers; because many managers do not understand some religions, and this has created discrimination against religions which are not followed by managers (Borstorff and Arlington, 2011). In their research, Borstorff and

Arlington (2011) looked at data from an online survey of 141 individuals with regard to the issues that are of common importance for religions. These issues are holidays and time-off provision, dress codes, food and accommodation, affinity networks and their acceptance, and office space decoration. The importance of religion can be seen in the research, because participants defended their beliefs against religious discrimination. A common view of participants is that businesses should have a diversity policy in their structure through state regulation. Legislation can guide employers to introduce company regulations. So, employers should give great importance to religious diversity and respect it. If they do not respect religious diversity, litigation can be brought into the agenda, which can outweigh the cost of accommodating discrimination.

Religion and spirituality are directly related to work, because religious obligations can sometimes be strict in workplaces. In other words, some workers may avoid working in a particular job because of religious constraints, such as Catholic nurses who may not be involved in abortion, Hutterites who may not want to drive cars and Muslims who may refuse to work in a company that produces alcoholic drinks (Haddad, 2002). For that reason, even if some avoidance exists in workplaces because of religion differences, religious diversity must be managed by organisations at a permissible level (Bouma et al., 2003). For instance, religious holy days (e.g. Sunday for Christians, Saturday for Jews and Friday for Muslims) are occasions of legitimate absence. On the other hand, religions can regulate how people dress, so toleration of religious diversity can create a peaceful workplace. Bouma et al. (2003: 52) point out the key features of religion/spirituality that may concern individuals: 'Beliefs about the ultimate nature of reality, including hope, destiny, purpose and the relationship of the now to the eternal, the changing to the persistent, the human to the more than human'; and 'Practices, rites and rituals through which the religion is expressed, related to life and the beliefs inculcated and put into practice'. A specific example of tolerance with regard to religion is the study of Ball and Haque (2003). They outline the meaning of Islam and the regulations of that religion concerning the workplace. They state (2003: 317): 'Islam comes from the word salama which means both surrender to God and peace. The word Muslim comes from the same root and it means one who surrenders or submits to what God has ordained'. In order to understand the workplace environment from the perspective of Islam, some rules must be examined. In Ball and Haque (2003), these rules include: 1) meeting spiritual needs (praying five times a day), 2) dietary needs (fasting in the Ramadan period) and 3) dress code (avoiding dressing to be physically attractive). Therefore, when religions regulate their followers regarding the workplace, then discrimination against diversity can be seen. If religions do not impose restrictions, individuals cannot identify the religion of workers. Namely, actions or behaviours in the workplace with regard to beliefs clearly indicate the worker's religion, so policies related to diversity are crucial in order to provide a peaceful workplace environment.

Discussion activity 8.2

Discuss the regulations in your country from the perspective of both diversity issues and religious discrimination. Give at least one organisational example of religious discrimination.

Religious diversity: a comparative approach

This section will examine religious diversity from macro and micro level approaches. The macro level approach will encompass religious diversity across the world in terms of regional differences among the religions which have the most believers around the world. At the micro level, we will discuss the UK and Turkey in terms of different state structures and freedoms in their legislations.

The Pew Research Center obtained data related to religious diversity around the world. The study focused on widely followed religions: Christianity, Islam, Buddhism, Hinduism, Judaism. These religions encompass three quarters of the world population. The remainder of the global population was categorised in three additional groups: the religiously unaffiliated (atheists, agnostics or nothing in particular), traditional religions (such as Chinese folk religions, Native American religions and Australian Aboriginal religions), and other religions. Table 8.1 summarises religious diversity as found by the Pew Research Center (2014).

Table 8.1   Regional religious diversity (per cent)

	Very high	High	Moderate	Moderate	Low	Low
	Asia–Pacific	Sub-saharan Africa	Europe	North America	Latin America Caribbean	Middle East–North Africa
Christians	7	63	75	77	90	4
Muslims	24	30	6	1	<1	93
Unaffiliated	21	3	18	17	8	1
Hindus	25	<1	<1	1	<1	1
Buddhists	12	<1	<1	1	<1	<1
Folk religions	9	3	<1	<1	2	<1
Jews	<1	1	<1	2	<1	2

Source: Pew Research Center, *Global Religious Diversity Report*, April 2014.

Christians and Muslims are in a majority around the world, as indicated in Table 8.1. After identifying these rates of diversity across the world, the Pew Research Center created the Religious Diversity Index (RDI). This index has four levels which are: very high (7–9.5 or higher), high (5.5–6.9), moderate (3–5.4) and low (0.0–2.9). The Religious Diversity Index has great importance for understanding the amount of diversity in countries. Within this chapter, after looking at macro level figures for religion across the world, the UK and Turkey have been chosen as countries which have both different levels of religious diversity and different religious issues at the micro level. Thus, Table 8.2 summarises the UK's and Turkey's RDI indexes and religious diversity.

Table 8.2   Religious diversity in the UK and Turkey

Country	RDI	Christian (%)	Muslim (%)	Unaffiliated (%)	Hindu (%)	Buddhist (%)	Folk religion (%)	Other religion (%)	Jewish (%)	2010 country population
Turkey	0.4	0.4	98.0	1.2	<1	<1	<1	2	<1	72750000
UK	5.1	71.1	4.4	21.3	1.3	0.4	0.3	0.8	0.5	62040000

Source: Pew Research Center, *Global Religious Diversity Report*, April 2014.

Even though, as Table 8.2 illustrates, Turkey has a large Muslim population, a conceptual conflict exists in the country. This concerns Alawism. One of the famous legal forums of Alawism describes this conflict as:

> The main discussion related to Alawism and Islam is whether Alawism can be examined in Islam or not. Some Alevi authors wrote that Caliph Ali was the same person both in Alawism and in Islam. Thus, this assumption brought the knowledge of Alawism in Islamic approaches. However, these Alevi authors did not explain the common or distinctive points in Shiah Islam or Sunni Islam. Alawism cannot be only explained through Islamic perspectives. If the perspectives take this into consideration, the other factors of Alawism will be excluded and this will have a detrimental effect on wisdom of Alawism. Evaluation of Alawism should not be done through political preferences and worldview. It is an ethos. However, it does not mean that Alawism does not have a part of Islam (aleviforum.net, 2014).

As is indicated in the passage, some Muslims accept that Alawism is an Islamic approach, but most Muslims do not accept Alawism as a part of Islam. The research by the Pew Research Center does not give importance to this conflict in its study; for that reason discrimination studies with regard to religious minorities in Turkey become crucial, as such studies could project the level of religious pluralism in the country.

RDI values also indicate that religious diversity is low in Turkey (RDI = 0.4) in comparison with the UK (RDI = 5.1). However, according to the Summary Report of the RELIGARE Project (2013), three models can be identified in the European region (which includes Turkey) about approaches to religious issues. These models are given in Table 8.3.

Table 8.3   Models and examples of approaches to religious issues

Model	Example
Strict separation between states and religious groups	France, Turkey
States with established majority church	UK, Denmark
Agreements by churches and religious communities with states	Italy, Spain, Germany

Source: Summary Report of the RELIGARE Project (2013); www.religareproject.eu.

These models indicate that Turkey and the UK have different perspectives on religion. While Turkey is secular, the UK system is not. Understanding the structure of states and legislations will make clear the freedoms related to religion and within the scope of this chapter.

Legislation and prevention of discrimination

In this section legislation in the UK and Turkey will be presented. Then, the two countries will be compared within the context of their legislation frameworks.

The UK as a European Union (EU) member follows EU legislation. Table 8.4 outlines the UK approach to freedom of religion.

Table 8.4   UK legislation and religion

Legislation	Definition
Directive 200/78/EC of 27 November 2000 establishing a general framework for equal treatment in employment and occupation.	The concepts of religion and belief are not explicitly defined. The introduction to the Directive expresses respect for the principles of the European Convention on Human Rights (ECHR). The concepts of religion and belief should therefore be read consistently with Article 9 of ECHR. Mainly Article 9 emphasises the freedom of religion manifestation in public as teaching, practice and observance
Employment Equality (Religion and Belief) Regulations (S1/2003/1660)	Section 2 (1): In these regulations, 'religion and belief' means any religion and belief. There is no specific definition of religion
Racial and Religious Hatred Act 2006	Schedule 1, amending Public Order Act 1986: 'Religious hatred' means hatred against a group of people defined by reference to religious beliefs or lack of religious belief

(Continued)

(Continued)

Legislation	Definition
Equality Act 2006	The Act introduces a broad definition of religion or belief with the goal of prohibiting discrimination in the provision of goods and services and amends the 2003 Regulations to make the definition consistent. There is no longer any requirement that a belief should be similar to a religion and it protects lack of religion and belief
	Section 44 Religion and Belief
	In this
	(a) 'religion' means any religion
	(b) 'belief' means any religious or philosophical belief
	(c) a reference to religion includes a reference to a lack of religion, and
	(d) a reference to belief includes a reference to a lack of belief
Equality Act 2010	Section 10 of Religion or Belief emphasises
	(a) 'Religion' means any religion and a reference to religion includes a reference to a lack of religion
	(b) 'Belief' means any religious or philosophical belief and a reference to belief includes a reference to a lack of belief

Source: Prochaska, E. (2013) *The Definition of Religion or Belief in Equality and Human Rights Law*, Equality and Human Rights Commission.

In contrast to the UK, Turkey has its own legislation regarding freedom of religion. Legislation in Turkey does not explicitly define the concept of religion and belief. Instead of a definition, the Constitution of the Republic of Turkey emphasises freedom of religion in Article 24:

Everyone has the freedom of conscience, religious belief and conviction. Acts of worship, religious rites and ceremonies shall be conducted freely, as long as they do not violate the provisions of Article 14. No one shall be compelled to worship, or to participate in religious rites and ceremonies, or to reveal religious beliefs and convictions, or be blamed or accused because of his religious beliefs and convictions. Religious and moral education and instruction shall be conducted under state supervision and control. Instruction in religious culture and morals shall be one of the compulsory lessons in the curricula of primary and secondary schools. Other religious education and instruction shall be subject to the individual's own desire, and in the case of minors, to the request of their legal representatives. No one shall be allowed to exploit or abuse religion or religious feelings, or things held sacred by religion, in any manner whatsoever, for the purpose of personal or political interest or influence, or for even partially basing the fundamental, social, economic, political, and legal order of the State on religious tenets.

Article 14 of the Constitution is related to violation of indivisible integrity of the state, its territory and nation, and to endangering the existence of the democratic and secular order of the Republic-based human rights. Turkish legislation uses these two articles to allow freedom of diversity. Other acts in the Constitution relating to freedom include labour law. Therefore, evaluation of freedom and restrictions is subjective rather than objective. Table 8.5 lists European Court of Justice Decisions with regard to specific cases in Turkey and where the Court decided in favour of applicants. This indicates the subjective restrictions on freedom related to religion in Turkey, because articles in the legislation of Turkey are open-ended. Court decisions in Turkey regarding complaints of discrimination can be decided with regard to individual judgement rather than specific articles of legislation in Turkey.

After reviewing the legislative perspective relating to freedom of religion, we will now compare the two countries regarding legislative freedom and the states' approach

Table 8.5 Turkey: cases in the European Court of Justice – religion

Case name	Problem	Court decision
Ahmet Aslan v Others (2010)	The applicants, 127 members of a religious group known as Aczimendi tarikati, complained of their conviction in 1997 for a breach of the law on the wearing of headgear and of the rules on wearing religious garments in public, after having toured the streets and appeared at a court hearing wearing the distinctive dress of their group (made up of a turban, baggy trousers, a tunic and a stick)	The Court found a violation of Article 9, holding in particular that there was no evidence that the applicants had represented a threat to the public order or that they had been involved in proselytism by exerting inappropriate pressure on passers-by during their gathering. The Court emphasised that in contrast to other cases, the case concerned punishment for the wearing of particular dress in public areas that were open to all, and not regulation of the wearing of religious symbols in public establishments, where religious neutrality might take precedence over the right to manifest one's religion
Sinan Isik (2010)	A member of the Alevi religious community, the applicant in 2004 unsuccessfully applied to a court requesting that his identity card feature the word 'Alevi' rather than the word 'Islam'. It was obligatory in Turkey for the holder's religion to be indicated on an identity card until 2006, when the option was introduced to request that the entry be left blank. His request was refused on the grounds that the term 'Alevi' referred to a subgroup of Islam and that the indication 'Islam' on the identity card was thus correct	The Court found a violation of Article 9 which had arisen not from the refusal to indicate the applicant's faith (Alevi) on his identity card but from the fact that his identity card contained an indication of religion, regardless of whether it was obligatory or optional. The Court underlined that the freedom to manifest one's religion had a negative aspect, namely the right not to be obliged to disclose one's religion

Source: European Court of Human Rights (2013) *Factsheet – Freedom of Religion*, July.

to freedom of religion. In Table 8.6 the UK and Turkey are compared in terms of freedom of religion.

Table 8.6 Comparison of freedom of religion in the UK and Turkey

	Legislation	Discrimination against religion	Structure of state	Approach to freedom of religion
UK	EU legislation	Private sector oriented discrimination can be seen. Therefore, the private sector has most equality and diversity policies	Non- secular	Non-secular liberal
Turkey	Constitution and international agreements (European Court of Human Rights)	Mostly, public sector oriented discrimination can be seen. Labour law mentions freedom with regard to the Constitution, but there is no implementation against religious discrimination in the private sector, because employers can create some other reason to fire an employee or not accept him/ her for a job. However, some companies have diversity policies under their human resources departments, but these are not professional such as those in UK companies	Secular	Secular conservative

The UK has a *non-secular liberal* ethos which means that the official religion is Christianity, and there is no formal separation between the state and the Church. Therefore, there is no need to intervene in religious diversity within the context of the public sphere. However, discrimination can be seen in the private sector owing to bias for religions. On the other hand, Turkey has a *secular conservative* ethos which means that protection of secularism is more important than freedom. Constitution Article 24 mentions freedom, however Article 14 mentions restrictions on freedom. Violation of secularism has been strictly prohibited and the boundaries of this violation have not been clearly identified. Thus, freedom can be easily restricted with regard to ideologies of the legislative body. Muslim populations are high in Turkey, so secularism perceives Islam as a potential violation to the structure of the state. Therefore, the government sector, rather than the private, is affected by secular thought in the Turkish context.

Summary and recommendations

In this chapter, the concepts of religion, spirituality, workplace, diversity, discrimination and religious diversity were introduced. Religious diversity in the world at the macro level, and in the UK and Turkey at the micro level was examined. Understanding religion as an aspect of diversity was discussed. Legislation in Turkey and the UK was examined in relation to freedom of religion and preventing discrimination against religious diversity. From evaluation of the legislation of both countries, we could see that Turkey has a secular conservative ethos and the UK has a non-secular liberal ethos regarding religion. This indicates that the state sector in Turkey has a highly protectionist tendency towards secularism. The cases of Ahmet Aslan and Others, and Sinan Isik showed the subjective perspective of Turkey regarding religious issues in the state sector. Examination of the secondary data provided through research papers and court decisions, identified discrimination against religious diversity in the state sector in Turkey. On the other hand, the UK has freedom of religious diversity within the government sector owing to not having a secular state structure in terms of separation of state and church. However, discrimination against religious diversity has been seen in the private sector because of bias with regard to some religions (e.g. Islam) in the opinions of some business owners.

Within this chapter, macro and micro level approaches have been used to understand religious discrimination. The macro level encompasses the state or government, the micro level encompasses organisations within states. When Turkey and the UK are looked at, Turkey has not enough regulations and legislation to prevent religious discrimination. The UK has regulations and legislation. However, there are still some cases related to religious discrimination in organisations, as indicated in Organisational insight 8.1. For that reason, in order to have a good system for preventing religious discrimination, legislation related to discrimination, and control of implementation of this legislation, must be considered first. Organisations must clearly indicate their diversity policies to the public. There must be strict legal punishment for organisations that discriminate against religions. The state education systems and discourses of politicians must be inclusive rather than discriminatory. A ranking system must be developed to identify the most diverse organisations and this should be a source of good publicity for those organisations. The media and political parties must advocate diversity as a policy for organisations. In this way, a united community of people can be created within a state.

Discussion questions

1. How do you interpret the difference between religion and spirituality?
2. What is the role of international organisations which focus on discrimination issues and cases, and how effective are they?
3. What is the difference between non-secular liberal and secular conservative concepts?
4. Is there any relation between government and religious minorities from the point of discrimination? If yes, how?

CASE STUDY

HSBC and Ziraat banks

HSBC

HSBC is one of leading banking and financial organisations in the world. It has 9,500 offices in 85 countries. The bank provides a comprehensive range of services to millions of customers. The main location of the bank is in the UK. This retail banking network encompasses over 1,500 branches across England, Wales, Scotland and Northern Ireland; however, the range of services varies between commercial, corporate, premier and private banking services. The UK is the home of the bank's global headquarters and more than 8,000 people across hundreds of different roles are employed there. HSBC is also one of the oldest banking groups in the world. The origin of the company goes back to 1865. The HSBC Group is proud of having such a long history in the banking sector and the success of HSBC is directly relevant to the way that it does business today.

The HSBC Group has some expectations of individuals who want to be employed. When its main priorities are considered, it gives great importance to matching the values of companies and individuals in the selection process. Therefore, the HSBC Group wants applicants to show their skills, experience or qualifications, and also wants an applicant to prove that he/she is an HSBC person. It outlines its values in order to explain the meaning of being an HSBC person. Success at the global level has been built on this approach. The HSBC Group knows that goals of candidates indicate their ability to adapt to organisational values and practices.

Three core values have been introduced by the HSBC Group: Open, Connected and Dependable. These values have been elaborated as follows:

HSBC people are Open. The meaning of this value is to be honest and straight talking. Treating others in the organisation with respect and fairness are other criteria for being open. An employee should listen to other ideas and collaborate for the efficiency of the team.

HSBC people are Connected. The ability to establish strong relationships with customers, colleagues and the community where an employee works is one of the expectations of HSBC Bank. A member of HSBC must empathise with others.

(Continued)

(Continued)

HSBC people are Dependable. The HSBC group expects a candidate to be committed to quality in everything she/he does. Challenging circumstances, taking responsibility for decision making and standing up for the right course of action have great importance for being dependable.

How to show that a candidate shares their values

In the interview process of the HSBC Group, candidates are asked to describe occasions when they have shown the qualities that HSBC is looking for. The HSBC group advises candidates to start thinking about some examples related to their openness, connection and dependability. Thus, candidates should be prepared for those questions. HSBC Group expects at least one strong example for each value. Inherently, behaviour and communication throughout the recruitment process will be important for candidates to show how they are open, connected and dependable.

The main goal of the HSBC Group is to create easy and straightforward application and recruitment processes for candidates. Thus, HSBC provides a guide to different stages of the recruitment process. This means that each step in the recruitment process will create an awareness in candidates about where they are. Then, when candidates are contacted to find out if they have been successful, they will know what the next step will be.

HSBC is different

HSBC claims that diversity has great importance in its roots. The main proof of this claim is that is was founded nearly 150 years ago with the goal of creating financial trade between Europe and Asia. Its aim was to bring diverse people and cultures together for mutual benefit, and it has the same principle today.

It believes that diversity brings benefits for customers, businesses and people. HSBC has different approaches to creating the most innovative products and solutions. For those reasons, in order to meet the demands of its hugely diverse global customers, it needs a diverse workforce. It describes this as true diversity. Thus, it tries to create a working environment which is open, supportive and inclusive at every level. Fairness and

(Continued)

(Continued)

equal opportunity through a diverse workforce are the main rationale of the HSBC Group.

> I would like people to view HSBC as a responsible institution, which is aware of its role in the community, is trusted by its customers, is a good and fair employer, and offers a stable, attractive and positive return to its shareholders (Stuart Gulliver, HSBC Group Chief Executive)

Key facts from the HSBC Group

- A culturally diverse team of international managers made up of more than 50 nationalities.
- HSBC has more than 30 employee network groups, covering areas such as gender, ethnicity, age, sexuality, disability, religion, culture and working parents.

Ziraat Bank

Ziraat Bank is a leading bank which has great importance in shaping the Turkish banking sector. The history of the bank goes back to 1863. It claims that it is always on its customers' side with ATMs, video teller machines, internet branches, call centres, telephone and mobile banking, and other channels. It also has the largest international service network of all the Turkish banks. The main goal of the bank is to contribute to Turkey as a strong and competitive service provider, having a leading position in the sector and operating on a global scale. Ziraat Bank provides services to the entire country with 1,425 domestic branches, and is the sole provider of banking services in 404 of those locations. Among the innovative projects of Ziraat Bank, 1,234 branches have changed to the 'Bank Customer Business Model' in order to provide more efficient and higher quality services in those branches. In the near future, this model for branches will be completed. Additionally, it is planning to open 150 more branches, particularly in Istanbul and the big cities in Anatolia.

Ziraat Bank provides many services related to payment systems, credit, chequing accounts and investments, with a broad range of products. In addition, it offers customer-friendly products with the most favourable terms and pricing options.

(Continued)

(Continued)

Vision and mission

The vision of Ziraat Bank is to be:

> a bank that is universal, respected and has high market value; a bank that provides extensive, reliable service everywhere in Turkey and the world at the same quality, and meets the needs of every segment; a bank that sees human resources as its most valuable asset; a bank that continuously makes a difference and creates value in a way that benefits its deep-rooted past; a bank that promises more from a bank at every stage and serves as a model for its competitors.

The mission of Ziraat Bank is to be:

> a bank that understands customer needs and expectations, thereby offering them the best solutions and value recommendations from the most appropriate channel; a bank that brings to every segment of society a wide range of products and services in the fastest, most effective way through its extensive network of branches and alternative distribution channels; a bank that operates with profitability and productivity at global standards by recognising its ethical values and social responsibility; a bank that holds customer satisfaction to be more important than anything else.
> www.ziraat.com.tr/en/OurBank/AboutUs/Pages/VisionAndMission.aspx

Being an employee in Ziraat Bank

Ziraat Bank knows its leading position in the sector. Therefore, the goal of its people-oriented human resources policy is to provide its employees with a future-oriented perspective combined with self-confidence. Other features pursued are the requirements of the age: openness to change and development, team players, success oriented, with a developed sense of responsibility.

Ziraat Bank has a continual development philosophy, which is about supporting employees through their careers. Ethical values and trust, effectiveness, quality and productivity are key concepts for the brand and it expects the workforce to be conscious of these features of the bank.

Broad career opportunities

Ziraat Bank places great importance on job satisfaction in all domestic and international branch networks. Thus, job roles in the bank are appropriate to

(Continued)

(Continued)

the skillset of workforce. Moreover, training programmes are provided to enhance knowledge and skills for career goals.

Making a difference in the sector

The workplace in Ziraat Bank supports skills and knowledge to make a difference in the sector. In this context, the bank is also a source of qualified people within the sector in general.

A career at Ziraat Bank

On the website of Ziraat Bank (www.ziraat.com/tr/en/index.html), a career in the bank is described as follows:

> Ziraat Bank provides a range of career opportunities and a range of training programmes to its employees. The main reason for creating such opportunities is due to having the biggest and most well established bank structure in Turkey. The vertical career levels are open to employees who can make good progress in terms of position and area of responsibilities with regard to human resources policies. In addition, the bank is conscious that each position creates different value within the context of the new-position structure of the bank. Therefore, horizontal transfer opportunities among positions are offered to employees through preferment exams and training.

Questions

1. In this chapter, we have examined regulations which encompass diversity issues in both Turkey and the UK. Based on the regulations of both countries, what is missing from the information given for both banks in terms of human resources policies with regard to diversity?
2. If you were to belong to a religious minority group in Turkey, and you thought you had encountered clear discrimination because of your religion, what would be the legal procedures that you would need to follow in response to this discrimination? Please also answer this question for the UK.
3. The main difference in both cases is the country of origin of the banks. HSBC is located in the UK, a member of the EU, and Ziraat Bank is located in Turkey which is in the EU membership process. What are the implications for organisations of being or not being a member country of the EU in terms of diversity policies and the recruitment process for candidates?

Further reading

Ben-Nun Bloom, P., Arikan, G., & Sommer, U. (2014) 'Globalization, threat and religious freedom', *Political Studies*, 62(2), 273–91.

King, J.E., & Williamson, I.O. (2005) 'Workplace religious expression, religiosity and job satisfaction: clarifying a relationship', *Journal of Management, Spirituality & Religion*, 2(2), 173–98.

Weaver, G.R. & Agle, B.R. (2002) 'Religiosity and ethical behavior in organizations: A symbolic interactionist perspective', *Academy of Management Review*, 27(1), 77–97.

References

Acker, J. (2006) 'Inequality regimes: gender, class, and race in organizations', *Gender & Society*, 20(4), 441–64.

Adler, N.J. and Gundersen, A. (2008) *International Dimensions of Organizational Behavior*. New York: SouthWestern.

aleviforum.net (2014) *History of Alawism and Relationship with Islam* (access date: 25 May 2014).

Ataov, T. (2002) *Discrimination and Conflict*. Amsterdam: Sota Publications.

Bae, J. and Lawler, J.J. (1998) 'Overt employment discrimination by multinational firms: cultural and economic influences in a developing country', *Industrial Relations*, 37(2), 126–52.

Bailey, J.R. and Eastman, W.N. (1994) 'Positivism and the promise of the social sciences', *Theory & Psychology*, 4(4), 505–24.

Ball, C. and Haque, A. (2003) 'Diversity in religious practice: implications of Islamic values in the public workplace', *Public Personnel Management*, 32(3), 315.

Borstorff, P. and Arlington, K. (2011) 'Protecting religion in the workplace? What employees think', *Journal of Legal, Ethical and Regulatory Issues*, 14(1), 59–70.

Bouma, G., Haidar, A., Nyland, C. and Smith, W. (2003) 'Work, religious diversity and Islam', *Asia Pacific Journal of Human Resources*, 41(1), 51–61.

Cacioppe, R. (2000) 'Creating spirit at work: re-visioning organization development and leadership – Part II', *Leadership & Organization Development Journal*, 21(2), 110–19.

Conlin, M. (1999) 'Religion in the workplace: the growing presence of spirituality in corporate America', *Business Week*, no. 3653, 150.

Cox, T.H. Jr (1993) *Cultural Diversity in Organizations: Theory, Research & Practice*. San Francisco: Berrett Koehler.

Cromwell, J.B. (1997) 'Cultural discrimination: the reasonable accommodation of religion in the workplace', *Employee Responsibilities & Rights Journal*, 10(2), 155–72.

DiTomaso, N., Post, C. and Parks-Yancy, R. (2007) 'Workforce diversity and inequality: power, status, and numbers', *Annual Review of Sociology*, 33(1), 473–501.

Dubow, E.F., Pargament, K., Bower, P. and Tarakeshwar, N. (2000) 'Initial investigation of Jewish early adolescents' ethnic identity, stress, and coping', *The Journal of Early Adolescence*, 20(4), 418–41.

European Court of Human Rights (2013) *Factsheet – Freedom of Religion*, July.

Fleury, M.T.L. (2000) 'Gerenciando a diversidade cultural: experiências de empresas Brasileiras', *Revista de Administração de Empresas*, 40(3), 18–25.

Fox, J. (2000), 'Religious Causes of Discrimination against Ethno-Religious Minorities', *International Studies Quarterly*, 44(3), 423–50.

Haddad, Y.Y. (2002) *Muslims in the West – From Sojourners to Citizens*. New York: Oxford University Press.

Harrison, D.A. and Klein, K.J. (2007) 'What's the difference? Diversity constructs as separation, variety, or disparity in organizations', *The Academy of Management Review*, 32(4), 1199–228.

Harvey, J.B. (2001) *Reflections on Books by Authors Who Apparently Are Terrified About Really Exploring Spirituality and Leadership*. Greenwich: Elsevier Inc.

Herring, C. (2009) 'Does diversity pay? Race, gender, and the business case for diversity', *American Sociological Review*, 74(2), 208–24.

Hicks, D. (2002) 'Spiritual and religious diversity in the workplace: implications for leadership', *The Leadership Quarterly*, 13(4), 379–96.

Hicks, D.A. (2003) *Religion and the Workplace: Pluralism, Spirituality, Leadership*. Cambridge: Cambridge University Press.

Hinnells, J.R. (1997) *A New Handbook of Living Religions*. New York: Penguin.

Johnson, P.G. (1997) *God and World Religions: Basic Beliefs and Themes*. Shippensburg, PA: Ragged Edge Press.

Kelly, E.W. Jr. (1995) *Spirituality and Religion in Counseling and Psychotherapy: Diversity in Theory and Practice*. Alexandria, VA: American Counseling Association.

Konrad, A.M. (2003) 'Defining the domain of workplace diversity scholarship', *Group & Organization Management*, 28(1), 4–17.

Kuran, T. and McCaffery, E.J. (2008), 'Sex differences in the acceptability of discrimination', *Political Research Quarterly*, 61(2), 228–38.

Lawler, J.J., and Bae, J. (1998) 'Overt employment discrimination by multinational firms: cultural and economic influences in a developing country', *Industrial Relations: A Journal of Economy and Society*, 37(2), 126–52.

Loden, M. and Rosener, J. (1991) W*orkforce America. Managing Diversity as a Vital Resource*. Homewood, IL: Business One-Irwin.

Mendoza-Denton, R. and España, C. (2010) 'Diversity science: what is it?', *Psychological Inquiry*, 21(2), 140–5.

Milbank, J. (1990) *Theology and Social Theory: Beyond Secular Reason*. Oxford: Blackwell.

Mitroff, I.I. and Denton, E.A. (1999a) 'A study of spirituality in the workplace', *Sloan Management Review*, 40(4), 83–92.

Mitroff, I.I. and Denton, E.A. (1999b) *A Spiritual Audit of Corporate America: A Hard Look at Spirituality, Religion, and Values in the Workplace*. San Francisco: Jossey-Bass.

Morgan, J.F. (2004) 'How should business respond to a more religious workplace?', *S.A.M. Advanced Management Journal*, 69(4), 11–19.

Morrison, A.M. (1996) *The New Leaders: Guidelines on Leadership Diversity in America*. San Francisco: Jossey-Bass.

Özcan, K., Özkara, B. and Kizildag, D. (2011) 'Discrimination in health care industry: a research on public hospitals', *Equality Diversity and Inclusion: An International Journal*, 30(1), 22–40.

Pew Research Center (2014) *Global Religious Diversity Report*, April. www.pewforum.org/2014/04/04/global-religious-diversity/

Poole, E. (2000) 'Framing Islam: an analysis of newspaper coverage of Islam in the British press', in Hafez, K. (ed.) *Islam and the West in the Mass Media*. Cresskill, NJ: Hampton Press, pp. 157–80.

Prochaska, E. (2013) *The Definition of Religion or Belief in Equality and Human Rights Law*, Equality and Human Rights Commission.

Rao, A. (2012) 'Managing diversity: impact of religion in the Indian workplace', *Journal of World Business,* 47(2), 232–39.

Reeves, T.C., McKinney, A.P. and Azam, L. (2013) 'Muslim women's workplace experiences: implications for strategic diversity initiatives', *Equality, Diversity, Inclusion: An International Journal,* 32(1), 49–67.

Regmi, K., Naidoo, J. and Regmi, S. (2009) *Understanding the Effect of Discrimination in the Workplace: A Case Study Amongst Nepalese Immigrants in the UK.* Bingley: Emerald Group Publishing.

RELIGARE Project (2013) *Summary Report.* www.religareproject.eu

Revell, L. (2010) 'Religious education, conflict and diversity: an exploration of young children's perceptions of Islam', *Educational Studies,* 36(2), 207–15.

Richards, P.S. and Bergin, A.E. (2000) *Handbook of Psychotherapy and Religious Diversity.* doi:10.1037/10347-000.

Schaeffer, C.B. and Mattis, J.S. (2012) 'Diversity, religiosity, and spirituality in the workplace', *Journal of Management, Spirituality & Religion,* 9(4), 317–33

Wendell, L.F. (2003) *Human Resources Management.* New York: Houghton Mifflin.

Wing Sue, D. and Sue, D. (2008) *Counseling the Culturally Diverse: Theory and Practice* 5th edn. Hoboken, NJ: John Wiley & Sons.

Sexual minorities in the workplace

9

Mustafa Bilgehan Ozturk and Nick Rumens

Intended learning outcomes

After reading this chapter, you will be able to:

- Understand the variety of issues and challenges that may influence the employment experiences of sexual minorities
- Differentiate the main theoretical approaches which attempt to explain why and how sexual minorities are marginalised and discriminated against in various work settings
- Apply legal, political and social contextual factors in order to develop multi-faceted understandings of sexual minority employment in the UK and cross-nationally
- Recognise the critical influence of relations of power and inequality in the workplace, and how these affect the organisational practices designed to provide sexual minority employees with a voice in the workplace
- Explain the variations in workplace experiences of sexual minorities on the basis of influencing factors such as employment sector, organisation size and equal opportunity and diversity practices in regard to sexual orientation

Introduction

The term 'sexual minority' has traditionally been understood and used to collectively identify lesbian, gay and bisexual individuals. In this sense, sexual minorities are groups of people whose sexual orientation or sexual characteristics are different from the majority of the population who are presumed to be heterosexual. Transgender individuals (men and women who identify as the opposite gender) have also been referred to as 'sexual minorities', regardless of whether they have undergone any form of gender-reassignment. Transgender people may identify sexually as heterosexual, gay, lesbian, bisexual or simply 'trans' (LGBT), demanding more sensitive understandings about how sexuality and gender intersect in ways that influence how these individuals identify belonging to sexual and gender minority groups. Although LGBT individuals can suffer from different types of sexual and gender discrimination (e.g. homophobia, biphobia, transphobia, sexism), the term 'sexual minority' can also be used to indicate a shared sense of discrimination among minority groups who fall outside prevailing sexual norms. Looked at this way, the term 'sexual minority' typically refers to those people whose sexual characteristics and practices are socially and legally less accepted. As such, the understandings and meanings associated with what groups of individuals constitute a sexual minority are historically patterned, changing at any given time and from one cultural context to another. Crucially, however, sexual minority is a term that is often used to describe groups of individuals who experience rejection, disapprobation, ridicule and misrecognition, not because they are inherently 'deviant' or 'unnatural', despite vociferations to the contrary, but simply because they differ from what is routinely experienced and understood as 'normal' by the presumed majority.

In this chapter, we consider sexual minorities (LGBT) in the context of workplace relations. We first review the contributions made by a range of theoretical traditions to our understanding of the type and extent of discrimination faced by LGBT employees. We then explain how the impact of context on the workplace experiences of sexual minorities helps us to understand that sexual stigma and prejudice do not exist in a vacuum. Rather, they take particular forms and expressions depending on a range of social, legal, political and organisational contextual factors. For example, organisational contextual factors such as workplace culture, company size and employment sector, together with wider social and legal contextual factors, are considered in this chapter. Similarly, this chapter argues that an analysis of the employment experiences of sexual minority employees remains incomplete without adequate attention devoted to underlying relations of sexual and gendered power within the workplace, which may constrain or encourage the development, shape and purpose of organisational practices designed to give sexual minority employees a voice in the workplace, which may allow them to participate openly as LGBT in organisational life. The chapter ends with recommendations for good practice in addressing the inequalities experienced by sexual minority employees at work. These recommendations will resonate with those who are charged with improving the workplace experiences of sexual minority employees, such as equality and diversity practitioners, managers, industry-wide and sector-specific professional bodies and policy makers.

Theories for understanding the workplace experiences of sexual minorities

There are different theoretical approaches that attempt to explain the workplace issues and challenges faced by sexual minorities. Chief among these approaches are economic, psychological and poststructuralist theories. Economic studies have usually focused on explaining labour market distortions and inequalities as a result of discrimination on the basis of sexuality (e.g. Badgett, 1995; Drydakis, 2009; Weichselbaumer, 2003). Wage penalties suffered as a result of sexual minority status in the marketplace have been a primary focus in this literature. These studies have been complemented with experimental field research that has demonstrated the difficulties faced by LGBT individuals in securing employment. More recently, in the context of greater social acceptance of LGBT people in and outside work in many Western countries, the economic approach has also investigated the impact of LGBT workplace inclusion on company performance.

In contrast, psychology theories have focused on examining issues of disclosure of sexual orientation (often termed as 'coming out' as LGBT) and identity management in the context of discriminatory workplaces, noting the consequences for sexual minority workers' mental and emotional well-being (e.g. Griffith and Hebl, 2002; King and Cortina, 2010; Ragins, 2008). For instance, in this approach, scholars have theorised sexual orientation as a form of invisible stigma, socially constructed, that affects how, when and where LGBT employees can or cannot disclose their sexuality at work, examining how disclosure can negatively and positively influence organisational outcomes such as employee satisfaction and company performance. The psychological approach has focused also on how the perceived and actual sexual prejudices of co-workers, customers/clients and managers can influence LGBT employees' decisions about to whom they disclose as LGBT, under what conditions and to what extent. (For a wider understanding of psychological perspectives on diversity that goes beyond LGBT concerns, refer to Chapter 2.)

Finally, poststructuralist theories focus on revealing how power relations within organisations may privilege some sexualities over others (e.g. Bendl et al., 2008; Ozturk and Rumens, 2014; Rumens and Kerfoot, 2009; Ward and Winstanley, 2003). Poststructuralist-inspired studies of LGBT employees have examined how heteronormativity, a term used to describe how gender and sexuality are separated into hierarchically organised categories, reinforces restrictive binaries such as heterosexual/homosexual, man/woman and masculine/feminine. In each case, one element of the binary is privileged over another. For instance, heterosexuality is privileged over homosexuality, with the latter considered to be 'deviant' and 'abnormal' in regard to heterosexuality which is considered 'neutral' and 'normal'. Poststructuralist analyses question these enduring binaries, interrogating how they are reproduced in and through organisations, constraining the conditions of possibility for sexual minorities to participate openly in the workplace.

Economic theories

One of the earliest economic analyses of sexual orientation discrimination was carried out on the wage effects of sexual prejudice in labour markets. There is now widespread evidence from different labour market contexts that LGBT individuals have consistently suffered a wage penalty in the workplace. In a seminal study of US wage differentials in respect of sexual minorities, Badgett (1995: 726) found that 'gay and bisexual male workers earned from 11% to 27% less than heterosexual male workers with the same experience, education, occupation, marital status, and region of residence'. According to the same study, lesbians and bisexual women also seem to earn considerably less as a consequence of pay discrimination based on sexual prejudice, although the results are not as consistent in the case of gay and bisexual men. Later studies have documented similar differentials in earning power, with gay and bisexual men experiencing the brunt of discriminatory pay regimes, with the weight of the penalty reaching as much as 30 per cent under-remuneration (Carpenter, 2007). These results are replicated in many employment contexts around the world, even in the case of 'gay-friendly' countries such as Sweden, with substantial negative pay outcomes reported for sexual minority workers (Ahmed and Hammarstedt, 2010). More recently, Martell (2013) demonstrates that there is an enduring variation in sexual minority earnings power from that of the general population of workers, even after taking into account a plethora of differences in workers' characteristics and abilities. According to Martell, relative invisibility of sexual orientation status allows some sexual minorities to 'pass' as heterosexual, which accounts for some moderation of the wage penalty. However, given that many LGBT individuals appear to prefer coming out from the corporate closet, they may end up paying a wage penalty as a result of a persistent income–disclosure trade-off.

Another strand of economic research has considered the challenges faced by LGBT people in finding employment. For instance, Weichselbaumer (2003) conducted experimental research where hypothetical job applications, which were comparable in all aspects except for sexual orientation, were submitted to prospective employers in Austria. Study findings showed that the job interview invitation rate for lesbian women was up to 13 per cent less than for heterosexual women. A similar experimental design investigating discrimination-based distortions in hiring decisions in the case of Greece found that discrimination against gay male applicants lowered their ability to secure a job interview by as much as 26 per cent (Drydakis, 2009). In the most recent audit study of this type, Tilcsik (2011) demonstrates that gay men in the US are substantially less likely to be invited for job interviews, but the level and amount of hiring discrimination varies significantly based on regional social attitudes and equality laws in place in different states. Both wage discrimination and hiring discrimination studies of this kind document the persistent, pervasive and harmful employment discrimination against LGBT employees in different labour markets.

Against this backdrop of labour market discrimination, there is a growing literature that makes the business case for the full equality and inclusion of LGBT individuals in the workforce. The business case argues that the acceptance and inclusion of LGBT employees in the workplace can help not only improve job satisfaction and participation among LGBT employees, but also help organisations to improve productivity and efficiency. Some organisations have taken great strides to badge themselves as 'gay-friendly', developing a strong corporate social responsibility ethos of diversity and inclusion. Profit motivated 'gay-friendly' organisations may elicit higher interest in company stock due to market expectations that a more inclusive workforce policy will entail better corporate productivity (Badgett et al., 2013). For instance, analysing the stock performance of companies with a positive corporate equality index (CEI) score (a measure of LGBT inclusion in a corporation), Wang and Schwarz (2010) find a good CEI score received in a particular year is, statistically speaking, likely to lead to improved stock performance in the following year.

Organisational insight 9.1

Finance

The global finance industry has a strong masculine bias in terms of what type of employee personalities, leadership styles and on-the-job behaviours are valued by the employers. While in many occupations cooperation and teamwork are touted as highly prized qualities of an idealised model employee, the archetypal successful finance worker is pushy, aggressive and greedy, with a highly dramatic work attitude. According to Prugl (2012: 22), 'the financial sector is one of the few bastions of virtually uncontested masculine privilege remaining in the aftermath of feminism'. The hyper-competitive industry norms are especially acute in trading, a line of work that has been viewed as the straight man's natural employment habitat. Being a trader represents the epitome of a testosterone-driven, macho orientation to work, where 'guys' are locked in a zero-sum game in the markets; and for there to be winners, there must be losers, a status which must be avoided at all cost. Companies actively seek out those who can fulfil a heroic vision of a conqueror of the markets in their employment processes. The fall of the once-illustrious, big four global investment banking firm Lehman Brothers has been explained by this constructed masculinist drive to conquer, where risks are downplayed, and gains are sought with aggressive abandon, and the emergent suggestion is that the 2008 financial meltdown could have been averted if Lehman Brothers were possibly more like Lehman Sisters (van Staveren, 2014).

Psychology theories

Psychological approaches have been particularly concerned with investigating the negative consequences of stigmatisation for sexual minorities, especially the influence on employee well-being in the workplace. It is demonstrated that discrimination on the basis of sexuality has strong negative ramifications for sexual minority workers' mental and emotional well-being (King and Cortina, 2010). Conceptualising non-heterosexual orientation as a source of invisible stigma (i.e. a non-readily observable trait), there is often concern that LGBT individuals who perceive discrimination in their work environments may be forced to limit how they express their sexual identities in the workplace (Ragins and Cornwell, 2001). The issue of which work colleagues know about an individual's actual or presumed sexual identity can serve to amplify fears associated with workplace disclosure decisions among LGBT employees (Ragins et al., 2007). Organisational supportiveness is taken as a major dynamic of positive contextual change, which enhances sexual minority workers' job satisfaction, and reduces anxiety and stress at work (Griffith and Hebl, 2002). Sexual minorities who are more satisfied in their roles as a result of non-discrimination, and who therefore also feel less anxiety and stress, are shown to have greater commitment to their companies. This has been framed as a recommendation for businesses to engage with sexual minorities in the workplace (King and Cortina, 2010).

Another strand of this literature is that sexual minorities often use sexual identity management strategies to cope with workplace contexts that actually or potentially discriminate against them. An early but enduring model of workplace identity management specifies three specific workplace disclosure strategies which sexual minorities undertake; namely, counterfeiting, avoidance and integration (Woods and Lucas, 1993). Counterfeiting indicates actions taken to deliberately portray a heterosexual image and persona at work, which amounts to passing as a non-LGBT employee. Avoidance is an intentional strategy of omitting displays of behaviour or disclosure of information that may signal one's sexual minority status to colleagues. Finally, integration involves being open about one's sexual identity and freely revealing details that indicate a minority sexual identity, but with the aim of being folded into the heterosexual majority.

With changing societal attitudes as well as the wider introduction and implementation of progressive legal safeguards, many sexual minority workers in Western European, and increasingly US, work contexts eschew counterfeiting, and instead opt for either avoidance or integration strategies. In developing nations, where there are limited legal safeguards to tap into and where strong anti-gay prejudice may go unchecked or even be encouraged, counterfeiting or avoidance remain the principal identity management strategies. Aside from such identity management strategies, employees often adjust their openness from one colleague/client to another according to different encounters and interactions within the same workplace (Button, 2001), or disclose to varying degrees along a changing continuum based on differences in perceived threats (Ragins and Cornwell, 2001). In this sense, disclosure as LGBT is not a one-off event but an ongoing process. Finally, sexual minority workers may often face public–private tensions in the form of disclosure disconnects, where they choose to be open in one sphere (e.g. private life) and remain closeted in another (e.g. work life), and thus experience 'psychological stress, role conflict, attributional ambiguity' as a result (Ragins, 2008: 210).

Poststructuralist theories

Poststructuralist theories within the organisation literature attempt to uncover and problematise dominant (e.g. heteronormative) discourses that construct sexual minorities as subordinate subjects in the workplace. This approach takes the workplace not as a container for sexuality and sexual minorities, but treats sexuality and the workplace as mutually influencing, not only in the sense that places of work shape how sexualities and sexual minorities are understood and experienced, but also in the sense that the workplace is sexualised through how sexualities and sexual minorities are constructed and attributed meaning at work. For example, LGBT employees who fit in with heteronormative expectations about how they should behave and dress professionally are likely to be attributed recognition as viable, productive human components of organisational life (Rumens and Kerfoot, 2009). LGBT employees who are unable or who choose not to conform to heteronormative discourses may be discursively constructed as 'abnormal' and 'deviant' and, in some cases, experience a sense of silence or erasure from organisational life. According to Ward and Winstanley (2003), silence can take many forms: 1) silence as reactive (where colleagues react to coming out as a sexual minority with silence, as opposed to extensive talk of straight people's private lives); 2) silence as a means of suppression (where talk of homosexuality is eschewed in the organisation to 'invisibilise' sexual minorities); 3) silence as censorship (where for instance laws can drive sexuality underground in social life).

Rumens and Kerfoot (2009) also draw on poststructuralist theories to examine how gay men working in 'gay-friendly' work contexts face specific identity dilemmas as they construct themselves as professionals. This is because the concepts 'professional' and 'professionalism' are often linked to heteronormative expectations of what it is to behave and embody these constructs, which typically involves a separation of sexuality from professionalism. This can limit how gay men might use sexuality as a source of professionalism in the workplace (just as it might be the case for heterosexuals too), as well as heightening their vigilance about how discourses of homosexuality that associate it with perversion and paedophilia can have a devastating impact on maintaining a professional identity as an openly gay man at work.

Poststructuralist analyses may also be used to challenge and dismantle harmful sexual binaries. Research that draws on queer theory, a set of conceptual resources partly rooted in poststructuralist theories, seeks to destabilise heteronormativity. For example, queer theory is deployed in a strategic manner to question the very diversity management discourses which are supposed to create the conditions whereby sexual minorities may be included in the workplace. Analysing diversity management theory and practice from a queer theory perspective, Bendl et al. (2008) reveal how diversity management discourses sustain a heteronormative notion of diversity that constrains how sexual difference and sexual diversity are understood, experienced and managed in the workplace. This research highlights the need to critically examine even those organisational discourses and practices which are purportedly designed to help sexual minority groups achieve inclusion in the work context. A queer theoretical perspective exhorts us to question ideas which seem, at first glance, reasonable, natural or normal. In this context, Bendl et al. (2008) invite us to consider the contention that diversity management policy and practice supports sexual minorities only in ways that affirm heteronormative understandings of organisational sexuality. (Refer to Chapter 3 to review policy and practice of diversity management in the workplace in general.)

Discussion activity 9.1

Compare and contrast the economic, psychological and poststructuralist theories outlined above. What approach to explaining the work experiences of sexual minorities do you prefer, and why? What implications for management and organisational practice can be drawn from the insights derived from these theories? Can you think of any other issues that may have a bearing on the work lives of sexual minorities, which these approaches have not considered?

Contextual detail: sexual minority employees in the UK

Over the past two decades or so, the UK has experienced a progressive socio-cultural shift, where previously restrictive and unsupportive attitudes toward sexual minorities have been substantially liberalised. Weeks (2007) asserts that a social world that was predicated upon sexual restraint and orthodoxy, where practising homosexuality was previously a criminal offence in the UK, has been revolutionised to a point of appreciation and acceptance of sexual diversity. Indeed, the Civil Partnership Act (2004) and the Marriage (Same Sex Couples) Act (2013) have been key milestones in helping LGBT people to gain recognition as citizens and take their place in society's basic building block, family life, alongside heterosexuals. This progressive normalisation of sexual minority identity is highly significant, as it can potentially constitute a critical aspect of the social justice case for greater support and valuation of sexual minorities in the workplace. These UK legal reforms – together with the Employment Equality (Sexual Orientation) Regulations (2003) and the Equality Act (2010), which protect sexual minorities from prejudice- or fear-based discrimination in the workplace – have been important as another driver for equality action. Previously, social justice and business case arguments for addressing sexual orientation at work served as the stimulus for employers to develop formal 'gay-friendly' signals, such as policies that include sexual orientation, LGBT networks and support groups. Typically, organisations in the public sector have been in the vanguard here, although many private and third sector organisations are making significant advances in this respect. Legal reform by itself is insufficient to eradicate employment discrimination towards sexual minorities but it does provide provisions that allow victimised sexual minorities to seek legal redress through the courts. Legal reforms may also serve a legitimating function at the level of society for sexual minorities, which have opened up previously restrictive notions of citizenship to LGBT people, and shape more inclusive business environments.

Progressive contextual changes in the UK have also conditioned the possibility for the rise of the 'pink pound', defined as the substantial buying capacity of members of the LGBT population in the UK, which has influenced a corporate view of sexual minorities as customers/clients. Sexual minorities, who are often stereotyped as having more disposable income, and so may command significant monetary power in the marketplace, are valued highly by some organisations as potentially affluent consumers. As such, some work organisations are increasingly motivated, as part of a business case rationale, to support their sexual minority workers on the basis that these employees possess insider knowledge about the preferences and demands of potential LGBT consumers. At the same time, such strategies are problematic for their tendency to stereotype LGBT people (particularly gay men and lesbians) as affluent and middle class, ignoring the realities of those sexual minorities on lower incomes. Demographically, sexual minorities are more diverse than stereotypes give credit for, but not enough is known about the position and participation rates of LGBT people in the UK labour market given the paucity of statistical data on this issue. Some surveys suggest that the number of openly LGBT people is about 5 per cent of the total population (Hayes et al., 2012). It is likely that this number would be around 10 per cent, if LGBT people could come out without fear of negative consequences. These survey results must be treated with caution, but they can operate as a critical factor in support of the business case for full sexual minority equality and inclusion in the workplace.

Discussion activity 9.2

What kinds of further legal and socio-cultural progress may be necessary to reach full equality for sexual minorities in UK workplaces? What new diversity and equality policies may be necessary to capitalise upon the gains made by progressive legal and socio-cultural reforms? What are the limits of legal reforms for eradicating sexual prejudice in the workplace? Are there also organisational-level differences in the way companies approach diversity and equality in regard to sexual minorities?

Go online and review the diversity management policies in five UK companies. Identify the similarities and differences there are within a UK context.

Cross-national contextual detail: sexual minorities in the workplace

Around the world, contextual realities of being a sexual minority vary drastically from one country to another. Areas outside the EU are particularly noted for potential workplace rights gaps in respect of sexual minorities, although even within the EU, there is variation in the degree to which sexual minorities are protected from sexual prejudice. Globally, the vast majority of nations fail to uphold the most basic human rights of LGBT individuals, let alone protect sexual minorities from discrimination at work. Nor are the rights violations or abuses against sexual minorities following a trajectory of linear decline. According to a multinational societal attitude survey conducted by the Pew Research Center (2013), the global divide on the issue of sexual minorities is very strong, with some countries such as Uganda (96 per cent) and Nigeria (98 per cent) demonstrating extremely high animosity to homosexuality at the level of the general public. Consistent with such public sentiments, both of these countries have recently pursued an aggressive criminalisation of same-sex conduct, with long prison terms imposed upon individuals identified to be sexual minorities.

The recognition of and advances towards sexual diversity are routinely thwarted and even reversed, with some countries showing momentary progress only to regress at a later point in time in terms of their legal provisions for equality. For instance, among BRIC countries, Russia and India serve as instances of recent high-profile assaults on sexual minority rights, broadly construed. In Russia, in 2013, authorities passed legislation that would outlaw any promotion of homosexuality as a viable or normal identity to children. The wording of the Russian anti-LGBT legislation is so vague that it could potentially apply to any speech or supportive action in favour of LGBT individuals (Lenskyj, 2014), with the possible result that workplace rights of sexual minorities are now under increasing attack. The Indian Supreme Court decided in 2013 to reinstate Section 377, a colonial-era law banning same-sex intimate relations, which had been overturned some years previously by a lower court. There is now a discouraging precedent in India, where the prevailing impression is that even hard-won rights can be taken back from sexual minorities at one stroke. The wider significance of the Indian Supreme Court decision has been to delegitimise the standing of sexual minorities in society, and as a result their position in the employment sphere could be at greater risk.

In the Middle Eastern context, in an in-depth qualitative study of lesbian, gay and bisexual employees in Turkey, Ozturk (2011) found evidence of substantial discrimination in the employment sphere, ranging from seemingly mild but ridiculing jokes, to name-calling and mental abuse, to job termination, and even threats of violence. This study underscores the socio-cultural constitutive elements of such discrimination, where both patriarchy and heteronormativity work in tandem to render sexual minority work lives unliveable, or otherwise impose substantial penalties upon the free expression of sexual minority status. Sadly, in the Turkish case, sexual orientation discrimination is upheld in both public and private spheres, with family members' complicity in the perpetration of violence of various kinds. Ozturk and Özbilgin

(2014) provide a range of critical cases that include honour killings against sexual minorities, job terminations in schooling and de-licensing in football refereeing, to demonstrate the encompassing nature of homophobia in the Turkish system of values. Turkey is a remarkable case study because the country is purportedly the first Islamic society with a Western-style, democratic governance structure based on free and fair elections, although it has a nascent autocratic political elite, which has been widely protested in recent years, culminating in the now notorious Gezi Park events.

In the US, there is a mixed picture regarding legal protection and rights for sexual minorities. Despite recent advances with regards to LGBT marriage equality, LGBT individuals do not yet have the nationwide right to form marriages. With no access to formal state acknowledgement of their relationships, sexual minorities are deprived of the legitimating effect of an important societal institution. Partly as a consequence, there is also no national anti-discrimination employment regulation across the US, and at present in many States, sexual minorities can be fired for simply disclosing their LGBT status. Notwithstanding this challenging context, over the past two decades there has been a steady proliferation of safeguards to thwart discrimination against LGBT workers in both the public and private sectors. A large number of state legislatures and municipal authorities have passed statutes that prohibit LGBT discrimination. Executive Order 13087 signed by former President Bill Clinton banned sexual orientation discrimination by non-military federal departments as well as federal contractors, while Executive Order 13672 signed by President Barack Obama extended the scope of this protection to include gender identity, both of which provisions have afforded legal protection against discrimination to countless LGBT workers. The 2010 repeal of a longstanding US military policy, popularly known as 'Don't Ask, Don't Tell', which prohibited lesbian, gay and bisexual service members from disclosing their sexuality at work, expanded federal protections further. In the private sector, many large corporations have adopted sexual orientation and gender identity non-discrimination policies in an effort to recruit and develop their human resources based on talent in order to compete more productively in the global marketplace.

Discussion activity 9.3

In the above section, contextual details relating to Russia and India were discussed with a view towards understanding what may be some challenges for sexual minority employees in these countries. The other two countries in the BRIC group, Brazil and China, also have room for progress on the sexual minority equality front. Conduct an online search as to the existing LGBT rights in these two countries, considering both similarities and differences. What are the challenges associated with progress on the equality and diversity areas in these countries? Discuss how the work lives of sexual minorities can be improved in Brazil and China.

Power relations and inequality: issues of silence and voice for sexual minorities in the workplace

As mentioned earlier in the chapter, existing research demonstrates the disempowerment and subjugation of sexual minorities at work through a process of silencing (Ward and Winstanley, 2003). This is partly because sexual minorities often suffer from an invisible stigma (Ragins, 2008). Compared to other minority strands such as race and gender, they are a lot less visible in an immediate sense. (Refer to Chapters 4 and 5 to review gender and race and ethnicity concerns in the workplace.) For instance, while sexist and racist attitudes can be questioned by pointing out the low numbers of women and racial minorities in top management echelons, it is less obvious how to point to a disadvantageous numerical imbalance in the case of LGBT employees. The invisible nature of the social stigma in effect sustains the very conditions of possibility that uphold heterosexuality, leaving the status quo unchallenged. This contributes to the erasure of the presence of sexual minority employees. As well, workplaces, populated mainly as they are with heterosexual majorities, seek to stabilise norms and expectations of behaviour according to heterosexual values, diminishing LGBT workers' capacity to self-express fully at work. Overall, the atmosphere of silence and silencing leads to an inequality regime (Acker, 2006), where one group of employees (the sexual majority) with privileged status receive all the benefits of their empowered position, and set in place a system and process designed to operate according to their needs, creating a lower order of power, privilege and claim for recognition for a disadvantaged Other group (sexual minorities). Challenging this unequal order is difficult, as sexual minorities have less discursive power, as they function in a heteronormative organisational system.

Extant research also indicates that sexual minority employees have found that silence itself may be a way of challenging the status quo by refusing to partake in the functioning of heterosexist hierarchies (Ward and Winstanley, 2003). A sexual minority who choose silence may be negating the destructive language of organisational homophobia by reducing its available repertoire in the organisational discourse. Furthermore, deployment of voice and silence may depend on whether sexual minority employees, who may wish to challenge an organisational homophobia, are tempered radicals (i.e. individuals who are deeply committed to an organisation while simultaneously seeking change that is anathema to organisational values). Previous research on LGBT priests, exemplars of tempered radicals, shows they use both silence and voice interdependently, as 'when you are saying one thing, you are not saying another' (Creed, 2003: 1503). Here, the aim is to minimise damage to an organisation to which one is committed, while achieving success in a particular reformation of the organisational order. Similar tempered radicalism relates to workplace experiences of school teachers, Boy or Girl Scouts organisations and the military, indicating the complexity of silence as part of the lived experienced of a wide variety of sexual minority employees.

Positioned against the idea of silence serving as a strategy to defy heteronormativity, Bell et al. (2011) emphasise the importance of voice, which they define as the sum of all active efforts to transform an unfavourable organisational dynamic rather than passive disengagement with the problem and eventually exiting the organisation. Thus, according to Bell et al. (2011: 140), diversity management practitioners and organisational employment relations strategy must pay special attention to facilitating voice through putting in place and supporting enabling mechanisms of individual and collective action, for instance, intra- and extra-organisational LGBT networks, sexual orientation champions, organisational sexual orientation initiatives and LGBT-focused organisational training opportunities.

Voice and silence challenges facing sexual minority employees

An important caveat to the above-mentioned literature is that processes of voice and silence may be contingent, where the underlying mechanisms work differently based on sectoral and organisational size contexts. A small business is likely to have a relatively more informal human resources function, which is potentially insufficient to advance a clearly articulated diversity policy. A multinational enterprise, on the other hand, is likely to have a well-developed and strategically focused human resource function, usually with a clear diversity and equality strategy. Whereas in small businesses voice may take the form of individual efforts by sexual minorities to underline their presence at work and convince owner-managers to commit to the rights of sexual minority employees, in large organisations there are opportunities for collective action. For instance, Colgan and McKearney (2012) find that despite a decline in unionisation, in large organisations sexual minorities increasingly create alliances and employee networks that help to advance LGBT equality at work. Additionally, as large private organisations have significant reputational concerns in a highly competitive business arena, they wish to project a strong corporate social responsibility ethos to various stakeholders in the marketplace. Corporate social responsibility can be powerful enough to make businesses conscious of human rights requirements, superseding the business vs social justice arguments to give initiatives for LGBT rights and equality at work an enhanced position of influence, strengthening voice opportunities and greatly widening the range of available mechanisms (Colgan, 2011). On the other hand, public sector organisations, which may be expected to perform better on sexual minority equality and diversity at work, are not necessarily as advanced as desired. In many public sector settings, the UK public equality duty may serve as a deceptively comforting mechanism of voice, while in practice fundamental challenges exist and remain unaddressed. In particular, despite its pioneering status in equalities issues, the public sector has started to lag behind the private sector as a result of the new public management (NPM) discourse in the UK (Colgan et al., 2009). NPM's predominantly business case arguments for LGBT inclusion have a stifling impact on the variety of voice mechanisms available to LGBT employees. Furthermore, in the public sector there is a gap between hard knowledge of legislation on equality and diversity, and soft knowledge of day-to-day equality practice (Senyucel and Phillpott, 2011), which may reduce actual feasible voice opportunities.

A proviso in this analysis is that regardless of public vs private sector status or size-related HR capacity variations, an important differentiator in terms of voice and silence mechanisms is the gendered nature of the industry setting in which the organisation is located. For instance, employers in the construction industry, a sector of employment dominated numerically and culturally by men and masculinities, are shown to be less responsive to claims of sexual orientation discrimination in the workplace (Wright, 2013), with the industry failing to follow emerging market norms of inclusion toward sexual minorities. In explaining this deficit, Rumens (2013) problematises the dominance of men in the construction industry as well as the scholarly literature on construction, and explains that advances can only follow through the disruption of ubiquitous essentialist practices of sex and gender categories in construction. In the police service, another traditionally male-dominated work domain, despite recent advances, sexual minorities still face the necessity to manage their identities at work through the use of sophisticated strategies (Rumens and Broomfield, 2012), which may have considerable psychological costs negatively impacting on their work lives. On the other hand, sexual minorities who wish to fashion a particular identity, for instance, a butch lesbian persona, may draw strategic benefits from prevailing masculinist practices in a male-dominated industry. For example, lesbian firefighters may be more easily accepted into the watch as compared with heterosexual women, perhaps due to male firefighters' perception of lesbians' stronger compliance with the masculine work culture (Wright, 2008). However, this still falls short of full acceptance, and sexual minorities may simply face a different type of discrimination, such as unwanted jokes or colleagues' lack of interest in private lives in the context of workplace social relations, as opposed to sexual harassment directed at heterosexual women.

Discussion activity 9.4

Break into small groups and discuss five ways in which sexual minorities can be given voice at work. What are the different responsibilities of top management, supervisors, colleagues and equality and diversity officers in an organisation in facilitating voice mechanisms for sexual minority employees? What are the variety of possible business and social justice costs associated with the silencing of sexual minority employees at work? It may be useful to consider the example of James presented in Organisational insight 9.2.

Organisational insight 9.2

Firefighting

The fire service is an industry with a long-held reputation for projecting a conservative staffing outlook. Existing academic scholarship has described members of the fire services crews as well as their management ranks as a group largely comprised of heterosexual, able-bodied men. Aside from a gender under-representation, which may be considered the visible part of the iceberg, there is the largely silent homophobia that potentially pervades all layers of the forces. While gender imbalance is now acknowledged and some remedial action is being taken by fire services, when it comes to sexual minorities, there is much room for improvement.

For over a decade, James served as a highly successful operational staff member of a large fire and rescue service in the UK. Since he joined the service more than ten years ago, until his promotion last month, James was engaged in a carefully constructed identity management strategy of covering (see Woods and Lucas, 1993). However, once he reached a senior management level, James finally put his guard down, and discreetly started to inform his colleagues that he is gay. Although colleagues have responded positively, most of them declined to speak to James about his sexuality at length. James has thus felt unable, despite now wanting to do so, to share his private life at work, while his straight colleagues openly ask one another about their partners and children. More worryingly, his boss Alan, who had long served as a mentor for him and had always shown support for his career advancement, has lately distanced himself from James. In fact, Alan now shows a marked indifference to James's existence in the organisation, sometimes seemingly avoiding interpersonal contact intentionally. Although Alan has made no disparaging remarks to James about his sexuality, at meetings he pointedly looks at other colleagues and always averts his eyes from James. Feeling stressed and discriminated against, James is now seriously considering changing jobs and quitting his beloved occupation.

Summary and recommendations

This chapter has first considered the economic, psychological and poststructuralist theoretical approaches to understanding the workplace experiences of sexual minorities. Based on the economic approach, it is clear that sexual minorities even in legislatively 'gay-friendly' contexts suffer from pay and promotional penalties. One intervention to help remedy existing disparities may be to carry out intra-organisational, sectoral (for instance, private vs public) and industrial audits to ensure that systematic under-earning and managerial under-representation of sexual minority employees are reported and addressed. Company pay policies must be developed with specific attention paid to sexual minority employees' remuneration and non-monetary benefits, especially in legal contexts where same-sex partnerships have no legal standing. Countering hiring dis-crimination is challenging given that it is rarely acknowledged openly in recruitment and selection processes, but helpful here is the presence of a strategically aligned human resource function that has input into the people resourcing function of the organisation. Regarding the psychological and emotional welfare of sexual minority employees, it is important to support sexual minority employees who may have job dissatisfaction, stress and anxiety, and other well-being challenges as a result of sexual prejudice in the work-place. LGBT organisational networks and support groups may help to provide such support as well as leveraging wider organisational change in how employers engage with sexual minorities at work. Poststructuralist accounts of sexual minorities in the workplace favour strategies that disrupt and destabilise workplace heteronormativity. This is likely to require creating queer-conscious organisational policies challenging the uncontested and socially naturalised place of heterosexuality as the standard bearer of organisational relations. That is, organisational policies should be developed, not with the unarticulated assumption that organisational members are heterosexual and have heterosexist needs and expectations, but instead organisational members (heterosexuals as well as LGBT people) have a variety of equally valid sexualities, and policies at all levels must reflect this diversity of sexualities.

Contextual details covered earlier in the chapter point to a wide variation in legal and socio-cultural support for sexual minorities. There is little indication of a linear positive transformation for sexual minorities over time, as recent reversals in the for-tunes of LGBT people in Russia and India illustrate vividly. One recommendation is for multinational companies as well as international human rights NGOs to lobby for more protective and supportive legislation. Global companies make large-scale invest-ments in infrastructure and mobilise job opportunities for substantial numbers of citizens. Although difficult and potentially unpopular among some global organisa-tions, many can exercise power to leverage the advantageous consequences of their presence in a given country to support progressive agenda shifts for sexual minorities.

It is also important to consider context at a lower level of analysis, when it comes to public vs private sector employment, industry, and organisational culture and size. For instance, in the UK despite a public sector equality duty, explained above, many sexual minorities have still to experience inclusivity within public organisations. In some cases, private sector organisations have surpassed their public counterparts, and thus it is important to not make sector-based assumptions as to which sector is better or more 'gay-friendly' over the other. In terms of industries, this chapter points to tra-ditional, male-dominated industries as being particularly homophobic employment spaces, where sexual minorities often face complex challenges. One recommendation to challenge such industry-wide problems is to coordinate industry-wide action plans to confront and eradicate homophobia by publicity campaigns, trade conferences and symposia, and industry-defined employment practices that push for a greater equality and inclusion agenda. The recent 'kick homophobia out of football' campaign in the UK, which challenged both homophobic fans and, importantly, homophobic club management and field team members, is a good example of industry-coordinated action. This chapter has also indicated that in small-sized organisations with informal HR systems, issues of minority sexuality may be overlooked or insufficiently addressed. Although small businesses may not individually have resources to hire equality and diversity officers and spend time and money on intra-organisational diversity policies, small and medium enterprise (SME) associations and government programmes that are in place to support SME firms can invest in creating a set of sexual minority inclusive policies, guidance and training programmes to ensure that such firms are well-served and capable of serving all their employees well. Finally, various interventions at the level of individuals and organisations can also potentially change the current status quo of unequal workplace relations. This chapter explains that unequal power relations and organisational silencing of sexual minorities are widespread and now normalised features of organisational life. Recommended actions to take in order to give sexual minority employees more voice can be greater recognition of issues of organisational sexuality in union discussions, plans and programmes, organisational champions for sexual minority issues, top management sexual minority employees who can serve as mentors to those on lower rungs of the organisational ladder, sexual minority/majority workplace alliances and sexual minority networks. Admittedly, the plethora of interventions and recommendations may have a cost dimension, but failure to take action on all fronts and at all levels can have even greater costs for individual employees and organisations alike.

Discussion questions

1. Imagine that you are the CEO of a global finance company. Based on this chapter and your reading around the topic, explain the main equality and diversity issues that influence sexual minority employees in your company. Create a plan of strategic support for your employees with a view towards achieving full equality. Think about what specific individual-based actions can be taken to help sexual minorities with their career advancement and mentoring needs.
2. Conduct a small informal qualitative study with five interviewees who identify as heterosexual. You could select them from different employment sectors and/or industries. Ask them what their views of sexual

(Continued)

(Continued)

minority employees are, whether they work alongside any sexual minorities currently and what suggestions they would provide in combating sexual inequalities at work. If they have issues with working alongside sexual minority colleagues, ask them to explain the reasons for their beliefs and attitudes. Based on their suggestions and reasons, discuss organisational policy and practice recommendations that will strengthen support for sexual minority employees.

CASE STUDY

Religious freedom vs sexual minority employees

Hallow Hill School is a faith-based school in Sydney, Australia. Since the founding of the school by a group of devout evangelical missionaries, its policies have been developed to uphold a strict scriptural interpretation of the Bible. The mission and values statements of the school have been put together based on the teachings and doctrinal leanings of evangelical Christianity. In over two decades of operation, Hallow Hill has become a virtual magnet for families who wish to send their children to be schooled according to conservative principles of their religion, and the school recognises that they have a strong sense of duty to impart the sensibilities and tacit knowledge and understandings that the parents wish their daughters and sons to be given. Accordingly, it is the express expectation of the school management that all members of staff respect and abide by the school code of ethics, which has its basis in Bible teachings, and which provides guidance on acceptable and non-acceptable behaviour on the part of the school employees. Additionally, members of staff cannot be associated with any activity, even outside the school premises, if such activity is against the school's interpretation of Christian teaching and practice. While the school has been positive towards its diverse staff, it has shown a clear lack of tolerance of diversity when it comes to sexual minorities. Through a variety of means of communication, Hallow Hill continually propagates the message that it will not employ sexual minorities under any circumstances, as it believes employing sexual minorities would be against the deeply held religious convictions and sentiments of the school personnel, parents and the students.

(Continued)

(Continued)

Jane Cassandra Levkinsky is a seasoned mathematics teacher, and has been serving as both a teacher and the Head of Science and Mathematics at Hallow Hill for the past year. Jane has achieved very strong results in the classroom environment, with many students obtaining high marks and showing increased commitment to their studies. Due to Jane's consistent, innovative, positive and constructive approach, some pupils who had previously done very poorly in their maths studies blossomed and reached far superior results compared to their previous record, which has prompted a number of parents to contact the school to provide thank you messages lauding Jane's accomplishments. Hallow Hill's management has also been highly impressed with Jane. Their appreciation of her teaching excellence is further enhanced by their observation that Jane has been a first-rate strategic thinker who has revolutionised her team's approach to teaching, and has both motivated her staff to aim for stronger student results and allowed herself to be an invaluable resource for pragmatic and useful ideas when one of her team members needed guidance.

All of this changed one day last month, when Adam, another teacher in Hallow Hill, checked out Jane's new Facebook page. Upon his visit, Adam thought that Jane had some pictures where she was hugging another woman in a way which was suggestive of a high degree of intimacy. Coupled with these pictures, a few oblique comments made by Jane and her friends on the Facebook page gave the impression to Adam that Jane is a lesbian, and the woman in the pictures is her partner. Adam immediately notified the Hallow Hill management and they held a 'crisis meeting' with Jane. At this meeting, Rev. David Jackson, the principal, bluntly asked Jane if she was a lesbian. Jane avoided answering the question a few times, and at long last told the attendees as well as the principal that her private life was her business, and she would not like to disclose whether or not she is a lesbian.

The unfortunate treatment of Jane worsened over the weeks that followed. The previously supportive management team, which had repeatedly indicated their satisfaction with Jane's work, started questioning Jane's decisions at every turn, micromanaging Jane's work day to the minute, publicly suggesting that Jane's budget had inaccuracies which might have harmed the school, and finding fundamental faults with some of the innovative teaching methods and techniques Jane introduced, arguing that these were not fit for purpose and seemed insufficiently evidence-based to be used in the Hallow Hill classroom contexts.

(Continued)

(Continued)

Finally, Jane felt that her work was no longer appreciated by the Hallow Hill staff and management, and that she was not welcome in the classrooms or corridors, which for her meant that she could not function as a teacher and a team leader. Jane provided the principal with her resignation letter, in which she came out as a lesbian and explained that the events depicted above amounted to constructive dismissal, for which she would seek legal remedies in Australian courts. Principal Jenkins responded that her resignation was accepted, as she could not serve as a lesbian staff member, which would be in violation of the school's faith-based teaching ethos which rejected sexual diversity. The principal explained that all of this arose out of communication issues, and as a change in policy in the aftermath of this case, the school would henceforth ask all job candidates if they are a sexual minority or not, and those who affirmed sexual minority status or those who declined to answer the question would be denied jobs. Finally, the principal also vigorously denied that Jane was made to leave her job under duress, as a result of a campaign to push her out.

Attitudes toward sexual minorities in Australia are amongst the most positive around the world. For instance, the Pew Research Center's global survey on homosexuality finds that 79 per cent of Australian respondents believe that society should accept homosexuality. Additionally, according to federal legislation ratified recently in Australia, the Sex Discrimination Amendment (Sexual Orientation, Gender Identity and Intersex Status) Bill 2013, there is now a nationwide employment non-discrimination law designed to protect sexual minorities in the workplace. However, this law provides an exemption clause for faith-based schools that wish to exclude sexual minorities from serving as staff, although the constitutionality of this aspect of the law is yet to be fully contested in courts at the highest level. Despite great positive strides made in support of sexual minorities in the Australian workplaces, there is still contestation as to the expansiveness of protection. The question whether sexual minority employees should be protected in all areas of work is still not fully or satisfactorily answered, as per Jane's experiences.

Questions

Discuss the issue of competing minority rights, in this case, religious vs sexual minorities. Do you see an inherent conflict? Are there possibilities for reconciling these rights contradictions, and if so, what are the conditions for cooperation and mutual understanding?

(Continued)

(Continued)

1. What rights should be prioritised in deciding equality and diversity policies at the national level? Explain what issues are at stake in favouring one set of rights over another.
2. What role should a faith-based school take in delving into the private lives of its staff? Is private legal activity off-limits or fair ground for access or questioning for employers to start an enquiry?
3. To what extent can an institution, which is allowed to legally discriminate, claim to support, espouse or pursue equality and diversity goals? What is at stake in allowing legal discrimination on any basis, nationally, industry-wide or in terms of individual employees?

Further reading

Browne, J. (2014). *The Glass Closet: Why Coming Out is Good Business*. London, Random House.

Colgan, F. & Rumens, N. (Eds.). (2014). *Sexual Orientation at Work: Contemporary Issues and Perspectives*. London, Routledge.

Sue, D.W. (2010). *Microaggressions in Everyday Life: Race, Gender, and Sexual Orientation*. New York, John Wiley & Sons.

Ward, J. (2008). *Sexualities, Work and Organizations: Stories by Gay Men and Women in the Workplace at the Beginning of the Twenty-first Century*. Abingdon, Routledge.

References

Acker, J. (2006). Inequality regimes: gender, class, and race in organizations. *Gender & Society*, *20*(4), 441–64.

Ahmed, A.M. & Hammarstedt, M. (2010). Sexual orientation and earnings: a register data-based approach to identify homosexuals. *Journal of Population Economics*, *23*(3), 835–49.

Badgett, M.L. (1995). The wage effects of sexual orientation discrimination. *Industrial and Labor Relations Review*, *48*(4), 726–39.

Badgett, M.V., Durso, L.E., Mallory, C. & Kastanis, A. (2013). *The Business Impact of LGBT-Supportive Workplace Policies*. Los Angeles, CA: Williams Institute.

Bell, M.P., Özbilgin, M.F., Beauregard, T.A. & Sürgevil, O. (2011). Voice, silence, and diversity in 21st century organizations: strategies for inclusion of gay, lesbian, bisexual, and transgender employees. *Human Resource Management*, *50*(1), 131–46.

Bendl, R., Fleischmann, A. & Walenta, C. (2008). Diversity management discourse meets queer theory. *Gender in Management: An International journal*, *23*(6), 382–94.

Button, S.B. (2001). Organizational efforts to affirm sexual diversity: a cross-level examination. *Journal of Applied Psychology*, *86*(1), 17.

Carpenter, C.S. (2007). Revisiting the income penalty for behaviorally gay men: evidence from NHANES III. *Labour Economics*, *14*(1), 25–34.

Colgan, F. (2011). Equality, diversity and corporate responsibility: sexual orientation and diversity management in the UK private sector. *Equality, Diversity and Inclusion: An International Journal, 30*(8), 719–34.

Colgan, F. & McKearney, A. (2012). Visibility and voice in organisations: lesbian, gay, bisexual and transgendered employee networks. *Equality, Diversity and Inclusion: An International Journal, 31*(4), 359–78.

Colgan, F., Wright, T., Creegan, C. & McKearney, A. (2009). Equality and diversity in the public services: moving forward on lesbian, gay and bisexual equality? *Human Resource Management Journal, 19*(3), 280–301.

Creed, W.E.D. (2003). Voice lessons: tempered radicalism and the use of voice and silence. *Journal of Management Studies, 40*(6), 1503–36.

Drydakis, N. (2009). Sexual orientation discrimination in the labour market. *Labour Economics, 16*(4), 364–72.

Griffith, K.H. & Hebl, M.R. (2002). The disclosure dilemma for gay men and lesbians: 'coming out' at work. *Journal of Applied Psychology, 87*(6), 1191–9.

Hayes, J., Chakraborty, A.T., McManus, S., Bebbington, P., Brugha, T., Nicholson, S. & King, M. (2012). Prevalence of same-sex behavior and orientation in England: results from a national survey. *Archives of Sexual Behavior, 41*(3), 631–9.

King, E.B. & Cortina, J.M. (2010). The social and economic imperative of lesbian, gay, bisexual, and transgendered supportive organizational policies. *Industrial and Organizational Psychology, 3*(1), 69–78.

Lenskyj, H.J. (2014). *Sexual Diversity and the Sochi 2014 Olympics: No More Rainbows*. Basingstoke: Palgrave Macmillan.

Martell, M.E. (2013). Differences do not matter: exploring the wage gap for same-sex behaving men. *Eastern Economic Journal, 39*(1), 45–71.

Ozturk, M.B. (2011). Sexual orientation discrimination: exploring the experiences of lesbian, bisexual and gay employees in Turkey. *Human Relations, 64*(8), 1099–118.

Ozturk, M.B. & Özbilgin, M. (2014). From cradle to grave: the lifecycle of compulsory heterosexuality in Turkey. In Colgan, F. & Rumens, N. (Eds.). *Sexual Orientation at Work: Contemporary Issues and Perspectives*. Abingdon: Routledge, pp. 151–65.

Ozturk, M.B. & Rumens, N. (2014). Gay male academics in UK business and management schools: negotiating heteronormativities in everyday work life. *British Journal of Management, 25*(3), 503–17.

Pew Research Center (2013). *The Global Divide on Homosexuality: Greater Acceptance in More Secular and Affluent Countries*. Pew Research Center Report. Washington, DC.

Prugl, E. (2012). 'If Lehman Brothers had been Lehman Sisters...': gender and myth in the aftermath of the financial crisis. *International Political Sociology, 6*(1), 21–35.

Ragins, B.R. (2008). Disclosure disconnects: antecedents and consequences of disclosing invisible stigmas across life domains. *Academy of Management Review, 33*(1), 194–215.

Ragins, B.R. & Cornwell, J.M. (2001). Pink triangles: antecedents and consequences of perceived workplace discrimination against gay and lesbian employees. *Journal of Applied Psychology, 86*(6), 1244–61.

Ragins, B.R., Singh, R. & Cornwell, J.M. (2007). Making the invisible visible: fear and disclosure of sexual orientation at work. *Journal of Applied Psychology, 92*(4), 1103–18.

Rumens, N. (2013). Queering men and masculinities in construction: towards a research agenda. *Construction Management and Economics, 31*(8), 802–15.

Rumens, N. & Broomfield, J. (2012). Gay men in the police: identity disclosure and management issues. *Human Resource Management Journal, 22*(3), 283–98.

Rumens, N. & Kerfoot, D. (2009). Gay men at work: (re) constructing the self as professional. *Human Relations*, *62*(5), 763–86.

Senyucel, Z. & Phillpott, S. (2011). Sexual equality and diversity in UK local councils. *Equality, Diversity and Inclusion: An International Journal*, 30(8), 702–18.

Tilcsik, A. (2011). Pride and prejudice: employment discrimination against openly gay men in the United States. *American Journal of Sociology*, *117*(2), 586–626.

Van Staveren, I. (2014). The Lehman Sisters hypothesis. *Cambridge Journal of Economics*, *38*(5): 995–1014.

Wang, P. & Schwarz, J.L. (2010). Stock price reactions to GLBT nondiscrimination policies. *Human Resource Management*, *49*(2), 195–216.

Ward, J. & Winstanley, D. (2003). The absent presence: negative space within discourse and the construction of minority sexual identity in the workplace. *Human Relations*, *56*(10), 1255–80.

Weeks, J. (2007). *The World We Have Won: The Remaking of Erotic and Intimate Life*. London: Routledge.

Weichselbaumer, D. (2003). Sexual orientation discrimination in hiring. *Labour Economics*, *10*(6), 629–42.

Woods, J.D. & Lucas, J.H. (1993). *The Corporate Closet: The Professional Lives of Gay Men in America*. New York: Free Press.

Wright, T. (2008). Lesbian firefighters: shifting the boundaries between 'masculinity' and 'femininity'. *Journal of Lesbian Studies*, *12*(1), 103–14.

Wright, T. (2013). Uncovering sexuality and gender: an intersectional examination of women's experience in UK construction. *Construction Management and Economics*, *31*(8), 832–44.

PART III

FUTURE OF DIVERSITY MANAGEMENT

Part III Contents

Work–life balance

10

Jawad Syed

Intended learning outcomes

After reading this chapter, you will:

- Understand how issues of time and place of work are relevant to employees and managers in modern organisations and also how they are relevant to diversity management
- Have learnt about the changing nature of the workplace and its implications for the family and vice versa
- Have learnt about the notions of flexible work, employee well-being and work–life initiatives, such as childcare and employee assistance
- Have learnt about work–life related issues for single parents and single people with weak family ties
- Have become aware of some recent debates on time and place of work, virtual workplaces, job stress, and current organisational approaches and practices
- Understand the significance of legislative and demographic context for work–life balance and have reviewed some cross-national examples

Introduction

Previous chapters in this book have dealt with issues unique to specific diversity groups, such as women (Chapter 4), Lesbian, gay, bisexual and transgender (LGBT) persons (Chapter 9) and ethnic minority groups (Chapter 5). A common observation in these chapters and also in the diversity literature overall is that employees in general face the challenge of having to balance their professional and personal lives on an ongoing basis. The present chapter discusses the issue of how organisations and employees can manage work–life balance (WLB) in an increasingly global competitive environment. It discusses the notion of WLB and examines the factors that have caused an increase in attention to WLB, and how the issue is addressed within diversity management. The chapter identifies important changes within society and organisations which have contributed to an increased focus on WLB within organisational policies. The chapter explores organisational examples in order to assess how diversity management policies address WLB and how this affects employees and organisations. The chapter offers a critical review of the literature and organisational policies that identifies some gaps in diversity policies surrounding the issue of WLB.

The world of work is changing rapidly and so are the needs of employees. Baby boomers (i.e. those born between 1946 and 1964) are ageing and there is an increasingly ageing society in most industrialised countries. Also, with the kick-start from the internet generation, new opportunities and applications of technology are on the march. Migration and globalisation mean that there are important changes in ethnic and religious diversity which need to be taken into account in designing and implementing organisational policies. Family dynamics are also changing, with the increasing growth and acceptance of single-parent and non-traditional families. In this context, WLB is about developing working approaches that are equally beneficial to individuals and organisations (DfEE, 2000).

The concept of WLB represents the conviction that personal life and paid work may be viewed as complementary, not competing, elements of life (Holliday and Manfredi, 2004; Lewis, 2000). This balance can be achieved by conceptualising WLB as a two-way process that considers the needs of employees as well as those of employers (Lewis, 2000).

Employee demographics in Europe and elsewhere have changed dramatically since World War II, and more recently due to globalisation and migration. There are an increasing number of women in the workplace and also in managerial roles, many of whom are still heavily burdened in terms of their family-related responsibilities. Today's workforce also comprises dual-earner couples, something which is now routine rather than an exception in the labour market. Such workers have to take care of not only their jobs but also children or elderly dependents (Bond et al., 1998).

Moreover, due to the recent financial crisis (2008–12), governments and organisations are seeking to make employees redundant while also trying to lengthen the work week. This situation is particularly challenging and unnerving for dual-career couples and other employees who need time to attend to their family-related roles (Hill et al., 2001). A survey of 5,000 US households found that 63 per cent have high levels of job-related stress (Jayson, 2012). Increased stress levels resulting from lack of WLB have become more frequent, and represent a major challenge for employees and organisations.

Definitions

Felstead et al. (2002: 56) define work–life balance as 'the relationship between the institutional and cultural times and spaces of work and non-work in societies'. Expanding on this definition, Hill et al. (2001: 49) refer to WLB as 'the degree to which an individual is able to simultaneously balance the temporal, emotional, and behavioral demands of both paid work and family responsibilities'. Clark (2000) defines WLB as 'satisfaction and good functioning at work and at home, with a minimum role of conflict'.

Kirton and Greene (2010) define WLB as employment policies facilitating the balancing of work and life outside of work – implicitly extending beyond parenting/caring responsibilities. According to RCN (2008), WLB denotes the working practices that acknowledge and seek to support the needs of staff in achieving a balance between their homes and working lives.

While there is a consensus on the benefits of WLB, Grzywacz and Carlson (2007) note that ambiguity revolves around how WLB should be defined, measured and researched. In other words, the theorising of the subject is still a work in progress.

Evolution of WLB and interface with diversity

In this section, a contextual and historical discussion of how WLB has evolved is offered.

Historical context

The roots of WLB go back to the nineteenth century when workers and unions successfully campaigned against long working hours in factories, and it became apparent that a decrease in working hours had no significant impact on production (Bosworth and Hogarth, 2009). During the early twentieth century, the campaign for a maximum cap on working hours was also reflected in pioneering studies in the field of WLB (e.g. Myers, 1924). The studies emphasised the role of motivation, human relations and conditions under which reduction in working hours may improve productivity. In 1938, the US government introduced the *Fair Labor Standards Act* with a maximum workload of 44 hours per week (US Department of Labor, 2013). Finally in the 1980s, companies began to introduce family-friendly policies, such as telecommuting and flexible scheduling. Even though such policies were originally focused on women, in practice they accommodated both women's and men's needs. In this context, the current notion of WLB gained currency, with a view to protect family life in an increasingly competitive workplace and career-driven society (Parakati, 2010).

According to Bosworth and Hogarth (2009), a number of indicators represent the current policy mix in terms of WLB, i.e. health and safety at work, equality, a flexible labour market and international competitiveness. Today, WLB is recognised as a major issue for both employees and employers to manage. Indeed, many of the challenges related to WLB can be seen as by-products of a poorly managed WLB – examples being stress, absenteeism, retention, ill health and morale.

Demographic change

An important factor that affects WLB is demographic change in societies and labour markets. An example of this is the ageing workforce. The 2006–7 Human Solutions Report showed that one-third of all workers in the US were aged 45–64. Those in this age bracket are likely to be more susceptible to health issues. However, WLB policies are equally important to younger workers. In terms of age, Smith and Gardner (2007) show that young employees tend to make more use of WLB policies such as compressed work weeks, flexitime and telecommuting. In terms of gender, Allen (2001) found that women are more likely to benefit from WLB policies than men, mostly for maternity and childcare.

WLB and gender

Clark (2000) shows how the conventional model of male breadwinner and female homemaker has started to change since the 1970s, with an increased focus on the implications of work for the family and vice versa. Naturally, the debate surrounding WLB has not only considered the emergence of dual-career and single-parent families, it has also affected how gender equality is theorised and implemented as a part of diversity management in organisations.

Brief and Nord (1990) identify a number of factors that have contributed to increased attention to WLB, i.e. increasing numbers of single parents, increased participation of women in the labour market, popularity of part-time and casual work, changing worker expectations, and a substantial growth in the social value associated with a father's involvement within the home. Each of these changes is important in terms of how organisations manage WLB within their diversity management practices.

Managing WLB is particularly important for women, as they are traditionally assumed to have, and many of them still have, the role of homemaker. Thus, it is important to consider how changes in work routines and structures affect women's WLB. Indeed, the debates about WLB cannot be complete without taking into account the personal and financial situation of women, as well as those of other historically disadvantaged employees. From a critical feminist perspective, Slaughter suggests that women can achieve far better career–family balance – that women can 'have it all' – but not until major cultural shifts against masculine structures, which dominate the economy and society, take place (Slaughter, 2012).

Özbilgin et al. (2011) recognise that diversity management policies in many organisations are derived from government laws and directives, thus it is important to recognise their impact on WLB. Current equality laws and policies regarding WLB in the UK are largely derived from the Maternity and Parental Leave etc. Regulations 1999, the Employment Rights Act 1996 and the Work and Families Act 2006. Table 10.1 offers a comparative perspective on maternity leave policies across the world. However, much of the legislation provides only limited rights for working women with care commitments (Conaghan and Rittich, 2005). This legislative oversight may be attributed to an assumption that a traditional nuclear family is the norm, i.e. the male breadwinner and female homemaker model. However, non-traditional forms of family are becoming increasingly common. For example, in the US only around 17 per cent of married couples are composed of working men and unemployed wives. In contrast, 26 per cent are headed by single women, while nearly 5 per cent of married families are composed of working women and unemployed husbands (US Department of Labor, 2004). This lack of regard for contemporary social changes has led to the slow development of WLB and diversity initiatives in organisations (Özbilgin et al., 2011).

Table 10.1   Maternity leave policies around the world

Australia	Paid parental leave (government funded) began 1 January 2011. Up to 18 weeks paid at the national minimum wage
China	The minimum length of maternity leave was increased in May 2012 to 98 days
Germany	Germany introduced a system of parental leave benefit, the so-called Elterngeld, on 1 January 2007, replacing a much less generous system called Erziehungsgeld. The new system offers a 67% replacement rate of previous labour earnings (from employment or self-employment) for either father or mother for up to 12 months post-childbirth
Italy	Maternity leave lasts for 5 months (these are paid at 80% of mother's usual salary). Additional parental leave lasts 6 months per parent (with a maximum of 11 months per child), and parents receive 30% of their usual salary
Japan	Mothers in Japan are guaranteed 14 weeks maternity leave, including 6 mandatory weeks post-childbirth. Pay depends upon the employer and various other elements. In addition, mothers have access to childcare leave, which lasts until the child's first birthday.
Netherlands	Women receive a guaranteed 16 weeks paid maternity leave (six weeks before and 10 weeks after childbirth). In addition, women can take 13 weeks of full-time leave or six months of part-time leave before their child's eighth birthday
India	Under the Maternity Benefits Act of 1961, women are entitled to maternity benefits at the rate of their average daily wage for a maximum period of 12 weeks (6 weeks before delivery and 6 weeks after). This provision is available only to those who have worked at least 80 days in their organisation in the past 12 months (ILO, n.d.)
Norway	9 weeks compulsory maternity leave, 100% salary. May also take parental leave for 44 additional weeks at 100% salary. May also take an additional year of unpaid leave
Russia	Women receive 140 days maternity leave, 70 of which are to be taken prior to birth, with 70 taken after birth, with up to 100% of salary as a ceiling. The maternity leave is mandatory
UK	26 weeks of Ordinary Maternity Leave and 26 weeks of Additional Maternity Leave making one year in total. The combined 52 weeks is known as Statutory Maternity Leave. A recent amendment makes it mandatory for women to take a minimum of 2 weeks' maternity leave immediately after childbirth (4 weeks minimum for factory workers). Pregnant employees may also be eligible for a one-time, tax-free payment, offered to low-income mothers to buy supplies for the baby, which does not have to be paid back

Sources: Catalyst, 2013; ILO, n.d.

WLB and dual careers

For female employees, WLB has been long related to their dual responsibilities, also described as double shift. According to a study in the Indian State of Kerala, most women have a dual role, which includes pursuing their career and taking care of their family. This may result in work–family conflicts (Thomas, 2013). Thomas' study in Kerala showed that the major problem of WLB is time pressure, i.e. women do not have enough time to achieve the competing tasks at work and home. The amount of work from their full-time employment causes them frustration when they cannot find sufficient time to take care of their family-related duties. Having these problems while trying to balance their work and life, some women choose to gain flexibility by finding seasonal or part-time jobs. According to the UK labour market statistics (ONS, 2012), significantly more women in employment work part-time (43%) compared to men (13%). This suggests that in addition to part-time employment, non-permanent employment too may be a source of flexibility for female employees.

According to Houston and Marks (2005), a major reason for women participating in part-time jobs is the presence of children. Childbirth, nursing and caring tends to perpetuate traditional divisions of work and caring roles for most couples (Houston and Marks, 2005). Although the norms of society are changing, and women are no longer just housewives and men are not the only ones to work, women still take up large responsibilities in taking care of their children. Hakim (2000) argues that some women do not want to make a choice between work and family – they want both. As a matter of fact, there are more women taking part-time jobs than men. However, as noted by Schaffer (2013), 'you can have it all, but not at the same time'. In practice, it is a challenge for all employees, and women in particular, to be a successful employee and a successful parent/carer at the same time. This reflects the need to find solutions in achieving WLB.

Discussion activity 10.1

Royal Bank of Scotland (RBS) offers a number of policies that recognise the importance of WLB, e.g. flexible working and the 'your time' scheme. The 'your time' scheme recognises the need for unexpected time off work due to emergent family and other commitments. The scheme won an HR excellence award for flexibility. The scheme amongst other initiatives has helped RBS in being recognised as a family-friendly organisation and has also boosted its recruitment (RBS, 2013).

Discuss what could be some possible reasons for a positive effect of WLB on recruitment. Find examples of WLB policies in organisations in your local area or region which may be compared to the flexible working facilities offered by RBS.

WLB and sexual orientation

An important aspect of WLB is an individual's sexual orientation. Increasingly, lesbian and gay couples are participating in non-traditional families. Some lesbian and gay couples are also adopting children and need to balance their commitment at work and their family. A failure by an organisation to properly facilitate lesbian, gay, bisexual and transgender (LGBT) individuals can leave them feeling isolated and unwelcome, which in turn can lead to job stress and poor WLB. The Out and Equal Workplace Summit Report (2012) states that a lack of accommodation for LGBT persons results in the fear of being 'found out' taking over from concentration on the job role. Counselling Directory (2013) statistics showed that 68 per cent of gay men had been verbally abused within the past five years in the workplace. Organisations need to pay attention to creating an inclusive environment in which LGBT workers not only feel valued and safe, but also have equal access to the privileges and rights available to other employees, such as family leave, partner medical insurance and invitations to social events.

Organisational insight 10.1

Two contrasting examples of WLB and sexual orientation

Not all organisations pay attention to the WLB-related issues of LGBT employees. Accenture plc, however, creates an inclusive work environment for its LGBT employees, including the provision of leave and flexible employment. Accenture is a Fortune Global 500 company, operating in multinational management consulting, technology services and outsourcing. Its incorporated headquarters are in Dublin, Ireland. The company sponsors several gay-friendly events such as the LGBT workplace summit and the Lesbian and Gay Film Festival in London. The organisation takes into account non-traditional family structures and grants equal leave, flexible work and other facilities to LGBT employees. The organisation was voted by leading gay associations as the most LGBT-friendly organisation to work for. Aside from the acclaim, Accenture trains all employees to understand LGBT individuals. It has set up a thorough support network so that no-one is left feeling alone. This support ensures LGBT employees can operate to their full ability and are productive members of the organisation (Accenture, 2012).

While Accenture is an example of how an organisation should deal with LGBT employees, Wal-Mart has been criticised as an example of how not to. According to The National Gay and Lesbian Task Force, a gay advocacy group based in Washington, DC, Wal-Mart has a poor record when it comes to gay and lesbian employees. The advocacy group said that Wal-Mart's policies

(Continued)

(Continued)

provide little to no protection for, and at times show hostility towards, their LGBT employees. Activists have criticised Wal-Mart for denying employee benefits to same-sex partners and for failing to prohibit discrimination based on gender identity (Harris, 2011).

WLB and religion

Religion is a major factor influencing an employee's WLB. The topic of religion within the workplace often sparks debate. There is a hugely controversial grey area for management regarding what to facilitate, without disrupting harmony with individuals of diverse faiths/atheists. The poor management of religious diversity within a WLB context can lead to negative effects for the organisation. The affected individuals are likely to be demoralised, feel isolated and dissociate themselves from the organisation. Another more generic problem for organisations to deal with is individuals requesting time off work, whether it be for prayer time or a religious festival such as the Sabbath or Eid. The usual practice in some organisations is that any time lost due to religious commitments is made up out of contractual hours, thus evening out any qualms over bias. This practice on the whole seems a fair and justifiable method of dealing with work–religion conflicts that arise. In faith-based societies such as Israel and Saudi Arabia, special provisions are made in governmental laws and organisational policies to accommodate the religious requirements of people of Jewish, Islamic and other faiths.

Discussion activity 10.2

Sav et al.'s (2014) qualitative study shows how Australian Muslim men cope with potential conflict and try to achieve balance between their work, family and religious roles. The study shows that personal coping strategies, such as time management and workplace adjustment, are more effective in achieving WLB and coping with conflict as opposed to external ones such as supervisor support. The study shows that Muslim men in Australia use these strategies to actively achieve WLB while also avoiding potential conflict.

Should organisations expect their ethnic minority employees to change their lifestyle and ethnic or faith-based practices to fit the organisational requirements? What could be a fair boundary-line for such expectations and adjustments?

WLB and intersectionality

WLB has specific implications for people who face multiple disadvantages due to two or more layers of identity. While the overlapping of the protected characteristics of gender, race and disability is of particular importance in terms of WLB, it is often ignored within legislation and consequently diversity management policies. While the Equality Act (2010) in the UK takes into account intersectionality as a legal policy, this feature is lacking within legislation in the US where same-sex partnerships are not covered within the Family and Medical Leave Act, which is a central piece of legislation governing WLB.

Furthermore, research suggests that culture and ethnicity can also affect WLB. In a study of Pakistani and Bangladeshi heritage women living in the UK, Dale (2005) observed that these women face greater challenges in achieving a balance between employment and family roles. This may be attributed not only to the style of work, which is arguably geared toward Western social and capitalist norms, but also to the home, where traditional expectations of women as homemakers remain common (Bradley et al., 2005). Similarly, many other issues arising from intersecting and multiple identities may be ignored within WLB policies, which means that such workers may not fully benefit from governmental or organisational WLB initiatives.

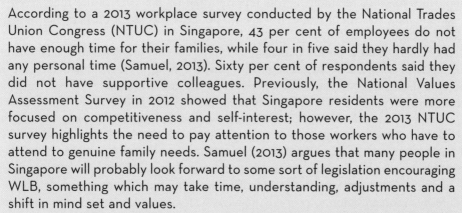

Discussion activity 10.3

According to a 2013 workplace survey conducted by the National Trades Union Congress (NTUC) in Singapore, 43 per cent of employees do not have enough time for their families, while four in five said they hardly had any personal time (Samuel, 2013). Sixty per cent of respondents said they did not have supportive colleagues. Previously, the National Values Assessment Survey in 2012 showed that Singapore residents were more focused on competitiveness and self-interest; however, the 2013 NTUC survey highlights the need to pay attention to those workers who have to attend to genuine family needs. Samuel (2013) argues that many people in Singapore will probably look forward to some sort of legislation encouraging WLB, something which may take time, understanding, adjustments and a shift in mind set and values.

Do you think that legal intervention is sufficient to encourage and implement WLB policies in the workplace? What other interventions and strategies may be needed?

WLB is useful for all employees

While the preceding sections have highlighted WLB for certain groups, it is important to consider that WLB is attractive to and useful for all employees, in terms of improvement in employee engagement and commitment. Wasay (2013) shows that maintaining WLB can be a win–win strategy, helping employees to effectively handle their personal and professional commitments, and employers to retain skilled and engaged employees. Indeed, employees in general are attracted to organisations that treat their employees well and are flexible enough to pay attention to individuals' needs and circumstances. Baral and Bhargava (2010) suggest that supervisors' support and work–family culture are positively related to job satisfaction and employee commitment. Empirical research conducted by Smith and Gardner (2007) suggests that employees who recognise higher levels of supervisor support are more likely to use WLB initiatives. Galinsky and Johnson (1998) suggest that those employees that are offered flexible working arrangements are generally more satisfied, show more initiative and are more likely to remain in the job, than workers without access to such arrangements.

Previous research shows that remote working has a healthy effect on individual and organisational performance. A study from the University of Texas at Austin (2012) found that employees who work from home are able to add up to seven hours to their work week compared to those who work exclusively at the office. Another study revealed that telecommuting may increase productivity and decrease absenteeism and employee turnover (Noonan and Glass, 2012). Cisco's experience shows that the company was able to enhance efficiency, productivity and job satisfaction by allowing its employees to work remotely. It was reported that 60 per cent of the time saved by telecommuting was spent working while 40 per cent was spent on personal business (Cisco, 2009).

Conversely, WLB if poorly managed can have adverse implications for employees and organisations. Likely negative results attached to a work–life imbalance are an increase in family conflicts, work-related stress, fatigue and health and mental problems. Stress alone costs UK businesses an estimated £3.7 billion a year and a loss of 80 million working days. Furthermore, there will be a probable decrease in creativity, morale, productivity and general engagement (Hitt et al., 2009). Based on her analysis of macro statistics in Canada, Crompton (2010) notes that 27 per cent of workers describe their lives on most days as 'quite a bit' or 'extremely' stressful. The majority of highly stressed workers (62%) identified work as their main source of stress. A failure by an organisation to properly manage WLB can lead to a work–life imbalance and consequently negatively affect the employees and their productivity. Research conducted by Janssen (2013) reveals that 72 per cent of the workers in the study were not entirely happy with their WLB.

Discussion activity 10.4

There is considerable diversity in how much time people spend at work across the Organisation for Economic Co-operation and Development (OECD) countries. Turkey is the country with by far the highest proportion of people working very long hours, with more than 46 per cent, followed by Mexico with nearly 29 per cent and Israel with nearly a fifth of employees. Overall, men spend more hours in paid work and the percentage of male employees working very long hours across OECD countries is 12 per cent, compared with less than 5 per cent for women.

Are the countries with highest working hours per week necessarily the most productive and advanced economies? And to what extent does a national culture of intensive work affect WLB in organisations?

Ways for organisations to provide better WLB

In many countries, there is a wide spread of employer policies on WLB and their take-up by employees. In the UK, a recent survey (CIPD, 2012) suggests that most employers (85 to 96 per cent, depending upon the company size) offer some form of flexible working to their employees. A wide range of flexible working arrangements are offered by employers, with part-time working (88 per cent) the most commonly offered type of flexibility. About 63 per cent of employers provide a right to request flexible working for all employees. Working from home on a regular basis (54 per cent) is the next most commonly offered flexible working option. On the flipside, arrangements such as time off to work in the community are offered by less than a quarter of employers.

An important way in which organisations may help all employees, particularly women, in achieving better WLB is by providing flexible working arrangements. Employees wish to have greater flexibility in terms of working hours, and taking breaks from work and workplaces (Alison and Jeff, 2005). By providing flexibility to employees, organisations may give them freedom to choose their time and place of work. When raising children, women (or men) can be allowed to take breaks, and they can also choose to work at home to save time due to the lack of a commute, and this extra time can be spent with the family. Flexible work arrangements mean that employees do not necessarily have to resign from their full-time job or take part-time jobs, hence worry about reduced income can be relieved. In other words, employees do not have to trade-off between their family and careers.

Flexible working arrangements, however, may create some issues for organisations when there is a shortage of workers in a particular department due to the nature or demands of work. This is the reason why organisations may have to offer different incentives and training to keep employees engaged and also to ensure high productivity. This explains why some companies may be reluctant to adopt flexible working arrangements.

Pay inequality is often identified as a problem related to WLB. Employees in general like to have equality of pay and other conditions for flexible and standard jobs (Alison and Jeff, 2005). While some employees, women in particular, try to gain more flexibility by working in non-standard jobs, this may have a negative impact on their earnings. If the equal pay rule is imposed, women can have fewer worries about their income as they will be sure to receive salaries in accordance with the time they work. It is however recognised that even highly paid women (and men) are subject to time- and stress-based conflict between work and home.

The problem with the equal pay rule is that it is hard to measure the contributions of standard workers and non-standard workers. Studies found that training opportunities are more likely to be available to full-time workers than to those working part-time (Alison and Jeff, 2005). Moreover, full-time workers may have a greater motivation to perform better in their tasks to gain bonuses and promotions, while for part-time workers such options may not be available.

Each employee may have her or his own reasons to need WLB. While some may need time to take care of their children, others may need financial support or subsidy to pursue further studies. All of these activities require time and/or money from the employee. Organisations can consider providing financial help or flexible scheduling of work to their employees based on their issues and needs. This may also motivate employees to put in more effort because they have reduced personal worries. However, organisations may not be willing to spend extra money on their employees when they are not sure whether this investment will provide sufficient returns. Misuse by people who do not really need flexible work or subsidies may happen, and other employees may consider it unfair when they do not qualify for such benevolence.

Organisational insight 10.2

MITRE Corporation

MITRE is a not-for-profit engineering company chartered in the US. In 2003, it was listed among the '100 Best Companies for Working Mothers' by *Working Mother* magazine (USA Today, 2004). The company is rated as

(Continued)

(Continued)

a top employer in terms of work–family balance. According to another report, MITRE was ranked amongst the top 25 companies to work for in 2012, and was specially appreciated for its attention to work-life balance (Giang, 2012).

MITRE offers flexible work arrangements to its employees, both in their working time and working places. A variable working schedule is allowed and employees can have flexible working hours subject to company and customers' needs. These have provided an incentive for employees to work there and have catered to their needs for flexible work.

Employees face different problems, such as child and elder care, financial issues and other family issues. In order to help employees achieve WLB, MITRE has contracted with another company to provide consultation, information and referral services to their employees. This is to make sure that their employees are not under stress without being noticed or helped.

'Companies are responding to pressure from both men and women who demand a balanced life. Work–life benefits are here to stay', said an employee of MITRE (USA Today, 2004). It is important that the organisation is willing to listen to feedback from their employees and apply changes.

Employees in MITRE requiring time away from work for personal matters are paid for these days off. They are able to take 21 paid days away from work. Moreover, they can also take up to eight weeks off as a sabbatical for their personal business or development after seven years of service.

According to Diane Hanf, an employee at MITRE, she decided to join the company after 23 years of service in the Air Force because of the company's WLB policies. She said that MITRE offered the balance that she needed in view of her family situation, young son at home, and the need to balance family and work (Hanf, 2003).

The example of MITRE shows that part-time hours are not the only solution to WLB. Companies can introduce innovative and better policies and working arrangements so that employees' needs for WLB are adequately addressed while not having an adverse impact on their earnings.

Country study: WLB in Russia

With increasing economic relations with Western Europe and other countries, Russia has, in recent years, assumed a regional and global role through its memberships in the Group of Eight (G8), the Group of Twenty (G20), and Asia-Pacific Economic Cooperation (APEC). Russia is shaping its own unique profile in addressing the major challenges of the twenty-first century as the chair of APEC in 2012, and the G20 in 2013 (World Bank, 2014). Given its enormous size in terms of area, population and economy, it is important to understand how the country is responding to issues of WLB.

The Russian population in 2013 was estimated to be 142 million people with 71 per cent of the population between 15 and 64 years of age. Within this group approximately 52 per cent are women. The country is currently experiencing negative population growth (−0.02 per cent) due to a low birth rate (1.2 per cent). With a GDP of US$2.555 trillion, Russia has in the past few decades moved from a centrally planned economy to a more market-based and globally integrated economy. Economic reforms in the 1990s privatised most of industry, with notable exceptions in the energy- and defence-related sectors. However, the private sector remains subject to heavy state regulation. The labour force is estimated to be 75.24 million, mostly concentrated in services (64.7 per cent), followed by industry (27.4 per cent) and agriculture (7.9 per cent). The current unemployment rate is 5.7 per cent (2012 estimate) (CIA Factbook, 2014).

Since the Soviet era, the Russian Federation has had a long tradition of female employment and also institutional arrangements for childcare. During the transition period there was some decline in female employment and public expenditure on the family was also cut (Ovcharova and Papova, 2005). The governmental family allowance is quite low and has not taken into account the increasing cost of childcare. Parental leave is paid for children under 18 months and additional unpaid leave may be taken until the child is three (Pailhe, 2009).

Since the break-up of the Soviet Union in 1991, the development of family policy in Russia has experienced the turmoil of transformation, privatisation of enterprises, and rising unemployment affecting citizens' social rights and lifestyle (Teplova, 2007).

Putin's speech to the nation in 2006 exhibited clear pro-natalist intentions. Not only were benefits increased but the most important measure, the so-called maternity capital, was introduced in 2007, giving mothers the right to attractive non-monetary benefits. The maternity grant given at childbirth amounted to 6,000 rubles on the condition that the mother had registered with a medical establishment during pregnancy. For early registration she was awarded an extra 300 rubles (Council of Europe, 2005). According to Zakharov (2008), changes in family policies during the 1980s led to a short-term baby boom in Russia, which was mostly due to women giving birth to children earlier than planned or catching up with previously postponed births.

Thus, despite underfunding and turmoil during transition, WLB remains an important feature of governmental laws and organisational policies in Russia. In terms of health and well-being, the Russian government, through the obligatory medical insurance system, covers medical and emergency care for employees working in the public sector. Contributions are required from employees as well as employers for the obligatory medical insurance fund. Despite the growing private health care sector, most Russians still prefer government-affiliated hospitals which provide free obligatory care. Physical fitness centres have become popular with employees and are available throughout major cities (Engle et al., 2010).

There are also specific provisions for parental leave and care of children. A pregnant woman is legally entitled to paid maternity leave of 70–84 days before childbirth and of 70–110 calendar days after childbirth. Maternity pay comes from a government Social Security Fund to which both employees and employers contribute. The government also supports a childcare leave programme in which a mother can take off up to three years from her position to care for her child. During this time she receives a government allowance equivalent to half of her annual salary and the company guarantees her the same level of position upon her return. Women are legally protected from dismissal when taking maternity leave or leave to care for a child (Engle et al., 2010).

In terms of flexibility, approximately 17 per cent of Russian companies offer flexible work options to full-time employees. In some Russian-owned companies, managers prefer to have their staff working within a zone of their effective control, thus discouraging remote working arrangements. In terms of commuting, organisations help their employees by providing special buses to transport employees to and from the office. In some companies, some employees, particularly those working in field sales jobs, are provided with company cars (Engle et al., 2010).

According to the OECD Better Life Index (OECD BLI, 2013), the Russian Federation has made progress over the past decade in improving the quality of life of its citizens. The BLI statistics show that people in Russia work 1,981 hours a year, about 11 per cent higher than the OECD average of 1,776 hours. However, only 0.2 per cent of employees in Russia work very long hours, much lower than the OECD average of 9 per cent. While men spend more hours in paid work across the OECD, in Russia there is hardly any difference (OECD BLI, 2013).

Questions

1. Compare the historical context and current policies of WLB in Russia with those in your own country. What similarities and differences do you identify?
2. To what extent do governmental, political and ideological approaches to work and family affect work–life balance policies in organisations?
3. What steps do you suggest for organisations in Russia to effectively manage WLB?

Summary and recommendations

Although organisational policies are a key factor influencing WLB, there are driving forces behind the decision to implement such policies. The driving forces identified in this chapter are related to individual dimensions of diversity, such as gender, family responsibilities, sexual orientation, and demographic and religious background. In the interest of employee well-being and productivity, it is imperative for an organisation to properly manage WLB. Failure to do this can result in adverse implications, not only for employees but also for organisations.

While part-time working is often presented as a solution to the WLB challenge, the disadvantage of part-time work is reduction in salary and wages and an adverse impact on career trajectory. Clearly, economic and societal structures, including organisational structures, remain masculine and ethnocentric, thus providing unequal opportunities and an imbalanced environment for women and other disadvantaged groups. Many women who work part-time do so not because they seek lower stress levels via reduced job responsibilities but because the time demands and rigid scheduling of many full-time positions do not easily enable individuals to meet the demands of their caregiving role. And in addition to pay, another issue with part-time work is underemployment, which is its own source of WLB-related stress.

To conclude, there has been an increasing demand for a better WLB from employees. To achieve WLB, organisations may develop strategies that deal with the diverse needs of their employees, so that employees can have greater flexibility in their work while the organisation too can gain value from their work. Indeed, WLB is not just about family and childcare, nor is it about working less. It is about 'working smart', about being fresh enough to give all one can to both work and home, without trading one for the other (OBU, 2007).

Discussion questions

- What advantages can an organisation expect to have by introducing family-friendly policies?
- What are the usual constraints and challenges facing managers in implementing flexible working and other WLB initiatives in organisations?
- How can an organisation tackle WLB when often those who are most time-deprived and stressed are the very managers who should be leading the way to solutions?
- To what extent does individual identity affect the WLB requirements of an employee?

CASE STUDY

Yahoo!

One of the first internet pioneers and leaders, Yahoo! is currently struggling in the fast-changing world of technology. After the departure of three CEOs in a short span of four years, a new CEO was needed who could lead the company into the future (Fisman, 2013). On 16 July 2012, Marissa Mayer was appointed President and CEO of Yahoo!, and with her appointment the corporation's search for direction was about to end.

Marissa Mayer, then 37, was the youngest and one of the few women leading a Fortune 500 company, and probably the only one that was five months pregnant at the time of her appointment. Before taking over at Yahoo!, Mayer had joined Google in 1999 as the company's first female engineer (Fisman 2013; McLean, 2014). After the appointment of the new CEO, a pregnant woman, many employees at Yahoo!, especially women, thought there was finally someone who understood what it meant to be a mother and working at the same time. They seemed to be proved wrong. In March 2013, Mayer surprised both her employees as well as independent analysts by decreeing that there will no longer be a remote working option for Yahoo! staff. A company memo leaked to the media stated, that with effect from June 2013, employees would no longer be permitted to work remotely, in order to create a more productive and connected organisational culture (Goudreau, 2013). The leaked memo reads in part:

> To become the absolute best place to work, communication and collaboration will be important, so we need to be working side-by-side. That is why it is critical that we are all present in our offices. Some of the best decisions and insights come from hallway and cafeteria discussions, meeting new people, and impromptu team meetings. Speed and quality are often sacrificed when we work from home. We need to be one Yahoo!, and that starts with physically being together. (Goudreau, 2013)

This policy is expected to affect hundreds of remote workers. It was alleged that the new policy was aimed at getting rid of rogue employees while keeping only those deemed committed and productive (Fisman, 2013; Weinberger, 2013).

(Continued)

(Continued)

After the announcement, a veritable outcry went through the internet, causing a debate on WLB. It was alleged that more than 20 years after a strong movement towards WLB, Yahoo! was falling back in time. Headlines like 'Boohoo, not Yahoo: Are we moving backwards on work–life balance?' (Total Trust, 2013) circulated on the internet. Following Yahoo!'s announcement, Silicon Valley echoed with debate on the role and future of flexible work in the modern workplace. Currently, a large number of people in Silicon Valley work from home or have other flexible arrangements in place (Weinberger, 2013). Overall 10 per cent of US employees work at least one day from home (Shah, 2013). However, the question remains as to why Yahoo! decided to take this road. After giving birth, Mayer only took two weeks off before returning to her office. After the ban on remote work, it transpired that she had rented an office next to her own with a private nanny for her baby, so they could be close (Reynolds and Neild, 2013). That bothered many employees, since due to the policy, they couldn't work from home and had to leave their babies at home, while their CEO enjoyed the privilege of a private nursery right next to her office.

This obviously caused demotivation in the existing staff. In fact, there was talk of Silicon Valley competitors using flexible schedules as bait to recruit Yahoo!'s competitive employees (Kedleck, 2013).

To be fair, one should also consider the intended or alleged benefits to be gained from the new policy. Companies in the technology sector critically depend on innovation and new developments. A major argument, as emphasised in Yahoo!'s leaked memo, is that some of the best ideas and decisions come from hallway and cafeteria discussions, therefore it is important that employees are present at the workplace. Previous research shows that despite modern IT and communication facilities, business leaders still spend 80 per cent of their time in face-to-face meetings (Fisman, 2013). The reason for this is, in order to cut through complex agendas and work on new innovative ideas, quite often people need to have face-to-face meetings.

The media attention given to the Yahoo! case shows that many people feel affected by WLB. It remains to be seen whether Yahoo!'s new policies lead to success. It may be the right choice over the short and medium run, given the company's current economic situation. However, its long-term implications in terms of staff turnover, motivation and productivity remain far from certain.

(Continued)

(Continued)

This case study can also be analysed in the context of current debates on the problems of presenteeism and flexible working. Presenteeism is generally defined as a tendency to attend work even when one feels unhealthy. It applies to employees attending work while sick and also to those employees who routinely work overtime for the sake of performance, money or corporate citizenship (Johns, 2010; Simpson, 1998). The Yahoo! example by way of illustration highlights the CEO's view that people need to be physically at work.

Questions

1. To what extent do you agree or disagree with Marissa Mayer's policy of requiring employees to be physically at Yahoo! instead of remote working? Why?
2. What would you do if you were in Marissa Mayer's place?
3. To what extent are issues of WLB linked with an organisation's approach to diversity and inclusion?
4. How do you analyse the Yahoo! case study in the context of current debates on presenteeism? Find a couple of examples in other organisations where presenteeism is encouraged.

Acknowledgements

Thanks to Greg Innes, Katy Wright, Tarek Belhous and Yeuk Yiu Wai for contributing to lively class debates on this topic and also assisting in the literature review.

 # Further reading

Hill, E.J., Miller, B.C., Weiner, S.P. and Colihan, J. 1998. Influences of the virtual office on aspects of work and work/life balance. *Personnel Psychology*, 51(3), 667–83.

Houston, D.M. 2005. *Work-Life Balance in the Twenty-First Century*. London: Palgrave.

Hughes, S. and Bolton, T. 2002. *Work–Life Balance*. Spiro Press.

Kaiser, S. and Ringlstetter, M.J. (Eds) 2010. *Work-Life Balance*. Berlin, Heidelberg: Springer-Verlag.

Smithson, J. and Stokoe, E.H. 2005. Discourses of work–life balance: negotiating 'gender blind' terms in organizations. *Gender, Work & Organization*, 12(2), 147–68.

References

Accenture 2012. *Accenture's commitment to the LGBT community: a workplace of equality.* Available at: www.accenture.com/SiteCollectionDocuments/PDF/Accenture_Lesbian_Gay_Bisexual_Transgender.pdf. [Accessed 14 April 2013.]

Alison, L.B. and Jeff, F. 2005. *Gender and Work-Life Flexibility in the Labour Market, Work-Life Balance in the Twenty-First Century.* Basingstoke: Palgrave.

Allen, T. 2001. Family supportive work environments: the role of organisational perceptions, *Journal of Vocational Behaviour*, 58: 414–35.

Baral, R. and Bhargava, S. (2010) Work-family enrichment as a mediator between organizational interventions for work-life balance and job outcomes, *Journal of Managerial Psychology*, 25(3): 274–300.

Bond, J.T., Galinsky, E. and Swanberg, J.E. 1998. *The 1997 National Study of the Changing Workforce.* New York: Families and Work Institute.

Bosworth, D. and Hogarth, T. 2009. *Future horizons for work-life balance.* Institute for Employment Research, University of Warwick. Available at: www.beyondcurrenthorizons. org.uk/wp-content/uploads/ch4_hogarthterence_futurehorizonsforworklifebalance20090116. pdf. [Accessed 1 April 2013.]

Bradley, H., Healy, G. and Mukherjee, N. 2005. Multiple burdens: problems of work-life balance for ethnic minority trade union activist women. In Houston, D.M. (Ed.). *Work-Life Balance in the 21st Century.* Basingstoke: Palgrave Macmillan.

Brief, A. and Nord, W.F. 1990. Work and the family. In Brief, A. and Nord, W.F. (Eds). *Meanings of Occupational Work.* Lexington, MA. Lexington Books.

Catalyst 2013. *Catalyst quick take: family leave – U.S., Canada, and global.* New York: Catalyst. Available at: www.catalyst.org/knowledge/family-leave-us-canada-and-global. [Accessed 21 January 2015.]

Chartered Institute of Personnel Development (CIPD) 2012. *Flexible working provision and uptake.* Survey Report May 2012. Available at: www.cipd.co.uk/hr-resources/survey-reports/ flexible-working-provision-update.aspx. [Accessed 21 January 2015.]

CIA Factbook 2014. *Russian Federation.* Available at: www.cia.gov/library/publications/the-world-factbook/geos/rs.html. [Accessed 21 January 2015.]

Cisco 2009. *Cisco study finds telecommuting significantly increases employee productivity, work-life flexibility and job satisfaction.* Available at: http://newsroom.cisco.com/dlls/2009/ prod_062609.html. [Accessed 4 April 2013.]

Clark, S.C. 2000. Work/family border theory: a new theory of work/family balance, *Human Relations*, 53(6): 747–70.

Conaghan, J. and Rittich, K. 2005. *Labour Law, Work and Family.* Oxford: Oxford University Press.

Council of Europe 2005. *Russia 2005. 4 Maternity.* Excerpt from the MISSCEO database. Available at: www.socialcohesion.coe.int/MISSCEO/IndexCountry.aspx?year=2005. [Accessed 26 May 2012.]

Counselling Directory 2013. *Discrimination and minority groups.* Available at: www.counselling-directory.org.uk/abusestats.html. [Accessed 14 April 2013.]

Crompton, S. 2010. What's stressing the stressed? Main sources of stress among workers. Available at: http://www.statcan.gc.ca/pub/11-008-x/2011002/article/11562-eng.htm. [Accessed 12 November 2014.]

Dale, A. 2005. Combining family and employment: evidence from Pakistani and Bangladeshi women. In Houston, D.M. (Ed.). *Work–Life Balance in the 21st Century*. Basingstoke: Palgrave Macmillan.

Department for Education and Employment (DfEE) 2000. *Changing patterns in a changing world*. Scotland Office. Available at: http://dera.ioe.ac.uk/8789/1/52_1.pdf. [Accessed 3 April 2013.]

Engle, R., Usenko, L.N. and Dimitriadi, N.A. 2010. *Work–life in Russia*. Boston College Center for Work and Family. Available at: https://www.bc.edu/content/dam/files/centers/cwf/research/publications/pdf/BCCWF_EBS_Russia.pdf. [Accessed 21 January 2015.]

Felstead, A., Jewson, N., Phizacklea, A. and Walters, S. 2002. Opportunities to work at home in the context of work–life balance, *Human Resource Management Journal*, 12: 54–76.

Fisman, R. 2013. CEO right: Yahoo workers must show up. *CNN*. Available at: http://edition.cnn.com/2013/02/26/opinion/fisman-yahoo/index.html. [Accessed 4 April 2013.]

Galinsky, E. and Johnson, A.A. 1998. *Reframing the Business Case for Work–Life Initiatives*. New York: Families and Work Institute.

Giang, V. 2012. The 25 best companies to work for in 2012. The Business Insider, June 28. Available at: www.businessinsider.com/the-25-best-companies-to-work-for-2012-6?op=1&IR=T [Accessed 21 January 2015.]

Goudreau, J. 2013. Back to the Stone Age? New Yahoo CEO Marissa Mayer bans working from home. *Forbes*. Available at: www.forbes.com/sites/jennagoudreau/2013/02/25/back-to-the-stone-age-new-yahoo-ceo-marissa-mayer-bans-working-from-home/. [Accessed 4 April 2013.]

Grzywacz, J.G. and Carlson, D.S. 2007. Conceptualizing work–family balance: implications for practice and research, *Advances in Developing Human Resources*, 9(4): 455–71.

Hakim, C. 2000. *Work–Lifestyle Choices in the 21st Century: Preference Theory*. Oxford: Oxford University Press.

Hanf, D. 2003. *Transitioning from the military to MITRE: in search of the right work–life balance*. MITRE, November. Available at: www.mitre.org/employment/employee_spotlight/diane_hanf.html. [Accessed 13 April 2013.]

Harris, B. 2011. Gay groups join fight against Wal-Mart. *The New York Times*, March 2. Available at: http://cityroom.blogs.nytimes.com/2011/03/02/gay-group-joins-fight-against-wal-mart/. [Accessed 21 January 2015.]

Hill, E.J., Hawkins, A.J., Ferris, M. and Weitzman, M. 2001. Finding an extra day a week: the positive influence of perceived job flexibility on work and family life balance, *Family Relations*, 50: 49–58.

Hitt, M., Miller, C. and Colella, A. 2009. *Organisational Behaviour* 2nd edition. New York: Wiley.

Holliday, M. and Manfredi, S. 2004. *Work-life balance. An audit of staff experience at Oxford Brookes University*. The Centre for Diversity and Policy Research. Available at: www.brookes.ac.uk/services/hr/cdprp/resources/wlb_report.pdf. [Accessed 3 April 2013.]

Houston, D.M. and Marks, G., 2005. Working, caring and sharing: work–life dilemmas in early motherhood. In Houston D.M. (Ed.), *Work–Life Balance in the 21st Century*. Basingstoke: Palgrave.

Human Solutions Report (2006–7) *Under pressure – implications of work–life balance and job stress*. Available at: www.grahamlowe.ca/documents/182/Under%20Pressure%2010-06.pdf. [Accessed 16 April 2013].

International Labor Organisation (ILO) n.d. *The Maternity Benefit Act 1961 in India*. Available at: www.ilo.org/dyn/travail/docs/678/Maternity. [Accessed 21 January 2015.]

Janssen, J. 2013. *A poor work–life balance is bad – both for the employees and the employers*. Available at: www.netsurvey.se/en/2013/01/30/a-poor-work-life-balance-is-bad-both-for-employees-and-employers/. [Accessed 16 April 2013.]

Jayson, S. 2012. Burnout up among employees. The slow-to-recovery economy is taking a new toll on workers. *USA Today*. Available at: www.usatoday.com/story/news/nation/2012/10/23/stress-burnout-employees/1651897/. [Accessed 7 April 2013.]

Johns, G. 2010. Presenteeism in the workplace: a review and research agenda, *Journal of Organizational Behavior*, 31: 519–42.

Kedleck, D. 2013. Memo read round the world: Yahoo says no to working at home. *TIME*. Available at: http://business.time.com/2013/02/26/memo-read-round-the-world-yahoo-says-no-to-working-at-home/. [Accessed 4 April 2013.]

Kirton, G. and Greene, A.M. 2010. *The Dynamics of Managing Diversity – A Critical Approach*, 3rd edition. London: Routledge.

Lewis, S. 2000. Workplace programmes and policies in the United Kingdom. In Haas, L., Hwang, P. and Russell, G. (Eds). *Organisational Change and Gender Equity*. London: Sage, p. 105.

McLean, B. 2014. Yahoo's Geek Goddess. Vanity Fair. January. Available at: http://www.vanityfair.com/business/2014/01/marissa-mayer-yahoo-google. [Accessed 12 Nov 2014.]

USA Today 2004. Working Mother magazine's top 100 places to work. USA Today, September 21. Available at: http://usatoday30.usatoday.com/money/books/2004-09-21-working-mom-list_x.htm [Accessed 21 January 2015.]

Myers, C.S. 1924. *Industrial Psychology in Great Britain*. London: Cape.

Noonan, M.C. and Glass, J.F. 2012. *The hard truth about telecommuting*. Bureau of Labor Statistics, USA. Available at: www.bls.gov/opub/mlr/2012/06/art3full.pdf. [Accessed 4 April 2013.]

OECD BLI 2013. *OECD Better Life Index. Russian Federation*. Available at: www.oecdbetterlifeindex.org/countries/russian-federation/. [Accessed 21 January 2015.]

Out and Equal Workplace Summit 2012. *Work-life balance – empty words or promising pathway?* Available at: http://outandequal.wordpress.com/2012/08/16/2012-out-equal-workplace-summit-new-workshops/. [Accessed 16 April 2013.]

Office of National Statistics (ONS) 2012. *Gender working patterns*. Available at: http://www.ons.gov.uk/ons/about-ons/business-transparency/freedom-of-information/what-can-i-request/index.html. [Accessed 12 November 2014.]

Ovcharova, L. and Popova, D. 2005. *Child Poverty in Russia. Alarming Trends and Policy Options*. Moscow: UNICEF, Independent Institute of Social Policy, pp. 14–15.

Oxford Brookes University (OBU) 2007. *Work–life balance for all*. Available at: www.brookes.ac.uk/services/hr/eod/wlb/. [Accessed 7 April 2013.]

Özbilgin, M.F., Beauregard, T.A., Tatli, A. and Bell, M.P. 2011. Work–life, diversity and intersectionality: a critical review and research agenda, *International Journal of Management Reviews*, 13: 177–98.

Pailhe, A. 2009. Work–family balance and childbearing intentions in France, Germany and Russian Federation. In Conference Proceedings: *How Generations and Gender Shape Demographic Change: Towards Policies Based on Better Knowledge*. United Nations Economic Commission for Europe. Geneva: United Nations Publications, pp. 57–64.

Parakati, V. 2010. The history of work–life balance: it's not as new as you might think. *Examiner. com*. Available at: www.examiner.com/article/the-history-of-work-life-balance-it-s-not-as-new-as-you-think-1. [Accessed 2 April 2013.]

Royal Bank of Scotland (RBS) 2013. Available at: www.rbs.co.uk. [Accessed 17 April 2013.]

Royal College of Nursing (RCN) 2008. Spinnig plates: Establishming a work-life balance. Available at: https://www.rcn.org.uk/__data/assets/pdf_file/0007/156166/003214.pdf. [Accessed 12 November 2014.]

Reynolds, D. and Neild, B. 2013. Tech excess question Yahoo's work-from-the-office edict. *CNN*. Available at: http://edition.cnn.com/2013/02/26/tech/remote-working-yahoo-mobile/index. html. [Accessed 4 April 2013.]

Samuel, J. 2013. Making work–life balance work. *The Straits Times* [Singapore] 21 March. Available at: www.straitstimes.com/premium/forum-letters/story/making-work-life-balance-work-20130321&. [Accessed 21 January 2015.]

Sav, A., Harris, N. and Sebar, B. 2014. Australian Muslim men balancing work, family and religion: a positive look at a negative issue, *Personnel Review*, 43(1): 2–18.

Schaffer, J. 2013. Female faculty struggle to balance family and work commitments, *The Stanford Daily*, 31 March. Available at: www.stanforddaily.com/2013/03/31/female-faculty-struggle-to-balance-family-and-work-commitments/. [Accessed 21 January 2015.]

Shah, N. 2013. More Americans working remotely. *The Wall Street Journal*, March 5. Available at: http://online.wsj.com/articles/SB10001424127887324539404578342503214110478. [Accessed 12 November 2014.]

Simpson, R. 1998. Presenteeism, power and organizational change: long hours as a career barrier and the impact on the working lives of women managers, *British Journal of Management*, 9: S37–S50.

Slaughter, A-M. 2012. Why women still can't have it all. *The Atlantic*, June 13. Available at: www. theatlantic.com/magazine/archive/2012/07/why-women-still-cant-have-it-all/309020/. [Accessed 21 January 2015.]

Smith, J. and Gardner, D. 2007. Factors affecting employee use of work–life balance initiatives, *New Zealand Journal of Psychology*, 36: 3–12.

Teplova, T. 2007. Welfare state transformation, childcare and women's work in Russia, *Social Politics*, 14(3): 284–322.

Thomas, K.C. 2013. *Work–Life Balance: A Sociological Study of Women Professionals in Kerala*. Kerala: Mahatma Gandhi University.

Total Trust 2013. *Boohoo, not Yahoo: Are we moving backwards on work/life balance?* Available at: www.trustiseverything.com/blog/boohoo-not-yahoo-are-we-moving-backwards-on-work-life-balance/. [Accessed 12 November 2014.]

University of Texas at Austin 2012. *Telecommuting increases work hours and blurs boundary between work and home, new study shows*. Available at: www.utexas.edu/news/2012/12/03/telecommuting-increases-work-hours-blurs-boundary-between-work-home-new-study-shows/. [Accessed 4 April 2013.]

US Department of Labor 2004. *Women in the Labor Force: A Databook*. Washington, DC: US Department of Labor. Available at: www.bls.gov/cps/wlf-databook.pdf. [Accessed 22 April 2013.]

US Department of Labor 2013. *Fair Labor Standards Act of 1938*. Available at: www.dol.gov/oasam/programs/history/flsa1938.htm. [Accessed 3 April 2013.]

Wasay, B. 2013. An investigation of the relationship between work–life balance and employee engagement, *Strategic HR Review*, 12(4).

Weinberger, D. 2013. What Mayer misses out on work–life balance? *CNN*. Available at: http://edition.cnn.com/2013/03/02/opinion/weinberger-work-from-home/. [Accessed 21 January 2015.]

World Bank 2014. *Russia: Overview*. Available at: www.worldbank.org/en/country/russia/overview#2. [Accessed 21 January 2015.]

Zakharov, S. 2008. Russian Federation: From the first to second demographic transition, *Demographic Research*, 19(24): 907–72.

Intersectionality in the workplace

11

Harry J. Van Buren III

 Intended learning outcomes

After reading this chapter, you should have a firm understanding of the concept of intersectionality and how it differs from analyses of oppression and discrimination that focus on individual-level categories. You should also be able to apply intersectional analyses to the organisational context as they relate to the management of diversity.

You should be able to:

- Define intersectionality
- Discuss why and how the concept of intersectionality developed
- Explain why the concept of intersectionality adds to our understanding of oppression and discrimination
- Identify opportunities for intersectional analysis, especially with regard to analyses of discrimination in organisations
- Discuss the implications of intersectionality for organisational action
- Discuss the challenges that intersectionality poses for public policy
- Apply intersectional analyses to diversity management

Introduction

We talk all the time about discrimination on the basis of sex, race, ethnicity, disability status, and sexual orientation, among other forms of disadvantage and oppression. Why do we need another diversity concept? Doesn't intersectionality just confuse the issues related to managing organisational diversity?

Imagine that you are talking to a well-meaning person who opposes oppression and discrimination. He wants to do the right thing, and believes that he would never knowingly harm another person, irrespective of that person's background. This person gets that not everyone is treated equally and that one's life chances do not solely (or even largely) depend on personal effort. Yet if you talked to that person about 'intersectionality,' you might get the kinds of questions that are posed at the beginning of this section. What is intersectionality, and why do we need the concept to understand better how forms of oppression and discrimination reinforce each other?

Intersectionality is challenging because it forces us to think systematically about human experiences holistically and systemically. Intersectional analyses force us to look beyond single-variable analyses of oppression and discrimination, and toward understanding systems of oppression in which one form thereof reinforces and intensifies the effects of other forms. It can make us feel uncomfortable because thinking through the additive and systemic effects of discrimination is challenging, whether we want to make our organisations more just or to change public policy in ways that promote justice. It may also cause us to wonder how we can make progress towards eradicating discrimination and oppression. And yet, intersectional analyses matter because oppression and discrimination come in myriad forms as experienced by different people, and *systems* of oppression do not correspond simply to individual categories of difference. McCall (2005) has noted that in social science fields such as sociology, the concept of intersectionality has brought about new research that has explored the multiplex nature of subordination. Intersectionality similarly can and should enrich our understanding of diversity management as we seek to make our organisations more just.

In this chapter, I'll take up these questions and others. I'll start by discussing the development of intersectionality as a concept (including the three types of complexity that inform work in the area) and discuss some of the current critiques of intersectionality research. I'll then consider the European Union (EU) and US contexts vis-à-vis intersectional analysis, focusing on the forms that anti-discrimination legislation takes and how an intersectional approach would be a useful addition to existing legislation and regulation. With the help of a case study focusing on veiled Muslim women in the EU, I'll discuss approaches to using intersectional analyses in organisations and conclude with a set of recommendations.

The concept of intersectionality

The concept of intersectionality, at its root, seeks to understand how forms of oppression and discrimination intersect in ways that reinforce each other. Someone who is a black woman, for example, is not just black and not just a woman from the perspective of others in her society or from the standpoint of how she understands her life experiences. Rather, her experience can only be understood by considering how her race and sex *together* affect how she is seen and treated by others. The discrimination she is wrongly subject to based on her race intersects with the wrongful discrimination she experiences based on her sex. If she is discriminated against because she is a black woman and then wants to pursue legal remedies, existing laws related to discrimination on the basis of single variables are often inadequate to the task.

Now, let's add layers of complexity. If she has a physical disability, that experience intersects with her race and sex, and her experiences of discrimination will be different to those of a black woman who does not have a physical disability. Other forms of disadvantage, such as being gay in a society that is strongly homophobic or being an undocumented migrant, add to the complexities of personal identity and experiences of discrimination. In this respect, the same individual can not only be subject to multiple forms of discrimination based on elements of his background and life experiences, but the discrimination itself takes on a different character based on the intersection of different forms of oppression as experienced by him. Without the concept of intersectionality, we would not be able to name or to theorise about the multiple forms of disadvantage that some individuals face in society. The concept of intersectionality also allows us to move beyond binary, single-category models of discrimination towards a richer understanding of how individuals relate to their settings in myriad ways. It also, as will be discussed later, offers a framework for critiquing the existence and definitions of the categories themselves. Acker (2012) notes that the notion of intersectionality adds needed complexity with regard to the study of inequality regimes as they are related to gender.

This might seem like common sense, and perhaps it is. And indeed the essential insight of intersectionality can be found in the writing of black activists in the US dating back to the late nineteenth century (Cole, 2009). Intersectionality 'provides a concise shorthand for describing ideas that have, through political struggle, come to be accepted in feminist thinking and women's studies scholarship' (Phoenix and Pattynama, 2006: 187). The emergence of intersectionality came out of a particular history in the US that bears examination.

In the 1970s, a group of black feminists who collectively made up the Combahee River Collective (1986) wrote a manifesto that sought to connect their experiences of racially based oppression to oppression based on their sex. This manifesto brought forth the analogous concept of 'simultaneity' (1986). There had been a long history of black feminist critiques of dominant strains of feminism (Holvino, 2010) that informed their work. Intersectionality as a concept reveals something that is highly relevant to understanding organisational diversity: human experience cannot be neatly categorised on the basis of any one personal attribute or characteristic. The work of bell hooks (1984), writing in the radical and black feminist traditions, challenged the notion that gender was the primary determinant of a woman's fate, especially for black women. The concept of intersectionality has radical implications for how we manage diversity in organisations and how government regulation might function in ways that promote justice, and the insight that forms of oppression and discrimination are multiple and intersecting has been expressed for more than a century.

The origin of the *term* 'intersectionality' has been credited to the legal and critical race scholar Kimberlé Crenshaw (1989, 1991). She wrote that (1991: 140), 'because the intersectional experience is greater than the sum of racism and sexism, any analysis that does not take intersectionality into account cannot sufficiently address the particular manner in which Black women are subordinated'. In a more recent review, Choo and Ferree (2010: 131) note that there are:

> three dimensions of theorizing what intersectionality signifies: the importance of including the perspectives of multiply-marginalized persons and groups; an analytic shift from addition of multiple independent strands of inequality toward a multiplication and thus transformation of their main effects into interactions; and a focus on seeing multiple interactions as overlapping in their co-determination of inequalities to produce complex configurations from the start, rather than 'extra' interactive processes that are added on to main effects.

The complexity of intersectional analyses should be evident. It can be hard enough to understand the discrimination that someone who is not similar to you has faced in his or her life. It is even harder to understand how forms of discrimination and disadvantage intersect, and in so doing, intensify the experience of discrimination for some people in society. There are myriad ways of categorising how individuals differ in ways that lead to discrimination, as will be discussed. However, we also need to understand how intersectionality is used in research about diversity and discrimination, especially as categorising people into discrete categories that are then the basis for intersectional theorising can be highly problematic if done in uncritical ways.

McCall (2005: 1772) has noted that 'intersectionality has introduced new methodological problems'. Doing research about discrimination and societal diversity is complex on its own when dealing with one form of human difference. Bringing together multiple forms of difference into an analysis of how they intersect and create harm adds greater complexity, and in so doing might make research about intersectionality and discrimination both harder and less fruitful: harder for obvious reasons related to the complexity of identifying and empirically testing research questions, less fruitful because intersectionality research might not lead to easily understandable and actionable conclusions. In further unpacking the complexity that the application of intersectionality brings to analyses of discrimination, she specifies three types of complexity: anticategorical, intercategorical and intracategorical. Each approach adds to our understanding of difference, discrimination and diversity.

Anticategorical complexity seeks to deconstruct categories such as 'race' and 'sex'. Rather than reifying these categories as immutable, anticategorical complexity seeks to interrogate them because they are 'simplifying social fictions that produce inequalities in the process of producing differences' (McCall, 2005: 1773). Here the existence of the categories themselves is the root of oppression; they are not even useful fictions. Rather, categorisation 'inevitably leads to demarcation, and demarcation to exclusion, and exclusion to inequality' (McCall, 2005: 1777). The categories continue to exist because people act as if they exist, an insight consistent with work related to performativity (Austin, 1962; Butler, 1997; McDowell, 2008; Styhre and Eriksson-Zetterquist, 2008; Winker and Degele, 2011). Anticategorical complexity might then seem to be not intersectional at all. Anticategorical complexity in intersectional analysis seeks to question the existence of particular categories, such as gender. Gender, in an anticategorical sense, cannot be reduced to biological sex and indeed sex is not itself a male–female binary (Fausto-Sterling, 2000, 2008). In this respect anticategorical complexity 'subverts race/gender [and by extension, other binaries] in the service of theorizing identity in a more complex fashion' (Nash, 2008: 89).

Intercategorical complexity (sometimes called 'categorical complexity') 'requires that scholars provisionally adopt existing analytical categories to document relationships of inequality among social groups and changing configurations of inequality among multiple and conflicting dimensions' (McCall, 2005: 1773). Intercategorical complexity represents the other end of the continuum from anticategorical complexity in that it 'focuses on the complexity of relationships among multiple social groups within and across single social groups, single categories, or both' (McCall, 2005: 1786). Inequality and discrimination in this analysis thus is understood as multi-dimensional and changing over time.

Intracategorical complexity takes a middle path between anticategorical complexity and intercategorical complexity. It does not reject categories completely, as does anticategorical complexity, and it is more sceptical about the usefulness and veracity of categories than intercategorical complexity. While recognising that categories have shortcomings, intracategorical complexity also recognises that as social constructions, categories are necessary for understanding society and the lived experiences of individuals in it; here intracategorical complexity (much like anticategorical complexity) recognises that categories are performative in nature. Taking a middle path allows researchers to 'identify a new or invisible group – at the intersection of multiple categories – and proceed to uncover the differences and complexities of experience embodied in that location' (McCall, 2005: 1782). In naming groups that have been hidden by traditional categories, intracategorical complexity also reveals the extent of difference within those categories.

As can be seen, intersectionality is complex, and scholars working in this area use multiple conceptualisations of it. However, the core idea of intersectionality – that discrimination and oppression cannot be understood through recourse to a single, binary classification – holds across work in the area. Intersectionality interrogates questions related to discrimination – and by extension, power – in novel ways.

Power and intersectionality

In some sense, intersectionality is all about power – who has it and who lacks it. Intersectionality focuses on how human differences intersect in ways that bring about subjugation. In this context, 'differences' are those variations that help explain who has power and who lacks it in a particular society. Intersectional analyses uncover power dynamics that are often hidden from view and thus unaddressed.

Power-based analyses informed the work of early intersectional theorists. The initial work in intersectionality came out of the experiences of black women in the US who were left out of their society in multiple ways. As people who were black, they experienced discrimination that was shaped by the historical experience of slavery and later Jim Crow laws that legalised their subjugation. As women, they were left out of the power structures of a society that gendered social relations in ways that advantaged men. Feminism, in seeking to unmake maleness as normative, had a blind spot in that it treated the experiences of white women as normative. bell hooks (1981), in critiquing the feminism of the time, decried the implication that all women were white and all blacks were men. Black women were doubly oppressed, and their experiences could not be understood without an intersectional analysis. Intersectionality as a conceptual framework, therefore, surfaces power dynamics in a society and provides a fuller explanation for why some people are discriminated against.

For each type of complexity – anticategorical, intercategorical and intracategorical – power-based analyses are essential. Anticategorical complexity addresses power directly; the power to determine what social classifications matter and to police the boundaries of those classifications itself is a marker of and basis for the maintenance of power structures. Indeed, anticategorical complexity theorists posit that the categories themselves are the problem; destroying the categories and the boundaries they enforce is the necessary condition for destroying power imbalances. Intercategorical complexity seeks to uncover how 'membership' in multiple disadvantaged groups causes some people to lack power and to suffer discrimination. Intracategorical complexity surfaces new groups of people – hidden by existing classifications – who are discriminated against based on the intersection of categories that are simultaneously subject to criticism and useful for describing contemporary social relations.

Power based on maleness, economic status or membership in the dominant racial group of society is perhaps easier to understand than powerlessness based on the intersection of less-favoured categories. As will be discussed, much anti-discrimination regulation addresses single-category-level discrimination. However, a more fully developed analysis of power and powerlessness – whether in an organisation or a society – requires attention to intersectional analysis. When someone is being discriminated against, it is important to ask why. Power, or rather the lack thereof, is a critical explanation for why some people are treated well and others poorly. The initial work done on intersectionality sought to address the lack of power of black women, whose double membership in powerless groups had not been adequately addressed in previous activism, government action or scholarship. The challenge for organisations and governments is to expand their analyses of power, powerlessness and discrimination to take in how categories of difference intersect in ways that sustain existing power structures.

Critiques of intersectionality

There have been a number of critiques of intersectionality. As a relatively new construct – even though the core insight has been present in activism and scholarship for a long time – intersectional scholarship does not have a strong degree of convergence or an established methodology. Further, while intersectionality has considerable face validity, its usefulness for organisational practice has not yet been well established.

Lack of explanatory power

Intersectionality is a powerful heuristic and way of looking at the social environment. However, it is less clear what it is trying to explain, in part because the concept seems to be vague in its definitions (Nash, 2008). Is it trying to provide a general theory of identity? Describe how discrimination in a society might be remedied? Predict who will suffer discrimination in an organisation? Here Choo and Ferree (2010) note that intersectional analysis can be group-centred (focusing on multiply marginalised groups and their perspectives), process-centred (seeking to understand how multiple forms of disadvantage multiply as in intercategorical complexity, or uncover previously unknown groups experiencing disadvantage as in intracategorical complexity) or system-centred (focusing on the social system as a whole), although the particular claims made by scholars working within the field are often less than clear. While not every concept needs to make testable claims or to explain particular phenomena, intersectionality offers a potential way forward to study and then ameliorate forms of discrimination and oppression in a society – but scholarship in this area needs to give more attention to increasing its explanatory power.

Levels of analysis

Another critique of intersectionality is that it is fuzzy on which level(s) of analysis it seeks to be operative at. It might seek to explain how particular individuals experience discrimination. It might function at the group level; for example, intracategorical intersectionality seeks to surface previously hidden groups in order to name and ameliorate their oppression. Intersectionality might also be useful at the organisational level of analysis, seeking to understand how organisational systems and cultures affect the extent and bases of discrimination. It might function at the national level, although this is an area of research that has been left largely unaddressed (Gottfried, 2009). It might even be useful in transnational research (Yuval-Davis, 2006). Intersectionality seems particularly useful in cross-level analyses of discrimination, another potential area for research (Winker and Degele, 2011). More work disentangling the multiple levels of analysis for which intersectional analyses can be useful is needed.

Neglecting the actions of the powerful

Intersectionality focuses on the experiences of those people who have been oppressed. However, in so doing it neglects the aetiology of how oppression emerges. Walby et al. (2012: 230) argue that 'it is important not to focus only on the disadvantaged people since this obscures the role of the powerful within sets of unequal social relations ... the consequence of this focus of attention is that the ontology of the inequality is often too shallow and unitary'. In focusing on the experiences of those who are harmed by discrimination and oppression, the actions of those whose behaviour sustains discrimination and oppression is often left unaddressed. This relates to the previous discussion of what the goals of intersectionality research are and should be.

Categories that are frequently left out of intersectional analyses

It is not surprising that Nash (2008) notes that black women are the quintessential intersectional subjects, given how the concept emerged, and intersectionality analyses have included women generally (Acker, 2012; Shields, 2008). However, other categories have been largely left out of intersectionality research. Class, given that it is an outcome of disordered and unjust social relations, has received some attention from intersectionality scholars (Holvino, 2010), but merits much more (Nash, 2008). Religion is an important element of one's identity and an all-too-common basis for discrimination, but it has not been well explored in the intersectionality literature (see Arifeen and Gatrell, 2013, and Rahman, 2010, for notable exceptions). Age discrimination is well known in almost every society, yet age merits more attention vis-à-vis intersectional analysis (Warner and Brown, 2011). There is a paucity of research that addresses categories such as migrant workers (but see Alberti et al., 2013, and Buitelaar, 2006) or forms of disadvantage such as lookism (Winker and Degele, 2011). And sexuality in all of the forms that it takes – which has significant implications for how gender is theorised (and enforced by the powerful, usually men, who are members of majority racial and ethnic communities, in ways that disadvantage women and gay men) – while a growing area for intersectionality research, is still receiving less attention than needed (Bowleg, 2008; Dworkin, 2005; Rahman, 2010). Further, intersectional analyses that do not include women as their subjects – say, for example, addressing discrimination against gay Muslim men (Rahman, 2010) – are few and far between. Other important categories of difference, such as religion, have similarly received little treatment (Arifeen and Gatrell, 2013; Yuval-Davis, 2006).

Intersectionality is a powerful way of conceptualising and understanding oppression and discrimination. Of course, scholars should be free to define their work as they fit. But for the concept of intersectionality to fulfil its promise, more categories of disadvantage need to be examined and linked together into a broader analysis of unjust social relations.

Lack of an established methodology and empirical work

As noted before, intersectionality has considerable face validity in that it describes the social world as it is found and experienced. We know intuitively that forms of disadvantage intersect with each other. However, the movement from intersectionality as framework and heuristic to intersectionality as a research paradigm with well-established methodologies that give rise to robust empirical work is far from complete. Nash (2008: 6) points out that there is 'a tremendous gap between conceptions of intersectional methodologies and practices of intersectional investigations', ironically leading to the replications of identity that early intersectional theorists sought to critique. Crenshaw (1989, 1991) focused on the lived experience of black women, and yet her focus on them precluded an examination of the other ways in which they might be mistreated (Nash, 2008). While intersectionality is useful as a research paradigm in fields as diverse as gender studies (Acker, 2012), globalisation (Gottfried, 2009), the management of work (Özbilgin et al., 2011), political science (Hancock, 2007) and psychology (Cole, 2009), there is a danger that intersectionality can be used so loosely as to rob the concept of its distinctive contribution to our understanding of discrimination and diversity.

Further, while there has been significant progress in developing theoretical frameworks for intersectional analysis (although more needs to be done here; Nash, 2008), there is a paucity of empirical work using intersectionality as the organising research principle. There are, of course, many different and valid ways of creating knowledge; in this regard, Zander et al.'s (2010) call for action research with regard to intersectionality in organisations seems particularly apt. However, claims made related to intersectionality have not been well tested empirically (qualitatively, quantitatively or mixed methods) or even been the subject of methods development to that end. Without empirical work, intersectionality runs the risk of being more of a heuristic rather than a research field in its own right, that in turn informs work done in other research fields.

Lack of application to organisations

Finally, there is the issue of the extent to which intersectionality has been well applied to the organisational content. It should be evident that intersectional analyses should be useful to diversity management. Zander et al. (2010), in describing intersectionality as a new approach for international business research, argue that it is 'partially formulated to address the management of social relations, which are changeable, varying, and multi-layered'. They propose that it can be brought to bear on topics such as career patterns. Similarly, Özbilgin et al. (2011) apply intersectional analysis to work–life balance concerns. However, given the importance of organisations to questions of power and discrimination, the lack of intersectional analysis in this context is curious. Much of the purpose of this chapter is to make the case that intersectionality is useful to the study and practice of diversity management.

Section synopsis

- Intersectionality offers a different perspective on the analysis of discrimination and oppression. Rather than seeing forms of difference as separate from each other in terms of their negative effects, intersectionality seeks to understand how they intersect in ways that create disadvantage for some people within a society.
- Three types of complexity – anticategorical, intercategorical and intracategorical – inform work on intersectionality, with different goals for and analyses of why discrimination persists.
- The experience of black women has been foundational to work on intersectionality; one topic of debate is the inclusion of categories beyond race and sex in intersectional analyses.
- Academic work on intersectionality has focused more on theory building than theory testing and organisational application.

Intersectionality legislation in the EU and the US related to discrimination in employment

Both the EU and the US have legislation that seeks to prevent discrimination in employment, but this legislation tends to focus on specific categories rather than an intersectional analysis of why discrimination occurs and how it might be remedied. Lombardo and Verloo (2009: 479) note that 'from Article 13 of the Treaty of Amsterdam onwards, "equality" in the EU has to do with combating discrimination on grounds of sex, racial and ethnic origin, disability, age, religion, and sexual orientation'. Verloo (2006: 224) argues that 'an individualistic anti-discrimination policy is insufficient'. Similarly, through legislation such as the Civil Rights Act of 1964 and the Americans with Disabilities Act of 1990, the US has sought to ban discrimination in the employment arena (although there is not at present national-level legislation banning discrimination on the basis of sexual orientation). In the EU, discrimination legislation started largely with gender-related concerns (Lombardo and Verloo, 2009). In the US, for historical reasons having to do with the legacy of slavery and Jim Crow laws, discrimination legislation started with concerns related to race and broadened to take in gender, disability and age. Both the EU and the US have significant requirements for organisations to prevent discrimination and to report on their efforts to do so.

In both the EU and the US, 'political and policy practice has seldom referred to intersectionality when trying to deal with multiple inequalities' (Verloo, 2006). In both places, anti-discrimination legislation has focused on specific categories rather than taking a more systemic analysis of discrimination and disadvantage in the employment setting. In the US, the Equal Employment Opportunity Commission requires that organisations track data related to the racial and gender composition of their work-forces, and other US labour regulations have similar requirements (Robinson et al., 2005). However, requirements that US organisations think in intersectional terms with regard to discrimination do not exist, and there is little evidence that intersectionality is even discussed by policy makers at the legislative and agency levels of analysis. Similarly, Lombardo and Ronaldson Agustín (2012), in coding a sample of 66 EU texts related to gender equality, found only 34 occurrences of intersectional references across the entire sample. As in the US, the preference in the EU is for focusing on 'specific inequality axes' in EU labour regulation (following Lombardo and Ronaldson Agustín, 2012). In the EU, there is some discussion of how intersectionality might be useful in remedying discrimination, but there is little evidence to date that this has affected public policy.

There is, in short, a marked preference in the EU and US contexts for labour regulation regarding discrimination that addresses single categories of disadvantage rather than intersectional analyses of discrimination. In neither the EU nor the US are there specific employment regulations banning discrimination based on the intersection of categories. Arguably, this is because the discourse related to intersec-tionality has not achieved the same level of use in public policy processes as have gender, race-based and other forms of discourse about discrimination. It also may be the case that the lack of conceptual clarity and specific policy recommendations have made intersectionality a useful framework to discuss the intersection of bases for discrimination, but have not yet allowed intersectionality to play a robust role in the policy environment.

Intersectionality is challenging for policy makers because existing regulatory regimes related to discrimination are set up for binary categories that are easy to clas-sify, assess and report on. While existing anti-discrimination regulations share with intersectional theories a concern about discrimination, the difficulty of assessing how combinations of disadvantage can be empirically assessed for (a) reporting purposes, (b) 'intensity' of disadvantage requiring regulatory attention and (c) determinations that discrimination has occurred and requires remedy, has caused intersectionality to be used more as a frame of reference than as a basis for regulation. In this respect political policy makers face the same challenges as do organisational decision makers, as will be discussed in the next two sections.

Making intersectionality useful in diversity management

The case study on p. 329 offers some clues as to how intersectionality might be made useful in the field of diversity management. For those people who are involved in diversity management practice, intersectionality offers a critical framework for assessing who has privilege in their organisations and who does not. As there are more questions than answers in contemporary intersectionality research, it is appropriate that the application of intersectionality to the practice of diversity management should focus on raising new questions, which can then be provisionally answered in ways that promote greater justice and fair treatment. Unlike other areas of diversity management, there is not an extant 'intersectionality toolkit' that can be applied in organisations.

Intersectionality has myriad dimensions and definitions, using different research paradigms. It is an important concept that can enrich scholarly work in diversity management, in addition to practice. But the current lack of conceptual clarity, empirical work and attention to organisational implications mean that it needs to be translated for the practice of diversity management. Two additional ideas for implementing intersectionality in diversity management are intersectionality impact assessments and meta-focus groups.

Intersectionality impact assessments

Lombardo and Ronaldson Agustín (2012), in their analysis of EU employment regulation and its treatment of intersectionality, suggest that regulators create intersectionality impact assessments. These assessments would push policy makers to think about discrimination differently. Rather than focus on specific and discrete categories, an intersectionality impact assessment would create (p. 495) 'a more institutionalized and systematized approach to the inclusion of intersectional considerations'. This sort of practice could usefully be brought to human resource management (HRM) and diversity management. Organisations committed to fairness and inclusion could conduct internal intersectionality impact assessments, seeking to understand patterns of preference and prejudice that exist through the intersection of interpersonal differences.

Meta-focus groups

As there are not yet well established methods for conducting intersectionality research, engaging in internal intersectionality impact assessments would be rather difficult for the practitioner. One way forward would be to adopt Zander et al.'s (p. 462) suggestion of a meta-focus group, but apply it to the organisational context. Here a meta-focus group would gather researchers from those who have conducted research on different dimensions of diversity together (p. 462), 'to develop new theories by jointly producing an understanding of intersectionality, its consequences, and the interplay between social interaction and power structures'. This analytic method could be usefully applied to the organisational context, in which the diversity manager would bring together a diverse group of employees to discuss how they experience discrimination and their impressions of how differences intersect in ways that sustain and intensify disadvantage.

There is a critical need for diversity management scholarship and practice to integrate an intersectional perspective on discrimination in organisations. There is not an extant method for engaging in such analyses, however. Intersectionality represents a frontier for diversity management research and practices, and offers new perspectives on why discrimination persists. For the diversity manager, the starting point is to think in intersectional terms about who is favoured in the organisation, who is not, and how forms of difference intersect in ways that lead to ongoing discrimination that is either not named or named in binary and single-category terms.

Summary and recommendations

Intersectional analyses add complexity to our understanding of diversity management. However, the concept of intersectionality has significant implications for employees, managers, organisations and governments. Intersectionality holds much promise for advances in diversity management, but more academic work and attention to organisational application is needed in order for it to fulfil this promise.

For employees, intersectionality is helpful in two ways. First, thinking in terms of intersectionality helps them think about their own experiences; when they are feeling discriminated against, why is that so? Equally important is how intersectionality helps an individual employee understand how others are being treated – and mistreated – so that he or she can take affirmative steps to contribute to the creation of a truly just environment. Intersectional thinking helps individual employees make sense of their environment, their reactions to it, and how their organisations might change to become more diverse and just.

Managers with responsibility for employees, which includes anyone having one or more direct reports, should use intersectionality as a way of understanding the organisational environment and their contributions to it. Dismantling discrimination in organisations is never simple, and intersectional analyses help managers think through the ways in which barriers to fair treatment intersect and affect the experiences of employees. Further, intersectionality helps a particular manager better relate to employees through a clear-eyed analysis of why he or she feels as if relations with each individual are 'good' or 'bad', and then use that analysis to think critically about each relationship in turn and how it might be improved. To the extent that better or worse relationships are affected by intersecting differences between managers and individuals, ensuring fair treatment is more complicated. Managers might also think about what their 'ideal' employees look like, believe and act – and then interrogate those preferences on their own terms and in terms of what they say about the application of intersectionality in their contexts.

Traditionally, organisations have managed diversity through recourse to specific categories such as race and sex. This is to be expected, given how laws related to discrimination evolved. Intersectionality helps organisations think beyond binaries and single categories towards a more systemic understanding of discrimination and diversity. In particular, organisations often have taken-for-granted archetypes for 'acceptable' behaviour that are not only highly gendered and based on dominant racial and social classifications, but also affected by attitudes towards other forms of human difference. In suggesting how organisations might use intersectional analyses, the US Human Rights Network and the Rutgers Center for Women's Global Leadership (2013) ask this final set of clarifying questions:

> Is there any group of people in your community who are undercounted (or not counted), invisible and whose culture and way of life are rejected and negated by the mainstream society? Who are they? What are their multiple identities – ethnicity, race, sexual orientation, gender, gender identity, religious or faith tradition, national origin, citizenship status, or economic and social status? Have you accounted for them in your presentation? Have you made space in your presentation for the existence of such groups, whether or not you know of their existence? Why or why not?

The complexity revealed by analyses of discrimination may seem daunting to the individual who wants to use intersectionality in diversity management. Managing diversity on the basis of discrete categories seems easier than on the basis of an intersectional analysis of who has advantage in an organisation and who does not. However, intersectionality is an important perspective in making organisations more diverse through making them more just. Grappling with intersectionality is thus at the leading edge of diversity management scholarship and practice. When personnel responsible for organisational diversity management think in intersectional terms, they are thinking more deeply and systemically about discrimination and fairness.

Key terms

Intersectionality is the analysis of how forms of disadvantage in society reinforce each other.

Anticategorical complexity seeks to question and deconstruct social categories, believing that only when these categories are shown to be false will discriminatory regimes be dismantled.

Intercategorical complexity seeks to document relationships of inequality *among* social groups and changing configurations of inequality among multiple and conflicting dimensions, believing that such analyses help show how forms of disadvantage reinforce each other in regimes of inequality.

Intracategorical complexity takes a middle path between anticategorical and intercategorical complexity. While finding categories of difference useful as social fictions, it also seeks to interrogate their boundaries to find new groups hidden from view that are subject to discrimination.

Discussion questions

1. Intersectionality as a concept developed out of the experience of black women scholars and activists, and as Nash (2008) has pointed out, black women have been used as the 'quintessential intersectional subjects'. Discuss and begin to formulate an intersectional analysis for another marginalised group in your society.
2. Suppose you have been promoted to be the head of HRM of your organisation. You and your organisation are committed to fair employment practices. How can the concept of intersectionality help make your organisation fairer?
3. There is little empirical research using intersectionality theory. Outline an empirical study, including the research question, research subjects and methods used, that draws on ideas from intersectionality theory.
4. Is the lack of a defined 'intersectional methodology' (Nash, 2008) a strength or a weakness, and why?
5. What does the concept of intersectionality add to our understanding of diversity management?
6. The EU has started to shift its policies on gender equality towards an intersectional approach (Lombardo and Ronaldson Agustín, 2012). Is this a good idea or a bad idea, and why?

CASE STUDY

Veiled Muslim women in Europe

Because intersectionality has largely been part of academic discourse rather than the world of practice, there is not much case-based evidence for how it might be used with regard to diversity management. Muslim women in Europe will be the subject of this case study as a means of discussing how intersectionality might be used to study discrimination and diversity management.

Muslim women in Europe are appropriate subjects for an intersectional analysis of discrimination and diversity management because, as women, Muslim and in many cases migrants, they are subject to bias in the employment setting. Women, as previously discussed, are frequently subjects of intersectional analyses of discrimination. (While men can and should be

(Continued)

(Continued)

subjects of intersectional analysis, for it to be appropriate, the men in question would need to be members of two socially disfavoured groups; see Rahman (2010) for an example using the case of gay Muslim men in Europe.) As Muslims, they are frequently subject to discrimination, as they are members of a religion that is perceived negatively and whose members are subject to significant discrimination (Brüß, 2008; Karlsen and Nazroo, 2013). Muslims are subject to negative social evaluations (Helbling, 2014). If the Muslim women are migrants, they are subject to social opprobrium based on membership in that 'group' (Brüß, 2008; Safi, 2010). Being female, Muslim and overtly religious, irrespective of whether they are migrants or not, Muslim women in the EU who wear headscarves are subject to discrimination on multiple fronts. Their experiences, and how organisations can respond to discrimination against them, can be analysed through an intersectional analysis.

In contrast to male Muslims, many female Muslim women wear specific markers of their religious beliefs such as headscarves. This automatically marks them as Muslim and as women. As Vakulenko (2007: 186) argues, 'the "Islamic headscarf" is an obviously intersectional issue: the very term, used by the European Court of Human Rights, suggests that the garment in question is religious in nature'. Male Muslims, in contrast, might come from countries and ethnic heritages in which not everyone is Muslim, and so have a kind of 'plausible deniability' when it comes to religion while also being members of the favoured sex. A Muslim woman who demonstrates her religious identity by wearing a headscarf is therefore subject to discrimination based on her membership in two categories that are treated as suspect: women and Muslims. A woman wearing a headscarf is also identifying herself as explicitly religious; in the EU context, overt religiosity is also seen as less than ideal in a Europe that is becoming more secular (Jiménez Lobeira, 2013; Lehmann, 2013).

At issue in the present context is not the legality of wearing the headscarf in the EU, an issue that has been in part settled through legal cases filed under the European Convention for Human Rights (Vakulenko, 2007) but is also the subject of considerable controversy related to the extent of genuine protection for religious and cultural rights of ethnic and religious minorities in the EU (Edmunds, 2012). What is not in dispute is that Muslims in Europe are the subjects of negative evaluations from non-Muslim Europeans, and Muslim women who wear headscarves are particularly subject to discrimination based on their membership in the categories of women, Muslims and

(Continued)

(Continued)

religious people. In a study using female Muslim confederates and testing actual organisational behaviours, Ghumman and Ryan (2013) found that women in Europe who wore headscarves were more subject to formal discrimination, such as not being called back for interviews after a job application, and informal discrimination, such as a lack of interest expressed by organisational representatives. They perceived – correctly – that they were less likely to be favourably evaluated and to receive job offers. Less-diverse organisations were more hostile to Muslim women job applicants than more-diverse organisations.

Now suppose you are the head of human resource management for your organisation. You know from your training that there are a variety of subtle barriers (Van Laer and Janssens, 2011) to the advancement of women and the advancement of members of ethnic minority groups. You may be aware that there is discrimination against Muslim women who wear headscarves and indeed against Muslims generally. You may or may not be aware of prejudices against people in Europe who are overtly religious. Bilge (2010) argues that Muslims who wear headscarves are subject to two dominant (mis)readings of Islam: women's subjugation to men and Muslims' opposition to Western culture. How do you think about making your organisation a welcoming place for Muslim women, and especially those women who choose to wear the headscarf?

A traditional approach to this issue might be to write a memorandum or policy statement about respect for religious diversity. You might think about this issue as something that affects a category called 'Muslim women who choose to wear veils', which would be a non-intersectional approach. But let's think about this issue differently, using intersectional analysis. You might start by thinking about these questions:

- What biases do women face in our organisation?
- What biases do Muslims face in our organisation?
- Is there a bias against people who are overtly religious in our organisation?
- Is there bias against migrants in our organisation (for Muslim women who are also migrants)?

These are traditional questions focusing on discrimination on the basis of a single category. But now you want to think deeper. Think about these questions (adding migrant status as appropriate):

(Continued)

(Continued)

- What biases do Muslim women face in our organisation?
- What biases do women who are religious face in our organisation?

These questions start to get at intersectional analysis. An intersectional analysis does not simply add the level of discrimination based on membership in one category to the level of discrimination based on membership in another category, as if forms of discrimination were simple additives. Rather, you would want to think about how attitudes towards different categories intersect. Does, for example, the fact that a woman wears a headscarf not only exhibit overt religiosity, but also reinforce negative attitudes about the assertiveness of women? Does a female Muslim who wears a headscarf seem to be more 'other' than men who are native to the country and of the majority race, and if so (which is likely) what does this say about your organisation's attitudes toward difference?

After thinking about these questions, you might start to think about the policy implications of an intersectional analysis of discrimination against Muslim women who wear headscarves. You would certainly want to think about this specific case as one example of diversity management in your organisation, with implications for organisational policies and procedures related to applicant evaluation, promotion and interpersonal relations. You might decide to do training on this specific topic. But an intersectional analysis allows you to go deeper, helping you assess what the archetype of the 'ideal' employee is, and assess whether it is based on genuine organisational needs or preferences based on prejudicial attitudes (Young, 1991).

Questions

This case study addresses the case of veiled Muslim women in Europe from an intersectional perspective. It uncovers some of the biases faced by them and how organisations might start to remedy them. Intersectional analysis is useful in multiple contexts and for answering questions about diversity management.

1. Identify, using intersectional analysis, another group that faces discrimination in your culture or society based on membership in two or more disfavoured classes. After defining this group and what sources of disadvantage intersect for it, develop a research proposal for how you would study discrimination against members of this group.

(Continued)

(Continued)

2. In almost every society, men who are members of the majority race or ethnic grouping in that society comprise the largest portion of elite positions: CEOs, directors, and so on. Much of the analysis of diversity management for elite positions focuses on single variables of disadvantage: sex, race or ethnicity, religion, and sexual orientation to name but four. First, identify the archetype of the 'ideal CEO' or the 'ideal' for some other elite position in your society, using as many descriptors (demographic, personality, etc.) as you can. Then, using intersectional analysis, discuss how organisations in your society should change the ways in which they operate to ensure fair treatment for people seeking that type of elite position.

 # Further reading

Acker, J. (2012). Gendered organizations and intersectionality: problems and possibilities. *Equality, Diversity and Inclusion: An International Journal*, 31, 214–24.

Alberti, G., Holgate, J. & Tapia, M. (2013). Organising migrants as workers or as migrant workers? Intersectionality, trade unions and precarious work. *International Journal of Human Resource Management*, 24, 4132–48.

Crenshaw, K. (1991). Mapping the margins: intersectionality, identity politics, and violence against women of colour. *Stanford Law Review*, 43, 1241–99.

McCall, L. (2005). The complexity of intersectionality. *Signs: Journal of Women in Culture and Society*, 30, 1772–800.

Nash, J.C. (2008). Re-thinking intersectionality. *Feminist Review*, 89, 1–15.

Styhre, A. & Eriksson-Zetterquist, U. (2008). Thinking the multiple in gender and diversity studies: examining the concept of intersectionality. *Gender in Management: An International Journal*, 23, 567–82.

Winker, G. & Degele, N. (2011). Intersectionality as multi-level analysis: dealing with social inequality. *European Journal of Women's Studies*, 18, 51–66.

References

Acker, J. (2012). Gendered organizations and intersectionality: problems and possibilities. *Equality, Diversity and Inclusion: An International Journal*, 31, 214–24.

Alberti, G., Holgate, J. & Tapia, M. (2013). Organising migrants as workers or as migrant workers? Intersectionality, trade unions and precarious work. *International Journal of Human Resource Management*, 31, 4132–48.

Arifeen, S.R. & Gatrell, C. (2013). A blind spot in organization studies: gender with ethnicity, nationality and religion. *Gender in Management: An International Journal*, 28, 151–70.

Austin, J.L. (1962). *How to Do Things with Words*. Oxford: Clarendon Press.

Bilge, S. (2010). Beyond subordination vs. resistance: an intersectional approach to the agency of veiled Muslim women. *Journal of Intercultural Studies*, 31, 9–28.

Bowleg, L. (2008). When Black + lesbian + woman ≠ Black lesbian woman: the methodological challenges of qualitative and quantitative intersectionality research. *Sex Roles*, 59, 312–25.

Brüß, J. (2008). Experiences of discrimination reported by Turkish, Moroccan and Bangladeshi Muslims in three European cities. *Journal of Ethnic and Migration Studies*, 34, 875–94.

Buitelaar, M. (2006). 'I am the ultimate challenge': accounts of intersectionality in the life-story of a well-known daughter of Moroccan migrant workers in the Netherlands. *European Journal of Women's Studies*, 13, 259–76.

Butler, J. (1997). *Excitable Speech: A Politics of the Performative*. London and New York: Routledge.

Choo, H.Y. & Ferree, M.M. (2010). Practicing intersectionality in sociological research: a critical analysis of inclusions, interactions, and institutions in the study of inequalities. *Sociological Theory*, 28, 129–49.

Cole, E. (2009). Intersectionality and research in psychology. *American Psychologist*, 64 (April), 170–80.

Combahee River Collective (1986). *The Combahee River Collective Statement: Black Feminist Organizing in the Seventies and Eighties*. Latham, NY: Kitchen Table, Women of Color Press.

Crenshaw, K. (1989). Demarginalizing the interaction of race and sex: a black feminist critique of antidiscrimination doctrine, feminist theory, and antiracist politics. *University of Chicago Legal Forum*, 140, 139–67.

Crenshaw, K. (1991). Mapping the margins: intersectionality, identity politics, and violence against women of color. *Stanford Law Review*, 43, 1241–99.

Dworkin, S.L. (2005). Who is epidemiologically fathomable in the HIV/AIDS epidemic? Gender, sexuality, and intersectionality in public health. *Culture, Health & Sexuality*, 7, 615–23.

Edmunds, J. (2012). The limits of post-national citizenship: European Muslims, human rights and the hijab. *Ethnic and Racial Studies*, 35, 1181–99.

Fausto-Sterling, A. (2000). *Sexing the Body: Gender Politics and the Construction of Sexuality*. New York: Basic Books.

Fausto-Sterling, A. (2008). *Myths of Gender: Biological Theories about Women and Men*. New York: Basic Books.

Ghumman, S. & Ryan, A.M. (2013). Not welcome here: discrimination towards women who wear the Muslim headscarf. *Human Relations*, 66, 671–98.

Gottfried, H. (2009). Gender and employment: a global lens on feminist analyses and theorizing of labor markets. *Sociology Compass*, 3, 475–90.

Hancock, A.M. (2007). When multiplication doesn't equal quick addition: examining intersectionality as a research paradigm. *Perspectives on Politics*, 5, 63–79.

Helbling, M. (2014). Opposing Muslims and the Muslim headscarf in Western Europe. *European Sociological Review*, doi: 10.1093/esr/jct038.

Holvino, E. (2010). Intersections: the simultaneity of race, gender and class in organization studies. *Gender, Work & Organization*, 17, 248–77.

hooks, b. (1981). *Ain't I A Woman?* Boston, MA: South End Press.

hooks, b. (1984). *Feminist Theory: From Margin to Center*. Cambridge, MA: South End Press.

Jiménez Lobeira, P.C. (2013). Veils, crucifixes and public sphere: what kind of secularism? Rethinking neutrality in a post-secular Europe. *Journal of Intercultural Studies*, 35, 385–402.

Karlsen, S. & Nazroo, J.Y. (2013). Influences on forms of national identity and feeling 'at home' among Muslim groups in Britain, Germany and Spain. *Ethnicities*, 13, 689–708.

Lehmann, D. (2013). Religion as heritage, religion as belief: shifting frontiers of secularism in Europe, the USA and Brazil. *International Sociology*, 28, 645–62.

Lombardo, E. & Ronaldson Agustín, L.R. (2012). Framing gender intersections in the European Union: what implications for the quality of intersectionality in policies? *Social Politics: International Studies in Gender, State & Society*, 19, 482–512.

Lombardo, E. & Verloo, M. (2009). Institutionalizing intersectionality in the European Union? Policy developments and contestations. *International Feminist Journal of Politics*, 11, 478–95.

McCall, L. (2005). The complexity of intersectionality. *Signs: Journal of Women in Culture and Society*, 30, 1772–800.

McDowell, L. (2008). Thinking through work: complex inequalities, constructions of difference and trans-national migrants. *Progress in Human Geography*, 32(4), 491–507.

Nash, J.C. (2008). Re-thinking intersectionality. *Feminist Review*, 89, 1–15.

Özbilgin, M.F., Beauregard, T.A., Tatli, A. & Bell, M.P. (2011). Work–life, diversity and intersectionality: a critical review and research agenda. *International Journal of Management Reviews*, 13, 177–98.

Phoenix, A. & Pattynama, P. (2006). Intersectionality. *European Journal of Women's Studies*, 13, 187–92.

Rahman, M. (2010). Queer as intersectionality: theorizing gay Muslim identities. *Sociology*, 44, 944–61.

Robinson, C.L., Taylor, T., Tomaskovic-Devey, D., Zimmer, C. & Irvin, M.W. (2005). Studying race or ethnic and sex segregation at the establishment level: methodological issues and substantive opportunities using EEO-1 reports. *Work and Occupations*, 32, 5–38.

Safi, M. (2010). Immigrants' life satisfaction in Europe: between assimilation and discrimination. *European Sociological Review*, 26, 159–76.

Shields, S.A. (2008). Gender: an intersectionality perspective. *Sex Roles*, 59, 301–11.

Styhre, A. & Eriksson-Zetterquist, U. (2008). Thinking the multiple in gender and diversity studies: examining the concept of intersectionality. *Gender in Management: An International Journal*, 23, 567–82.

US Human Rights Network and the Rutgers Center for Women's Global Leadership (2013). *Framing Questions on Intersectionality.* www.ushrnetwork.org/sites/ushrnetwork.org/files/framing_questions_on_intersectionality_1.pdf, accessed June 6, 2014.

Vakulenko, A. (2007). Islamic headscarves and the European Convention on Human Rights: an intersectional perspective. *Social & Legal Studies*, 16, 183–99.

Van Laer, K. & Janssens, M. (2011). Ethnic minority professionals' experiences with subtle discrimination in the workplace. *Human Relations*, 64, 1203–27.

Verloo, M. (2006). Multiple inequalities, intersectionality and the European Union. *European Journal of Women's Studies*, 13, 211–28.

Walby, S., Armstrong, J. & Strid, S. (2012). Intersectionality: multiple inequalities in social theory. *Sociology*, 46, 224–40.

Warner, D.F. & Brown, T.H. (2011). Understanding how race/ethnicity and gender define age-trajectories of disability: an intersectionality approach. *Social Science & Medicine*, 72, 1236–48.

Winker, G. & Degele, N. (2011). Intersectionality as multi-level analysis: dealing with social inequality. *European Journal of Women's Studies*, 18, 51–66.

Young, I.M. (1991). *Justice and the Politics of Difference.* Princeton, NJ: Princeton University Press.

Yuval-Davis, N. (2006). Intersectionality and feminist politics. *European Journal of Women's Studies*, 13, 193–209.

Zander, U., Zander, L., Gaffney, S. & Olsson, J. (2010). Intersectionality as a new perspective in international business research. *Scandinavian Journal of Management*, 26, 457–66.

Conclusion

Future of diversity management

Mustafa Özbilgin and Jawad Syed

 Intended learning outcomes

After studying this chapter, you should be able to:

- Identify the utility of studying diversity management from international perspectives
- Analyse and reflect about key themes of diversity recurring in this book
- Explore how diversity can be studied by asking elementary questions
- Consider futuristic orientation and expansion of diversity management

Introduction

Studying international perspectives on diversity management provides a wealth of insight into how diversity may be managed under different national systems and institutions such as education, employment and law. International perspectives can help us understand and transcend the path dependent visions of managing diversity in domestic contexts.

Drawing on a host of contextual and organizational examples of approaches to various dimensions of diversity, chapters in this book have demonstrated that diversity management is a complex and multifaceted phenomenon. In this book, we capture this complexity by bringing insights from sociology, psychology, international relations, history, management, business and organization studies. Diversity management has also multiple levels of analyses, including macro-international and supranational levels, meso-organisational and group levels, and micro-individual levels.

Diversity management is treated in different ways across domestic systems in terms of its place in the organizational structure and national political discourses. Tatli and Ozbilgin (2012) demonstrate that diversity management has gained different meanings, enjoyed divergent perspectives and afforded varied repertoires of practices and actions even across three neighboring countries that operate under the legal umbrella of the EU, i.e. Britain, France and Germany.

Key themes in this book

Chapters in this book highlight a number of themes and issues related to diversity that are not mutually exclusive but interact and overlap. Among the most powerful themes to emerge include:

- the influential role of factors in the external, international environment on business in general and diversity management in particular;
- a need to consider diversity management at a number of levels, particularly at the macro national and international level, the meso or organisational and group level, and the micro individual level;
- the emerging debate about the convergence, and divergence of diversity management practices across the globe and the emerging practice of crossvergence;
- the conflicting, perceived or actual, implications of diversity for organisational performance, whereas reality is to be found somewhere between creativity and conflict, productivity and tensions, inclusion and power imbalances etc;
- the overlapping of diversity with business ethics and social responsibility;
- the difficulties surrounding the implementation and consistency of diversity policies within organisations.

In recent decades, global institutional developments, such as the policies of the World Trade Organization, International Labour Organization, and the European Union (EU), have promoted the cause and practice of equality and diversity in the workplace. Moreover, national regulations and global corporate practices have served as converging forces that have specific implications for diversity and inclusion at work. However, the enactment and implementation of such laws and the roles of governments and their enforcement agencies are not consistent across national contexts.

An explicit acknowledgement of the macro-level factors provides insights into the convergence/divergence debate. Although globalisation of business, culture, knowledge and technology transfer, and international standards has occurred and has contributed to increased attention to diversity management across the globe, particularly in North America, Europe, Australia, and BRICS countries, the chapters in this book demonstrate that the particular arrangements in national economies and societies may result in divergent approaches to gender and diversity in different countries.

A very strong theme running through the book is the importance of understanding diversity and inclusion in terms of not only the macro-environment, but also the meso-organisational and micro-individual levels. This approach enables us to consider the influence of collective factors operating within the organisation, such as vision and strategy of diversity, allocation of resources, demographic composition of employees and customers etc. The approach also enables us to take into account the issue of intersectionality and multiple identities that a person may hold.

By acknowledging the influence of these multiple levels, it is possible to explicitly think about the development, implementation and international transfer of diversity management policies and practices (Syed and Özbilgin, 2009). Examples from diverse geographical and industrial contexts highlights how diversity policies and practices are not value-neutral; instead, they involve making choices subject to industrial and societal influences, resulting in the development of policies, or lack of policies, that may have ethical and equality related implications for employees, other stakeholders and the broader society.

Another key theme emerging from this book concerns the variety of stakeholders who have interests in diversity management and its outcomes. For instance, employees, the community and governments have a stake in the diversity initiatives and their outcomes. Once again, depending upon the institutional, cultural and other contextual forces, such stakeholders may have varied levels of interest in and influence on the diversity agenda.

Overall, the book brings to fore the international development and growth of diversity management, especially emerging from globalisation, knowledge transfer and contextual influences, suggesting that the existing Western-centric approaches to diversity require re-evaluation.

Back to basics: some elementary questions for diversity management

As a way forward, this chapter takes a step back to ask a number of straightforward questions – such as *where*, *when*, *why*, *what* and *how* to explore diversity management from international perspectives.

In order for us to make sense of diversity in multiple domestic environments, we need to identify its unique meanings and substance, not only through standardised and etic approaches but also locally embedded insights. Asking these elementary questions is always helpful to explore any management concept from contextual perspectives. In order to understand diversity management as it manifests in each unique domestic setting, the following questions can be posed (see Figure 12.1).

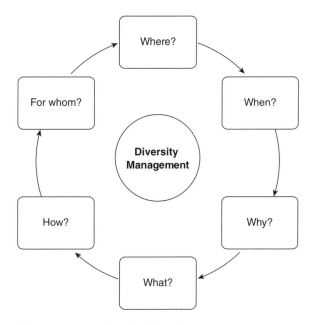

Figure 12.1   Some elementary questions for diversity management

Where? (the place)

It is important to note place, as in the country, sector, organisation, team, in which we are exploring diversity. Research shows that diversity management does not happen in the same way in different places. Starting with the where question requires the setting to be described.

When? (the history)

Diversity management is path dependent and historically embedded. National and institutional approaches in diversity can be understood if we attend to the history of diversity in the specific setting of the organisation or the country.

Why? (the rationale)

There are different reasons and rationale for take up of diversity management interventions. While some organisations are driven by shareholder considerations, others may pursue contribution to their organisational goals, or pursue diversity management as a way to deal with compliance with industry and legal demands. Attending to rationale for diversity management can reveal the significant drivers, beneficiaries and activities of diversity.

What? (the practice)

Diversity management practices range from information giving and receiving practices, to practices that aim to change structures and institutions, and to practices which seek to change people, cultures and thinking. Practice of diversity gains shape according to the national, institutional and group priorities of diversity.

How? (the process)

Antecedents, correlates and consequences of managing diversity is bounded contextually. It is therefore important to explore the process by which diversity activities are organised, under what considerations, in which order and in order to generate what kind of consequences, in their unique setting.

For whom? (the beneficiaries)

Diversity management can have benefits for people, performance and the environment. Beneficiaries could be kept narrow or broad depending on the particular approach to diversity management. Beneficiaries of diversity as well as people who are responsible to craft its strategy and deliver its practices chart out stakeholders in the politics of diversity.

Future: expansion of diversity management

Diversity management, as a concept, originates from North America, although management of differences at work is not new. There are a number of ways the concept and practice of diversity management have been expanding, which also outline its direction in the foreseeable future.

Diversity as a problem to diversity as a resource

Managers worldwide have to deal with the challenges and possibilities of dealing with differences at work and among stakeholders of their organisations with varying degrees of effectiveness. The way diversity is sometimes treated with antagonism, where differences at work are considered as problematic. Yet in some other organisations, some forms of diversity can be construed as a resource, a valuable asset for the organisation and the wider context in which the organisation is situated. The recent years have seen the expansion of the treatment of diversity not only from an antagonistic point of view but from the perspective of resource. The polarisation of the treatment of diversity in organisations along the axes of 'diversity as problem' and 'diversity as resource' has also been recently challenged with more balanced perspectives, where organisations seek to both combat the negative consequences of diversity such as difficulties of communication, industrial conflict, and disharmony at work; and to benefit from diversity as a resource in ways to promote performance, innovation, creativity and problem solving at work.

Diversity as fixed to diversity as dynamic

Categories of diversity such as gender, ethnicity, age, sexual orientation, disability and religion can be treated in two different ways. First, differences can be attributed to particular attributes of categories of workers, such as women being good at certain kinds of roles, and men being better in others. Some scholars argue that treatment of differences as absolute among different diversity groups is problematic as it disregards the construction of the roles associated with different diversity categories. For example, socio-economic position and roles of women and men are socially and historically constructed. As such it is unwise to make fixed distinctions among women and men without understanding how construction of gender identity changes over time and across settings.

One of the consequences of fixing differences among diversity categories is to believe that such differences are universally valid. Conversely, comparative research shows that the meaning of categories of 'different' are differently shaped due to different construction of these differences in different settings. For example, travelling across national borders can subject an individual to different forms of ethnic bias, or ethnic privilege, depending on the social construction of the value of their ethnicity in these different locations. Furthermore, individuals sharing the same ethnicity can display highly varied forms of behaviour and attributes. There is also a temporal dimension as treatment of ethnic category may change over time. Progressive formulations of diversity should recognise the constructed and dynamically changing nature of diversity. This requires moving away from fixed categories to evidence-based emic approaches which can capture how diversity categories are treated at a given locale and at a specific point in time.

Diversity as siloed to diversity as intersectional

Diversity categories such as gender, ethnicity, age, sexual orientation, and disability have different terminology for managing diversity. Siloed treatment of diversity management has led to formulations of strategies dealing with single categories of differences. As gender equality is the most legally supported category of difference, there is a tendency to consider gender as the primary category of diversity management in many organisations globally. Resultantly, other categories may be treated as an afterthought. Yet, in progressive theorisation around diversity management, there is a need to move from siloed approaches to an intersectional approach, where multiple categories of difference are considered together in order not to reduce the complexity of diversity at work to single reasons.

Focus on individual to focus on community

Diversity management is sometimes criticised for its focus on the individual at the expense of the community and solidarity, which pushed the agenda for equality by gender, ethnicity, disability etc. Loss of solidarity and community in formulations of diversity management has been recently challenged. As a result, we see that community organising is brought back into diversity management. The expansion of diversity from individual level differences to solidarity and community manifests itself by engaging internal and external diversity networks, in order to bring collective interests of diversity groups.

Focus on business case to focus on triple bottom line and global value chain

Early formulations of diversity management focused on the contribution of differences on the performance of organisations. Performance for diversity management is increasingly defined as a triple bottom line term, as performance of the organisation in terms of profitability (financial viability), people (stakeholders including workers, managers, shareholders, customers, and wider society) and planet (environmental impact and sustainability). Connecting diversity management with these wider range of foci facilitated a wide range of impacts to be measured in terms of contribution of diversity management to organisational life. In recent times, it has been suggested that the triple bottom line should be expanded to also include a focus on the value chain, which leads to imbalanced developments across different functions and regions in which an organisation operates. For example, the gender inequalities in manufacturing facilities of a global textile company can become invisible by that organisation's success in promoting women to leadership positions in the headquarters. A triple bottom line focus incorporating a value chain approach is useful in ensuring that diversity is managed in a fair and responsible way across the value chain of the organisation.

Voluntarism to regulation

Diversity management is sometimes viewed as a voluntary measure for organisations to deal with differences at work. Yet, voluntary approach without supportive legal and sectoral regulation is found to be ineffectual. Diversity management interventions in organisations, despite claims of voluntarism, are keenly connected to and mirror the rationale of legal and sectoral regulation. Therefore, recent formulations of diversity management transcend simple voluntaristic agendas in favour of promoting advancement of regulation at sectoral, national, supranational and global levels.

Individual responsibility to shared responsibility

Diversity management is increasingly considered a shared responsibility, which diversity professionals are tasked to coordinate. Considering diversity as the sole responsibility of an individual at work does not create the engagement that most organisations need to achieve system change. What needs to happen is for the diversity professionals to engage all segments of the organisation with a view to cascade the diversity management policy across the organisation. This approach requires that diversity management is considered everyone's responsibility.

Domestic to global

What appears to be universal considerations of diversity that emanated from the North American context are indeed domestic formulations which cannot be directly transferred to other national contexts. In recognition of this, there has been an expansion of diversity management language and practices in different domestic settings, and emergence of national diversity management practices. Differentiation between national practices of diversity leads to complexities of coordination. In order to coordinate differently structured diversity efforts across multiple domestic settings, there were attempts to formulate international and global approaches to diversity management (Syed and Özbilgin 2009; Tatli and Ozbilgin, 2012). Thus, diversity management has been expanding from its modest domestic formulations to multi-domestic and global framing of the management of differences.

Concluding remarks

Much more than a politically correct governmental or corporate lip service, diversity remains relevant in socio-cultural and economic terms in different national and international contexts. However, approaches to diversity management remain influenced not only by employee and customer demographics but also by many other multi-level factors within and without the workplace.

Figure 12.2 summarises our discussion in terms of critically expanding diversity management to have a more positive, dynamic, intersectional, community-oriented and responsible focus in a global workplace.

This chapter suggests that in order to have a futuristic and proactive approach to diversity, policy makers and business leaders need to look beyond the conventional

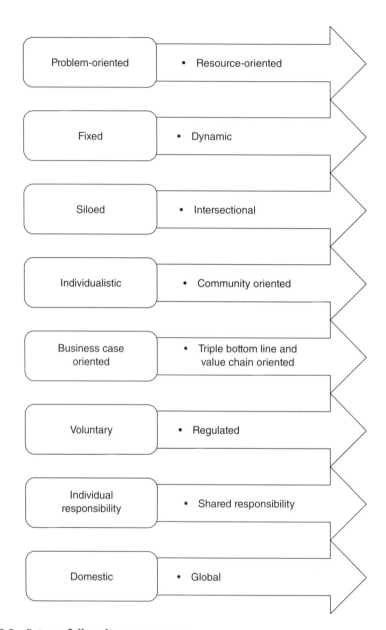

Figure 12.2 Future of diversity management

business case for diversity management. Leaders that frame workforce diversity as a key strategic priority may wish to adopt a more future-oriented approach and a long-term vision of diversity management. Workforce diversity policy as a long-term consideration connects the past of the organisation with its present and future. Indeed a key challenge for the new starters is to perceive diversity as a resource and an opportunity, instead of a challenge and a liability. While a focus on the organisational performance and national productivity is a good starting point, it is equally important to incorporate a triple bottom line and global value chain focus and a consideration of the dynamic, intersectional and contextual nature of diversity and its management.

While most organisations and governments still use a business case argument to justify an increased focus on diversity management, it is a fact that the business case emphasises the shareholder over all other organisational stakeholders, e.g., employees, families, society (Kossek, 2005). Thanks to the increased awareness, advocacy and legislation, business organisations continue to be held increasingly accountable to multiple societal goals, such as promoting social change (Anft, 2002; Syed & Kramar, 2009).

Thus, in addition to the economic or business benefits, organisations as well as government policy makers may consider a socially responsible approach to diversity management, taking into account a long term vision of social and economic well-being. At the very least, the business case should explain how diversity can be managed as a shared responsibility across the organisation, in order to dilute business risk, lower risk-taking behaviour and 'future proof' the organisation, because the global business environment will become increasingly diverse (Jonsen et al. 2013). Within academic scholarship and organisational practice, it is important to develop intersectional solidarity, i.e., common willingness among champions of different diversity strands, such as gender, ethnicity, sexual orientation, age and religion, with a view to easing tensions among them and to building a stronger and more coherent drive towards inclusion in the workplace.

We anticipate that this book will provide insights into the contextual framing and operationalisation of diversity management across the globe. Today, all organisations operate in a global, international labour market and all have to deal with diversity in one form or the other. The dynamic and varied nature of the international context provides an opportunity for diversity and inclusion to be reconceptualised, and provides many wonderful opportunities for scholars and practitioners.

Discussion questions

1. What is the significance of the elementary questions about diversity management?
2. Why is it important to have a multi-level perspective of diversity management?
3. In your view, what is the future of diversity management? What will be the shape of the organisational practice of diversity in the next 50 years?
4. Is the theory and practice of diversity management currently converging, diverging or crossverging?

CASE STUDY

Dynamic context of diversity: the National Health Service in the UK

The National Health Service (NHS) represents the publicly funded health-care systems in the UK. Primarily funded through central taxation, the core principle of the NHS is to provide a health service that is free of cost for everyone. The NHS has clear values and principles about equality and fairness for both patients and employees.

As a public body, the NHS is bound by the Equality Act 2010 and Public Sector Equality Duty to work towards reducing inequalities in employment and service provision. NHS organisations are required to give fair treatment to everyone regardless of their background or circumstances and to take full regard of individual differences. The specific diversity categories include those identified in the Equality Act 2010: age, gender, disability, ethnicity and race, gender reassignment, marriage and civil partnership status, caring responsibilities, sexual orientation, and pregnancy and maternity.

The degree of public interest and scrutiny, the organisation's size and scale, and its rapid pace of change are key considerations in the NHS diversity policy. In a complex and devolved system, which is made up of almost 500 organisations, it is difficult to attain consistency in the management of diversity, particularly in semi-autonomous organisations. An interview with the NHS's head of equality, diversity and human rights uncovered a major political shift in the language of diversity and its impact on the NHS. Leadership in the NHS needs to maintain momentum as new structures and systems are being imposed. A range of legal and voluntary measures is used in the NHS to promote equality, fairness and diversity. However, given the governmental austerity and budgetary controls, a recent trend has been a shift in resourcing away from diversity to other areas in the organisation. To maintain the momentum in a changing political environment, equality and diversity leaders in the NHS need to adopt a new political discourse. This entails engaging stakeholders, using social media and other means, to mobilise 'bottom-up' support. In the backdrop of these political developments, diversity gaps in some areas remain most dominant. For example, in London, where ethnic minority representation in the population is 45 per cent, only 8 per cent of the NHS Trust board members are from ethnic minorities, and just 2.5 per cent of chief executives and chairs (Faragher, 2014).

(Continued)

(Continued)

Questions

1. What factors are affecting the NHS to shift resources and attention away from diversity?
2. If you were a diversity manager at the NHS, what would you do in this situation?
3. What lessons do you draw from this case study?

(source: adapted from Ozbilgin et al., 2014)

Further reading

Nkomo, S. & Hoobler, J.M. (2014). A historical perspective on diversity ideologies in the United States: Reflections on human resource management research and practice. *Human Resource Management Review, 24*(3), 245–57.

Olsen, J.E. & Martins, L.L. (2012). Understanding organizational diversity management programs: A theoretical framework and directions for future research. *Journal of Organizational Behavior, 33*(8), 1168–87.

Özbilgin, M. & Tatli, A. (2011). Mapping out the field of equality and diversity: rise of individualism and voluntarism. *Human Relations, 64*(9), 1229–53.

Syed, J. & Boje, D.M. (2011). *Antenarratives of Negotiated Diversity Management. Storytelling and the Future of Organizations: An Antenarrative Handbook,* 47.

References

Anft, M. (2002). Toward corporate change: Businesses seek nonprofit help in quest to become better citizens. *The Chronicle of Philanthropy*, September, 10, 12.

Faragher, J. (2014). NHS to face 'regulatory consequences' for failure to improve racial diversity. *People Management, CIPD*, August 1. Available at: http://www.cipd.co.uk/pm/peoplemanagement/b/weblog/archive/2014/08/01/nhs-faces-regulatory-consequences-for-failure-to-improve-racial-diversity.aspx

Jonsen, K., Tatli, A., Özbilgin, M.F. & Bell, M.P. (2013). The Tragedy of the uncommons: reframing workforce diversity, *Human Relations, 66*(2), 271–94.

Kossek, E. (2005). Workplace policies and practices to support work and families: Gaps in implementation and linkages to individual and organizational effectiveness. In S. Bianchi, L. Casper, K. Christensen & R. Berkowitz King (Eds), *Workforce/workplace mismatch? Work, family, health and well-being* (in press). Mahwah, NJ: Lawrence Erlbaum Associates.

Ozbilgin, M., Tatli, A., Ipek, G. & Sameer, M. (2014). The business case for diversity management. The Association of Chartered Certified Accountants. Available at: www.accaglobal.com/content/dam/acca/global/PDF-technical/human-capital/pol-tp-tbcfdm-diversity-management.pdf

Syed, J. & Kramar, R. (2009). Socially responsible diversity management. *Journal of Management and Organization, 15*(5), 639–51.

Syed, J. & Özbilgin, M. (2009). A relational framework for international transfer of diversity management practices. *The International Journal of Human Resource Management, 20*(12): 243–53.

Tatli, A. & Özbilgin, M.F. (2012). An emic approach to intersectional study of diversity at work: a Bourdieuan framing. *International Journal of Management Reviews, 14*(2): 180–200.

Index

Page numbers in bold indicate terms within a table, and in italic indicate terms within a figure.